GRANVILLE STUART, AGED 75

Forty Years on the Frontier

As Seen in the Journals and Reminiscences of Granville Stuart,
Gold-Miner, Trader, Merchant, Rancher and Politician

Granville Stuart

Edited by Paul C. Phillips

INTRODUCTION TO THE NEW BISON BOOKS EDITION BY
Clyde A. Milner II and Carol A. O'Connor

UNIVERSITY OF NEBRASKA PRESS
LINCOLN AND LONDON

© 1925 by The Arthur H. Clark Company
Introduction to the new Bison Books Edition © 2004 by the Board of
Regents of the University of Nebraska
Manufactured in the United States of America

First Nebraska paperback printing: 1977

Library of Congress Cataloging-in-Publication Data
Stuart, Granville, 1834–1918.
Forty years on the frontier as seen in the journals and reminiscences
of Granville Stuart, gold-miner, trader, merchant, rancher and
politician / by Granville Stuart; edited by Paul C. Phillips;
introduction to the new Bison Books edition by Clyde A. Milner II and
Carol A. O'Connor.
p. cm.
"This Bison Books edition combines the two volumes of the original
edition"—T.p. verso.
Originally published: Cleveland: Arthur H. Clark Co., 1925, in series:
Early western journals, no. 2.
Includes bibliographical references and index.

ISBN 0-8032-9320-8 (pbk.: alk. paper)
1. Stuart, Granville, 1834–1918. 2. Frontier and pioneer
life—Montana. 3. Pioneers—Montana—Biography. 4.
Montana—History. I. Phillips, Paul C. (Paul Chrisler), 1883–1956.
II. Title.
F731.S9115 2004
978.6'031'092—dc22   2004009380

This Bison Books edition combines the two volumes of the original
edition. Part 1, "Prospecting for Gold" (formerly volume 1), begins on
arabic page 13. Page numbering begins over again in part 2,
"Pioneering in Montana" (formerly volume 2), and begins on arabic
page 7. The text remains unaltered.

CLYDE A. MILNER II AND CAROL A. O'CONNOR

Introduction to the new Bison Books Edition

Granville Stuart (1834–1918) lived an extraordinary life. What he experienced and what he wrote intersected with major themes in the history of the nineteenth-century North American West. He lived long enough to connect to the West of the early twentieth century as well, and many Montanans consider Stuart the state's quintessential pioneer. Indeed, in the preface to *Forty Years on the Frontier*, Stuart asserts his primacy. "I was here to greet the brave men and noble women who . . . lay the foundation for this magnificent state" (pt. 1, 20).

Stuart is most readily remembered for helping launch Montana's gold rushes of the 1860s and for leading vigilantes against horse thieves in the mid-1880s. Stuart panned gold, punched cows, and hanged thieves. And he did much more. Throughout his adult life, he collected guns and books. He taught himself Shoshone, French, and Spanish. He did pencil sketches of Montana scenes and kept extensive notes about weather, vegetation, and landscape. A free thinker, Stuart denounced formal religion, especially Christianity, but he remained a staunch member of the Democratic Party. His political loyalty led to his appointment from 1894 to 1898 as the U.S. minister to Paraguay and Uruguay.

Although not always directly attributed to him, scenes from Stuart's life have reached large audiences—in A. B. Guthrie's novel *These Thousand Hills* (1956); in director

Arthur Penn's film *The Missouri Breaks* (1976); and in the multimedia, multivolume epic launched by Larry McMurtry's *Lonesome Dove* (1985). Even more fascinating than these fictions are the many ways Stuart's real life parallels—and surpasses—that of the cowboy vigilante hero of the first major western novel, Owen Wister's *The Virginian* (1902). For example, as did Wister's hero, Stuart used lynchings to uphold his own brand of justice, but he hanged more men than in the novel. In the aftermath of this violence, Stuart, like the fictional Virginian, wed a young schoolteacher, although she was his second wife rather than the first. The novel ends with an idyllic honeymoon in the Rocky Mountains, whereas Stuart soon lost his ranch, dispossessed most of his children, and had to find new ways to make ends meet. Stuart lived through the very era of Wister's novel and confronted some of the same moral dilemmas as its hero. But Stuart's life story is not a romantic parable; it is a western saga for grownups.

Not all the troubles and tragedies, the struggles and challenges of Stuart's life appear in this posthumously published memoir, but the full title does capture the scope of what the original two volumes (now combined here) contain: *Forty Years on the Frontier as seen in the Journals and Reminiscences of Granville Stuart, Gold-Miner, Trader, Merchant, Rancher and Politician.* Much more might have appeared in this remarkable 1925 publication, but Stuart's second wife, Allis Isabelle Brown Stuart, and the editor of what did appear in print, Paul C. Phillips, had their own difficulties with each other and with the manuscript that the old pioneer left behind.[1]

Stuart's life spanned eighty-four years, yet his manuscript mentions his first wife only once and gives little information about his children and his domestic life. Even his vital relationship with James, the oldest of his three brothers, omits any mention of this sibling's untimely death. His memoir does show that they forged a close attachment from their childhood in the Midwest, when Granville, on the winter ice, coasted to school holding James's coattails. Together in 1852 the two brothers took the overland route to the gold fields of California. Over the course of the next five years, they tried their luck on numerous claims in placer and hydraulic mining. They fraternized with gamblers, observed the work habits of the Chinese, and contributed to the decimation of the Native population. James joined a company of white men who, with the assistance of several Chinese, carried out a raid against the Concow Indians. If the Stuarts arrived in California too late to hit pay dirt, they got to what became Montana too early. Less than half a year after sickness halted their return to Iowa, and the Mormon War diverted them northward, the brothers found gold in Alder Creek in present-day Powell County. This April 1858 discovery eventually made the brothers famous, but it never made them rich.

Stuart's published reminiscences indicate the various social settings in which he and his brother moved, but not all the personal stories appeared in print. British, Mexicans, French Canadians, Nez Perces, Bannocks, Shoshones, Flatheads, Blackfeet, and individuals of other cultural backgrounds intermingled in what became southwestern Montana. They also intermarried. James fathered a son in 1863. The mother was French Canadian and Nez Perce, and the son grew up in Idaho living among the Nez Perces.[2] Later James married Ellen LaVatta, of Mexican and Native parentage. They produced three sons, the youngest of whom died of convulsions in 1873. As for Stuart, a brief liaison with the daughter of a French Canadian was followed by his marriage to Awbonnie Tootanka, a young Shoshone woman about fifteen years old. By the time their first child was born, the gold rush to Montana had begun.

Within a few years Montana would change from an informal meeting ground of many peoples into an official territory of the U.S. government. That this shift occurred while the Civil War was raging meant that Montana attracted deserters and other ignoble characters who wished to avoid the conflagration in the East. In 1862 and 1863, Granville and James faced down bandits. Though neither brother joined the vigilantes in Bannack and Virginia City in early 1864, they approved of the hangings of road agents and other presumed outlaws that occurred there.

For a time in the mid-1860s, the brothers' roles as leaders of the new territory seemed secure. James led two early expeditions to the Yellowstone country. He served as Missoula County's first sheriff, presided over Montana's first legal execution, and won a seat in the territory's first legislature. Meanwhile, Stuart wrote the first book about the territory, *Montana As It Is* (1865). He served on the board of the territorial prison, secured election to the legislature, and promoted Deer Lodge for the state capital. Nevertheless, as the end of the Civil War brought thousands of new settlers into the territory, the two brothers could not help but note the dominant society's disapproval of their mixed-race families. Eager to succeed on social and financial terms, the brothers discussed leaving their wives.

A letter that Stuart wrote to James in April 1873 suggests his dilemma. After more than a decade of living with Awbonnie and with the couple's fifth child on the way, Stuart wrote disparagingly of "such an outfit as mine." He encouraged James, whose second marriage had collapsed, to "keep clear of any entangling 'liaison.'" Apparently Stuart was toying with the possibility of "closing out" his own "family arrangements" and taking a "high toned" wife. He told James that "there is no woman of wealth or position so high that either of us should despair of getting her." As for "the wild reckless adventurous life" the two brothers had lived, in Stuart's opinion, far from precluding a favorable marriage, it increased their attractiveness as suitors. "Outside of this particular vicinity we could marry almost who we please."[3]

Five months later James died at Fort Peck of a liver ail-
ment. Stuart was distraught: "Oh! inexorable Death! Why
did not you take me instead of him?"[4] Over the following
months Stuart dealt with his grief by writing "A biograph-
ical sketch of James Stuart. One of the pioneers of Montana." Published in 1875 in the first volume of contributions to the Montana Historical Society, the essay secured
the older brother's reputation as a man of action (and
showed how quickly pioneer memoirs became a trope).
Stuart turned James into a western hero. In later years, he
followed a similar process for himself when he wrote his
own memoir. Stuart's presentation of his brother hero said
nothing about James's marriages, his children, or his financial problems. (He had declared bankruptcy in 1870.)
Nor did it mention his last wealth-making scheme: James
went to eastern Montana to profit from the trade in buffalo hides, and he kept meticulous records in his personal
ledger of what he paid for the sexual companionship of
young Indian women.[5]

Although James's death robbed Stuart of his primary
relationship, it cleared the way for him to draw closer to
his wife and children. Together he and Awbonnie adopted
two of James's sons. Stuart's letters for the winter 1879–
80 reflect this new devotion. On the birth of his eighth
child, Stuart wrote cheerily to a friend, Charley Warren: "I
would call that boy Charles if I had not one of that name
already—in fact if this thing keeps up I will have to import
some names as I will have the usual list exhausted." Soon,
however, the news grew grim. Stuart wrote to his youngest
brother, Thomas, "Awbonnie was confined on the 26th
and has been sick ever since. & then the measles started
in and there is Eight of the children down with it & the
ninth one looks as tho he was starting in." Four weeks later
he told his friend Reece Anderson, "My poor little baby
died last night & was buried today. . . . Awbonnie has been
insensible about half the time since its death—she has a

fearful abscess of the breast." Before 1880 was over, Stuart lost another child—five-year-old Emma—to pneumonia.[6]

Although *Forty Years on the Frontier* contains little such information about Stuart's family and his marriage to Awbonnie, it does incorporate extensive accounts of his years as a cattleman. This new enterprise, conducted during the 1880s, probably represented Stuart's last chance to strike it rich in Montana. Equally important, ranch life offered a rare opportunity for the members of his mixed-race family to succeed. His sons and nephews earned respect for their skills as horsemen and marksmen. His daughters had numerous suitors. Indeed, Mary Stuart married Teddy Blue Abbott, whose cowboy memoir *We Pointed Them North* (1939) pays tribute to his years on the DHS (Davis-Hauser-Stuart) Ranch.

Among the sources that shed light on this time in Stuart's life is a tape of his daughter Mary Stuart Abbott, at the age of eighty-eight, addressing a gathering in Lewistown, Montana.[7] Mary describes the family's move in 1881 from Helena to their land just east of the Judith Mountains. Treating the two-week trip like a grand vacation, Stuart chose the most beautiful spots for nightly campsites. When they arrived on the Musselshell Range, the grass was shoulder high and exceedingly beautiful.

From Mary's point of view, the good times continued. She describes the near-weekly dances, the roller-skating craze, the family's interest in education. She also speaks of her father's efforts to teach the children Shoshone. Her parents regularly conversed in Awbonnie's native tongue. The children could understand Shoshone, but, in Mary's words, "We never got the hang of how to talk it."

Even before his family joined him at the new ranch, Stuart found that he would need to consider violent action to maintain any claim to the open cattle range. He complained bitterly about Indians crossing the "British line" from Canada to take horses and kill cattle. But he recognized that the Indians no longer had buffalo to hunt. He knew that livestock and not people were being threatened. Yet he did not hesitate to suggest killing thieves. Despite the presence of his mixed-race family, he regularly denounced "half-breeds," whom he suspected of stealing horses. He considered the soldiers at nearby Fort Maginnis inept at stopping Indian raiders, and he accused military patrols of butchering his cattle to supplement their rations.

In a letter to his mother in West Liberty, Iowa, dated March 19, 1881, Stuart told of the need to guard their horses day and night "in Indian proof corral with a big lock on the gate & cabins & stables at the corners with portholes to shoot out of & some of us sleeping in there with one eye & both ears open. Our ranch looks like an arsenal. More Winchester rifles & revolvers & cartridge belts hanging round the walls than are in a whole county in Iowa & when we ride out each man has a repeating rifle, a revolver & two belts full of cartridges. It seems odd to me to look back to the days when Father hunted in the bottoms of Cedar River with a flint lock muzzle loading gun—even the Indians all over this western country have breech loading guns."[8] Eventually Stuart advocated raising a private army of fifty men to wipe out the Indians and "half-breeds" on the range but then relented when he figured the cost of such an operation. By the summer of 1884 he did ride with a private force of vigilantes, and in later years he continued to advocate similar violent initiatives.

As the manager of the largest open-range cattle herd in Montana, Stuart directed the slaying of at least fifteen suspected horse thieves during the summer of 1884. One of those extra-legal executions, the hanging on July 3 of Sam McKenzie, took place only a mile or two from the ranch. His daughter Mary, only fourteen, was taken by her cousin to view McKenzie's body. She had learned that before the hanging, members of her father's outfit had taken McKenzie to the bunkhouse at the DHS, where they forced him to dance and fiddle.[9] Why did Stuart, the owner of a three-thousand-book library and a four-term veteran of the territorial legislature, take the law into his own hands? Why, when he was widely acknowledged to have been the man behind the lynchings in 1884, was he appointed the U.S. minister to Uruguay and Paraguay in 1894? In his memoir, Stuart mentions McKenzie's death but gives none of the details that his daughter later recalled, and he avoided providing any names of the vigilantes who carried out the killings.

For the members of the Stuart family the years at the DHS represented the classic best and worst of times. Financially the ranch did not succeed. Too many other entrepreneurs had had the same idea. Their stock overgrazed the range; the weather proved a disaster. Eventually Stuart's financial partners deserted him. The vengeance Stuart showed toward horse thieves may have partly been his lashing out at forces that undercut his success. The contemporary treatments of "Stuart's Stranglers" in such sources as *Harper's Magazine* present Stuart as a hero whereas later accounts depict him as a villain (such is the case in the film *The Missouri Breaks*). Stuart's vigilantism far from contradicting his position in society stemmed from it. He was a leader on the range for a distinct brand of law and order. Among his colleagues in the Montana Stockgrowers Association, which supported his actions, were many of the new western elite, including Theodore Roosevelt, then a president in the making, and Russell Harrison, the son of one U.S. president, Benjamin Harrison, and grandson of another, William Henry Harrison.

Stuart was gambling on the cattle business both to bring him the pecuniary rewards he believed his courage and intelligence warranted and to provide a place in society for his marginalized mixed-blood family. Summer drought and a terrible winter produced the Great Die-Up, which killed 60 percent of Stuart's cattle in 1886–87. Personal losses followed in the wake of financial devastation. Aw-bonnie died in 1888, followed by the passing of Katie, the oldest and favorite of his children, in 1889. Stuart kept trying to restructure his personal debt with his creditors and partners but failed to receive any relief despite his constant pleadings.

In 1890 Stuart married Allis Isabelle Brown Fairfield, a schoolteacher twenty-nine years his junior. He also left the DHS Ranch, moved to the booming city of Butte, and packed off the five still-dependent surviving children from his first marriage. Three children were sent to live at the St. Ignatius Mission. Two others were taken in by recently married Mary and Teddy Blue. (Two other sons and the two adopted nephews were old enough to strike out on their own.)

Throughout the rest of his life, Stuart saw little of his children. Socially he moved in Allis Belle's orbit; financially he depended on his political connections. More and more he allowed himself to be identified by such titles as "Montana's first pioneer" and "the discoverer of gold in Montana." As a speaker, writer, and creator of western identity, Stuart played to the prejudice that smart and daring white males like himself had made Montana work.

Perhaps his happiest times came not in Montana but during a three-year interlude in Paraguay and Uruguay, where he served as the U.S. State Department's chief diplomatic representative with the rank of minister. Stuart wrote glowingly of his life in Montevideo, Uruguay's capital city. He and Belle enjoyed swimming and socializing. He sought out new opportunities for developing mines and raising cattle and hinted in his letters that he might not return to the United States. But violence still shaded his life. Uruguay plunged into a revolution fought mostly in the countryside. Montevideo remained eerily peaceful until the assassination of Uruguay's president—an event that occurred directly in front of Stuart. Less than six months after this dramatic event, a change of U.S. presidents ended Stuart's diplomatic career. Once again the prospects for personal fortune failed to pan out, and he returned to Montana.

Back in his home state, Stuart still sought a pathway to prosperity. He tried to broker the sale of mining properties, and he had Allis Belle seek out investors for timberlands in Oregon. He launched a prolonged and frustrating legal suit against Samuel Hauser, the prominent Montana banker. Stuart believed that Hauser had sold mining investments belonging to him. The case eventually reached the U.S. Supreme Court, but Hauser prevailed. For nearly a decade, Stuart lived in Butte and served as head of the Butte Public Library. Once more he was nurtured by his love of books, but his salary was modest. During this time the courtly, aged pioneer found himself in a political feud with the socialist mayor of Butte. Stuart survived the confrontation and then retired to a small ranch south of Missoula. Here he spent his final years composing a pioneer history of Montana while also writing his personal memoir.

Not surprisingly, *Forty Years on the Frontier* ends when Stuart leaves the cattle range of central Montana. His life from 1890 onward is not examined, although a manuscript chapter does exist concerning his travels as the state land agent.[10] Paul C. Phillips made numerous decisions in editing the two volumes that first appeared in 1925. His own introduction and footnotes explain some of his choices. Phillips selected the title over the objections of Allis Belle. She asserted that her husband had spent sixty-five years on the frontier and that Phillips had picked out a "chestnut" used as the title for "almost every frontier book."[11] In two letters to the publisher, the Arthur H. Clark Company of Cleveland, Ohio, Phillips claims that Allis Belle Stuart gave him a manuscript "fully three times as large as the one I sent you and I told her it could not be published in that form at all." He also explained "in regard to Mrs. Stuart's objections to the title, I limited it to forty years from the gold rush to California to the end of the cattle range."[12]

Allis Belle survived Stuart by twenty-nine years. Left with nothing but his name and papers (he had cashed in his life insurance in the desperate winter of 1890–91), Allis Belle was forced to work as a cook. She sold some of his papers, claimed others were stolen, and locked horns over the issue of ownership with the editor of Stuart's memoir as well as with one of her stepsons. The dispute continued into the middle decades of the twentieth century. All this helps explain why Stuart's papers are scattered among three separate archives and why many items, especially the vigilante materials, remain in the hands of private collectors.

Stuart's writings, including what he may have planned to put in his reminiscences, could fill multiple volumes. An old friend, Thomas Irvine, visited him during his last years and recalled that "he had a room full of diaries he had kept since 1856, what a pity he died before he saw his book in print." Irvine had helped Stuart find the rangelands for the DHS Ranch in 1880 and believed the old pioneer had nearly completed his history of Montana as well.[13]

For Stuart the story compiled in his declining years became his final commodity. It gave him little financial success, but it assured him of social and historical prominence. His life story changed to fit his own expectations of what was important and also met the larger society's expectations of what a heroic life in the West should be. The multiracial frontier that welcomed Stuart in what would become Montana exists in the narrative that he recreated in his advanced years. Yet his biracial first family is nearly absent. Free-thinking, irreligious statements do not appear. The story presented in the memoir is selective. It obscures much of the larger saga of a pioneer who outlived the frontier. Yet it remains, and deservedly so, a classic account of life in the far West of the United States.

NOTES

1. Boxes 8 and 9, MSS 1534, Granville Stuart Collection, Harold B. Lee Library, Brigham Young University (BYU), Provo UT. These boxes hold manuscripts, written by Granville Stuart in his advanced years, copies of some writings in the hand of Allis Belle Stuart, and typescripts. Much of this material served as the basis for the first volume of *Forty Years on the Frontier*, but some of it was changed or not included in the published work. Most of the drafts for the second volume of the work have not been located.

2. Entry for James Stuart, born in October, 1863, *An Illustrated History of North Idaho Embracing Nez Perces, Idaho, Latah, Kootenai, and Shoshone Counties, State of Idaho* (n.p.: Western Historical Publishing Company, 1903), 459.

3. Granville Stuart (GS) to James Stuart, April 24, 1873, Granville Stuart Collection, Box 1, Folder 5, Montana Historical Society (MHS), Helena MT.

4. Entry under October 23, 1873, Weather and Meteorological Journal, 1872–1879, Granville Stuart Collection, Box 3, Folder 4, MHS.

5. James Stuart Ledger Book, Western Americana MSS S-1969, Folder 5, Beinecke Rare Book and Manuscript Library, Yale University, New Haven CT. James recorded his relations with young Native women between January 21, 1871, and January 15, 1873. The notations were written in pencil upside down on the plain paper at the front of the book before the lined account pages.

6. GS to Chas. S. Warren in Butte, December 31, 1879; GS to Thomas Stuart in Deer Lodge, January 4, 1880; GS to Reece Anderson, January 28, 1880, Letterpress Book, Granville Stuart Collection, Box 1, Folder 3, MHS. Although a footnote in Paul Phillips's edition of *Forty Years on the Frontier* (note 56 on p. 206 in this edition) states that Awbonnie (or Aubony in his spelling) gave birth to nine children, the correct total is eleven: Katie, Tom, Charley, Mary, Lizzie, Emma, Sam, George, Edward, Harry, and Irene.

7. Mary Stuart Abbott and Oscar O. Mueller, "Lectures to the Montana Institute of the Arts," Lewiston MT, June 21, 1958, Oral History Collection #66, MHS.

8. GS to Nancy Stuart at West Liberty, Iowa, March 19, 1881, vol. 1, pp. 328–31, Letterpress Book, Beinecke, Yale.

9. Abbott and Mueller, "Lectures."

10. "To the Kootney," Box 6, Folder 10, MSS 1534, Harold B. Lee Library, BYU.

11. Allis Belle Stuart to Paul C. Phillips, June 30, 1925, Arthur H.

Clark Co. files, Spokane WA. Our thanks to Robert A. Clark for providing copies of these letters.

12. Phillips to Arthur H. Clark Co., December 3, 1924, and February 6, 1925, Arthur H. Clark Co. files.

13. Thomas H. Irvine to L. A. Huffman, March 13, 1919, Huffman Collection, McCracken Library, Buffalo Bill Historical Center, Cody WY.

Prospecting for Gold

From Dogtown to Virginia City,
1852–1864

Contents

Illustrations

Introduction

Granville Stuart had a knowledge of the far western frontier that was intimate and varied. He saw it at its beginning, and he was a part of every development until its end. As a boy in the pioneer agricultural settlements of Iowa, with the gold rush to California, and then through many years as miner, Indian fighter, trader, packer, merchant, and cattle baron, he lived every phase of frontier life. In his experience we see the seamy side of the gold craze in California and we learn something of the back wash from the tide of this great western movement. As a trader and packer he watched the currents that surged over the Immigrant road to the gold fields. Through his vision and luck, combined with that of his companions, the mountains of the Northwest, abandoned by the trapper and fur-trader, became the Mecca of thousands of gold seekers. For many years he lived the life of the gold camps. He saw its beginning in the craze for wealth; he saw its passions, its heartlessness, and crime. He also saw it in its happier moods, its drinking, its dancing, and its sports. Then as a merchant he grappled with the problems of transportation over thousands of miles of wilderness, and of distributing his goods to widely scattered customers. As pioneer conditions in the mining camps began to recede he sought a new frontier. He went into the Great American Desert east of the mountains, and was one of the first of the great cattle men of the Northwest, and as a cattle man he saw the end of the frontier.

Granville Stuart wrote in his journal, the daily experiences of more than forty years. The journals remain now, some in small memoranda books, some in account books, and others in large sized blank books. The day-by-day story of these years is so vast that many large volumes of print would not contain it.

Realizing this fact Mr. Stuart devoted the later years of his life to condensing these journals and making them into a narrative that would tell the outstanding experiences of his life. Not content with this he was busy collecting materials to explain more fully the history of the frontier, and especially the history of Montana. He sought and received sketches from many other pioneers, and he searched letters and other old papers for material. All of this he had drafted into a voluminous manuscript when death stopped his labors. The journals, the manuscript, and the other papers were put into the hands of the editor to prepare for publication.

The task was not a simple one but statement of what was done is due the reader. First the contributions of the other pioneers were excluded. Mr. Stuart had never fitted them into his narrative and the task of doing so after his death looked hopeless. Furthermore the extent of these contributions would make the work too large for publication. Mr. Stuart had been closely associated with Thomas J. Dimsdale and Nathaniel P. Langford, the historians of the "road agents" and the "Vigilantes," and had furnished them material for the writing of their books. In his last years he attempted to write the story again. He was influenced, however, by the writings of his friends to such an extent that his own contribution added little to what had already been published. For this reason the editor excluded that part of his narrative. Other parts of his manuscript had previously been published and that also was excluded. As Mr. Stuart had worked over his manuscript for years but had not finished it there were several sketches describing the same thing. The editor selected what he thought was the best and omitted the others. Finally the editor compared the completed manuscript with the old journals to verify their accuracy.

The history of Granville Stuart and his brother James is essentially a pioneer history. They broke the sod but others reaped the harvest. They gave to the world knowledge of the gold resources of Montana but they themselves panned but little of the precious metal. From their discoveries, however, there sprang up a host of millionaires. They were the first merchants of the gold mining era but others garnered the profits. And finally when Granville Stuart embarked in a business that brought him wealth, conditions beyond his control overwhelmed him with financial ruin. During all these years, however, the Stuart brothers were men of influence and character.

James Stuart was a man of action. He was an aggressive gold seeker, and he managed the mercantile business with daring skill. He was the first sheriff of a Montana county, and a desperate fighter of criminals. He led the Yellowstone expedition of 1863, and was active in the search for a direct route from the East to Montana. He was a man of tremendous energy and of violent impulses. He was a gambler, and a fighter, and a prince of good fellows. He showed marked political ability and was a man to whom the pioneers looked for advice and direction. An early death cut short a career that promised to be brilliant.

Granville Stuart was a dreamer and philosopher. He was a student of books and of nature, and a lover of all creation. He was a seeker after knowledge, and reflective both by nature and habit. He was a lover of music and art, and his pen and ink sketches, though crude, are well done. He had fine powers of observation, and he described sincerely what he saw. He had a talent for literary expression that was often enlivened by touches of bright humor.

Granville Stuart's writings are of real historical importance. He has given us the fullest description of life in Montana before and during the gold rush. He has sketched the last days of the old Hudson's Bay Company in the Northwest. He has given us glimpses of the Catholic Indian Missions when the white men were coming and the church was striving to control its converts. He has given us the best description of the old chief Victor and of the peaceful Indians, and he has presented the pioneer's views of the hostile redskins. The history of the cattle business in the Northwest is his most important contribution. No other leader in this great industry has told the story and probably no one else could tell it as well as he has done. He was with it at its beginning and throughout its whole turbulent life he was at the very center of its activities. He knew how it was financed, how it was organized, and how managed. He knew its personnel, and the plans, and ambitions, and schemes of all its members. He has described the downfall with a candor and breadth of view that carries conviction. His narrative is an important source for every student of the cattle range.

For thirty years after the end of the great cattle ranges Granville Stuart lived a life of varied fortunes. The loss of wealth had been a severe blow but his knowledge and experience on the range gave him hopes of recovering some of it. The memory of thousands of starved and frozen cattle, however, was too much for his sensibilities, and he turned his back on this business for himself. In spite of his feelings he stayed with the stockmen and for several years remained president of the Board of Stock Commissioners of Montana. This position carried heavy responsibility and no pay, but under his direction many stockmen were helped to rebuild their business on a different plan and the dangers from thieves and cattle diseases greatly reduced.

In 1891 Mr. Stuart was appointed state land agent and personally selected some six hundred thousand acres of land which the federal government had given to the state of Montana for school purposes. He had recently married Miss Isabel Allis Brown and the two of them explored every part of the state in search of desirable land. Mrs. Stuart remained his companion and helper during the remainder of his life.

In 1894 Mr. Stuart was appointed envoy extraordinary and minister plenipotentiary to the republics of Uruguay and Paraguay. As there was no direct steamship line to South America he went by way of Europe. During the five years of his mission there he traveled extensively. He went up the Paraguay river to the head of navigation and then across to the headwaters of the Amazon. On another trip he visited the great Parana Falls on the border between Brazil and Argentina. At the end of his mission he traveled around South America, stopping at every port and making many visits to the interior. The journals of his South American residence contain much information about the copper, nitrate, and other resources of that continent.

In 1904 Mr. Stuart was appointed librarian of the Butte (Montana) Public Library and there he began the preparation of his journals and reminiscences for the press. In 1916 he was commissioned by the state to write a history of Montana and was at work on this at the time of his death on October 2, 1918.

At eighty years of age Granville Stuart was a suave and courtly gentleman with an alert and inquiring mind. He regarded with reverence the sterling characteristics of pioneer life but he could laugh at its eccentricities. His retentive mind, broadened by a wealth of experience, and study, and living was engrossed by an intense desire to finish his work so that the new generation could understand the pioneers who had made the West. How well he succeeded is left for the reader to judge.

PAUL C. PHILLIPS

Preface

These reminiscences are written for the purpose of presenting, as best I can, a pen picture of the life of the "Montana Pioneer."

Civilization has moved forward so rapidly that in the short span of my life I have seen the tide of emigration sweep from the Mississippi river to the Pacific coast, and from the Rio Grande to Alaska. I can remember when there was not a single railroad west of the Mississippi, when there was not a telephone or telegraph line in existence, and a tallow dip was our best means of illumination.

The great expanse of country between the Missouri river and the Rocky mountains was put down on our maps and in our geographies as, "The Great American Desert." I crossed that desert when there was not a habitation from the Missouri river until the small Mormon settlement at Salt Lake was reached; nor one from Salt Lake until the Sierra Nevada mountains were crossed. I came to what is now our magnificent state of Montana when it was a trackless wilderness, the only white inhabitants being Jesuit fathers, and a few Indian traders and trappers at the missions and trading posts; when the mountains and valleys were the homes of countless herds of buffalo, elk, deer, moose, antelope, bear, and mountain sheep; when the streams swarmed with fish and beaver and the Indians were rich and respectable. I have watched the frontier push from the Mississippi river to the Rocky mountains, there to join hands with the settlements that had advanced from the Pacific coast; and from the Rio Grande to the Yellowstone, there to greet civilization that moved down from Hudson Bay. I saw in the valley of the Yellowstone the last of the buffalo, the last of the wild free Indians, the last of "The Great West that Was."

Now I see fields of alfalfa and waving grain where were once the bunch grass and the wild sage. Electric trains travel smoothly along o'er what once were trails, and tunnel through the mountains over which I have climbed with much difficulty. Automobiles spin along on splendid highways which but a few short years ago were my hunting trails, difficult to travel even on my sure-footed Indian pony. Where I was wont to cross streams on hastily constructed rafts I now see splendid bridges of steel and concrete. The places where I pitched my tent for a few days hunt or a prospecting trip are now the sites of thriving cities and villages illuminated by electric light. The placer mines have given place to the mines of copper and zinc. On the bank of the Missouri where I sat and sketched the falls, with one eye on my work and the other casting about for the hostile Sioux, is a great city and the largest smelter and copper reduction plant in the world. I have seen the time in Montana when there was not so much as a scrap of printed paper to read. Now every town supports one or more good newspapers; and libraries well stocked with books and periodicals are in every town and hamlet.

I was here to greet the brave men and noble women who left their homes and civilization, crossed the plains, suffering toil and privations and attacks by hostile Indians, to lay the foundation for this magnificent state. I have bidden farewell to many of these same splendid men and women who, after finishing their labors here, have crossed the Great Divide. Now there are but few left of the little band of Montana pioneers.

I leave these recollections written that those who come after may know something of the hardships endured, perils encountered, and obstacles overcome by this warm-hearted, generous, self-sacrificing band of men and women who suffered so much to attain their ideals. No finer type of men and women ever lived on this earth than were these pioneers, all of whom I hope to meet and greet some time, just over on the other side.

I see our work carried forward by the splendid young men and women of Montana and rest in confidence that it will be excellently done. To this younger generation as well as to the pioneers I am indebted for the assistance and financial aid that has enabled me to complete this work.

GRANVILLE STUART

Early Life

I was born in Clarksburg, Virginia, August 27, 1834, of Scotch descent. The Stuarts seem always to have been pioneers. An old memorandum book of my grandfather's, James Stuart, tells of his trading with Indians in Virginia in 1793. My father and mother, Robert Stuart and Nancy Currence Hall Stuart, with their two children, James and Granville, left Virginia in 1837 to try their fortunes in the then frontier state of Illinois.

They loaded their household effects on a steamboat at Wheeling, Virginia, and went down the Ohio river to its mouth and then up the Mississippi to Rock Island. Here they left the steamer and journeyed by wagon to Princeton, Bureau county, Illinois. They arrived in the early summer, having been one month making the journey.

There was a school in Princeton which my brother James attended and, although I was not of school age, I often accompanied him. The school teacher was not particularly desirous of my attendance at school and mother tried to persuade me to remain at home. Although it almost killed me to sit still so long I preferred that to remaining home alone.

My father succeeded in finding an old style compass, and he began surveying land for new settlers who were coming into the country in considerable numbers.

About this time the government purchased the land west of the Mississippi river from the Indians, and

Iowa territory was created and settlers began moving
into that fertile region.   In 1838 my parents also moved
across the river and took up a claim, number sixteen,
west of the river, on a stream called, "Wapsanohock" [1]
which means crooked creek in the Musquawkee [2] Indian language (which later in Montana, I found was
the same as Chippeway). The name, as is usual among
Indians, exactly describes that miserable muddy little
creek, which could not have been more crooked.

The bottom land, along this and other small creeks,
was covered with timber of good size; consisting of
walnut, elm, linden, hackberry, oak, hard maple (the
blessed sugar tree) butternut, hickory, and some other
kinds.   These strips of timber land, however, were
narrow, from a quarter to half mile wide, while all the
rest of the country was treeless, but covered with good
grass and many wild flowers.   The distances between
streams were great, often being from ten to twenty
miles.   After the grass became dry in the autumn, fires
of great extent, driven by high winds, became a source
of great danger and serious loss to the settler, who for
this reason usually built his cabin on the edge of the
woods where the fire could be more easily checked.

My father built his one room log cabin in the woods

---

[1] Wapsanohock creek in Cedar and Muscatine counties, Iowa. – ED.

[2] Miss Louise Kellogg, Fox Indian Wars during the French Regime in
Wisconsin State Historical Society Proceedings (1907), p. 142, states that the
Musquawkee are a branch of the Fox Indians. According to her, the Fox
Indians were also called "Mus quak kie" (Mus-quak-ku-uck). The Chip-
pewa and the Fox Indians, although bitter enemies, are both classed as
Algonquins by Frederick W. Hodge, in *Handbook of American Indians*.
(*Bureau of American Ethnology*, Bulletin no. 30, Washington, 1907). The
Potawatomi who were closely related to the Chippewa had one branch known
as Maskotens, meaning "people of the prairie." *Ibid*. These were also
known as "Maskoutechs which may be Musquawkee. They spoke the same
language as the Chippewa. It is possible that the Musquawkee were the
same as the earlier Maskotens. Miss Kellogg, however, does not believe
this. – ED.

a short distance from the creek, on a little run (the Virginia name for a small brook) which took its rise out on the prairie and flowed into the creek. This was pretty safe from the furious prairie fires, but Oh! Oh! the mosquitoes that swarmed there, and almost devoured us in the spring, summer, and fall, until frost came. Some idea of their incredible number may be gathered from the fact that the water in the run (which we had to use) was so full of their larvae, commonly known as "wiggletails," that we could neither drink nor use it until it was strained through a cotton cloth. I think that many of these mosquitoes must have carried the germs of malaria fever for we all had fever and ague, for several years, it being the worst in the autumn.

A few families of Musquawkee Indians lived in bark huts near us; my brother James and I used to play with the little Indian children of about our age and their good mothers would give us all the maple sugar we could eat, and then give us a cake of it to take home to our mother. These were good kind-hearted people although the whites were rapidly settling up their old hunting grounds, and exterminating the game. In about a year after we came, they moved further west and we saw them no more.

One of our neighbors, named Andrew Phillips, had three sons, William, John, and Solomon. One day the Phillips's, my father, James, and I were at the bridge crossing the creek, near where some Indians were camped. William Phillips, who was then about sixteen years old, was wrestling on the bridge with a young Indian of about his own age. Getting a good hold he flung the Indian over his shoulder, off the bridge and into the creek. He swam out in a furious rage, and ran to the camp to get his bow and arrows, saying he would kill young Phillips.   The older Indians and women caught and held the young one, and William's father and mine went to explain how it happened, gave them some trifling presents, and the trouble ended.   These Indians would listen to reason, and were not viciously inclined.

In the spring of 1840, my parents moved out of the creek botttom into a house on high ground, on the edge of the prairie.   There was more or less wind and consequently a few million less mosquitoes.   Near by, a small school house was built by the three or four families of the vicinity, and James and I went to school with five other young children.

The first school building I remember was a small cabin.   The logs composing it were not even hewed or peeled.   The windows – there were none – but in their stead a log was cut out of each side of the cabin, about three feet from the ground, and nearly the full length of the room, and in this space were fastened sheets of greased paper, which let in a somewhat dim and uncertain light, especially on dark cloudy days.   The door was at one end of the house, while a large open fireplace occupied the other end, and the floor was simply earth, wet and then beaten down smooth and solid. All the children attending the three months term of school in summer time, were barefooted.   The seats, however were triumphs of mechanical genius, being nothing more than rough unplaned slabs, without backs or desks of any kind.   It was pretty rough sitting I can tell you.   These slab seats were about ten inches wide and had slanting holes bored in them near the ends, into which short pieces of saplings were inserted for legs.   They were made so high that the children's feet were from six inches to a foot and a half from the floor. Of course the trustees were not to blame for the children being too short to fit the benches. At any rate the effect was to effectually double us up, and we could beat Wellington at Waterloo in wishing that night would come. For a teacher we had some young woman in the neighborhood whose educational possibilities were embraced in the three R's (reading, ritin, and rithmetic) and who was generally a little shaky on the last R. This fortunate young woman commanded the large salary of five or six dollars a month and the right to board in turn among the parents of her scholars.

I remember one of my first teachers giving me a reward of merit which was a kind of thumb stall which was put on my left thumb with which I held my book open, and was to keep my thumb from soiling the book. It was made with wings on each side and painted red and yellow to resemble a butterfly. I thought it very beautiful and kept it for long years afterward, until the house burned down and destroyed it along with my carefully preserved early school books. Perhaps this little work of art is responsible for my love for red and yellow colors to this day.

This summer saw the famous political campaign between the Whigs and Democrats. The Whigs nominated William Henry Harrison for president and the Democrats nominated Martin Van Buren. Harrison was familiarly called "Old Tippecanoe," because he defeated the Indians in the battle of that name, where the famous Indian chief Tecumseh was killed by Colonel Richard Johnson of Kentucky. While this campaign was in progress my father was building a frame dwelling house, and had in his employ several carpenters. Among them was an old chap named Ben Sailor, and I well remember one of his quaint sayings. There were large numbers of prairie chickens all about there, and in the spring when mating, they had a melodious song or refrain which sounded like "Boo-oo-oo Boo-oo-oo" long drawn out. One morning when the air was full of their music, Ben, who was an ardent Whig, said "There, listen to that, even the birds are saying, 'Tippecanoie-oo and Tyler-too-oo-oo.'" If the Democrats had any rallying cry it escaped my infantile memory.

During all this time we just shook, and shook, and shook, with the ague. We could only eat when the chill was on us, being too sick when the fever was on. I well remember how the cup would rattle against my teeth when I tried to drink and how, while trying to put the food in my mouth I would nearly put it in my ear, and how my spleen (commonly called the "melt" in those days) was swollen and felt hard as a piece of wood just below my ribs. This was known as ague cake. Almost everybody in that thinly settled part of Iowa would have the ague part of the time. Fortunately it was seldom fatal, but I can still see how thin and pale and woe-be-gone everyone looked.

In 1843 my parents moved a few miles to a farm on the bank of Red Cedar river, a lovely stream, about two hundred yards wide, with sandy bottom and water as clear as crystal. Best of all, it contained great numbers of fish, which were a welcome addition to the rather limited variety of our menu; although there was never any lack of enough, such as it was. In the winter of 1843 there was a two months term of school a mile and a half up the river, and on the farther bank at a little village called Moscow. The river was frozen over and brother James had a pair of skates, and we just flew up that lovely river to school. James did the skating and I just squatted down and held to his coat tail. For text books we had Webster's spelling book, with that discouraging frontispiece, a picture of a very lightly clad young man weakening when half way up a high mountain with a little cupola on top of it and on its front gable the word "Fame," in large letters, and a rough looking female ordering him to climb or bust. I attribute my failure to achieve greatness to that picture. The constant contemplation of it so impressed the difficulty of being famous (in that costume) upon my youthful mind that hope died within me. After we had worn our spelling books all to tiny little bits, we began on arithmetic, and each scholar seemed to have a different kind of a one. There were Doboll's, Pike's, Colbert's, and many others whose names as well as their contents have escaped me. Along toward the close of my education we had McGuffey's readers, which I thought were the very "ultima thule" of progress in the way of a reading book. Attending this school was a red-headed boy about ten or eleven years old who was a bright intelligent lad, named Erastus Yeager, who twenty-one years later was hung by the Vigilantes in Montana for being a road agent. In Montana he went by the sobriquet of "Red" and it was not until he was hanged that I learned he was my schoolmate in Iowa.[3]

[3] The road agents were a band of highwaymen who terrorized Montana during 1863. They were after gold dust and did not hesitate to kill in order to get it. Yeager was hanged January 4, 1864, by members of the vigilance committee who had organized to free Montana from the road agents. Before Yeager was hanged he confessed and gave the names of many other road agents. This assisted the committee in exterminating the band during the next two months. For an account of the road agents and vigilance committee in Montana see Thomas J. Dimsdale, *The Vigilantes of Montana* (first edition, Virginia City, 1865, third edition, Helena, 1915) and Nathaniel Pitt Langford, *Vigilante Days and Ways* (2 vols. in 1, New York, 1893). Stuart wrote that after Yeager was cut down "in his pockets were found letters addressed to him in his family name and post-marked from the little

The winter of 1843-4 was one of great severity in Iowa. Snow fell to a depth of two feet and laid nearly all winter with much weather below zero. The spring was very late. The ice in Cedar river did not break up until April 8, 1844, when we saw many fearful gorges, the ice piling up in hugh mounds and ridges, and all pushed far out of the river banks whenever the shore was low and flat. The snow was hard-crusted that winter, and many deer and wild turkeys perished from the extreme cold and the great difficulty of getting food.

In the summer of 1844 my father and two other men went up Red Cedar river with a pair of horses and a wagon on a hunting trip. There were but few people up the river in those days and they found plenty of elk and deer, where is now the town of Cedar Falls, and also many bee trees full of wild honey. They killed much game and trapped a few beavers. They dried a quantity of elk meat and filled a barrel with honey; then sold their horses and wagon, and made a large canoe out of a big walnut tree, and floated down the clear waters of Cedar river, feasting by the way on game and fish of all kinds which were there in greatest abundance. They met a few Indians, but they were all friendly. I remember well how we feasted on that dried elk meat, which was the first we children had ever eaten. The honey in the barrel was all candied and was delicious.

The big walnut canoe was so broad and steady that it could not be overturned by two men standing on one edge of it. Mother let brother James and me use it, and we soon became expert canoe boys and fearlessly

town of West Liberty, Iowa. When shown to James and me we knew that Red was Erastus Yeager. . ." – ED.

went everywhere in it. We very often paddled it at night for our father, who would place on its bow a tin lamp holding about a quart of lard with a rag wick in its spout which, when lighted, would cast a strong light for several yards in front of the canoe. The water of the river being as clear as glass our father could plainly see every fish as far as the light shone on the water. He used a three prong spear called a gig, with a red cedar shaft about ten feet long. Fish seemed attracted by the light and did not seem alarmed by the canoe. In two or three hours he would spear fifteen or thirty fine large ones of various kinds, with occasionally a gar, which was a fish three or four feet long, not fit to eat but which had a snout over a foot long filled with long sharp teeth. The next morning after a night's fishing my brother James and I had the task of carrying the surplus fish as presents to the neighbors.

About half a mile from our house there was a pretty little lake about seven hundred yards long and four hundred yards wide; along its shores on the west side were pleasant woods with some crabapple and plum thickets. Amid these beautiful surroundings on the shore of the lake the settlers of the vicinity built a small log school house which was rough plastered inside. It had glass windows and a real board floor, but best of all, there was a good swimming hole near by. We scholars just thought that anyone who wanted a better school house than that was too hard to please for any use. In this school house was held a summer school for three months (in 1844) where my three brothers and myself increased our small supply of knowledge.

At this time, 1843 to 1850, there was an abundance of game in the wooded creek bottoms and on the prairies and as my father was a good hunter we always had plenty to eat of squirrels, prairie chickens, wild turkeys, deer, and elk, and after the first year there were corn-meal and vegetables.   The scarce articles for the larder were coffee, tea, and sugar, although we had plenty of maple sugar and syrup, pure from the tree, something that one seldom ever gets in this year, 1916.

This was still the era of tallow-dip candles for light-ing and of open fire-place for heating and cooking and the cast-iron skillet and Dutch oven for baking.   The first cooking stove I ever saw was in 1845 and it was rather a crude affair, but a great relief from cooking over an open fire, although some of the first to use the new invention had more or less trouble getting used to it.   My father-in-law used to tell a story about an old couple who were the first to invest in a cook stove in his neighborhood.   They got the stove in St. Louis and brought it up the Mississippi river and home.   The neighbors came from near and far to view the stove and it became the center of interest and subject of gossip for the entire neighborhood.   Finally the excitement subsided, and little was said or heard of the new stove, when one day someone asked Mr. Jones how he liked the new stove by this time.   "Well," the old man answered, "the stove is all right I reckon, but mother and I are getting too old to lift the tarnal thing on and off the fire-place, so we jest cook the old way."

The guns used for hunting in those days were flint-lock rifles brought by the frontiersmen from Virginia and Kentucky.   They were full-stocked, that is, the wood of the stock reached to the muzzle of the barrel. They were heavy, weighing from eleven to thirteen pounds, all hand work with small calibres, running from about sixty round bullets to the pound of lead.   A cousin of mine bought a four-foot barrel, full stock rifle, carrying one hundred and fifty bullets to the pound of lead, for which he paid six dollars in cash. Money was very scarce in those days, nearly all trading being carried on by barter.

Father had two guns which I well remember, as it was with these guns he taught me to hunt. One was a flint-lock that he used when hunting along streams where there was timber and little wind. If the weather was cold and snow on the ground he could quickly start a fire with his flint-lock by which he would dress the deer he had killed. With the gun he was sure of killing a deer, if it was within one hundred and twenty-five yard distance. The other gun he used while hunting on the prairies or out in the wind. It was a small-bore rifle fired with percussion caps placed on the nipple. The cap would not blow off as did the powder in the pan of the flint-lock.

In our neighborhood was a widow with several children whose husband had been a good hunter. His rifle was a flint-lock half stock, of large calibre for those days, using forty round balls to the pound of lead. A half stock rifle was one in which the wood only extended along the barrel about one-third of the way to the muzzle, and from its end to the muzzle, on the under side of the barrel was a slender piece of iron called a rib, on which was soldered from two to four small pieces of iron or brass tubing called thimbles, in which the ramrod of tough hickory wood was carried. All rifles in those days were muzzle loaders and the Johnson one was the first half stocked gun I ever saw. My father used to borrow it occasionally because its large balls were more fatal to the deer than those of his small calibre rifle. When he was successful the Johnson family always received half of the venison. This

rifle was much better finished than most of the guns
then in use.   It had an oval silver box set in the butt
stock on the right side, a few inches forward was a hole
in which to carry an extra flint for the lock, and a
greased piece of rag to use in keeping the gun from
rusting if it got wet.   On the inside of this lid Johnson
had scratched or roughly engraved three letters, "B,"
and just below it, "D," and below that, "F."   After B
he marked the list of bucks killed by him (numbering
16) ; after D, the list of does (numbering 13) ; after F
the list of fawns (numbering 10).   My father, leaving
a little space after each of Johnson's list, added those
killed by him when he used the gun.   How I would
like to have that gun now as a souvenir of the ancient
days and conditions when life was just unfolding to me.

In the spring of 1849 the news of the discovery of
gold in California reached Iowa, and my father at once
determined to go to the gold fields.   He formed a traveling partnership with three other men and they bought
a wagon and four yoke of oxen and about four months'
supply of provisions, clothing and ammunition.   About
the middle of April, 1849, they started on the long
dangerous journey across the plains and mountains;
eighteen hundred miles through an unknown and uninhabited country, save the settlement of Mormons in
Great Salt Lake valley and the roving tribes of Indians
who had no fixed abode.

The emigrants, as these gold seekers were called, soon
learned that in union there was strength, and united
their scattered forces into trains of from ten to fifty
wagons, with from forty to two hundred men.   The
two principal starting places for these trains were,
Council Bluffs, Iowa, and St. Joe, Missouri.   Emigrants would come from all points, east and south and

when there were a sufficient number of wagons to form
a train, they would start out. The Indians rarely ever
attacked these large trains but were always lurking
around trying to steal their stock and they frequently
got away with a few scattered horses or mules. On the
western end of their route the Digger [4] Indians were
particularly annoying, as they were constantly stealing
cattle and horses.

On Black's fork of Green river the emigrant road
forked. The left hand road went up Black's fork to
Fort Bridger,[5] and then on to Salt Lake City. The
right hand road went up Ham's fork about thirty-four
miles and then crossed over some high clay ridges,
without any timber on them, to Bear river, then down
Bear river to Soda springs where it left the river and

[4] This name first applied to a small Shoshone tribe in Utah because they
practiced agriculture came to be applied to many tribes who lived on roots.
As most of these Indians were of low type the term became one of reproach.
Stuart probably referred to the tribes living between the Great Salt Lake
and Fort Hall. They were very degraded, living mostly upon roots and
insects. They seldom built habitations and had little clothing. They were
also often without shelter of any kind and were unable to purchase fire-arms.
The French called them *"Digne de pitie"* (worthy of pity). The Digger
Indians are sometimes classed with the Piutes, a more vigorous tribe. See
Thwaites's note in *Early Western Travels* (Cleveland, 1906) vol. xxviii, p.
312. Father De Smet described them with other tribes in 1841 in a letter
to Father Roothaan, General of the Society of Jesus. *Letters and Sketches*
. . . (Philadelphia, 1843) pp. 34-39. Also in Thwaites, *Early Western
Travels*, vol. xxvii, pp. 164-168. Fremont described the Diggers in 1845 as
follows: "They had the usual very large heads, remarkable among the
Digger tribe, with matted hair, and were almost entirely naked; looking
very poor and miserable, as if their lives had been spent among the rushes
where they were. . ." *Report of the Exploring Expedition to the Rocky
Mountains in the Year 1842* (Washington, 1845) p. 149. – ED.

[5] On the site of Fort Bridger was a small trading post in 1834. In 1843
Jim Bridger acquired it and started a blacksmith and repair shop and a
supply station for emigrants on the Oregon trail. Most travellers either to
Oregon or California passed this way for the conveniences of the post.
Grace R. Hebard and E. A. Brininstool, *The Bozeman Trail* (2 vols., Cleve-
land, 1922) vol. i, p. 48; Hiram Chittenden, *History of the American Fur
Trade in the Far West* (3 vols., New York, 1902) vol. i, p. 476.

went northwest to old Fort Hall on Snake river, then
down that stream for some thirty-five miles, then west
to the City of Rocks (which was a number of curiously
grouped granite pinnacles, which resembled buildings).[6]   At this place the branch roads reunited and
continued on as one until far down the Humboldt river.

This river should not be named Humboldt river for
this reason: In 1847 a party of Mormons found a man
named Peter Ogden, with his wife and children,
camped on Weber river, where now stands the city of
Ogden.   These Mormons were desirous of journeying
further west than the basin of Great Salt lake and Ogden told them of this river.   Following his directions
they found the river.   Ogden's wife's name was Mary
and she was the first white woman to travel down the
river, so out of compliment to her the Mormons always
called it the Mary Ogden river and so it should be
called.[7]   My father's party followed down this river

---

[6] This right hand road was known as the Sublette "Cut Off." While
shorter than the route via Fort Bridger it had no water and no supply
stations and was seldom used. *Ibid.*, vol. i, p. 478. The old Oregon trail
by Fort Bridger joined the Sublette "Cut Off" near Bear lake. The trail
by Salt Lake City went around the north end of Great Salt lake and down
the Humboldt joining the trail from Bear river and another from Fort Hall
as described by Stuart. – ED.

[7] Stuart is wrong regarding the date of Ogden's visit to this region.
Ogden became chief trader in charge of the Snake river brigade in 1824 and
left the mountains in 1831. Lewis and Phillips editors, *The Journal of John
Work* (Early Western Journals no. 1, Cleveland, 1923) pp. 28, 29. T. C.
Elliott, "Peter Skene Ogden, Fur Trader" in *Oregon Historical Quarterly*, xi,
no. 3, p. 23, thinks that Ogden penetrated this country in 1828. Traders and
trappers called this river Mary's or Ogden's river for a number of years
before the Mormons migrated to this country. Thomas J. Farnham, *Travels
in the Great Western Prairies* . . . in Thwaites, *opus citra*, xxviii, p.
113. This account was written in 1839. See also Chittenden, *American Fur
Trade*, vol. ii, p. 797. Ogden was one of the most daring of the Hudson's
Bay Company's fur traders. Mary, his wife, was an Indian squaw. Fremont named this river, the Humboldt, on his third expedition apparently not
knowing it was the Mary's river, he had previously hunted. John Charles
Fremont, *Memoirs of My Life* (Chicago and N. Y., 1887) p. 434. – ED.

some two hundred miles to Big Meadows where an old trapper named Larson had laid out a new route to the mines, which he claimed was the best and shortest road. They took that road, but found it went too far north, crossing the Sierra Nevada mountains near Goose lake and thence down Pit river into the head of Sacramento valley, being quite two hundred miles longer than the southern route by way of Carson river to Hangtown (afterwards Placerville). They reached Sacramento valley without a loss, late in the fall of 1849.

My father mined part of the time, hunted large game, elk, deer and antelope, which he sold at a good price.

In the winter of 1851 he returned home to Iowa via the steamship line to Nicaragua, across that country, and then by Garrison's steamer to New Orleans and up the Mississippi river. He kept a journal all the time but unfortunately our house burned down and with it many other valuable family records were destroyed. I remember well reading his journal which was a perfect pen-picture of the days of forty-nine.

Overland to California

In the spring of 1852, in company with my father, my brother James, and a jovial Irishman named Fayal Thomas Reilly, I started from near the village of West Liberty, Muscatine county, Iowa, on the long adventurous journey to California; overland across the vast uninhabited plains, then known on the maps as the "Great American Desert," but now (in 1916) forming the wealthy states of Nebraska, Kansas, Colorado, and Wyoming. Iowa then was very sparsely settled, and there was not a single railroad west of the Mississippi river, and I had never seen one, and never did until fourteen years later in 1866, at Atchison, Kansas.

Our outfit consisted of two light spring wagons each drawn by four good horses. In the wagon boxes we carried our supply of food and extra clothing. A loose floor of boards was placed across the top of the wagon boxes on which we placed our bedding, and on which we slept at night. The wagons had the usual canvas curtains which buttoned on to each end of the canvas roof. Inside we slept dry and comfortable through the worst storms. The storms along the Platte river were regular cloudbursts, accompanied by such fierce gales of wind as often to blow down the tents, which were used by most of the emigrants, and thoroughly soak their bedding. My father having had that disagreeable experience when he crossed this region in 1849, had so arranged that we slept in our wagons, using no tents, and thus were always dry, though many times we were obliged to picket the wagons to the ground to prevent their blowing over.

My father and brother occupied one wagon, and Reilly and myself the other. We each had a rifle and father had a small five-shooter revolver of twenty-five calibre, using black powder and round balls. I think it was called "Maynard's patent." No one would carry such a pistol nowadays, but revolvers were then just invented. This was the first one I had ever seen and I longed for the day when I could possess one, and bid defiance to whole villages of Indians, little knowing that the Indian with his bow and arrows, was quite beyond the reach of such a puny weapon. Our rifles were hung up in leather loops fastened to the sides of the wagon boxes, always loaded (they were all muzzle loaders) and ready for instant use. Our journey across the state of Iowa was a most disagreeable one. The western half of the state was very thinly inhabited. We had great difficulty in crossing the deep miry sloughs that at that period filled every low place. There being few people, there were still fewer bridges, and when our horses and wagons mired down, which usually happened about twice a day, we were forced to wade in mud and water up to our knees while unloading our wagons and then lift with all of our strength on the wheels to enable our horses to pull them out. Somewhere between Des Moines (then a small village) and Council Bluffs, we came to a Mormon village called Kanesville. These people, mostly Welsh and English, had wintered here in 1851 while on their way to Great Salt lake, and now found it profitable to stay this summer and repair the wagons and shoe the horses of the emigrants, who were passing through in large numbers on their way to California. We remained with them two days waiting our turn to get our horses shod and some small repairs to our wagons.

After many annoyances and much profanity we at last arrived at Council Bluffs on the east bank of the Missouri river. The village consisted of some twelve or fifteen one-story log cabins. We had to cross the river here, and when I saw the ferry boat, a flat scow, large enough to hold one team and wagon, the motive power of which was three men with oars, I looked at the wide swift flowing muddy river and thought we might possibly get across safely, but that the chances were rather poor. The price for crossing was ten dollars for each wagon and horses, which seemed to me exorbitant. However, we got across and from the way those oarsmen had to pull I concluded the price was reasonable enough. On the west side of the river to our astonishment, we found a considerable town of log houses, but every house was dismantled. We afterwards learned this had been the town where the Mormons had waited in 1846-47, until their leaders went on ahead and looked up a future abiding place for them. They called the settlement on the bank of the Missouri, "Far West." This is the site of the present city of Omaha. After crossing the river we traveled for several days across a gently rolling prairie country, till we came to Elk Horn river, a beautiful clear stream about fifty yards wide, with a fine strip of cottonwood timber along its banks. We crossed this river also on a ferry for which we paid five dollars for each team, but as we traveled up it for several miles we saw that if we had camped near the ferry and examined the stream for a few miles we could have forded it and saved our ten dollars.

From Elk river we crossed a prairie country and struck Platte river at Grand island and then traveled up its north bank for over two hundred miles. In this distance we saw only one lone tree which the emigrants had partly destroyed and doubtless not a vestige of it remained by July. In this long distance there was not a willow along this strangest of all rivers, with its yellowish, whitish water, which was usually over a half mile wide and in no place more than three feet deep, flowing with a swift current over a bed of quicksand dangerous to cross. The banks on either side were only from two or three feet high and the adjacent plains were covered with a fine growth of grass. It was while traveling up this stream that we encountered the most terrific storm that I had ever seen. Dark clouds appeared in the sky and distant thunder growled a warning. We lost no time in making ready and it was well we did. We buttoned our canvas covers down closely and tied one end of a stout rope to each wagon wheel and the other end to stakes driven deep into the ground, thus securely fastening the wagons so the wind could not blow them over. We had just finished our preparations when the storm broke. The wind blew a gale. Rain and small hail fell in torrents and we could not hear each other speak for the deafening peals of thunder which were preceded by blinding flashes of lightning. We expected every minute to have a wagon overturned or to be struck with lightning. The storm lasted about two hours, but without any serious damage to us. The tight canvas covers kept us dry and the picket ropes kept the wagons from turning over.

Next morning we passed a train that had set up tents. The tents were blown over and their blankets and provisions were soaked with water and they presented a dismal appearance trying to dry out their things and gather up their tents. The women and children looked particularly uncomfortable, but they greeted us with a cheery "Good-morning" and were all making the best of the situation.

Cholera was raging among the emigrants all along the road and many were dying. We drove as fast as our horses could stand it to get through this dreadful region of death, where we were seldom out of the sight of graves and saw many heartrending scenes. Abandoned wagons were numerous, and their former owners were in graves near by. We met a young woman driving a span of horses to a light wagon and with her were four little children, from two to seven years old. She stopped to talk with us. Her husband had died three days before and she was trying to return to Illinois, where her relatives lived. We gave her some sugar and coffee and did what we could to comfort her, telling her always to camp at night with some other wagons, that she would be meeting every day, for if any Indians saw her camped alone, they might take her horses, plunder her wagon, and abuse her.

One evening we camped near five abandoned wagons. Close by were freshly made graves and by one of the wagons was a large yellow dog, with a bushy tail. He was thin and nearly starved. While we were eating supper he came near us and stood looking longingly at our food. I could not stand that, so I coaxed him to me and divided my supper with him, which he devoured ravenously. He then went back and laid down by one of the graves and there remained all night. In the morning I called him to me and fed him well. He then went back to the same grave and laid down by it again. When we hitched up our horses and got ready to start I called him and we started to go. He followed a few steps, and then turned and went part of the way to the graves, stopped and began howling, Oh! so mournfully. We stopped to see what he would do. He quit howling and turned and came slowly to us, and when we again started he followed us. His pitiful howling was his leave taking of the loved one who lay there in the lonely grave. My eyes filled with tears of sympathy for him and I did my best to make him feel at home with us, little thinking that he was to save my life the next year. After he followed us a short distance I saw that he was too weak to keep up, for we traveled at a fast trot, so I took him up on the footboard of the wagon, where he lay part of the time, all the way to California.

The cholera did not extend above Fort Laramie,[8] and as soon as we struck the mountains we felt safe from it. How I did enjoy gazing upon them, and drinking clear ice-cold water from many lovely little streams. We continued up the North Platte river to the cañon and James and I went some distance from camp to take our first look at a mountain stream. Here the water was roaring and foaming over enormous boulders, with cliffs almost perpendicularly rising from one hundred to three hundred feet above the water, a

[8] Fort Laramie was located at the confluence of the Laramie and the North Platte. It was built in 1834 as a fur trading fort and named Fort William for William L. Sublette. Sublette sold it in 1835 to the fur trading firm of Fitzpatrick, Sublette, and Bridger who soon turned it over to the American Fur Company who renamed it Fort John for John B. Sarpy. The name Laramie gradually came into use and finally supplanted its official name. Chittenden, *opus citra*, vol. iii, p. 967.

Some years later Stuart wrote of Fort Laramie . . . "There are wood and water plenty; and, before many trains have passed, the grass is good above the fort. Mail station and post office here, with sutler's store, well stocked with travellers' outfits." *Montana As It Is* (New York, 1865) p. 132. – ED.

wonderful sight for two boys who had always lived in a level prairie country with sluggish muddy creeks.

In the summer of 1907 I traveled along this same strange river, in a luxurious car of the Union Pacific Railroad and saw all that was once a lonely stretch of plains, occupied by highly cultivated farms and fine residences, the owners of which were entirely unconscious that there were few fields bordering the view that did not have several unknown graves in them, where rested the bones of the hardy pioneers who fell by the wayside, when on their way to form a western empire on the shores of the far distant Pacific ocean.

Here we left the river and traveled several miles through red, desolate looking hills, passed Red buttes,[9] and then saw a pond of reddish looking water, where some good men (among the many who had preceded us) had put up a notice not to let horses or cattle drink of that water, as it was poisonous. The water carried so strong a solution of alkali as to make it dangerous to animals who drank it. Not far from the spring we saw two dead oxen and a horse. We took warning and did not stop, but kept on to a point where the water was less alkaline. We could now see Laramie peak, far away to the south, with patches of snow on it. This was our first look at snow in July and a wonderful sight it was. We passed Independence rock,[10] so named by the emi-

---

[9] Red buttes about one hundred fifty miles from Fort Laramie. *Ibid.*, pp. 132-133. – ED.

[10] Independence rock. The name originated long before 1842. Chittenden, *American Fur Trade*, vol. ii, p. 472, thinks it goes back to the Ashley expedition of 1823. Father De Smet described it in 1841, and even then he was not sure of the origin of the name. H. M. Chittenden and A. T. Richardson, *Life, Letters, and Travels of Father Pierre-Jean De Smet, S. J.* (N. Y., 1905, 4 vols.) vol. iv, p. 1348. John Wyeth visited the rock in 1832 and even that early the origin of the name was forgotten. Wyeth, *Oregon, or a Short History of a Long Journey*, edited by Thwaites, *Early Western Travels* (Cleveland, 1905) vol. xxi, p. 53. – ED.

grants of 1842, on their way to Oregon, who camped
near it on July 4.   It is an enormous lump of granite,
which rises about twenty-five feet above the plain of
sand and gravel.   It covers about a half acre and is
worn smooth by glacier action in past ages.   It is a
most remarkable object.   There are hundreds of names
and dates that passers-by have put on it with tar and
paint, and a few cut into the hard rock.   I saw a number bearing the date of 1849, and among them was my
father's name, Robert Stuart, July 29, 1849.

Just above Independence rock we came to a large
creek called "Sweetwater river," which is a branch of
North Platte river.   We forded this stream just below
"The Devil's Gate," where the river runs through a
high ridge between two perpendicular cliffs, one hundred and fifty to two hundred feet high.   What seemed
strange was that the river could have made a bend
around the end of the ridge without passing through it,
and probably did so in ancient geological times, until
an obliging earthquake made a big crack through it,
which the river at once took possession of.   This short-
ened its course a little.   This stream takes its name
from its beautiful clear cold waters having a sweetish
taste, caused by the alkali held in solution in its waters,
not enough, however, to cause any apparent injurious
effects.   In this vicinity we saw a most remarkable
pond, with water that looked white as snow.   On examination it proved to be not white water, but a bed of
pure white soda, several feet thick, deposited by the
evaporation of the alkali water, which had leaked in
out of the neighboring soil, during a long period of
time.   The Mormon emigrants took large quantities of
this soda to Salt lake and they said it was fully as good
as the commercial article.

We traveled up Sweetwater river three days when we came to Strawberry creek, where the road left the river and ascended a long rocky hill, known as "Rocky Ridge." Not much wood during these three days, but some large sagebrush and plenty of good grass and water. Somewhere in this vicinity was a grassy swamp, where we dug down about eighteen inches and came to a bed of solid clear ice. We dug up enough to put into water-kegs and enjoyed the luxury of ice-water all that hot day, while we traveled through the famous "South pass,"[11] of the Rocky mountains. There are no mountains near on either side, but only low grassy ridges with a slight depression through them where the emigrant road passed, but twenty miles on, more to the north was a range of snow-clad mountains, the highest one known as Fremont's Peak, because Lieutenant Fremont ascended it in 1842, and estimated its height as thirteen thousand feet.[12] The South pass is six thousand feet above sea level.

For several days I was greatly annoyed by frequent bleeding at the nose, which I afterwards ascertained was caused by the increasing altitude. I have never had any trouble with it since, when at much greater altitudes. On the west side of the pass we camped at Pacific springs, called because their waters flow into the Pacific ocean, by way of the Colorado river, which here is known as Green river because in the autumn, its water, where deep, has a beautiful green tint. Good

[11] South pass. Probably discovered in 1823 by Thomas Fitzpatrick. This opened the way for the discovery of a central route to the Pacific. Harrison C. Dale, *The Ashley Smith Explorations and the Discovery of a Central Route to the Pacific,* 1822-1829 (Cleveland, 1918) pp. 89, 90. For other claims see *ibid.,* p. 40. Seymour Dunbar, *History of Travel in America* (Indianapolis, 1915, 4 vols.) vol. iv, p. 1216, *note,* states that South pass is located on a map, by Melish about 1820. – Ed.

[12] J. C. Fremont, *opus citra,* p. 174. – Ed.

water and grass at the springs, no wood, but sagebrush.
From Pacific springs we traveled sixteen miles over a
sandy gravelly plain, with thin scattering grass, to Dry
Sandy creek.   No wood, but small grease wood and
sagebrush, water blackish, but drinkable.   "Sublette's
Cut Off" road turns off to the right here for Soda
springs, on Bear river, and Fort Hall on Snake river.
We took the left-hand road for Fort Bridger and Great
Salt Lake City.   From Dry Sandy to Little Sandy
creek was fifteen miles, over the same gravelly sandy
plain.   Here we found good water, but very little
grass.   Almost no fuel from here to Big Sandy creek,
eighteen miles of same kind of prairie.   Good water
here, but only grass in spots along the creek, fuel scarce
all the way from here to the upper ford on Green river.
Here was a ferry used during high water, but the
stream is fordable in the late summer and autumn.

At Green river we found plenty of grass and wood.
We went down this stream seven miles, to the lower
ford and ferry, where we found some Mormons, who
were ferrymen and traders.   We then traveled across
gravelly bench lands sixteen miles to Black's fork of
Green river.   All along here we had fine grass, plenty
of wood, and good water.   We journeyed up Black's
fork crossing and recrossing the river, traveling over
sagebrush valleys and rolling grassy hills to Smith's
fork.   This is a small branch of Black's fork coming
in from the south.   The road was good, but there was
very little grass.   No wood here, the hills are of hard
clay, bad land formation from Ham's fork all the way
to Fort Bridger, with many eroded buttes, scattered
about often resembling ancient castles and old ruins.
Fort Bridger like Fort Laramie was not a military fort
but a trading post.   There was a stockade with cabins

inside, built solely to trade with Indians, who were numerous through here, but were not hostile. We camped a few miles below the fort on the creek where we found plenty of grass and wood enough for our use. We did not lay over at Fort Bridger as we intended to stop at Salt Lake.

We traveled six miles across grassy hills to Muddy creek and on over to Sulphur creek. There were several fine springs of good water along the road, but wood was very scarce. Quaking Aspen hill between Muddy creek and Sulphur creek is the eastern rim of the Great Basin of Great Salt lake. All streams in this great basin run into the lake which has no outlet. Bear river is the first river we strike after entering the basin. It is a fine large stream of clear cold water. Here was a good camping place, plenty of wood, water, and grass. Bear river is easily forded excepting during the months of May and June, when the water is high and the ford becomes dangerous.

From Bear river to Red fork of Weber river, nineteen miles, is mostly through the wonderful "Echo cañon," which is bordered by the lofty pinnacles and cliffs of deep red sandstone forming some grand scenery. In this cañon, two miles below the cavern called "Cache cave," were good water and grass, but little wood. Here my brother James and I killed a deer. We had done scarcely any hunting and had seen little game. The emigrant trains were so numerous at that time that the wild game had all been driven away from the road and this was the first deer we had seen on the trip. At Spring branch, five miles below, the road leaves the river and strikes a little valley to the left. Here we saw a fine spring of clear cold water, to which we hastened to get a drink, which we as hastily spit out, for it was as salt as strong brine. It was the first salt spring we had seen, but we found several others between there and Salt Lake City.

Our next stop was at Beauchemin fork, nine miles. The road followed down Beauchemin fork to Big Cañon creek fourteen miles. In the first eight miles of this journey the road crossed Beauchemin fork thirteen times and was very dangerous in time of high water. At Cañon creek the road left Beauchemin fork and ascended Big mountain by way of a very steep ravine, to Big Cañon creek, where there was good water, wood, and grass. High mountain ridges all around. Then by way of Emigrant creek to Great Salt Lake city, ten miles. Our horses were greatly in need of rest so we stayed with the "Latter Day Saints," as the Mormons called themselves, for several weeks and were very kindly treated by them. In fact, I here got into better society than I have been in since, for I lived a month with one of the "Twelve Apostles" and his family. It was "Apostle John Taylor," a pleasant old gentleman, who succeeded Brigham Young, as head of the Mormon Church. He wore a snuff colored suit, and a rather rusty old plug hat. He owned a whole block and had an adobe house on each of the three corners, in which lived his three wives, each in her own house. I had the honor of living with the Apostle and wife no. 1, in house on fourth corner. She was a most amiable woman, a good cook, and a good housekeeper. She kept everything nice and clean, but the confounded bed bugs ran us out of the beds in the house, and we all slept out in the yard. Luckily it never rained. Mrs. Taylor felt greatly mortified about the bed bugs and said that she just couldn't keep them out, although she fought them all the time, and when one day, I pulled a piece of bark off a fir pole on a near by fence and found innumerable bed bugs under it, I knew why Mrs. Taylor could not keep them out of the house. The entire valley swarmed with them.[13]

When we camped on Weber river, where is now the city of Ogden, the sagebrush, just after sundown, swarmed with skunks, and I felt certain that Great Salt lake could beat the world for bed bugs and skunks. At this place I was stricken with a severe attack of mountain fever which laid me on my back in the wagon until we reached the Sierra Nevada mountains.

We had traveled one thousand miles since leaving Council Bluffs on the Missouri river, and the entire distance was uninhabited, except by a few Indian traders at Fort Laramie on North Platte, who live mostly like the Indians on wild meat straight – a few ferrymen on Green river and a few traders at Fort Bridger. We saw only a few Indians (Pawnees) on the trip, and they were friendly to the emigrants. We saw only a few straggling buffalo, as the great herds had passed on their annual migration north, while we were on the Platte river.

From Salt lake we took the emigrant road to Goose creek, up which we traveled something like seventy-five miles, then crossed over a divide into Thousand Spring valley. Most of the springs were hot. We passed over to the north fork of the Humboldt river. Here the emigrant road forks. One road follows down the river several hundred miles to its sink, and crosses

---

[13] Mr. Stuart wrote of Great Salt Lake city in 1865, "Feed for stock can be purchased here and so can any articles that the traveller may require, but the price will make his hair stand straight on 'end.' There is no camping place within two miles of the city and it is best either to stop near the mouth of 'Emigration cañon' or to cross to 'The other side of Jordan.'" *Montana As It Is*, p. 136.

a desert., distance of thirty miles, to Carson river. This was the southern route.[14] We took the other route and left the Humboldt river above its sink, going west across a desert forty-five miles wide, to Truckee river. Half way across this forty-five miles of sandy desert there was a very large boiling spring around which passing emigrants had left some surplus water barrels. These the departing emigrants would fill with hot water and leave to cool for those who were coming behind. In this way there was nearly always cool water in the barrels, awaiting the thirsty emigrant.

We started across the desert about four o'clock in the afternoon and reached the spring about midnight, where we rested an hour and watered our horses with the cooled water. We then filled everything with the hot water and started on, reaching Truckee river shortly after noon the next day. This river takes its source at Lake Tahoe and is a beautiful clear cool mountain stream flowing over a pebbly bottom, certainly a most refreshing sight to us coming from the heat, sand, and dust of the desert. It was full of magnificent trout, weighing from one to two pounds. We lost no time getting out fishhooks and lines, and during our stay here (two days) we feasted on trout.

We crossed the Sierra Nevada mountains by way of Beckwith pass, so named because old Jim Beckwith was living there and claimed to have discovered the pass. We found him living up in the valley leading to his pass. Many of the emigrants reaching his place were nearly starved. His nature was a hospitable and generous one and he supplied their pressing necessities,

---

[14] *Ibid.*, pp. 137-139. Here Mr. Stuart gives the itinerary for this southern route but not for the road his party followed. The details in his account of the trip from Fort Laramie to this place are the same as in the earlier book. – ED.

often without money, they agreeing to pay him later, which I regret to say a number of them failed to do. This so impoverished him that he was compelled to give up his place in the pass and resume a roving life, which he had long been accustomed to. The next place I heard of him was at Napa valley, California. Later he returned to Montana and resumed his old life among the Crows.[15]

After we crossed the Sierra Nevadas we came into American valley and halted at a wayside hostelry called the "American Ranch," which was the first ranch that I had seen. Here to our dismay, we learned that we had reached the end of the wagon road, as that part between there and Bidwell's bar on Feather river, a distance of fifty miles had not been constructed yet. A trifling detail that the robust liars on the Humboldt river (who were boosting for this route over the

[15] Beckwith should be spelled Beckwourth. For Beckwourth's account of this pass see *Life and Adventures of James P. Beckwourth*, edited by Charles G. Leland. (London, 1891) pp. 423-431, or edited by T. D. Bonner (New York, 1856) pp. 514-520. Stuart's manuscript here contains long accounts of Beckwourth taken from his *Life and Adventures* which the editor omits. Stuart's description of the last of Beckwourth's adventures is not contained in the Beckwourth book and is as follows: "In 1876 he was back on the Big Horn river in Montana with Captain John W. Smith, post-trader at Fort C. F. Smith. Beckwith had regained some of his former influence among the Crows. As soon as the troops came to the fort, Smith sent him to the river to bring up a large party of Crows that was camped there for the purpose of trading with them. Beckwith who was gettting old, was mounted on a spirited cavalry horse and seeing a small herd of buffalo he determined to kill one. His companions tried to persuade him not to attempt to run buffalo on such a horse, but he would not listen to them and started in pursuit. He soon was in the midst of the buffalo herd. His frightened horse became unmanageable, plunging and rearing among the running buffalo, and the old man was thrown and seriously injured. Some Indian women picked him up and placing him on a travois started with him for camp, but he died before reaching it. He was buried on the Big Horn in the hunting grounds of his adopted people." This story was apparently told Mr. Stuart by Tom H. Irvine one time sheriff of Custer county, Montana. – ED.

Sierra) neglected to tell when telling us this route was the nearest and best one to the Sacramento valley. We remained a few days at the "Ranch" eating three meals a day at one dollar a meal. The food was good, and I gained rapidly in strength. As the road from American valley into Sacramento valley had not been built, being only a pack trail for the greater part of the distance, we found ourselves bottled up, unable to go further into California with our wagons. We were obliged to sell them for a mere trifle; my recollection is that we got only twenty-five dollars for each of the spring wagons, which if we could have taken them on to Sacramento valley would have been worth two hundred dollars apiece. Our eight fine horses and harness we subsequently sold for sixteen hundred dollars. Getting some old saddles we took the pack-horse or rather mule trail for the Sacramento valley. This trail ran along across mountain ridges, often quite steep, and I can never forget how I suffered the next day, being still weak, and entirely unused to riding on horseback. It was all I could do to keep from falling off when going down the steep hills.

The first night out we staid at Balsein's ranch, on the divide between the middle and north forks of the Feather river. The food was excellent, but I was unable to eat and I was so exhausted I could scarcely stand up. The second day the road was much better, and we reached Bidwell's bar on Feather river. We crossed on a ferry, the first one we had seen since leaving Green river, east of Great Salt Lake City. We put up for the night at a hotel in Bidwell's bar. Here we saw our first orange tree. On this bar John Bidwell, who had about twenty Indians working for him, took out one hundred thousand dollars in gold dust during the years 1848 and 1849. Samuel Neal, who came into California with Lieutenant Fremont in 1844, also had about twenty Indians working for him. He took out of Feather river, during those two years, one hundred and ten thousand dollars in clear gold dust. I heard him tell that each Indian's task was to bring him one hundred dollars a day and that several of them often brought it by ten o'clock in the morning, and that they did not have to work any more that day, but laid in the sun and had all the fresh beef they could eat, and that was no small quantity. He and Bidwell had Spanish grants of land, each owning two leagues square, equal to one American township. The Indians belonged absolutely to the owners of the grant, but as far as my observation extended, this was not a great hardship to them, for they were taught to work and were well treated and well fed. As they were a gentle docile race they soon became semi-civilized and able to take care of themselves. When the Americans took possession of the country they became free, but most of them remained in their old homes, and lived practically as before. In the spring of 1850, Sam Neal, who had bought cattle and horses with some of his money had eighty thousand dollars on hand which he divided, and sent forty thousand dollars to his parents in Pennsylvania. The remaining forty thousand dollars he kept for himself.

To resume our journey. From Bidwell's bar we went down Feather river a few miles, and laid over at White Rock camp. We saw the river where a dam was placed across it, and all of that good sized stream turned into a large flume, for about a quarter of a mile, leaving the bed of the river practically dry. Here was a large number of men busily engaged in washing the

sand and gravel, and taking out large quantities of gold
dust so called, but very little of it was dust.   It was in
pieces from the size of a pinhead, some the size of
grains of wheat, and corn and pumpkin seed, and much
of it much larger than that called nuggets.   While we
were here the foreman of one gang of the miners came
up from the river with a sheet iron gold pan in which
he had about a gallon of gold of all sizes, which looked
mighty good to us.   The next morning we went on
down the river a few miles, and then crossed it on a
ferry, and went up Morrison's ravine, which split
Table mountain in two, and in a few miles emerged
into the famous Sacramento valley.   We went on across
Dry creek, reaching Sam Neal's ranch, where we
stopped at a large two-story hotel, on September 26,
1852.   Thus ended our trip of about two thousand
miles across the great plains and mountains.

Experiences in California

We spent a week at Sam Neal's ranch in the Sacramento valley, but as every meal we ate cost each of us one dollar James and I determined to leave and go up into the mountains to the gold mines. We went sixteen miles up in the foothills to a little village on the ridge between the west branch of Feather river and Little Butte creek. This little village was known as Butte Mills, because there was a sawmill near by run by water power from Little Butte creek, but it soon got its proper and well deserved name of Dog Town, for although there were only ten houses, there were sixteen fully developed dogs. From the edge of town one looked down into the West branch, where its waters flowed in a cañon a thousand feet deep, which in the course of about a million years it had worn down through talcose slate. This stream had been rich in placer gold, and was still being worked by many miners. James and I looked it over, but it was all claimed, and as we knew absolutely nothing about mining, we thought we had best hunt for some place that was easier to work than a small river that was full of large boulders, over which the water dashed and foamed.

We became acquainted with two young men, Wyatt M. Smith, eighteen years of age and Fountain J. Sweeney, age nineteen years, and being about our ages we were soon fast friends. They told us about six miles up Little Butte creek, there were some gulches

(ravines) known as "Tom Neal's dry diggins," that
they thought were rich, and they proposed to us to go
up there and go in with them in mining. They had
been in California for about a year, and already knew
a little about how to mine. We thought it a good
chance to learn from them and accepted their kind
offer. They already had some tools, and a part of a
kitchen outfit to cook with. James and I bought some
additional things and rolling up our blankets, with an
extra shirt apiece, took them on our backs and started
for the "diggins." Thus we entered upon a new,
strange, and untried life. Although our loads were not
very heavy, we found it necessary to sit down and rest
several times in going that six miles.

The country through which we passed was an open
forest with beautiful large trees of many kinds. We
selected a spot for our log cabin, near a clear cold little
spring in a wide gulch where the trees were smaller
and more suitable for building our cabin. This we
made sixteen feet square, and seven feet high at the
eaves, roofed it with clapboards that we made out of
sugar pine trees, which split so easily and accurately
that many of the clapboards were twelve inches wide,
and four feet long and only a half inch thick, and almost
as smooth as if they had been sawed. Never can I
forget the pleasure with which I roamed through the
beautiful forests that covered the region where we lived
and mined for a year and a half. There were the lofty
smooth-trunked sugar pines, six feet in diameter, three
hundred feet high; and from sixty to eighty feet from
the ground there was not a limb or a blemish. Many
large gray squirrels, almost double the size of the squirrels in the eastern states, made their home in the tree
tops. There were also yellow pine trees, a little smaller

than the sugar pines, and several species of fir trees and black oaks, large cedars, some beautiful madrona or laurel trees, dogwood trees, thirty feet high with large glossy leaves and snow white blossoms as large as a dollar, manzanita, and many other flowering bushes, that perfumed the air, and in the little open park-like spots, lovely flowers grew among the grass.   In the forests about here I saw for the first time birds putting away food for winter.   They were small, black and white woodpeckers, not very numerous, and always traveled in pairs, a male and female.   For a storehouse they selected a large dry limb on a pine or oak tree and carefully removed every particle of bark, then with their bills pecked small holes into which they deposited an acorn.   The acorns exactly fitted the holes and it was impossible to remove one without cutting it out with a knife.   The birds would fill large limbs just as full of acorns as they could possibly be filled.   It was a delight to me to watch these clever little woodsmen store their winter food and to listen to their cheerful cry of "Yacob, Yacob," repeated very rapidly.[16]

In the vicinity of our cabin were some patches of brush in which there lived a covey of California quails. Never was I guilty of killing one.   In going to and from work we often saw them scurrying along in the grass and undergrowth.

The large gray squirrels were interesting and beautiful also, but our appetites and love for hunting got the better of our tender-heartedness and we killed and ate any number of them.   My dog Watch, the one that

---

[16] The size and general description would suggest the Nuttall woodpecker (*dryobates nuttallii*) but the habits and call suggest either the ant-eating woodpecker (*melanerpes formicivorus*) or the Californian woodpecker (*M. f bairdi*).   Possibly Stuart saw all these different varieties and confused them. – ED.

I coaxed from his master's grave on the Platte river, was still my constant companion and he delighted to hunt squirrels and was an exceedingly clever squirrel dog.

Wyatt M. Smith and I each had a good muzzle loading rifle and we in turn hunted squirrels for dinner. The squirrels lived in the tops of the lofty sugar pines and fed on pine nuts and it was no easy matter to discover them high up in the tree. Watch had a very keen scent and he would track one to a tree and then bark until one of us came and shot it. We tanned the skins and made money bags out of them. When well tanned and carefully sewed they would last years and made a most excellent bag in which to carry gold.

I felt as though I had been transplanted to another planet. There was nothing here that I had ever seen or heard of before. The great forests, the deep cañons with rivers of clear water dashing over the boulders, the azure sky with never a cloud were all new to me, and the country swarmed with game, such as elk, deer and antelope, with occasionally a grizzly bear, and in the valleys were many water fowls. Tall bearded men were digging up the ground and washing it in long toms and rockers, and on the banks by their sides was a sheet iron pan in which were various amounts of yellow gold.

The gold coins used then were also different from any that I had seen. They were coined at the mint in San Francisco and were ten, twenty, and fifty dollar pieces. The great octagon fifty dollar pieces were especially strange to me.[17]

[17] John H. Landis formerly superintendent of the Philadelphia mint writes in the *Encyclopedia Americana* under COINAGE: "The largest gold pieces ever coined by the United States government are the six hundred $50 pieces coined as mementoes of the Panama-Pacific International Exposition." – ED.

These men had neither tents nor houses. They camped under lofty pine or spreading oak trees as the case might be, for it never rained there in the summer time. They were strong and healthy and lived a life as free as the air they breathed. No finer specimens of mankind existed anywhere than were these California miners of the days of forty-nine. Men without ambition never started for California. The faint-hearted turned back before they reached the Missouri river. The puny sickly ones either recovered or perished on the road. Only the courageous determined man crossed the plains and reached the land of gold.

Where all the gold came from was a much mooted question, and they pondered deeply over it and finally settled down to the belief that it must have been thrown out by volcanoes, as the country bore evidence of ancient volcanic convulsions. In 1851 a report was started (but no one knew who started it) that high up in the Sierra Nevada was a lake, evidently the crater of a large volcano, and that the shores of this lake were covered with gold so plentiful that there was little sand or gravel there. As soon as the miners heard this rumor they at once said, "That's just where we thought all this gold came from, and what is the use of us digging here in the mud and water for a few hundred dollars a day when we can go up there and just shovel it up by the ton?" And incredible as it now seems, several hundred of them abandoned rich claims and went up into the mountains and spent all summer looking for the "Gold lake." This of course did not exist, and when they came back in the fall, ragged and footsore, all their rich claims were taken by others. Later I personally knew two men who, in 1851, were working in Rich gulch on the West branch of Feather river, taking out three hundred dollars a day apiece. As soon as they heard of Gold lake they at once quit their rich claims and spent months and all the money they had searching for this imaginary lake, and on their return found their claims being worked by others and irrecov- erably lost to them.

I once asked some of those who, I knew had families in the states, "Why don't you quit drinking and gamb- ling and save your money and go back home to your families?" To which they all answered, "So I would, but don't you see that at the rate the gold is being taken out, by the time I got home with a lot of it it wouldn't be worth any more than so much copper, therefore, I am going to stay right here and have a hell of a good time while it is worth something." And so they stayed, and had that kind of a time. No such enormous amounts of gold had been found anywhere before, and as they all believed that the supply was inexhaustible, there was some justification for their thinking it would soon lose most of its value.

Even as at Great Salt Lake City I found myself in company with the twelve Apostles, so in the foothills of Sacramento valley I thought, in my eighteen-year-old innocence, that I must unconsciously have strolled into the Garden of Eden, for the good looking Indians who lived there wore no clothes, there were no fig trees there either; but they managed to get along, when the weather was cold, by wearing a small, I believe I am justified in saying, a very small apron, made of wisps of grass. These women felt no embarrassment because they were naked for they never knew what clothes were. They were as modest as their white sisters. In a short time we became accustomed to seeing them clad in their limited wardrobe and thought nothing of it.

FIELD OF THE BIG HOLE BATTLE

From an original pencil sketch made by Granville Stuart, May 11, 1878

These Indians lived in moderate sized huts dug partly in the ground. They would dig about three feet deep, then around that in a circular form would set up poles which would meet, tying them together with bark strings. On this they would put thatch and cover with mud mortar. The mud mortar was used to prevent their leaking. They had no fires in their huts. Their cooking was done out of doors. They had a small oval door about two feet in diameter at one side, by which they entered. These thatched huts were always warm. Their food in winter consisted largely of fish and acorn bread. There were quantities of acorns on the oak trees and in the fall the Indians gathered and stored them for winter use. They had baskets that held from one to two bushels of acorns. These were carried on their backs suspended from a broad band that passed across their forehead. These heavy loads caused them to stoop over and hold their heads low, consequently most of the older Indians were very stooped. They stored the acorns in little store-houses built upon poles about four feet from the ground. These little houses would hold from six to ten bushels of acorns. I was pleased to see that the men did as much work as the women and always carried the heavier load. They crushed the acorns with stone pestles into a sort of paste, and having no shortening they dug angleworms and crushed them up with the acorns. This made a sort of dough, which they made into little flat cakes and baked in hot ashes. This was their bread and largely their winter food. These little cakes of acorn bread were bitter to taste but highly nutritious.

The women also gathered many grasshoppers. On frosty mornings the hoppers would be stiff with cold and easily caught. After collecting a small basket half full they would put them in the edge of the fire and cover them with hot ashes. When they were roasted a nice brown they were scraped up carefully and restored to the basket. Then shaking them up and down and blowing them they got rid of the legs, wings, and ashes, leaving the body brown and crisp. They tasted like a bit of marrow.

These Indians were always anxious to work. They especially liked to go hunting with us. When we wanted to get a deer or elk we would have an Indian accompany us. They, being accustomed to those woods, would invariably see the game first. They would stop still and point to the brush and we could almost always get a shot before the game discovered us. After killing a deer we would give the Indian our hunting knife and he would butcher it. He always cleaned the paunch and filled it with the blood of the animal. This he carried home and made into a blood pudding, a great delicacy among them. He would then take the deer, tie its feet together and carry it to camp for us. His pay would be, head, neck and hide, though we usually gave him a quarter of the deer.

Often when passing under spreading trees he would discover wild pigeons and very often get one or more with his bow and arrow. These Indians were not allowed to have firearms at all. We often sent one of them to the village to get supplies. He would walk six miles to the store and return with fifty pounds of flour and as much bacon and other things, carrying it all on his back. His pay for this would be one hickory cotton shirt which cost seventy-five cents. They were strictly honest and never carried off anything that they were to bring us. After a few years the men wore clothes, but up to the time I left there the women had felt no need of additional clothing.[18]

In the years from 1852 to 1857 placer mining in California may be said to have been at its best. On all the streams in all the gulches and high up in the Sierras to the north, clear to the Oregon line every little camp was crowded with miners and gold was being taken out in such profusion as almost to lead one to believe that there would be an over-production and everybody seemed to be trying to find some way to spend all he had.

In the smaller towns the gambling halls were the chief attraction. They were magnificently fitted up with plate glass mirrors, brilliant lights shown from chandeliers, and upon a balcony at one end of the hall would be a string band, usually consisting of two violins, and banjo. About the room were numerous tables, large enough to accommodate eight people at each. All known gambling games were furnished, but monte and faro were the two favorite games. It was no unusual sight to see a man place a fifty dollar slug on a monte card or to place a thousand dollar bet on a faro card. Some won, some lost, but of course in the long run the dealers were sure winners. The supply of gambling suckers was endless. All of the halls would be crowded until two or three o'clock in the morning. Enormous sums of money changed hands in these places. Women gambled as well as men.

In an alcove at one side of the room would be a

---

[18] It is more difficult to classify the Indian of central California than it is the woodpeckers. There were many tribes in this region with customs similar to those described by Stuart. H. H. Bancroft, *Native Races of North America*, in *Works* (San Francisco, 1882-90) vol. i, p. 362 ff., describes these Indians in much the same way as Stuart does. – ED.

saloon bar stocked up with all kinds of choice liquors
and cigars.   The liquors were sold at twenty-five cents
a drink and the cigars at twenty-five cents each.   The
cigars were generally very good.   Considering the circumstances better order was preserved in these places
than could have been reasonably expected.   Of course
there was a great deal of drunkenness of all stages, from
gentle elation up to maudlin foolishness.   Quarreling,
shooting, and stabbing were comparatively rare.   It
was to the interest of the owners to keep as good order
as possible.   Many of the gamblers did not drink at
all.   They would keep sober and watch the game carefully, and sometimes make large winnings.

One night I strolled into one of these gambling halls
to listen to the music and watch the players and it was
here I lost my faith in the preachers of the Gospel.   At
our home in Iowa we had always attended preaching
regularly and our house had been a favorite stopping
place for the circuit rider, as mother was an excellent
cook and there was always plenty of nice chickens on
hand.

Of these preachers one, Brother Briar, gave a most
lurid description of hell-fire and painted a most vivid
picture of what would become of us if we did not
repent.   We hardly knew what we were expected to
repent of, but he scared us up plenty.   James and I
felt that we must do something quick in the way of
getting good or something terrible would happen.   We
would go home from meeting, climb up into the loft
where we slept, with our hair standing on end, and
dream all night of lakes of fire and brimstone and
devils, big and little with pitch forks.   We thought
Brother Briar a lucky man to be so good as to be safe
from such a pitfall.

Well time went on and in the many changes and events of our journey across the plains and the strange new life in California I had almost forgotten Brother Briar and his hell-fire sermons and certainly when I strolled into the great glittering room full of light and music and excited men and women crowded about the tables, betting their gold on the lucky or unlucky card, nothing could have been further from my thoughts than Brother Briar. When, lo! at one of the tables sat the self-same man coolly and calmly dealing faro. I said to myself then, he don't believe in hell-fire and never did, and neither do I.

Every Sunday there were horse racing, cock fights, and dog fights. In the larger towns of Marysville and Sacramento were the magnificent gambling houses, saloons, dance halls, music halls, theatres, horse races, and an occasional bull fight. Bull fighting never appealed to the miners and never became popular.

October 26, 1852, the rainy season set in with a downpour such as I have never seen since, not even in the tropics. It rained six days and nights without cessation. The west branch of Feather river rose fifty feet; sweeping away nearly all the miners' cabins on its banks and all of their tools, such as long toms, rockers, picks, shovels, and gold pans. The water poured down the hillside back of our cabin about four inches deep all over the ground. At no time during the six days could we get an armful of wood without being soaked to the skin (rubber coats and shoes were unknown at that time) but it was what we, of the dry diggings, had been waiting for.

We had finished our cabin, did some prospecting in the gulches in the vicinity, and found some ground that we thought would pay. We had a few boards hauled by wagon from the mill at Dog Town to within a mile of our cabin; but, there being no road further, we carried the boards the rest of the distance on our shoulders, which were sore for a week after. We used the boards for a door to the cabin and to make a long tom. We made our long tom in this manner – the bottom was a twelve-foot board twenty-four inches wide; nailed on each side of the bottom, and about three feet longer than the bottom were the sides which were about ten inches high. The projections beyond the bottom on each side were sloped up a gentle curve, from the end of the bottom up to the top of the two side boards and on the curve was nailed heavy sheet iron, the lower edge of which was closely nailed fast to the ends of the bottom. It was punched full of half-inch holes to the number of thirty-five or forty. The tom was placed in the gulch with the sheet iron end from twelve to twenty inches lower than the upper or open end, in which a considerable stream of water was turned from a water ditch. Under the iron end of the tom was placed a wooden box about four inches deep, and about the size of the perforated iron above it. This box was placed on the ground with the same slope as the tom above, and had several bars of wood about two inches high placed at intervals across the inside of its bottom.

In using the long tom after it was properly set in place, two of us took our places, one on each side of the tom, where, with pick and shovel, we dug up and shoveled into the tom the sand and gravel of the gulch, which the stream of water washed down to the perforated iron plate at the lower end where the third person was stationed with a shovel with which he stirred the sand and gravel back and forth on the half-inch holes down into the flat box underneath where the water carried all the sand and gravel off over the lower end of the box, leaving the gold, and some black sand, lodged against the two inch bars placed across the bottom of the box. The man at the plate threw out all the pebbles and rocks, which were too large to go through the holes, as soon as they were washed clean; but he had to carefully examine what he threw out, lest, as sometimes happened, there might be some nuggets of gold too large to go through the holes, in the iron. However, they were usually seen and picked up off the iron, which event, when it did occur, caused great joy and excitement, for a nugget too large to drop through the holes would be worth at least forty dollars, and might be large enough to be worth one hundred dollars or more. We had enough water in our gulches to work our long tom until about the first of March, but they did not prove as rich in gold as we anticipated. We could only make from three to five dollars a day, each one of us, but occasionally we would find some little nuggets worth from eight to sixteen dollars, which helped. One day just before our water supply failed I was digging on the right side of our long tom, with Wyatt M. Smith on the left side, and Fountain J. Sweeney at the iron plate, throwing out the rocks. On my side lay a flat rock about ten inches long and seven inches wide. I had dug past it, but as it slid about six inches of it stuck out of the bank right where I wanted to put my foot as I worked so I stuck my shovel under the side of it and gradually pried it up, when Lo!, there beneath it lay a bright nugget of pure gold that weighed sixteen ounces, which at sixteen dollars an ounce (the value of gold then) was worth two hundred and forty dollars. We also took out nine dollars in small gold that day, so that we made eighty-three dollars apiece, and there were three jovial boys in camp that night. This was the largest piece of gold I found while in California, although some localities yielded larger ones.

About the time the water failed in the spring in our gulch diggings, Sam Neal of Neal's ranch began to build a sawmill on Little Butte creek, about half a mile below Dog Town, and I hired to him to herd six yoke of oxen which were used for hauling pine logs to the mill.

In July the sawmill shut down and the oxen were taken down to Neal's ranch and I had to hunt other fields and pastures. During this time brother James had been prospecting for "diggins," and in company with other men had found a place on the West branch that looked good, so we bought a "rocker" and moved down into the deep cañon and went to work. There was a deep crevice in the soft talcose slate filled with sand and gravel amongst which there was considerable quantity of beautiful bright gold, resembling in size and shape muskmelon seeds, and up to the size of pumpkin seeds. It paid big, but in a week we dug it all out and although it was a good neighborhood in which to look for more, we accepted the opinion of our partners and abandoned it. This was unfortunate, for we learned later that much gold was taken out all around there that summer. We then fell in with two men who had mined over in Big Butte creek cañon. They said they knew of a spot in that creek that had not been mined out and that they knew it must be rich. They proposed to James and me that we go in with them, and turn the water out of the creek, which was then at a low stage, and work in the bed of the stream, taking out big returns in gold. We went with them carrying our blankets, tools, and grub on our backs about five miles. We did not need even a tent for shelter. We spent six weeks digging a small canal through the soft black slate on one side of the stream into which we turned the creek by building a dam across it as the head of our little canal. This dam we made by building two walls of stone about three feet apart and carrying the red soil of the hillside in sacks, and filling it in between the walls all of which was very hard work, and when done the greater part of the stream ran through our canal all right, but we then found, to our disgust, that quite a quantity of water seeped through the sand and gravel under our dam and this we could not stop, or at least we thought we couldn't. We found that there were many boulders of considerable size in the bed of the stream where we expected to work, which we had no means of moving. The seepage water running over and between these boulders was only a few inches deep and we could shovel up sand and gravel out of that water and get as high as twenty-five cents to a pan full. But that was very slow and unsatisfactory work, and our partners said we could not make it pay and that we had best abandon it, which we did. After we had, a year later, left that part of the state and saw mining elsewhere, I knew that if we had stayed there and used a little judgment we could have made enough to have paid us good wages for all our labor. James and I thought it highly probable that our two partners did that very thing, that they returned to the claim and worked it till the high water from the fall rains drove them out, thus getting the benefit of our labor for nothing.

We returned to Dog Town from our river claims and after a few days rest we, in company with a friend, Abe

Folk, went up to our gulch diggings and on our way passed by a gulch from which several thousand dollars of gold had been mined in 1850 (three years before) but the pay-streak gave out and no more could be found and it was abandoned. We began scratching in the bank at the side of the old workings and in a few minutes scratched out of the dirt, on the bed rock, four dollars in coarse gold. We then knew that we had found the pay-streak of the old workings where it left the gulch as it made a bend around the point of a hill and evidently went under the hill. We had neither paper nor pencil with which to claim the ground by putting up a notice stating the size and direction of our claim, so went on to our cabin about two miles beyond, intending to return and put up our claim notice the next morning, which was Sunday, but the next morning brother James and our friend took a notion to wash some clothes instead of going to our new found mine and putting up our claim notice. I had a feeling that we ought to do it without delay and told them so and urged them to go with me to the place and claim it. They laughed at me, saying that all that region was dry as bone and that there was no danger of anyone finding the pay or even coming into the district until just before the rains set in, which would be over two months yet, so I finally gave in and also washed clothes. It was by far the most costly washing that ever any three men indulged in, for when we went to the mine on Monday morning, Lo and behold! there was Tom Neal with several friends, with their notices up claiming the mine for a long distance, leaving us entirely out. Tom told us that he with a couple of friends happened along there on Sunday afternoon on their way to some gulches further up the ridge, and as he was of those who had mined there in 1850, he was showing them where he had mined and seeing where we had scratched out the place in the bank, and that convenient old case knife lying right there, he, as we had done, picked it up and began scratching in the place where we had dug. He soon found some pieces of gold and then he also knew that he had found the rich, lost pay-streak, and some of them having paper they at once claimed the rest of the gulch.

Now, if we had taken a little trouble to cover up the place where we had dug, with dry dirt and thrown that tell-tale old knife away Tom and party would doubtless have passed on, as he had often done before, and done no scratching. We were so confident that there was no chance of anybody coming along there that we did not even think of concealing the sign we had made. When the winter rains set in and furnished water in the gulch to wash the pay dirt, that party took out over twenty-five thousand dollars in beautiful coarse gold, some nuggets weighing from one hundred to three hundred dollars. To tide over the interval, before the winter rains set in, we busied ourselves making clapboards or shakes out of sugar pines. These were in good demand down in the valley and we made good wages.

In 1853 a man from Dog Town brought to our cabin a young man, just the age of brother James, who was very pale and weak. He was shaking with the ague every alternate day. He told us that his name was Rezin Anderson, that he had just crossed the plains from Iowa and come in by the Carson river route. Reaching Sacramento valley he was at once taken sick with the ague and no medicine would break it. The doctor there told him to go on up to the mines, the higher in the mountains the better. He got a little acquainted and met a man from Dog Town, who told him of men going up there with the ague and getting well in a short time. He managed to get there a few days later, and was told that there were two young men from Iowa in the dry diggings six miles further up in the mountains, so he hired a man to bring him to our camp and he told us that if we would take him into our cabin and mess, that he would work for us to pay what he would owe as soon as he got strong enough, for he was broke. Of course we did not refuse him and he became one of our mess, but his ague would not stop, and he looked so feeble that I feared he would not live more than a month or two.

Before we left Iowa James read and became interested in the Presnitz Water Cure System, just then coming into notice and into use in Germany. He told Anderson, if he would let him try, he believed he could cure him and Reece, as we ever afterwards called him, was glad to take the treatment. James stripped him and then rolled him up in a blanket wet with cold water and gave him hot tea to drink, at the same time covering him up with dry blankets. The cabin being quite warm, of course he soon broke into a profuse perspiration in which he was kept for an hour. He was then unrolled, rubbed dry, and put to bed for the night. After the second night the ague left him and after four nights of this treatment he was cured; his appetite, which had been poor, soon became good and he rapidly gained in strength. In two weeks he was able to do light work. His rapid convalescence I think was largely due to the large fat squirrels that my dog Watch and I got out of the lofty sugar pines in the neighborhood, which when nicely fried in bacon grease left nothing to be desired, except more squirrels.

One Sunday I happened to be at Dog Town and there being no amusement, except watching the several poker games that always ran on Sunday and as I never took any part or cared to look on at them, I took my rifle and went slowly down along the side of the cañon of West branch: occasionally sitting down on some projections of rock to enjoy the sunshine and soft air and watch the water dashing over the boulders far below. I heard something walking in the chapparal a little below me, so I picked up a stone and threw it where the slight noise seemed to come from, and out jumped a large deer with handsome horns. I at once shot, butchered, and quartered him, and went to Dog Town (only a little over a quarter of a mile away) and got three friends to help me bring up the meat, each of us carrying a quarter. When I got into the little town (in the West there are no villages, no matter how small they are they are always called towns) and the people saw the fine fat venison they wanted it, and in a few minutes I sold three quarters of it for twenty-one dollars and seventy-five cents. I have often thought that this little incident should have shown Brother and I a sure way of making a steady income, by buying two or three burros to pack, and then devote ourselves to hunting and delivering the meat to the various little towns scattered everywhere through the mines. It would have been a sure thing, as the demand was always good. But like everybody else in those days, we were bitten by the gold bug, and mine we must, and mine we did, which is not to be wondered at, when one considers the vast quantities of gold which were then being taken out in California, much of it with very little exertion.

At Dog Town we knew a man who in daytime followed the occupation of a crevice miner, and at night
that of a professional gambler. In the morning he
would put a little lunch in his pocket and taking a small
pick and a gold pan, and crevice spoon, he would go
down into the deep cañon of the West branch and carefully scan its shores along near the water; searching for
the fissures or cracks in the bedrock which often contained sand and gravel forced into them in past ages,
and in among which was usually considerable gold.
When he found one of these crevices he would dig its
contents up loose with his little pick and then scrape it
all out carefully with his crevice spoon, and put it into
the shallow circular iron pan, always called, "a little
gold pan," which he would then take to the edge of the
water, and squatting down begin to wash the sand and
fine gravel by a circular motion that would gradually
carry it out over the edge of the pan, leaving the gold
in the bottom. He told us he had been crevicing for
over two years and that he had learned where to look
for favorable places to hunt for rich crevices, but was
not always successful. We asked him what were his
usual gains in a day. He said that the first year he
would frequently find two or three ounces of gold a
day and some lucky day considerably more, but for the
past year he could only average one ounce a day for the
mines were now more carefully worked. One day he
returned to town about noon and joyfully showed me a
beautiful bright nugget of pure gold that he had just
found. It weighed six and one-fourth ounces and was
worth one hundred dollars. He said it was the largest
nugget that he had ever found, but that he had found
several of from one to five ounces.

In the summer of 1853 our father returned home to

Iowa by way of the Nicaragua route, which was by steamer from San Francisco to San Juan Del Sur, on the west coast of Nicaragua then across Lake Nicaragua thence down the San Juan river on Garrison's line of steamers and thence to New Orleans, thence up the Mississippi river to Dubuque and home.

In July, 1853, some Concow Indians, whose village was over on the North fork of Feather river, came over to the West branch and killed two Chinamen who were mining there and wounded two others. These Indians, in common with all those living on the western slope of the Sierra Nevada, were not allowed by the miners to have firearms and the Chinamen were killed with bows and arrows. Considerable numbers of Chinamen were by this time in California, mostly all engaged in mining on claims worked out and abandoned by white men. The Indians disliked them because they thought them other kinds of Indians, but I never heard of them killing any others, although they often robbed them. The West branch Chinamen brought their dead up to Dog Town for burial and their wounded excited much feeling against the Indians. The result was that the white miners offered to go and drive the murderers out of that part of the mines, if the Chinamen would go with them and carry their food and blankets, which they gladly agreed to do. My recollection is that sixteen well armed men went, accompanied by twelve Chinamen carrying food and blankets. The Indians discovered their approach and fled like deer, the miners firing on them as they ran. I think only two were killed and several wounded. A few of the Chinamen carried shot guns and when the miniature battle began the men said the Chinamen were widely excited and would shut both eyes and fire both barrels of their shot guns at once, the recoil nearly knocking them down, while the buckshot from their guns went tearing through the tops of the oak trees. The men said they were in greater danger from the Chinamen than from the Indians, because they did not know how to handle firearms. The little army was absent three days. I thought at the time that most of them were ashamed of the raid after it was over. The Indians moved and I never heard of them making any trouble afterwards. Brother James happened to be in Dog Town when the foray started and went with it. I was up at our diggings and knew nothing of it until he got back. The grateful Chinamen sent to San Francisco and presented each of their white allies with a large embroidered red silk handkerchief and a quart of brandy.

In the winter of 1852 after the rains began, the roads became so bad and the Sacramento valley was mostly flooded so that no food supplies could be brought up to Dog Town for over a month. Fortunately there was food enough of all kinds except flour. We had none of that for over two weeks, but we had beans and bacon and squirrels. When the pack train got in with the flour the packers swore that they would not make another trip that winter and demanded fifty dollars per one hundred pounds. We thought it well to buy a sack (fifty pound sacks were unknown until three years later) rather than to do without for the remainder of the winter and did so. By the time we had eaten half of it two pack trains loaded with flour arrived and the price fell to twelve cents a pound. Nearly all the flour used in California that winter came from Chile, South America. It had a yellow color and was first class. Large quantities of beans were also brought from there.

In fact if these two articles had not been brought from Chile everybody would have been reduced to meat straight.

In the spring of 1853 we grew tired of our diggings because we were entirely dependent on the rains for water and determined to seek a better place to mine. So James, Rezin Anderson, and I took our respective rolls of bedding on our backs and our rifles on our shoulders and started for Rabbit creek in Sierra county. We went by way of Morrison's ravine, then across Feather river at the ferry, then up the slope between Feather and Yuba rivers, stopping one night at Forbestown, first known as "Boles Dry Diggins," then up the ridge to "Mountain cottage," where we entered the snow of the Sierra Nevadas. We found the snow constantly becoming deeper, but here was a well beaten pack trail.

We arrived at Rabbit creek when the snow was sixteen feet deep. All the miners' cabins had steps cut in the snow down to the doors. There being no stoves, all cabins had open fire places, the chimneys of which were made to extend six or seven feet above the roof, so as to get to the surface of the snow. These chimneys gave plenty of air and the snow kept it so warm that the doors were open all day. The mines were all deep gravel channels from twenty-five to one hundred and twenty-five feet deep on the mountain spurs and ridges, and were worked by hydraulic pipes in which the water was piped down into the cuts and thrown against the banks which were composed of white quartz gravel and sand. These immense gravel beds were once ancient river beds before the mountains and ridges were upheaved, and all contained enough fine gold to pay richly for washing them away by hydraulic process. Through lines of sluice boxes the sand and gravel was dumped into the surrounding cañons which drained into the North fork of the Yuba river. Here the claims were two hundred feet square. No man could have more than one claim. All the claims along the water front were being worked so we located ours further back, but had to wait for those in front to wash their claims before we could work ours. Every mining district in California in those days had their own laws made by the miners and by them enforced. As we could not work our mines at once we went to work in a nearby mine where the gravel was forty feet deep. Part of us worked on day shift and the others on night shift.

We would work all week, but on Saturday night the miners would get up a stag dance, there being very few women in the camp. There were two fiddlers, one played first violin and the other played second. The first player was left handed but he was a good one and such fun as we would have. Among the young men was one named Clyde Hammon who, ten or twelve years later became one of the famous lawyers of California.

The Rogue River War

On Sunday, June 4, 1854, our cousin, Clinton Bozarth, who had been mining and running a pack train decided to return to his home in Iowa. He went by way of steamer from San Francisco to Nicaragua. This made us, who were left behind, rather homesick, but we were not yet ready to go home. While Bozarth was with us he told us that at Yreka, a town up near the boundary between Oregon and California, there were some flats that contained gold enough to pay well, if mined by hydraulic process. This news coupled with our inexperience and the desires of youth to seek better things though far away, determined us to go to Yreka. So on June 29, 1854, we quit work and bought two mules. On one we packed our blankets, clothes, and a little grub. One by one we took turns riding the other mule and started for Yreka, on pack trails that zigzagged along the western slope of the Sierras. We took this route to avoid the fierce heat of the route through the Sacramento valley, and to enjoy traveling among cool shady mountains. Our party consisted of James and Granville Stuart, Rezin Anderson, and John L. Good. Some parts of our journey were through unsettled regions, that were not occupied because no mines had been found there. James and I kept a brief diary of our trip, which I here insert.

JUNE 29, 1854. Left Warren hill and traveled seven miles and camped in the little village of Grass Valley.

JUNE 30. Nooned on top of Middle fork of Feather

river hill above the mouth of Nelson creek. Then
went down a long hill (said to be seven miles long and
our legs said it was ten miles, but our eyes said it was
only four and a half miles) then crossed the middle
fork and climbed up the big hill on the north side of
this awful steep cañon, and camped in the head of
American valley near where we entered it in September, 1852. Traveled twenty miles today.

JULY 1. Nooned on the divide between American
and Indian valleys and camped for the night down in
Indian valley. It was sure enough down, for it looks
just as if it had sunk right down for about one thousand
feet. Our knees before we got down the long steep
hill felt it was two thousand feet. Traveled eighteen
miles to-day.

JULY 2. Stopped for noon near the west end of Indian valley, and as our feet and legs felt sore, we stayed
there until the next morning. Only traveled eight
miles to-day. This valley is a long narrow one, with
steep timbered mountains rising up on each side and is
very beautiful, but has considerable tule swamp land
in it, but even the tules, six feet high and very dense,
waving in the wind like a green field are beautiful.

JULY 3. Nooned on the divide between Indian valley and the Big meadows, on the North fork of Feather
river, and there camped for the night in the lower end
of the Big meadows. Traveled eighteen miles to-day.
These meadows are in a beautiful little valley through
which runs the North fork of Feather river, a clear ice
cold stream about twenty-five yards wide and two and
a half feet deep. James rode over, leading the pack
mule and then came back and took us three across, one
at a time behind him. The mule nearly threw us in the
creek.

JULY 4. Camped on the head of Deer creek, a cold clear gravelly stream about sixteen feet wide and deep, which we thought we could wade at the crossing. We took off our boots and stockings, rolled up our pants and did wade it, but Oh! we never felt such cold water before and when we got across our feet and legs were almost paralyzed and ached frightfully. The cobble stones were so slippery and hurt our feet so that we had to wade slowly, and one and all said no more wading of creeks went with us while we had these mules for ferry boats. Traveled twenty-five miles today.

JULY 5. Started at sunrise as we feared we would find no water until we got down into the Sacramento valley, which lay like a map in plain sight below us, while we were parched with thirst under a burning sun. About noon the branch of the Old Larson emigrant road which we are now following, went down into the right hand cañon, but to our great discomfort, it was dry. We found a little water among some big boulders, but it was stagnant, and so hot that we could not drink it until we dipped it up with tin cups and waited a quarter of an hour until it partly cooled, and then we were afraid to drink it for fear it might be poisonous. We washed our mouths with it and wet our hair and went on. The road climbed out of the cañon up onto the other ridge. The day was very hot and there was no shade. We suffered greatly from the heat, and thirst. We reached the valley after dark and hearing frogs nearby we went to them and found a slough of warm stagnant water into which our mules and ourselves waded. We cooked our suppers which we enjoyed very much, having eaten nothing since daylight this morning. Traveled thirty miles.

JULY 7. Traveled twenty miles up the river and

camped at the "Blue Tent," which was a saloon, but as none of us drank any liquor, we were not desirable visitors.

JULY 9. Camped at the "Milk ranch," and had good fresh milk and bread and butter for supper. Traveled up the river for twenty miles.

JULY 10. Stopped in the town of Shasta at the St. Charles hotel. Traveled fifteen miles, weather red-hot.

JULY 11. Went up to the mountains, six miles. Camped a little below a rather lively little village called "Whiskey Town," and from the maudlin songs, yells, and cuss words, that enlivened the night we decided that the place was rightly named.

JULY 12. Went to "Mad Ox canyon," to look for placer diggins.

JULY 13. Prospected.

JULY 14. Moved three miles to Oak bottom on Clear creek. Now a very muddy creek, but the surroundings are beautiful.

JULY 15. Bought one-third of a water ditch and went to work on Oak hill with a small hydraulic. Lovely place to work, the hill being sparsely covered with oak trees. During July and August the thermometer often rose to one hundred and twelve degrees in the shade. As we were always soaking wet and mostly in the shade while working, we did not suffer much and we would all go and lie down in the creek with only our heads out of the water from twelve-thirty to one-thirty nearly every day. Frank Vandeventer and sister kept the Oak Bottom House across the creek and she made delicious pies, of which we bought many to eke out our miner fare. We worked here until September 28th and only made good our expenses from the time we left Warren hill until we sold out and quit work here. Bought a blue mare for seventy dollars and two mules for one hundred and thirty-one dollars and made another start for Yreka, being all mounted with one pack mule. Camped at Mountain House for the night. Traveled sixteen miles.

SEPTEMBER 28. Traveled twenty-two miles and camped at Seley's ranch on Trinity river, a beautiful clear swift stream, with some grassy meadows along it, but country mostly timbered. No mines on the river above here, but said to be many good placers a few miles below this point.

SEPTEMBER 30. Traveled sixteen miles and camped on Trinity five miles from the divide, between Trinity river and Scott's valley.

OCTOBER 1. Traveled eighteen miles and camped in Scott's valley which is perfectly beautiful, with a clear stream flowing through. The valley is different from most we have seen. There is beautiful yellow pine timber on the hills, and low mountains, while all the valley proper is covered with yellow bunch grass, knee high, and waving in the wind like fields of grain, being the first of its kind that we have seen in California.

OCTOBER 2. Traveled four miles and camped in same valley. In the night we were awakened by our mules snorting and trying to break loose from the picket pine. Getting up (we were sleeping in the open air without tents) we saw a huge grizzly bear shambling off and disappearing in the brush along the stream. We finally got our animals calmed down and went back to our beds, thankful that the bear had not come any nearer, and hoping that the next call would be on some-one else. During the night we heard continual splashing in the water near where we were sleeping, and couldn't imagine what kind of an animal was in the stream all night, as we had seen no sign of beavers in California. We would have gotten up and investigated, but as we didn't know just where that grizzly might be, we thought it safer to wait until morning. In the morning we went to the place whence came the noise and found that all that splashing in the river was caused by salmon fish, from three to four feet long, flopping and jumping in, forcing their way up the stream over the riffles where the water was not deep enough for them to swim. These were the first salmon any of us had ever seen. We walked in and killed one of them with a club, and while pounding her she splashed water all over us and soaked us plenty. We finally got her out and had fish to eat for two days, and being fish-hungry we enjoyed it hugely. Upon inquiry we were told that every fall these large fish came up from the Pacific ocean to the upper branches of all the streams as far as they can possibly go and there lay their eggs, then start back to the ocean, but most of them are so bruised and exhausted that they die on the way.

The bears follow along these salmon streams and in shallow places throw the fish out on the bank with their fore paws and then eat them at leisure. During this season bears become very fat. The grizzly that had so alarmed our horses and ourselves was only out on a little fishing trip and not looking for us at all.

OCTOBER 3. Camped six and a half miles from Yreka, fearing we would not find grass for our animals if we went any farther.

OCTOBER 4. Went to town and sent our animals out on a ranch to winter. Rented a cabin just west of town near the mines, examined the mining ground that we had come so far to secure and great was our disappointment. It lay so level and so low that it could not be worked by hydraulic process, and around it were only shallow gulches that would not afford any place for sluices to dump tailings, and would not drain much of the flat. The ground would not pay to work with pick and shovel, and to cap the climax the water was scarce in those mines and was already in use. None could be obtained except at high prices and winter was near at hand. Little work could be done as it was occasionally some degrees below zero, with a foot of snow. We began to wish ourselves back in Dog Town with its balmy climate.

We bought a claim for fifty dollars and worked it until cold weather set in and the ground froze. We purchased water from a ditch company for our sluices, all the water in this vicinity being taken from creeks to the mines on Yreka flats which caused much bitter feeling and no end of trouble. After the mines on the flat were discovered and much of the water turned from the creeks into ditches to supply these mines, other mines were discovered in the creek bottoms and many miners scattered along the creek bed were able to make good wages. During the summer months the water became scarce and there was not enough to supply all. The ditch company having first right to the water turned it all into the ditches for the Yreka flat diggins. This enraged the creek bottom miners and they cut the ditches and turned the water back into the creek. The ditch owners had a number of the miners arrested and placed in jail. This enraged their comrades and they swore that they would storm the jail and release the imprisoned men. Accordingly on the night of February 28, 1855, they made the attack.   Had they been secretive they might have succeeded, but so much talk and so many threats had been made that the officers of the law prepared for an attack and had the jail filled with armed men.   When the rescue party of miners attacked the jail they were met with a volley of shots with the result that four of their number were killed and fifteen or twenty wounded.   The wounded were carried off by their comrades and concealed in cabins scattered along the gulches near the creek.   Doctors sworn to secrecy, attended them at night for sometime.   If any more died it was not known.   The officers of the law let the matter drop and did not try to find the raiders.   They thought they were punished severely enough as it was.   None of the jail defenders were hurt.

MARCH 18, 1855.   We bought another placer claim for three hundred dollars, out of which we took considerable gold.   Rezin Anderson, being a blacksmith, hired to a shop in town at five dollars a day and did not mine with us anymore.

On the tenth of April, James joined a party of prospectors that was going around Mount Shasta (called Shasta Butte in those days) to the south side.   This proved to be an unprofitable as well as a most disagreeable trip.   They were gone a month and it stormed on them almost every day.   They had no tents and it rained and snowed so hard that they were unable to build fires half the time.   At night they rolled up in water-soaked blankets and shivered until morning.   They found no mines that would pay.   During this time I mined on Shasta river a few miles from Yreka and made some money.

About the twentieth of June, 1855, seven of us started on a prospecting trip about fifty miles up Klamath river, the party consisted of Hugh Bratton, John Cotton, Tom Burns, Tom Duffy, Ed. Tolts, and James and Granville Stuart. Duffy had a Shasta squaw for a wife and she told him that on a certain stream called Butte creek that came into Klamath river on the south side, that Indians knew where there was much gold. So we went in search of these supposed rich diggings. There being no trail up the Klamath we took the emigrant wagon road out to Klamath lake, then along the Oregon road to the crossing of Klamath river. Here we left the road and about ten o'clock in the morning started up along a well beaten trail which showed many barefoot Indian tracks. We had gone about a half mile when without warning a number of shots came from the steep timbered mountain side high above us. None struck us however. All the balls apparently passed over our heads as they always go high when fired down a steep mountain. We at once turned back and before the Indians could reload their guns (muzzle loaders) we got out of their sight behind a thick grove of cottonwoods. We went up the Klamath about a quarter of a mile and chose a strong position on a flat among some big oak trees, and awaited developments. In a short time several Indians appeared among the rocks on both sides of the river below us, but avoided exposing themselves to a shot. We called to them in Chinook jargon, which is understood by all Indians from here up to Russian America (now Alaska) and told them who we were, and asked them what was the matter and why they shot at us, but they only answered that they knew us, and would not tell us why they fired at us. Burns and Duffy by this time recognized several of them, one being the brother of Duffy's wife. Duffy tried to get him to come to us assuring him that he would not be hurt, but he would not come.   He as well as others had often been to Yreka and had been at Duffy's house.   His tribe were friendly Indians and there were no wars at this time with any of the tribes all of which made more unaccountable their conduct. Their actions were so suspicious that we became convinced that there was trouble brewing.   We saw several other Indians join the first ones.   We did not know how many more might be camped near where they fired at us.

This put a stop to our prospecting in Butte creek and we decided to return to Yreka.   We packed up at three in the morning and climbed up out of the cañon to the timbered table-land which lay between us and Klamath lake.   We traveled ten or twelve miles through the forest without any trail, when, coming to a meadow on the little creek, camped for the night.   At sunrise we saddled up and struck the emigrant wagon road a few miles from Klamath lake and from there to Yreka, we saw no Indians, and met with no further incidents.   .

We were not long in getting the key to the hostile conduct of these erstwhile friendly Shasta and Klamath Indians.   A few days after we had started on our trip the Indians on the Klamath river below where we were, had killed fifteen miners, who were scattered along the river for ten or fifteen miles.   Most of the poor fellows were murdered just after they had risen in the morning, without any suspicion of danger from the Indians who had been camped among them for months.   Those who fired on us knew about the massacre below, and some of them may have been implicated in it.   After we escaped their first fire and took up a strong position they knew us, and knew that we were all well armed with rifles and revolvers and if they followed up their attack many of them would be killed.

This kind of warfare is not liked by Indians. The miners whom they murdered were only one, two, or three, in a place and being taken unawares were killed without any risk to the Indians and their cabins robbed of everything. In some of them was considerable gold. The murderers soon fled across the Siskiyou mountains to Rogue river in Oregon, where, joining the disaffected Rogue river and Modoc Indians, they brought on the second Rogue river Indian war. The first one was in 1852-3, and Tom Duffy was in it and was shot twice through his thigh just above the knee at the Battle of the Cave. The bone was not broken and he did not limp.

Soon after our return to Yreka, Duffy and Burns saw two of the Indians that had fired at us and promptly had them arrested. They refused to talk and it seemed probable that, they, being acquainted in town, came in to see what the whites were intending to do about the murders. They were tried and sentenced to be hung. There was no moving for a new trial in those days (1855) for the purpose of defeating the ends of justice, as has now become the custom.

I will here give a brief account of the depredations committed by the Modoc and Rogue river Indians in 1852-53 and which finally led up to the second Rogue river war in which we enlisted.

The emigration by way of Snake river plains in 1852 consisted of large well equipped trains, and perhaps for this reason, was suffered to pass with less bloodshed than might have been anticipated, though there was much annoyance from pilferings and horse stealings. The emigration by the northern route was less favored.

This route crossed the Sierra Nevada by the old Lawson route and passed by Goose lake, Clear lake, Tule lake, and Klamath lake in northern California.   At the latter lake the road forked, the left hand road going to Yreka in Shasta valley, California, on the north side of Mount Shasta.   The right hand road turned north along the shore of Klamath lake, a sagebrush and lava bed country, then leaving the lake passed through a pine forest a few miles to Klamath river, which is crossed by a bad rocky ford and then ascended the pine clad Siskiyou mountains.   The summit is the dividing line between California and Oregon.   The emigrants from the States would separate at Klamath lake, part going to Oregon and part to California.   The road to California ran through the lake country.   Here in 1843 Fremont's camp was attacked, and here Capt. W. H. Warner, in 1849 was murdered while surveying for a Pacific railroad.   Parties traveling through this region were compelled to exercise extreme care, particularly at a pass now known as "Bloody Pass," where the road ran between an overhanging cliff and the waters of the lake.   In 1852, between sixty and one hundred men, women, and children died at the hands of the Modoc Indians, and a large amount of property was stolen or destroyed.

The first large train arriving at Yreka reported that they had not been molested, but that there were many companies on the road, some of them with families, and that the Indians were burning signal fires on the mountains which boded no good to travelers.

On this report Charles McDermit of Yreka raised a company of between thirty and forty volunteers to meet and escort these companies over the most dangerous portion of the road through the Modoc country.

At Tule lake the volunteers met a company of male emigrants going to Yreka. They sent two of their men, Smith and Toland, back with the emigrants to act as guides and guards. This party came through to Yreka without being attacked.

The next party to reach Tule lake consisted of about twenty poorly armed men five of them with families, and ten wagons. They found McDermit's company on the west shore of Goose lake and were warned of the danger ahead, and Toland with two of the volunteers accompanied them as guides. On coming to the high hill one mile east of the south end of the Tule lake on the nineteenth of August, no Indians in sight, the guides having in mind James Bridger's caution, "When there are no Indians in sight, then look out," decided to avoid a probable ambush by taking a northerly course across a sagebrush flat.

The women and children were placed in the wagons, and the covers fastened down to hide them from view, while the firearms were made ready for use. In this manner the company had nearly reached the open valley when the yells of Indians in pursuit disclosed to them that they were being pursued. By making all possible speed, open ground was reached just as a shower of arrows whizzed through the air. The emigrants replied with a volley from their rifles and the Modocs withdrew to the shelter of the rocks, but reappeared again on a high ridge, gesticulating and uttering demonical cries expressive of their rage and disappointment.

Seeing that they were working themselves up to a fighting pitch, and would probably attack at some other point, it was thought best to return to hold a talk. Acting on this plan, the wagons were corraled and

Toland with a half dozen others, making a great show of arms went back within speaking distance and challenged the Indians, through one of the guides, who could speak the jargon, to come and fight. Like all the people who practice treachery, they feared it, and not knowing what might be inside the wagon covers, declined, but the head chief proposed to meet the interpreter unarmed and talk with him.

While the talk was progressing, at a safe distance from the wagons, it was observed, by Toland, that every now and then a Modoc had tied his bow to his toe, secreted his arrows, and pretending to be disarmed, joined the chief in the sagebrush. The interpreter, on being warned ordered the Indians sent back, and the chief seeing no opportunity for obtaining an advantage, agreed to return whence he came, and leave the party to pursue its way unmolested. They had not proceeded far, however, before they discovered a reserve of Indians mounted, who had been placed where they could intercept any persons escaping from the narrow pass along Tule lake. Finding themselves outwitted, they also returned, hoping for better luck next time. Camp was made that night fifteen miles from Tule lake. A severe rain storm doubtless prevented a night attack, the Indians being unable to use their bows in wet weather. The train made a very early start next morning and thus averted further trouble.

On the twenty-third of August, at nine o'clock in the evening, Toland's camp was visited by a man on a poor and jaded horse, whose condition excited the utmost pity. He had to be lifted from his horse and fed and nursed back to life before he could give any account of himself. It then appeared that he belonged to a party of eight men who had been surprised by the

Modocs, and all killed except himself. His horse being shot he sprang upon another, which ran with him, carrying him several miles up the valley of Lost river, until he fell exhausted. From here the man whose mind was evidently unsettled by the shock he had received, wandered to Klamath lake, but seeing an Indian, turned back and the next day discovered his horse feeding. He remounted and rode, for three days without dismounting until he came to Toland's camp. He had eaten nothing, but had tied up a handful of rosebuds in his handkerchief as he said that he expected to be out all winter and should need them. This demented creature was taken by the company to Yreka, where his story in connection with the report of Toland and the guides of trouble in the Modoc country, led to the organization of a second company of volunteers.

A meeting was called on the evening of the twenty-fourth of August, at which means to put the men in the field was subscribed by the citizens and miners, and Ben Wright was chosen captain. He was at the time mining on Cottonwood creek, twenty miles distant, but by daylight he was in Yreka surrounded by men eager to assist the emigration through the dangerous country and to punish the Modocs for depredations already committed. A peculiar enthusiasm was imparted to volunteering by the fact that Toland's train was the first to arrive with women and children. The homeless miners were having their minds harrowed by the suggestion of what might have been the fate of these but for the warning and guidance given by McDermit's party, and what might even after all befall others on some part of the route. Three days were consumed in getting together the equipment of men and horses with provision wagons and everything necessary. On the

sixth day after the meeting at Yreka, Wright reached
Tule lake just in time to rescue a train that was surrounded and fighting the Modocs. The sight of
Wright's company advancing sent the savages into
places of concealment among the tules, and on the
island in the lake, and equally alarmed the emigrants
who mistook them for mounted Indians and prepared
for a yet more desperate encounter. Their fears were
changed to joy when Wright, discovering their alarm,
rode forward alone. This train was escorted beyond
danger, and the company returned to the Modoc country.

Wright found the mutilated bodies of the eight men
before mentioned and those of three of his acquaintances, members of McDermit's party, who had been
sent to guide trains and who had been killed. Filled
with rage and grief, Wright and his men made haste to
attack the Indians in their stronghold. To do this they
had to wade in water among the tules up to their arm-
pits, and fight the Modocs concealed in ambuscades
constructed of tules, having portholes. Such was the
vigor of their charge, however, that the ambuscades
were quickly depopulated, and thirty or more Modocs
killed while escaping to the rock island in the lake.

After the battle, Wright proceeded east to Clear
lake where he met a large party of emigrants and
planned a stratagem to draw the Indians out of their
stronghold on the island. He unloaded several ox
wagons, filled them with armed men, a few of whom
he clothed in women's apparel, and placed them in
wagons in plain sight, and loitering along in true emigrant fashion along the dangerous pass. But the Indians either had spies out who reported the trick, or

were too severely punished to feel like attacking white men again and they remained in their fastnesses.

Wright then went to Yreka and had boats built with which to reach the island, spending the time of waiting in patrolling the road through the Modoc country. In the meantime accounts of the massacres had reached Jacksonville, Oregon, and another company, commanded by John E. Ross of that place, proceeded to the Modoc country where it remained on the road until the season to travel was past. On the arrival of Ross, Wright returned to Yreka for supplies, and to bring out his boats. He was unable to find the Indians, who retreated to the lava beds, inaccessible then as now to white men.

That which Wright did find among the plunder left behind on the islands was women's and children's wearing apparel and many evidences that men, women, and children had been taken captive and cruelly tortured and murdered. One of the Indians captured by Wright had a cradle-quilt wrapped about his shoulders. He also learned that there were two white women held captive by the Modocs and however much he desired to exterminate these savages, he knew that the rescue of the women and the safety of all who passed through this section of country, depended upon a treaty with the Modocs.

Wright had an Indian boy for a servant who was part Modoc, and spoke their language. Using this boy as an ambassador, he finally persuaded four of their head men to visit his camp, for the purpose of discussing the terms of a treaty. His proposition was that if they would bring in the two captives, and the stock taken from the emigrants, he would leave their country and trouble them no more, or if they wished, he would trade with them for their furs and feathers. To this the chiefs gave their assent, and while one was sent to fetch the women and the property, the other three were detained as hostages. When the chief returned to camp instead of bringing with him the captive women and the stolen stock, he brought only a few broken down horses and a shotgun; but he was accompanied by forty-five armed warriors. When remonstrated with for his violation of his pledge, he replied that Wright had required three hostages, and now his men greatly out-numbering Wright's he should hold him and his company hostages for the good conduct of the white people. The place where Wright was encamped was on the north side of Lost river, near the stone ford, the Modocs encamping on the same side. The situation was critical, it being plain to Wright that a net was spread for him, which would surely close about him unless, he met the danger with a desperate measure.

The orders for the night were for the men to quietly slip out at midnight and conceal themselves in the sage-brush. They were arranged in groups of three and placed so that they could shoot into the Indian camp. They were to lay so concealed until they heard the crack of Wright's rifle when all were to fire simultaneously. The order was scrupulously carried out. The men rushing upon the surprised Indians at the crack of the signal gun finished the fight with their pistols. The fight was over in five minutes and forty Indians were slain. Wright had four men wounded. These were carried, on litters made by lashing guns together, fifteen miles to the nearest settlement. From there a messenger was sent to Yreka for aid. On the company arriving at that place – thin, sunburned, and nearly naked – they were met by cheers, and bonfires were built and banquets given.

The only regret felt was that the two captive women were left to the fiendish cruelty, which no one doubted, would end their lives before they could be rescued. As a matter of fact, they were never seen alive, but years after their bleaching bones were pointed out by the Indians to curious investigators of Indian history.[19]

Captain Ben Wright appointed agent for the Indians about the mouth of Rogue river, and Captain John Toland, of a volunteer company, were lured to an ostensibly friendly camp of Mackanotin Indians [20] and both cruelly murdered on February 22, 1856. Wright's heart was cut out, cooked and eaten by the Indians. They thought by so doing that they would become as brave as he was.[21]   Again the news came that the Rogue river Indians were in active hostility, aided and abetted by the Klamath Indians who had gone over to Rogue river.

The Oregon authorities called California to aid them in quelling these Indians as most of the hostiles were from across the line and the renegade Klamath Indians had incited the Rogue river Indians to take the war path.   California responded by raising a regiment of volunteers, known as the First California Mounted Riflemen.   They furnished their own horses, arms, and ammunition and received the promise of three dollars a day.

---

[19] These incidents of the Rogue river war are not found in the published histories. Stuart's description is from a remote part of the war. The condemnation he gives to the Indians is more severe than that given by other historians. – ED.

[20] Mackanotin. Bancroft, *Oregon*, vol. ii (*Works*, xxx) p. 405, spells it Mackanootenais. These were a group of the Rogue river Indians. – ED.

[21] This account of the renewal of hostilities is more specific than that in Bancroft. *Ibid.*, p. 369. – ED.

My brother James, Reece Anderson, and myself promptly enlisted. We were armed with muzzle loading rifles, Colt's navy cap and ball revolvers (brass cartridges had not been invented then) and were well mounted. We formed a part of Captain White's company of scouts and were sent to the Klamath lake lava beds to ascertain if possible whether the Modocs had joined the Rogue river Indians. Our company consisted of twenty-five men. Our supplies, food, blankets, and ammunition were carried on pack mules. We scouted all through the lake country until satisfied that the Modocs had nothing to do with the outbreak of the Rogue river Indians. We then returned home, having been gone a month.

On our return to Yreka we found that the Oregon troops assisted by the Californians had subdued the hostiles and the war was over. We were accordingly mustered out and disbanded. James, Reece Anderson, and I resumed mining near Yreka until the spring of 1856.

In July emigrant trains begun to arrive and the Modoc Indians again went on the war path and as these Indians had been so troublesome, constantly breaking treaties, it was decided to go after them good and strong and teach them a lesson that they would not forget.

The state again called for troops and James Stuart and Reece Anderson again enlisted. I remained at Yreka and continued mining, working our placer claims. This time one thousand men enlisted. They took boats out to the lakes and followed the Indians on to the islands and killed great numbers of them. It had been the custom of these Indians to carry stores to the islands in little rafts made of tules and leaving the

women, children and supplies, go out and attack any
emigrant train they could find unprepared and unsus-
pecting, then with their loot take to the islands again.
Without boats the whites were unable to follow them.
In 1856 the volunteers with their boats hunted the last
one down and either killed them or caused them to surrender. This put a stop to their depredations for that
season. The volunteers returned, disbanded and James
and Reece joined me at the mine and we continued
mining until June 1857.

From California to Montana

In the spring of 1857 we decided to visit our parents and our old home in Iowa. We arranged to cross the plains horseback, taking pack horses to carry our bedding and supplies. Others hearing of our contemplated trip wished to join us and soon there were eleven of us ready for the trip. Our party consisted of Frank L. Stone, P. H. Redick, S. S. Dickerman, Samuel B. Byall, James Chapin, Rezin Anderson, James Stuart, Granville Stuart, John Dickey, Enos Dickey, and Henry Buckingham.

All our preparations being made on the fourteenth day of June, 1857, we started from Yreka, California, on our journey east. Each man had a horse or mule to ride and a pack horse or pack mule for every two. Two of the party had double barreled shot guns. All the others had muzzle loading rifles and all had Colt revolvers. Each man had blankets and a change of under clothing, and food for about fifty or sixty days.

The first day we traveled twenty miles diagonally across Shasta valley, with Mount Shasta looming up grandly to the southeast. We followed the old emigrant road as far as Sheep rock, which is a rough granite upheaval covering about two acres and from one hundred to one hundred and fifty feet high (so called because many mountain sheep used it as a place of refuge from the Indians and their dogs, before the white men came). The Indians had no guns, but when the white men came they soon exterminated the unfortunate sheep with their rifles.

JUNE 15, 1857. We left the emigrant road which went east to the Klamath, Tule, Clear, and Goose lakes and turned to the southeast on a new road that had recently been opened through the woods to Pit river,[22] where it connected with the old Lawson 1849-road across the Sierra Nevadas.

JUNE 16. We traveled twenty miles and camped on a creek three miles from Pit river. No grass for our tired horses, the country being heavily timbered.

JUNE 17. Traveled ten miles and then camped in Pit river valley, where we found good grass for hungry horses. Traveled eighteen miles and camped at the ferry on Pit river. Here was a good hewed log house, stable, corral, and a small field fenced, but not a human being. The family that lived here had all been murdered by the Indians a short time before. We all bathed in Pit river, and enjoyed it greatly.

JUNE 19. We here took the old Lawson emigrant trail, went sixteen miles through open pine forest and camped for the night at a spring. We are now one hundred and eight miles from Yreka.

JUNE 20. Traveled eight miles and camped at a water hole. We found it safer to camp wherever we

---

[22] Pit river was so named because the emigrants, who crossed the plains to California in 1849 (of whom my father was one) found many pits about three or four feet wide and six feet long and from six to seven feet deep, in the game trails in the valley along this river. The dirt taken out of these pits and all taken away from the vicinity of the pits, they were then covered over with dry, almost rotten willow sticks, then lightly covered over with dry grass and leaves and a little sprinkle of earth put on so that it was similar to the ground around it. The Indians who made the pits would watch the deer, antelope, and elk that came into valley, and then surround and frighten them, when they would run in their old trails and some would jump on the covered pits and would at once give way and they would fall to the bottom. Unable to get out they fell a prey to the Indians. These Indians had no tools to dig with and these many pits were dug with prongs of deer and elk horns and the dirt carried away in little tule and willow baskets, a

found water, for in a strange country we did not know how far it might be to the next water.

JUNE 21. Traveled fifteen miles and camped at a spring. Road is rising all the time, with some stone stretches here and there. Since leaving Pit river we have been in open country, pine woods of rather poor scrubby trees, but no brush. Saw a few deer, but they always saw us first and fled.

JUNE 22. Traveled thirty-five miles over timbered ridges, stony, bad road. From the top of this ridge the plains of the Great Basin were in sight far, far, below us, and a good sized lake near the foot of the mountain. We made this long day's journey because we found no water. We passed no creeks since leaving Pit river, and not much grass. The descent down the mountain, which is the summit of the Sierra Nevada, was very long and very steep and was hard on our horses, although we walked and led them most of the way. We finally reached the lake which is called Honey lake and found good grass, but the water in the lake was hardly fit to drink. Men and horses all very tired. There are a few people living around the lake, but I would not care to live in such a disagreeable region. Not a tree or even a bush, since leaving the foot of the mountains, and the gnats and mosquitoes are bad. They almost devoured us and worried the horses greatly.

JUNE 23. Traveled fifteen miles over a stony road and camped on Little Willow creek (I do not know why it should be called Willow creek, as but few willows grow along its course). No trees anywhere, which

long hard labor which of course had to be done by the patient women. These Indians were not friendly to the whites and were dangerous. Along the road to Pit river were occasional little grassy parks in one of which called Elk park, we camped for the night.

makes me homesick for the noble trees of California. We are now one hundred and eighty miles from Yreka.

JUNE 24. Traveled eighteen miles over a stony road, camped at Mud springs, pretty fair grass, but no timber.

JUNE 25. Traveled eighteen miles and camped on Smoke creek. On the way we passed a pool of water under a shelving ledge of rock, and as we came to it about thirty or forty magpies flew up from it. Never saw so many together before. We camped on Smoke creek, a little crooked stream with not a bush on it, but in the narrow crooked bottom along the stream is the finest clover growing that I ever saw. It is as thick as the hair on a dog and fully three feet high. How our horses enjoyed it. They ate until they could hold no more and then laid down and rolled in it.

JUNE 26. Traveled twenty-five miles before we came to a spring. Much of the road rocky and bad. This spring is a wonderful one. It is about fifteen feet across, very clear, and apparently about eighteen feet deep. The water runs down a little slope about one hundred yards and then flows over a meadow of good grass about two hundred yards long by one hundred and fifty yards wide. The country around the spring is of a barren, sandy nature, with some small sage, but not a tree or bush in sight anywhere. The water is very cold and delicious, which is the more remarkable in a region where the water is usually bad and scarce, and where any is found, it is usually boiling hot. There are two other lovely springs in the group, all sending their water into the little meadow below them. There are no mountains or hills near these springs, and their

FRENCH GULCH, DEER LODGE COUNTY, M.T.
Here Mortimer Lott began mining gold shortly after the Stuarts began
operations on Gold creek
From an original drawing made by Granville Stuart, in 1869

GOLD CREEK MOUNTAINS, FROM DEER LODGE CITY (LOOKING WEST)
Scene of the first gold mining in Montana
From an original drawing made by Granville Stuart, August 22, 1865

water, after irrigating the little meadow, sinks in the thirsty desert plains.[23]

JUNE 27. Only traveled twelve miles when we came to a forked mountain of considerable size in the midst of sagebrush four and five feet high. At its foot we suddenly came to a lovely stream six or seven feet wide, and one foot deep of clear cold water. This stream comes out of a cañon that extends back into the forked mountain, on which we see a few scattering trees, apparently fir trees. The mountain is of granite and the creek is called Granite creek. These are the first trees we have seen since we left the Sierra Nevadas and they looked good to us. This lovely creek runs about one-half mile down through the big sage which it nourishes and then sinks in the bare white bed of a dry alkali lake. We camped here for the rest of the day and night, for we knew that there was no water ahead of us for sixty miles and the weather burning hot. There is much loose granite sand on the hillside where the creek emerges from its cañon into the plain and in this sand we find many tracks of mountain sheep. We possibly might kill one by climbing up the mountain, but we are too tired and besides the weather is very hot, so although we want fresh meat very much, we decided not to risk climbing mountains in this fierce heat.

JUNE 28. We started from Granite creek at daybreak. Our road lay over the smooth level dry bed of Mud lake. The greater part of the way this is white and so hard that our horses' feet scarcely made a mark. About half-way across we unexpectedly came to a big boiling spring that sent up lots of steam, but this water

---

[23] No doubt someone has a fine ranch there now with fruit and ornamental trees in plenty. – 1916.

did us no good, for we had nothing in which to cool it and besides it smelt badly. We feared it might be poisonous and there was not a blade of grass for our hungry horses. They have traveled thirty miles since daybreak in a boiling sun, but we did not stop. We were glad when the sun went down. About dark the road left the level bed of the dried lake and passed over low ridges with sagebrush and some greasewood brush. We arrived at Rabbit spring wells sometime after midnight. These springs do not flow any water, and are only a marshy piece of ground a few acres in extent. By digging holes from two to four feet deep we got some very poor alkali water in limited quantities, bad, but it was wet. There is no fuel here, but a few sprigs of greasewood and we are all too tired to hunt for it in the dark, so after picketing our horses on rather scanty grass and putting two men on guard, we made down our beds and slept sweetly until daybreak.

JUNE 29. Traveled fifteen miles to the Little meadows [24] on the Humboldt river. It is a pleasure to see our horses drink their full of its good clear water and eat all they could hold of the splendid grass and then lie down and roll in it with great grunts of satisfaction. We arrived here about two in the afternoon and for the benefit of our horses we remained all the rest of the day and all night.

JUNE 30. Traveled up the river twenty miles. Had good grass and good water. There was fine grass in the river bottom, with dense clumps of willows along the river banks. Back from the river the valley and low hills were covered with sagebrush. No timber along this curious river.

---

[24] Lassen's meadows. *Montana As It Is*, p. 138.—ED.

JULY 1. Traveled up the river twenty miles. We are traveling slowly to keep our horses in good condition. Good grass and good water, but no wood, use sagebrush for cooking. Road is often a mile or more from the river. Mosquitoes are very annoying. We are now in a section of country where the Indians are hostile and we do not camp near the willows along the river. We make a stop, cook our supper, then when it is quite dark, saddle up, travel five or six miles and make camp without fire or any noise. In this way we keep out of reach of any prowling bands of Indians.

JULY 3. Traveled only ten miles, as a big storm of some kind seems brewing. We made each of ourselves a kind of tent by cutting long slender willows about eight or nine feet long and sharpened both ends and bent them over and stuck them in the ground, thus making arches about three and one-half feet high and about three and one-half feet wide on the ground which we roofed over with a pair of blankets. Then we made down our bed on the ground, and under this shelter we were dry and comfortable. We had completed our shelters and were getting ready for bed when it began to rain. Two stood guard over the horses. Before morning it turned cold and snowed and then it was mighty uncomfortable for the guards. We do not leave our horses alone a minute on this part of the road, for although we have not seen any Indians we know that they are lurking near.

JULY 4. We did not move camp as it is impossible to travel in this storm. It rained and snowed in turn all day. We had no fire on account of the rain and stayed in bed when not on duty herding. In the evening it cleared up and we made a big fire of sagebrush, cooked our suppers, and partially dried out our clothes and bedding. Everything including our provisions was soaked. Both we and our horses have suffered severely during the past two days. None of us can say that we enjoyed the way we were compelled to celebrate the Glorious Fourth of this year 1856.

JULY 5. Traveled twenty miles to-day, passed Stony point, a very dangerous place on the road. Here some emigrants have been killed every year since 1848. Much of the trouble comes from carelessness on the part of the whites. Most of them know little about the habits of Indians and camp in dangerous places. They see no Indians and thinking there are none about become careless and allow their stock to stray too far from camp and the next thing they know the Indians have either stampeded and run off their stock or the train has been attacked. These Indians are mostly armed with bows and arrows and will not attack a train unless they can effect a surprise. We have seen no Indians, but being constantly on the lookout we have seen signs and every night we have seen their signal fires, but we keep our arms ready for instant use and never leave the horses unguarded nor do we camp in places where the Indians could slip up and surprise us. They are not apt to tackle eleven well armed men.

JULY 6. Traveled twenty miles and camped at Gravelly ford on the Humboldt river. Several Indians came into camp this morning and also in the evening. They are apparently very friendly, but as most of us kept our guns in our hands they had no chance to be otherwise. We are all well aware that "eternal vigilance is the price of safety" anywhere on the plains. We are now four hundred and forty-four miles from Yreka. Mosquitoes and gnats nearly set our horses crazy and also tapped us for a considerable quantity of blood.

JULY 7. Traveled twenty-five miles across the mountains to where we came to the Humboldt river again. Plenty of Indian signs, saw signal fires on the mountains to westward. Clouds of mosquitoes and gnats.

JULY 8. Traveled thirty miles up the river. Met two Mormons with a little one horse wagon and a loaded pack horse. They are the first white men we have seen since we left Honey lake valley, and the Sierra Nevada mountains of blessed memory. To-day saw a great many hawks for the first time on trip. The mosquitoes and gnats have tormented our horses and ourselves all day and everything and everybody are about played out.

JULY 9. Traveled thirty miles. Crossed the North fork of the Humboldt. Gnats and mosquitoes are untiring and still busy. Will they never let up? John Dickey rode ahead from our noon halt to try to kill a sage hen or rabbit. We heard him shoot twice and soon after saw him sitting on a big rock pounding the fragments of his double barreled rifle with another rock. He had beaten the stock of his gun into small pieces and bent the barrels into a curve and was busily engaged in beating the fine locks to pieces with another rock. When we asked him what was the matter, he said that he had fired twice at a sage cock and missed him both times and he'd be d—d if he was going to carry any such a d—d gun any further. The rifle was of German make and well finished and we felt sure that the fault lay with John and not with the gun. John was a man of passionate and ungovernable temper. He frequently beat his fine mule unmercifully without good cause. We are now five hundred and twenty-nine miles from Yreka. To-day we met one lone Indian riding a little colt. I am sure there are many Indians not far off or he would not be so bold.

JULY 10. Traveled twenty miles, crossed the river on an apology for a bridge and bade a long farewell to the Humboldt river. We have traveled up the Humboldt three hundred and two miles and it is quite a stream still. We camped at a spring on the mountain. Here plenty of Indians came into camp; they seemed very friendly and tried to talk with us, but as they did not understand English, or at least pretended they didn't (which is a common trick among Indians everywhere) and we did not understand the Snake language, we did not make much progress.

JULY 11. Traveled thirty miles. Pass through Thousand spring valley, a noted place and well remembered by all who crossed the plains in 1849. The valley is swampy owing to the many springs. We camped for the night at a spring to the left of the road. Today we passed a Mormon wagon in which were two men and a woman.

JULY 12. Traveled fifteen miles and then laid up on the head of Goose creek where we found good grass and good water. Here we met the first trains of emigrants bound for California. They looked very natural to us who went through the same experience five years ago. I could not help thinking of all the wonderful things I had seen and felt in that five years and now I had turned my back on them and was going home. Quite a number of wagons, mostly ox teams and about five hundred cattle passed us early this morning while we were cooking our breakfast.

JULY 13. Traveled twenty miles down Goose creek nearly north to where the road leaves it. Met lots of emigrants. Some of our party bought a few food supplies from them, mostly sugar, coffee, and bacon, which they sold us at a very reasonable price when one considers the twelve hundred to fifteen hundred miles they had hauled these things, across vast plains and mountains. Their teams were mostly in fair condition and would get through all right.

JULY 14. Traveled twenty miles. Bid a long farewell to Goose creek. Met scores of emigrants to-day and passed the forks of the roads. The right-hand one goes east to Great Salt Lake City and the left-hand one goes north-east and is known as the Hudspeth "Cut Off" [25] from Soda springs on Bear river to this place. It was considerably shorter than the old emigrant road, that went from Soda springs to Old Fort Hall on Snake river. Camped on West branch of Raft river at junction of Fort Hall road with the Hudspeth "Cut Off." Today we passed through the "City of Rocks," which is a great natural curiosity; huge rocks, some square, some round, some resembling houses, and all kinds of strange and fantastic shapes stand scattered over a space of about three miles long, and one mile wide. I never saw anything like this anywhere else in all my wanderings.

JULY 15. Traveled twenty miles and camped on the east branch of Raft river. Good camp, plenty of wood, water, and grass. The road crossed the river here. Here we found a couple of Mormons camped selling provisions to the emigrants.

JULY 16. Traveled twenty miles over hilly country and camped at a good spring where the grass is good

[25] *Ibid.*, p. 143. – ED.

and plentiful. Met many emigrant wagons mostly families with some small droves of cattle.

JULY 17. Traveled thirty-one miles to Malad creek sometimes called Gravel Bottom creek. Nice clear water, some wood and plenty of good grass. We passed over two high ridges and through two cañons. Leading up to and down through these there were some quaking aspen timber and some brush. But for twenty-two miles before reaching Malad creek we found no water and weather quite warm. The crossing of Malad creek is two hundred and forty miles north of Great Salt Lake City. Passed or rather met many emigrant teams. All were anxious to get to water as the teams were suffering greatly for it.

On the head of Malad creek, in the same region where I fell ill on my way to California in 1852, I was again taken sick. On July 17, 1857, I was so ill that my companions felt, that if I recovered at all it would be a long time before I would be able to travel. Accordingly it was decided that Reece Anderson and James Stuart remain with me and the other eight resume their long journey east. Here on the great Overland emigrant road about sixty miles north of where the town of Corinne was afterwards built, I lay for seven weeks too ill to travel. My brother succeeded in breaking the fever, but not until it had brought me nigh to death's door. My recovery was very slow.

Early one morning we heard a great hubbub followed by a number of shots fired into the camp of a train of emigrants camped nearby. They had let some of their horses graze away from their camp about two hundred yards. Suddenly four mounted Indians, who were concealed in a dense patch of willows, dashed out among them and with loud yells and shaking of their blankets stampeded all the loose horses. By the time the astonished emigrants got their rifles in action the Indians and frightened horses were three hundred yards away and going at full speed. A number of shots were fired, but no one was hit. The Indians stopped and fired back, wounding one man in the heel and then resumed their flight and were soon out of sight among the hills. They got away with eight horses. This sort of thing happened very often on the overland road because of the carelessness of the emigrants.

Camped near us was a man named Jake Meek, who some years before, had been in the employ of the Hudson's Bay Fur Company, carrying their mail and express between Fort Hall and Fort Boise on Snake river, near where is now the thriving town of Caldwell, Idaho. At the time of which I am writing both forts were in Oregon. Meek was engaged in trading ponies, dressed skins, and buckskin clothing to the emigrants, for money and tired out cattle and horses.

The emigrants at once accused him of being in league with the Indians in stealing their horses and made dire threats as to what they would do to him. He protested his innocence, but they were in an ugly mood and I think they would have killed him had not James Stuart and Reece Anderson taken his part. James told them that we had been camped near Meek for some time and knew him to be innocent; that only two days before the Indians had got away with two of his horses and came near getting ours and would have done so but for our always standing guard over them day and night. Eternal, sleepless, vigilance was the only way to save one's horses from being stolen when traveling through an Indian country.

During the time we were delayed here many important events had taken place. Brigham Young, President of the Mormon church, had, as we now learned, declared the state of Deseret now Utah, free and independent of the United States. In fact he had seceded from the Union.

I remember hearing Brigham Young in 1852 preaching and abusing the United States, calling them, "a Union with hell and the devil" and assuring the "Saints," "that the Mormon Church would overcome all its enemies, that the Lord would yet guide them back to Jackson, Missouri, that He would deliver the United States over to them and they would establish the Kingdom of God over the world." I thought at the time that Brigham was tackling too big a job, but I found that now five years later he had started in to make good. The government at Washington tried to reason him out of seceding, but Brigham refused to listen saying that, "The Lord was on the side of the Saints and that they could and would lick the United States, and all the legions of hell that were helping the United States." The government finally started five thousand troops commanded by General Albert Sidney Johnson to Utah to squelch him. While I lay sick Brigham declared Utah under martial law, organized and drilled the Saints and made it high crime to sell or give away any food or ammunition to a gentile, and got ready for war.

By this time the United States troops with long slow moving ox trains of supplies, were coming up North Platte and Sweetwater rivers and the Mormon troops patrolled and guarded all the roads, and when at last I was able to mount my horse, we found all the roads guarded, and we could neither go forward to the States nor back to California. To attempt it would cause us to be arrested as government spies and that meant sure death. A few persons found traveling were arrested and were never heard of afterwards. No doubt Brigham's corps of "Destroying Angels," under Porter ,Rockwell, and Bill Hickman, could have pointed out their graves. Five years later I became acquainted with Hickman at Gold Creek, Montana, and found him a genial sort of man. I think Byron's description of "The Corsair," "He was the mildest mannered man that ever scuttled ship or cut a human throat," would have fitted him quite well. We now found ourselves in a very dangerous situation. We could not long remain where we were, and if we tried to go anywhere else we ran the risk of losing our lives.

We discussed our forlorn situation with Meek, finding him familiar with the country generally. He told us that the past winter (that of 1856) he had wintered in Beaverhead valley some three hundred miles north, and that the Indians in that region were friendly, that the winters were not severe, and game was plentiful there, and that he intended to go there and winter as soon as the cattle and horses he had traded for had rested up enough to stand the trip. He said the best thing we could do would be to go with him and winter there and come back in the spring, as the Mormon war would probably be over then. We had never heard of Beaverhead valley, and knew nothing of the country, but as we could not safely go anywhere else we determined to go with him. Then came the problem of getting supplies in a hostile country in time of war. Meek told us that forty miles down the stream on which we were camped, was an outlying Mormon fort and a small settlement. He thought the bishop who ruled the settlement, as was always the case among the Mor-

mons, might possibly be induced by a good price to sell
us some food and ammunition secretly, in spite of
Brigham Young's prohibition against letting gentiles
have anything.   Brother James and Meek, who also
wanted supplies, went down to Bishop Barnard's fort
at Malad City, as these few adobe huts were called, and
found the bishop kind enough to sell them secretly a
limited quantity of flour, bacon, coffee, and sugar, provided Meek, who had bought a wagon and two yoke
of oxen from the emigrants, would bring his wagon to
the fort at midnight, and get his food and drive the
rest of the night, so as to be far away before day
dawned.   Of course these conditions were gladly accepted.   He also sold James a small quantity of powder, lead, and percussion caps, for our muzzle loading
rifles.   We were also armed with the old style powder
and ball Colt's navy revolvers and they were mighty
good weapons, too, as I often proved by killing deer,
antelope, and mountain sheep, with mine at one hundred yards distance.

While we were still at our camp on Malad creek preparing to go North, the massacre at Mountain meadows
in southern Utah took place.   On September 11, 1857,
there was murdered, in cold blood, by the Mormon
militia an entire train of emigrants, consisting of one
hundred and twenty men, women, and children.   Only
seventeen little children from three to seven years old
were spared alive.

This train of emigrants was camped at the meadows
resting their horses and cattle before starting across the
desert between there and California.   They were first
attacked by Indians and Mormon militia disguised as
Indians.   The train hastily entrenched themselves inside their corral of wagons and fought for four days.

Seven were killed and several were wounded and several Mormons were killed.

John D. Lee, who led the Mormons found the train too well equipped to be easily taken and decided to try another plan. His Mormons threw off their disguise and then appeared on the scene as a rescuing party. John D. Lee induced the train to surrender promising them protection and assistance to go to California. After giving up their arms all except the seventeen children before mentioned, were shot down in cold blood.[26]

The reason afterwards alleged for this dreadful massacre, by the Mormons, was, that this train was from Arkansas, where one of the twelve apostles of the Mormon church, Parley P. Pratt, was killed on May 13, 1857, by a man named Hector McLean, whose wife it was alleged Pratt had seduced. This was probably true, for Mrs. McLean left her husband and children and went with the Mormons to Salt Lake City. It was also alleged by the Mormons that the men of this emigrant train, while passing through the Mormon settlements, boasted that they were glad that Pratt was killed and that they would like to kill a lot more Mormons, and were abusive generally. The seventeen little children were sent back to their friends in Arkansas in 1859, by means of an appropriation made by congress for that purpose. Only one man was ever punished for this horrible crime. John Doyle Lee was duly

---

[26] R. L. Baskin, *Reminiscences of Early Utah* (1914) pp. 83-88, 108-149, gives a documentary account of the massacre and the evidence bearing on the guilt of the heads of the Mormon Church. His opinions are very hostile to the Mormons. Orson F. Whitney, *History of Utah* (3 vols., Salt Lake City, 1892) vol. i, pp. 692-709, blames the emigrants for hostile talk against the Mormons, and implicates only two white men in the massacre, Lee and Klingensmith. Even from his statement however there seems to be no doubt but that many other Mormons were implicated. – ED.

convicted of being the principal leader of those who murdered these emigrants and was taken to the spot of the massacre twenty years later and shot, March 23, 1877. The laws of Utah allowed murderers to choose whether they would be hanged or shot. Lee chose to be shot. Lee was convicted on the evidence given by a man named Philip Klingensmith, who turned state's evidence. He was second in command under Lee and ought to have been shot also, as he led the final massacre.

Had we known on the eleventh day of September, 1857, as we were packing up, of the dreadful deed being done at Mountain meadows, instead of traveling leisurely along, we would doubtless have traveled, without camping day or night, as long as our stock could go, in our desire to get as far away as we could in the shortest space of time. We did not hear of the massacre until June 26, 1858, when James, Anderson, Ross, and I went to Fort Bridger, Utah, for supplies.

We crossed the Rocky Mountain divide on the tenth day of October, 1857, where the station called Monida now is on the Oregon Short Line railroad. As soon as we had crossed the divide a wonderful change appeared in the country. Instead of the gray sagebrush covered plains of Snake river, we saw smooth rounded hills and sloping bench land covered with yellow bunch grass that waved in the wind like a field of grain. A beautiful little clear stream ran northwest on its way to join the Missouri river. This is now known as Red Rock creek. The forepart of October gave days of brilliant sunshine, warm and pleasant with no snow anywhere except on the tops of higher mountains and very little even there.

We had seen no game except an occasional lone antelope on the plains of Snake river. Soon as we came to the divide of the Rocky mountains bands of antelope of from four to five, to fifteen and twenty together, were in sight all the time, but the Indians had evidently been hunting them, for they were exceedingly shy, making it very difficult to get within gunshot of them on the smooth treeless benches of Red Rock creek. Our muzzle-loading rifles were not sighted for long range shooting, but we soon managed to circumvent them sufficiently to have meat. We also discovered as we moved on our way down the valley to Beaverhead that there was plenty of game, consisting of black tailed deer, big horn or mountain sheep, and also many bands of elk.

On the twenty-fourth of October we left Sage creek and crossed the rather high ridge of Blacktail Deer creek. That night a furious snow storm set in which lasted all the next day. Twelve inches of snow fell and it turned quite cold so that ice formed on pools of still water. Fortunately we were camped where wood was reasonably plentiful and we did not suffer. Having arrived at our destination, the Beaverhead valley, we chose as a camping place a spot in the valley at the mouth of Blacktail Deer creek. Here we remained until Christmas. At our camp were Reece Anderson, James Stuart, Jake Meek, Robert Dempsey with his wife, Antoine Le Clair and wife, and his two grown sons, and myself. We all lived in elk skin Indian lodges and were very comfortable. The winter was mild with very little snow. It was our custom to go hunting without a coat. There was plenty of game and the camp was kept well supplied with meat.

Fifteen miles further down the Beaverhead at the mouth of the Stinking Water was another camp of mountain men. Captain Richard Grant, an old Scotch gentleman formerly with the Hudson's Bay Company, with his family, John F. Grant and family, James C. Grant, Thomas Pambrun and family, L. R. Maillet, John Jacobs and family, Robert Hereford and family, John W. Powell, John Saunders, Ross, Antoine Pou·-rier, and several men in the employ of Hereford and the Grants.[27]   Captain Grant built a good three room log house for his family to live in, but the others occupied Indian lodges made of dressed elk skins.

A mile further down the river was Antoine Courtei and family, and two Delaware Indians, named Jim and Ben Simonds, both very large men, weighing over

[27] The families were Indian women and half-breed children with the exception of Captain Grant's family. His wife was a quarter-Indian from the Red river of the North and had been educated in a convent as were his three charming daughters. G. S. One of these daughters married C. P. Higgins of Hell Gate and Missoula. Angus MacDonald, a son of the old trader at Fort Connah believes that Mrs. C. P. Higgins made the contraction of an Indian sentence meaning, "Where the waters flow from opposite directions" to form the word Missoula. On the other hand his half-brother Duncan MacDonald asserts that Missoula came from an Indian expression *In May soo let que* meaning Quaking river. Father Palladino gives still another meaning. He believes that the expression *lm-i-sul-e* meaning "by the cold, chilling waters," is the origin of the word. *Indian and White in the Northwest* (Lancaster, Pennsylvania, 1922) p. 358.

Robert Hereford was a trader along the Emigrant road. It was probably he who informed the Stuarts of the signs of gold in Deer Lodge valley. Michael A. Leeson, *A History of Montana* (Chicago, 1885) p. 209. He was later in the Bitter Root associated with Major John Owen (*Fort Owen Journals* edited by Seymour Dunbar and Paul C. Phillips, 1925). He was engrossing clerk of the first territorial legislature of Montana, and later was assessor of Lewis and Clark county. MONTANA, *House Journal of First Legislative Assembly.* F. H. Woody, Sketch of the Early History of Western Montana in *Montana Historical Society Contributions,* vol. ii (Helena, Montana, 1896) p. 95. Maillet was a partner of Neil McArthur an old Hudson's Bay Company employe. He came into the Bitter Root in 1855, and had gone into the Beaverhead country to trade when Stuart met him. A semi-autobiographical sketch of his life is in *Montana Historical Society Contributions,* vol. iv (Helena, 1903) pp. 197-228. Thomas Pambrun is frequently mentioned in the *Fort Owen Journals.* Delaware Jim was for several years after this in the employ of Major Owen and accompanied him on many of his trading trips. Jake Meeks was also often associated with Major Owen. – ED.

two hundred pounds. These Indians had considerable quantity of goods to sell and trade to the Indians as did Hereford, and the Grants.

The time during the winter was passed trading with the Indians and in visiting one another's camps and in hunting. The price of a common horse was two blankets, one shirt, one pair of cloth leggins, one small mirror, one knife, one paper of vermillion, and usually a few other trifles. A dressed deer skin cost from fifteen to twenty rifle balls and powder; one elk skin, twenty to twenty-five balls and powder; antelope, five to ten balls and powder; beaver, twenty to twenty-five balls and powder; moccasins per pair, ten balls and powder. The Grants and the Hudson's Bay men generally, complained bitterly of the American hunters and adventurers for having more than doubled the price of all those articles among the Indians in the last ten years, which was doubtless true.

Simonds and Hereford each had considerable whiskey in their outfits but it was only for the whites, as they did not trade it to the Indians who were scattered about. These Indians were mostly Snakes and Bannocks, with a few Flatheads. They did not seem to crave liquor as most Indians do, but were quiet and unobtrusive, and as respectable as Indians ever get to be. The whites and half breeds drank enough while it lasted (which fortunately was not long) for themselves and all the Indians in the country. At times it seemed that blood must be shed, but the Providence that seems to watch over the lives of drunken men stood by them and the end of the liquor was reached before anyone was killed. As we three never drank, we often wished that the devil had them all.

Gambling was a popular pastime. The Indian is an

inveterate gambler and will gamble even the shirt off
his back and walk home naked. The mountain men
as a rule were almost as bad, and much of the time during these long winter nights and short winter days, was
taken up by playing the Indian gambling game of
"Hands." Those inclined for a game would collect at
some lodge. Inside there would be a pole usually a
lodge pole, about six feet long and on either side a
number of Indians and often white men. They would
sit and sing or drone a sort of song, all the time beating
on the pole with the sticks. One always knew by these
sounds that a game was in progress within the tepee.
The gamblers would sit opposite each other and they
would have a polished stick or bone about an inch long
and an inch or inch and a half in diameter. The man
who starts the game takes the piece of bone in his hand
and he shifts it back and forth holding his hands over
his head in front and behind him and when he thinks
he has sufficiently bewildered his opponent he stops and
the other guesses which hand the bone is in. If he
makes a right guess he wins and wrong he loses.

They take turns hiding the bone whether the man
who had the bone wins or loses the next man takes his
turn. They wager everything they possess on this
game; horses, blankets, belts, war bonnets, skins, robes,
vermillion paint, saddles, shirts, leggins, moccasins, and
tobacco. Usually the gambler has a pile of his belongings beside him and will wager first one article and
then another, and the pile grows or diminishes as luck
is good or bad. It is no uncommon thing to see one
man in camp with about everything in his possession
and next day perhaps be almost naked, having lost one
day what he has won the day before. The singing and
beating on the pole is not solely to furnish music to the

players. The musicians are usually unsuccessful gamblers, pounding and singing to make, "medicine," so that the next time they would be lucky.

On Christmas day Captain Grant invited Reece Anderson, Ross, James Stuart, Jacob Meek, and myself to dine with him. The menu consisted of buffalo meat, boiled smoked tongue, bread, dried fruit, a preserve made from the choke-cherries, and coffee. This was an elaborate dinner for those days. Supplies were scarce and hard to get, and most of us were living on meat straight.

Late in the fall some ten lodges of Nez Percé Indians came into the Beaverhead valley, and spent the winter camped there. They were peaceable among the whites and gave no trouble. A number of them had the smallpox during the winter, but it was of a mild type. We often met them riding along the trails all broken out with the disease. The weather was quite cold, with no snow on the ground, yet none of them died. They remained outside of our lodges when they called on us as they knew the disease was contagious. This was thoughtful of them and saved us the trouble of keeping them out of camp. A Bannock woman, the wife of Robert Hereford, took the disease and died. Strange to say her husband and three other white men who occupied the same lodge with her during her illness did not take the disease.

About January 1, 1858, there arrived ten men, under the command of B. F. Ficklin, who had been teamsters in the employ of Johnston's army. They were enlisted as volunteers, and sent out from the winter quarters at Fort Bridger to purchase beef cattle from the mountaineers. They were guided by Ned Williamson, and reported very little snow on the route. They could not purchase cattle on terms to suit them, and fearing to return in mid-winter, remained on the Big Hole until the general exodus in the spring, when they returned to Fort Bridger. They were compelled to eat some of their horses on their way, as indeed did also some of the mountaineers, game being very scarce. The spring was stormy and bad, although the winter had been mild and pleasant.

Just after Christmas we moved from the Beaverhead over on the Big Hole river a short distance below where Brown's bridge now stands and just above the curious ridge of naked broken rock known as the "Backbone." [28] We thought this a better hunting ground but the game was all poor and getting scarce. We decided that we would get out and go to Fort Bridger just as soon as the snow had melted enough to enable us to cross the divide. We were entirely out of provisions and had been for sometime living on wild game without salt. We knew that as soon as we crossed the Rocky mountain divide onto the sagebrush plains of Snake river, there would be no game of any kind and also none from there to Fort Bridger. We four visited Captain Richard Grant's camp at the junction of Stinking Water creek and the Beaverhead river. The Captain was getting ready to move his camp to Bitter Root valley by way of Deer Lodge valley and on down through it and Hell Gate cañon to the junction of the Hell Gate and Bitter Root rivers.

On the twenty-eighth of March, 1858, Reece Anderson, Ross, Brother James, and myself tried to cross the Rocky mountain divide at the head of Dry creek, above Pleasant valley (then known as "Lodge Pole Camp"). We had twenty horses and forced our way over near

---

[28] About thirty miles north of Dillon. – ED.

where the Summit stage station stood in 1876.[29]   Not far from where Monida now is, we encountered a driving snow storm and as the snow was about six feet deep and soft, the labor of breaking a trail was so severe that our horses became exhausted and night coming on we were compelled to return to our camp on Red Rock creek.   Here we discovered that the roots of the wild thistles which we dug out of the frozen ground with an axe, were large and firm and tasted very much like the inside of a cabbage stalk.   When boiled with our deer and antelope meat it improved it greatly.

It being found impossible to cross the Dry creek pass, and it was resolved to move over and try the next one south known as the Medicine Lodge pass.[30]   At this time everybody was reduced to meat straight and it took energetic hunting to get even that for game of all kind had become unaccountably scarce.

---

[29] Where the Oregon Short Line now crosses the mountains. – ED.

[30] This pass is southwest of the one above described. – ED.

The Discovery of Gold

While camped in Sheep Horn cañon, endeavoring to kill meat enough to do us over the divide, it became apparent that if we remained here longer, a resort must soon be made to horse flesh, so we resolved to go over to Deer Lodge where game was said to be abundant and kill and dry enough meat to do us to Fort Bridger. We were also actuated by a desire to investigate the reported finding of float gold by a Red river half-breed, named Benetsee, in the lower end of Deer Lodge, 1852.

On the fourth of April we moved to Deer Lodge valley and on the seventh made camp about where the town of Stuart now is. Reece Anderson and I went hunting in the mountains where the station of Durant now is. About the rocks in the cañon we encountered numerous bands of mountain sheep. I succeeded in killing one ewe that had not had kids that year and she was very fat; I also killed two yearlings. This was the first fat meat we had had for several months, and was a great treat to us. We packed the sheep on our horses and took them to camp and after dressing them carefully cut the meat in thin strips and dried it and used it as a seasoning for the poor antelope meat that we killed later.

We then went down the Deer Lodge valley to the mouth of Flint creek where we found John M. Jacobs camped with a small herd of cattle that he had taken from John F. Grant on the shares. Grant had gone to the Bitter Root. Here we luxuriated on milk and wild game. Jacobs had broken several cows to milk.

Later we joined camp with Thomas Adams now of Washington, D.C., and all moved up Flint creek to a point three miles above where the town of Philipsburg now is. Here we built a corral, strong enough to bid defiance to the Blackfoot Indians, into which we put our horses each night. We remained here but a short time as there was little game, and then moved down to the West fork of Flint creek near where the town of Hall now is. Here we were joined by Jacobs and we built another strong corral.

These Blackfoot Indians were not blood thirsty at this time, for they could have ambushed and killed us almost any day or night. But to be an expert and successful horse thief gave the Indian great prestige, and he was emphatically "It" among the damsels of his tribe. Except in actual war it was considered a greater achievement to get the horses without blood-shed and without being seen than it was to murder the owner in order to secure his horses.

Not long after this they succeeded in getting four of our horses. We had not seen any Blackfeet for sometime and had allowed our horses to run loose and feed on the luxuriant grass along the creek bottom. Just below us on the creek were camped eight lodges of Flathead Indians. They had a number of ponies that fed with ours. One morning I arose just at day break and went to bring our horses to camp as was our custom. I had gone only a short distance from the lodge when I saw hanging on a willow an old worn out pair of moccasins. Right then I knew what had happened. Investigation showed that four of our horses and eight of the Flatheads were gone. The Indians started out in pursuit but we knew it would be useless as the thieves had several hours start and as soon as they reached the top of the mountain about forty miles distant would be in the country of the Blackfeet. The Flatheads followed the trail to the divide and then returned. They knew that it meant certain death to them for a small party to go over into the enemies' country.

The Indians of the eastern states have always been described as a saturnian, gloomy, mirthless race, which may have been so, but it is not true of those living in the western states, for they love a practical joke and villages and encampments are often scenes of jollity and laughter. They have a keen sense of ludicrous humorous situations, as when that thief hung up his worn out moccasins where we would be sure to see them he told us very plainly, "I have walked until my moccasins are all worn out, and now I will ride home and you can take my old moccasins and walk in search of more horses."

John M. Jacobs had an English rifle made by Westly Richards, for tiger shooting in India, that he bought from a Hudson's Bay trader. It had a two foot barrel of sixty-five calibre, which chambered a one ounce round lead ball. It had a small back action lock of exquisite finish; also a spring to regulate the trigger pull, an iron ram-rod with a screw on its end for extracting balls, and moulds for making ounce balls, and a fine sole leather case for the gun, which only weighed eight pounds. Jacobs complained that he could not kill any game with it. I examined it carefully and made up my mind that the fault lay in Jacobs and not in the highly finished rifle, and offered to trade him my old reliable Kentucky rifle for it. He accepted my offer and we were both satisfied. I tried the rifle and found it a fine shooter when enough powder was used, and found that Jacobs used only half enough because he feared the recoil, which was tremendous, for it would turn me half around to the right every time I fired it.

Game of all kinds, found in this part of the Rocky mountains, was abundant in Flint creek valley and we were in no danger of starving especially after I traded for that mighty tiger rifle. With it I provided plenty of lean antelope, and deer meat without a speck of fat on it. This with plenty of clear water out of the creek was all we had. Our principal object in coming over into the Deer Lodge country was to kill game and dry meat enough to last us to Fort Bridger and to do a little prospecting.

We had been told that Benetsee, a half-breed from the Red river of the North had found gold on Benetsee creek, about twelve miles from where we were camped.

On May 2, 1858, James Stuart, Reece Anderson, Thomas Adams, and myself packed up the tools we had, which was an old square pointed spade with the hand hold broken out of the top of the handle, that Adams had found in his wagon when he had bought it in Salt Lake, and a tin bread pan that we had brought with us from California and started for Benetsee creek on a prospecting trip.

We followed up the creek about five miles carefully searching for any prospect or evidences of prospecting but found nothing. Near the bank of the creek at the foot of the mountain we sunk a hole about five feet deep and found ten cents in fine gold to the pan of sand and gravel. This convinced us that there were rich gold mines in this vicinity, but as we had no tools or provisions we could not do much prospecting. This prospect hole dug by us was the first prospecting for gold done in what is now Montana and this is the account of the first real discovery of gold within the state.[31]

It was now almost sundown and we built a fire and cooked our supper and sat around the camp fire dis-

---

[31] Stuart wrote in 1864: "About the year 1852, a French half-breed from Red river of the north, named Francois Finlay, but commonly known by the sobriquet of 'Benetsee,' who had been to California, began to 'prospect' on a branch of the Hell Gate now known as Gold creek. He found small quantities of light float gold in the surface along this stream, but not in sufficient abundance to pay. This became noised about among the mountaineers; and when Reece Anderson, my brother James, and I, were delayed by sickness at the head of Malad creek, on the Hudspeths 'Cut-Off,' as we were on our way from California to the states in the summer of 1857, we saw some men who had passed 'Benetsee's creek,' as it was then called, in 1856, and they said they had good prospects there, and as we had an inclination to see a little mountain life, we concluded to go out to that region, and winter, and look around a little. We accordingly wintered on Big Hole, just above the 'Backbone,' in company with Robert Dempsey, Jake Meeks, and others; and in the spring of 1858, we went over to Deer Lodge and prospected a little on 'Benetsee's creek;' but not having any 'grub' or tools to work with, we soon quit in disgust, without having found anything that would pay, or done enough to enable us to form a reliable estimate of the richness of this vicinity." *Montana As It Is,* pp. 7-8.

About 1875 Stuart again wrote of his party and the reasons for going to the Deer Lodge valley: "They were actuated by a desire to investigate the reported finding of float gold by a Red river half-breed, named Benetsee, in the lower end of Deer Lodge, in 1852, and its subsequent discovery, in 1856, by a party on their way to Salt Lake, from the Bitter Root valley." *Montana Historical Society Contributions,* vol. i (Helena, Montana, 1876) p. 37.

In 1876 Stuart again wrote: "In 1852 a Scotch half-breed from the Red river of the north, named Francois Finlay, but who was known among his associates as 'Benetsee' and who had just returned from California to the Rocky mountains, began to prospect on what is now Gold creek, in Deer Lodge county and found light float gold but as his prospecting was necessarily of a superficial character he found no mines that would pay. The fact of gold being discovered there, however became noised about among the mountaineers still in the country, and in the spring of 1856, a party among whom were Robert Hereford, late of Helena, John Saunders called Long John, Bill Madison and one or two others who were passing Benetsee creek on their way to Salt Lake from the Bitter Root valley where they had spent the winter trading with the Indians, and prospecting a little found more gold than had been obtained by Finlay. One piece weighed about ten cents and they gave it to old Captain Grant, who used to show it, up to the time of his death in 1862 as the first piece of gold found in the country. Granville Stuart, A Historical Sketch of Deer Lodge County, Valley, and City, July

cussing the situation until dark.   We decided to stick
to our original plan – kill and dry meat enough to last
us to Fort Bridger and then buy supplies and return
and prospect for mines.

4, 1876, *Montana Historical Society Contributions*, vol. ii (Helena, 1896)
p. 121.

Stuart wrote as a note to his Journals as follows: "Francois Finlay,
better known as 'Benetsee' perhaps did find a few colors of gold in Benetsee
creek, but his prospecting was of a very superficial nature and he was never
certain whether he had found gold or not.   I first became acquainted with
him in November, 1860.   I had located at a point where the Mullan road
crosses Gold creek; a village of Flathead Indians camped near me and
with them was Benetsee, who made himself known to me.   Naturally our
conversation was about gold in Gold creek.   I asked him if he had ever
dug a hole and he said 'No, I had nothing to dig with, and I never cared to
prospect.'   I am certain that this was true, because although we prospected
on Gold creek and in all the gulches and streams leading into the creek, I
never found the slightest trace of holes being dug or of any prospecting
being done and the slightest disturbance of the sod would be noticed by
us at that time.

"So far as I ever knew Benetsee was not an Indian trader and he posi-
tively never located a ranch on Gold creek nor made any particular place
his habitation in that vicinity.   In November, 1860, I built a log house at
Mullan road crossing of Gold creek and was the first person to build a
house and live on that stream, not a tree had ever been cut before that time,
and I found the least evidence that even a corral had ever been built anywhere on that stream.   He lived with the Indians and, as the Indians, lived
by hunting.   He roamed over the Flathead country as did the Flatheads,
going out to the plains to hunt buffalo and returning, after the hunt, with the
Indians.   I saw him occasionally so long as I lived on Gold creek, but when
I left there in 1863 I lost track of him."

Benetsee has a most loyal partisan in Duncan MacDonald of Dixon,
Montana, the son of Angus MacDonald who completed Fort Connah in 1847
for the Hudson's Bay Company and remained in charge for many years.
In 1916 he submitted a strong statement for Finlay which was quoted in an
article by Paul C. Phillips and H. A. Trexler, Note on the Discovery of
Gold in the Northwest in *Mississippi Valley Historical Review*, vol. ix, pp.
92, 93.

May 5, 1924, he wrote the editor another letter in which he says in part:
"As I have stated before about Benetsee Finlay which no one disputes in his
finding gold on a creek named after him in the early days long before Mr.
Stuart ever put his foot on the ground . . .   Sand Bar Brown yelled like
hell if Finlay did find gold, why did he not work the gravel?   A child, a
babe, knows better.   That Finlay was a British subject and had an Indian,
a Salish Flathead wife.   That under no circumstances that he could locate

The Blackfoot Indians were becoming very troublesome and horse stealing parties lurked about everywhere. `We selected a dense patch of willows near the
creek and as soon as it became quite dark so that we

a claim and was further advised by the H. B. Co. to never mention gold for
fear their fur business would be ruined, which is true. How did Stuart
or why did he turn from his winter quarters north in the spring? . . .
It was at his camping quarters towards spring that a gentleman from Fort
Owen enlightened him that a talk about gold being discovered by Finlay at
the creek in question. Instead of proceeding for his home, started for the
place mentioned and found the gold, but Finlay found it years before. . .
Angus McDonald sent seventeen pounds gold dust to Victoria for the H. B.
Co. obtained from the Pend' Oreille mines where the Clark fork runs into
the Columbia. . . Now Pend' Oreille mines was very rich and mined
for years. This was found by little Joe Morelle a teamster under Angus
MacDonald . . . Antoine Plant was one of the men with Finlay in
California; when he returned Finlay told him. He has an Indian wife
and a member of the tribe could not locate. . . And I ask again why did
Stuart start for that particular creek when he was to start direct for his
home? No, he did not start for Iowa but turned north made a straight line
for as we call Benetsee creek and when he arrived with others and sure
enough there was gold in the gravel but he never noticed any holes dug by
Benetsee Finlay. That is a rather weak excuse any man who has experience
regarding Montana streams knows that holes would be covered by first
high water."

In the *Fort Owen Journals* for Feb. 15, 1852, there is this entry: "Gold
Hunting found some." Charles S. Warren, The Territory of Montana in *Montana Historical Society Contributions*, vol. ii, p. 63, states: "In the spring
of 1852 Samuel M. Caldwell discovered gold on what was then known as
Mill creek, nearly opposite Fort Owen, west [east] of the Bitter Root river."

Lieutenant James H. Bradley in a letter to the *Helena Herald* of September 1, 1875, claimed the honor of first discovery for John W. Silver-
thorne who, he claimed brought about $1500 worth of gold to Fort Benton
in 1856. Letter quoted in Leeson, *Montana*, pp. 210, 211. Another pioneer,
Matthew Carroll, of good reputation for honesty claimed he knew Silver-
thorne well and that the gold brought to Fort Benton came from mines in
the Kootenai country in Canada.

The claims for the discovery of gold by Father De Smet and by Lieutenant
John Mullan rest on no definite evidence and other claims are nothing more
than rumors.

The evidence would seem to indicate that Finlay found gold in Gold
creek about 1852 and traded it at Fort Connah where he was cautioned not
to spread any report of his discovery. While the Stuarts were encamped
at Malad creek some one from the Deer Lodge country reported to them
the prospects for gold in this region. Led by this hope they turned north

could not be seen, we extinguished our fire and quietly led our horses into the center of the willows. Here each one selected the softest spot he could find, rolled up in his blanket and went to sleep leaving one man, gun in hand to keep watch over the horses and ourselves. The guard was relieved every two hours.

(see page 136) and discovered gold as described in the text. Finlay probably found the gold first but it was left to the Stuarts and their companions to spread the news. — ED.

Trading Experiences

Our horses were all in good condition; we had a supply of moose meat dried and on June 16, 1858, Reece Anderson, Ross, James Stuart, and myself packed up and started for Fort Bridger, intending to sell most of our horses (we had about twenty-five in all) purchase supplies and return. Adams remained on Flint creek with a small herd of cattle that he had taken from John Grant on shares. We were all well armed; James, Reece, and I each had rifles and Colt revolvers, and plenty of ammunition, Ross had a revolver.

We traveled up the south side of the Hell Gate river to where the town of Deer Lodge now is; then on the west side of Deer Lodge river past Warm springs; finding the river fordable we crossed and went through the gap known as "The Hump;" then recrossed the stream below Silver Bow and then went south through Deer Lodge pass, over the summit of the Rocky mountains and down Divide creek to Moose creek hill, which we crossed and struck the Big Hole river near where Melrose now is.[82] The river was very high; out of its banks over the low bottom and running ten miles an hour, frightful to look at and yet we must cross it.

A short distance below, where the Oregon Short Line railway bridge now spans the river, we found a few dead cottonwood trees. We cut these down and then cut them into twelve foot lengths. Finding a little

[82] This was the route of the old Northwest Company and Hudson's Bay Company fur traders. Major Owen crossed this pass in 1852. *Journal of John Work, opus citra*, pp. 100-101. – ED.

eddy and putting our logs in we lashed them together and made a raft. We tested it by all standing on it and found it would likely carry us and what little baggage we had.

We hewed out four good strong paddles and cut and piled a lot of brush on the middle of the raft. On this we put our clothes, keeping nothing but our shirts on ourselves. With our clothes we put our dried meat, two rifles and two revolvers and ammunition for them. Then we lashed all fast to the raft so that, if it wrecked, our things could not wash off and be lost. We could swim and push the raft to shore some place below.

We then saddled our horses putting half our blankets on them under the saddles and each man tied what clothes he had left to the saddle. We also tied one rifle and one revolver with ammuntion to the saddles. This was done so in case we lost the raft we would still have some blankets, a few clothes, and guns and ammunition. If dire necessity forced us to it we could kill a horse and dry the meat and we would not starve.

Having hedged in every possible manner against disaster, we each armed ourselves with a long slender willow pole and gathering the horses to a place where the bank sloped gradually into the water, we made a sudden rush upon them and with our poles we beat the poor things into the river. Some of them had swam rivers before and they at once struck out for the other shore and the others followed them. Great was our relief when we saw them ascend the bank after being carried down stream over one hundred yards by the swift current, and this, too, when the river was but a little over one hundred yards wide.

We then seized our paddles and seating ourselves two on the front end and two on the rear end of the raft we pushed out from the shore and paddled with all our might. The raft was a good one and did not overflow, but in spite of our efforts we drifted rapidly down stream and reached the other shore about fifty yards below where our horses landed. As we struck the bank we grasped some willows that stood in the edge of the water with one hand and hung to the raft with the other; the sudden stopping threw us down and the water rushed over us giving us a good soaking but our baggage on the brush remained dry. We hastily unloaded the raft, two holding it against the bank while the others carried our things on shore. Taking the ropes from the logs, that had served us so well, we regretfully saw them one by one float away.

We gathered our horses together, untied our clothes and weapons from the saddles, wrung the water out of them and spread them on the bushes to dry. We prepared a meal of dried moose meat, by cutting it into small bits and boiling it in our only kitchen utensil, a large frying pan, until it softened somewhat, then adding a little tallow, and frying it awhile so that we could chew it. After dark we saddled up and rode six miles to Birch creek. There selecting a place where there was good grass, we camped. Without any noise we picketed our horses and leaving one man at a time on guard, the others slept until dawn, when we arose, picketed our horses on fresh grass, prepared breakfast, like our supper; devoured it, saddled and packed up and lit out at a fast gait, for we expected to travel about fifty miles a day.

We reached the Beaverhead river at the mouth of Blacktail Deer creek where we had spent part of last winter. It too, was very high, but we searched until we found a place where we thought we could ford it.

Fearing it might be deep we held our most precious things in our arms and plunged in. Sure enough as we neared the farther bank the horses had to swim for about thirty feet. As usual we camped just before sundown and let our horses graze and cooked supper, and as soon as it was dark saddled up and went several miles up Blacktail Deer creek and silently made our all night camp.

Next day we passed Sage creek to Red Rock creek, then up Junction creek past the timbered butte and on over the Rocky mountains divide where is now Monida and camped in a pouring rain under some big fir trees just beyond Pleasant valley. The trees gave some shelter, but soon the water ran down the sloping ground and under our beds thoroughly saturating us. This was certainly a disagreeable night and we were glad when dawn came. We crawled out of our watery beds and finding some pieces of pitch wood in an old partially burned tree and lots of dry limbs we soon had a big fire and stood around it drying our dripping clothes and warming our benumbed bodies.

The sun rose in a clear sky and we were soon warm and dry. We saddled up and struck the trail. When we reached Camas creek, which had been a beautiful little clear stream flowing through the sagebrush, when we were there the preceding October, we found it out of its banks and about forty yards wide. We knew the channel must be deep but we had to cross it. Putting our saddles on the best swimmers among our horses we mounted and spurred them into the water, and away we went across that stream.

Our next stop was at Market lake so named because in the fall there were many wild water fowls here and the old trappers were always sure of fresh meat. They called going to the lake, "going to market" hence the name, "Market lake." This lake is fed from some under-ground cracks in the lava beds.

About two miles beyond Market lake is Snake river and at this time of year was at flood water. It was four times as large as the Big Hole river and was clear out of its banks, overflowing all the low ground on both sides and clear out into the sagebrush. At this place there was no timber to make a raft and there was no place where we could ford it, so we rode along down the bank looking for some opportunity to cross. A few miles further down there was a place where this large river turned up on edge and rushed through a crack in the solid lava about forty feet wide with another crack about twenty feet wide on the east side of the large one, forming a small island of hard lava about twenty feet wide and a hundred feet long. The water in these two cracks must have been a hundred feet deep and it went through them with such velocity as to make us poor devils giddy to look at it. Following on down the stream we finally spied some dead cottonwood timber in a little bend. The little bottom was all overflowed but we camped, stripped down to our shirts and waded out into the icy water to those dry trees. It was a close call to get them for while cutting them down we stood in the swift water to our hips, but we just had to have those logs. Even the old dry moose meat was getting low and we had exhausted our supply of tallow. We had not seen so much as a jack rabbit on the trip and there was no possibility of game between Snake river and Fort Bridger. As fast as we cut down a tree it was floated out to shore and when we had enough we towed them into a little eddy and constructed the raft. Then dividing our belongings as we did at the Big Hole river, we proceeded to make the crossing.

Our horses made most strenuous objections to taking the water. It looked quite as bad to them as it did to us and we had to use energetic measures to get them started into the turbid flood. They were swept down the river almost a quarter of a mile and landed on a small island, covered with a thick growth of willows, near the far shore. Now we were up against the necessity of making a landing on that island to drive the horses off.

The raft was all ready and we pushed off. When she struck the strong current, the water rushed over her about six inches deep and our hearts almost rose into our throats for we feared our raft was overloaded, but we paddled with all our strength and in a few seconds it rose and floated high in the water. Paddle as hard as we could we were drifting down stream very rapidly and it looked as though we would miss that island, but we managed to grab a bunch of over-hanging willows as we were being swept past the lower point of land, and although it almost jerked our arms off we succeeded in making the landing. Driving the horses off we returned to the raft: It was only about forty yards to the shore and we had no trouble in getting across.

At this place Ross discovered a raven's nest in a cottonwood tree a short distance from camp. He declared his intention of having fresh meat and, as the moose meat was about as dry and hard as flint and getting very scarce at that, almost anything in the way of food was tempting. Climbing the tree, in spite of the protests of the old ravens, he threw down four half grown birds, just one a piece he said, and in a short time he and Reece had them dressed and roasting before the fire. There was a peculiar flavor and smell about the flesh that soon sent James and me back to our dried meat, but Ross and Anderson picked the bones of all four and rose chuckling saying: "Such nice young fowls would not go to waste around us."

From this place we traveled down the river to near Old Fort Hall where we struck the Emigrant road leading to Oregon and California.

At Soda springs on Bear river we drank our fill of soda water from a spring on the bank, just above the river water. One can make excellent soda biscuits from this water, but at this time we had no flour.

We crossed Tommaws fork, a mean sluggish stream, on a bridge built by the emigrants. It was a pleasure to cross on a bridge, as we had had enough of constructing rafts.

We reached Fort Bridger on the evening of June 28, 1858, having eaten the last of our dried meat eight hours before. We had traveled six hundred miles in twelve days without encountering Indians or seeing any game.

We remained two weeks at Fort Bridger where we found several of those who had wintered in the Beaverhead valley where we had become acquainted with them. They treated us very hospitably and we enjoyed our stay. We then went to Camp Floyd where we remained about two weeks selling our horses to the soldiers and camp followers.

This fort reminded us strongly of the good old days in California. Money, all in twenty, ten, and five dollar gold pieces, was plentiful, and the way everybody drank, gambled, and scattered it around was almost equal to the days of forty-nine. A host of gamblers had congregated there and many of them were at the top of their profession. When the outsiders were "busted" they preyed upon one another and it was amazing to see the way they stacked up their coin on their favorite card. I saw them win and lose five thousand dollars on the turn of a single monte card.

We were unable to get mining supplies at Camp Floyd and we discovered that there was considerable money to be made by trading with the emigrants on the road to and from California and Oregon and thought best to try to increase our capital somewhat before returning to mining.

Reece Anderson and Ross purchased some supplies for the Indian trade, and went north to the Flathead country. We never again saw poor Ross. He was drowned in June, 1860, while attempting to drive a band of horses across Bear river, when the water was very high.

The latter part of July, 1858, James and I went to Green river, east of Fort Bridger and began buying and trading for poor and tired out oxen and horses, with the army supply trains and with the emigrants. On the long journey across the plains many of the horses and oxen became footsore and tired out and unable to travel. In this condition, they were a burden to the train. We would trade for, or purchase such stock for a very small sum and after caring for them and resting them up for a month or two, they were fit as ever and could then be disposed of for a good price.

Here I met Jim Baker, one of the trappers well known from the borders of Mexico to the British line. He was six feet, one inch high, and weighed two hundred pounds, a perfect blonde with large blue eyes. He remined me of pictures of the old Vikings who sailed the north sea. Jim was much too good natured to make a real genuine pirate. It made me sad to see him ruining himself drinking whiskey.

Robert Dempsey and his man, "Friday" Jackson, were there. They both kept saturated and, when in this state, Dempsey was said to be the best trader on the Emigrant road. He certainly had a faculty of sizing up the possibilities in a lame or jaded ox or horse and never paid too much for such an animal.

In October, 1858, we moved from the Emigrant crossing of Green river to Henry's fork, a distance of fifty miles. Here we remained until April, 1859. Near us was a French Canadian, named Marjeau, who had brought a lot of groceries and some trinkets for the Indian trade, in a big wagon with four yoke of oxen all the way from Council Bluffs. Dempsey and Jackson also came over here and camped near by, and later another French Canadian moved in with a stock of goods for the Indian trade. The winter was very mild with no snow, and bright sunny days. There was no game in the country and consequently there were no Indians.

Marjeau later moved down Green river to Brown's Hole, some thirty-five miles and there struck a village of Ute Indians and had a good trade, although the Utes were of a mean insolent character and difficult to trade with.

Hearing these Canadians speak French, put me in the notion of trying to learn the language, but only being with them occasionally I made little progress. It was my custom to make weekly trips, ten miles west, to Fort Bridger to get our mail. There I became acquainted with another French man named Ely Dufour, who finding that I was trying to learn French, presented me with a pocket dictionary of French and English, which I still have, in a somewhat damaged condition from frequent pressures of the lash rope on our pack horses.

In April we moved from Henry's fork to the mouth of Ham's fork, where we remained a month. Here I saw the first of the Pony Express riders. This rider did not stop to make any acquaintances, but came tearing up the road to the station, dismounted, threw his saddle on a fresh horse and was away again before I realized what had taken place.

The Pony Express was established by W. H. Russell of the firm of Russell, Majors, and Waddell, in 1860. The first trip was started April fourth. The route was from St. Joseph, Missouri, to Sacramento, California, a distance of nineteen hundred and fifty miles, through an uninhabited country infested with road agents and hostile Indians. There were relay stations along the route, where two minutes were allowed to change horses and mail. Each rider covered a distance of from sixty-five to one hundred miles, according to the character of the country. The dispatches were written on tissue paper, no rider carrying more than ten pounds. The horses used were California mustangs, noted for their sure footedness, speed, and endurance. The cost of delivering these dispatches was five dollars in gold for every half ounce. Although this seems to us at this day an exorbitant price, yet it did not cover one-tenth of the expense of maintenance to say nothing of the investment.

The time in which to make this trip was ten days and the wages paid the riders was one hundred and twenty-five dollars a month. As a tribute to the courage and fidelity of these riders be it said that never once during the two years that the Pony Express was in existence, did a dispatch reach its destination behind the schedule. The inaugural address of President Lincoln, March 4, 1861, was carried through in seven days and seventeen hours. Through rain and snow, across rivers, deserts, and mountain ranges, in the darkest nights, pursued by Indians, or robbers; often reaching a station wounded and dying; often finding their relief murdered, the station burned and horses driven off, nothing daunted, they kept right on until they delivered the goods and it never occurred to one of them that any obstacle, no matter what it was, was great enough to delay them one minute. I want to say right here that for nerve, courage, and fidelity, there never was a body of men that excelled the Pony Express riders.[33]

While camped here a mule train of sixteen wagons loaded with freight for Salt Lake City camped a short distance above us on the stream. In a few minutes we heard a shot fired and as there seemed to be some excitement we walked up to the wagons, and were shocked to see one of the drivers lying on the ground, shot through the heart. The wagon boss had gotten drunk at Green river, about fifteen miles back, was cussing the driver about some trifle, the driver had talked back and the "boss" who was J. A. Slade,[34] drew his revolver and shot the man dead. Later the teamsters dug a grave by the roadside, wrapped the dead man in his blankets and buried him. The train went on to Salt Lake and nothing was done about the murder.

[33] For a brief account of the pony express see Frederick L. Paxson, *Last American Frontier* (1910) pp. 182-185. – ED.

[34] For account of Slade see Dimsdale, *opus citra* (1913) pp. 143-151 and Langford *opus citra*, vol. ii, pp. 288-321. – ED.

Late in the summer we were joined by Reece Anderson, who brought twenty horses from the Flathead country, as Bitter Root valley was then called.

While here a tragic incident occurred that made me so mad that it was with great difficulty I kept from inflicting summary vengeance on two of the parties. Near by us was camped a man with a wife and five small children and a hanger-on friend of theirs. There came along a disreputable looking man with a five gallon keg of whiskey and camped with them. The three men at once proceeded to get drunk.

A few days prior to this time there came to our lodge a young man apparently about twenty years of age. He was on foot carrying a pair of blankets and a change of underwear. He was making his way to California and asked to stay with us until he could join some passing emigrant trains. We, of course, bade him welcome.

One day he told me that the drunken men, who were then nearing delirium tremens had threatened to kill him. I asked him what the trouble was and he said he did not know. I told him to keep away from them and gave him my Colt's navy revolver, telling him that if they came over to our camp after him to defend himself.

James, Reece and I went out to look after our stock and when returning, and about two hundred yards from our lodge, we heard three shots in rapid succession and saw the young man run out and fall close by. The three drunken men also came out, one of them limping, and went to their camp. When we reached the fallen man he was dead. We were furious, Reece and I were for going over and having it out with them, but James reasoned that we did not know who fired the fatal shot and that if we went over there while they were in their present condition we would likely have to kill them all and that we could not do on account of the women and little children. There was no civil law so James's council prevailed and we wrapped the unfortunate young man in his blankets and buried him beneath the cottonwood tree on which I would have liked to hang his murderers.

In October, 1859, we again moved over to Henry's fork of Green river with our horses and cattle and wintered near our former camp. There was very little snow and scarcely any cold weather; our stock came out fat in the spring, without having any shelter, excepting the willows along the streams, and nothing to eat, but bunch grass.

In April, 1860, we took our stock, and with our baggage loaded in a large wagon drawn by three yoke of oxen, started for Salt river valley, a branch of Snake river, and spent the summer there trading with the emigrants. This is the most beautiful spot that I have ever seen. In 1860 the bunch grass all over the valley waved in the wind like a field of grain. The creek in the center of the valley, bordered by a heavy growth of willows was clear as glass and icy cold, the home of many beautiful mountain trout.

In September, 1860, we raised camp and started for the Beaverhead valley, where we intended to winter and then in the spring to cross over to Benetsee creek and do some more prospecting for gold.

At the lower end of Salt river valley we found a little flat of some three or four acres that was as white as snow although the grass was green and beautiful all around. We camped near by and went to examine this white spot and found it to be a layer of pure white salt about four inches thick which had been deposited by a spring flowing from the side of a low bench about fifteen feet high. The spring furnished a stream of water, about four inches wide and two inches deep, of the strongest brine. This ran down into the little flat and covered it with salt as above described. We scraped up enough to fill a two bushel sack and took it with us. Later when the gold mines brought a rush of people to Montana and Idaho a company from Salt Lake established salt works there and supplied all this section with the finest quality of salt and from 1864 to the present time have paid dividends that far exceed those of any of the gold mines that we were interested in.

We traveled slowly allowing our horses and cattle plenty of time to graze. Snake river was now a clear beautiful stream, and we found a shallow place and forded it. We returned to Beaverhead by the same route that we had traveled before.

After we crossed the divide by way of Lodge Pole pass we found plenty of game and killed fat antelope whenever needed. On the Beaverhead river at the mouth of the "Pak-sam-ma-oi," [35] which in the Indian language means cottonwood grove, we established our winter camp. There game was abundant, the grass good, and the willows along the streams furnished shelter for our cattle and horses. We were soon joined by a middle aged trapper named Louis Simmons and a young Snake Indian boy named Tabbabo. This boy we employed as a horse herder, and he proved to be a good and faithful one.

---

[35] According to Mr. John E. Rees, an old Indian trader well acquainted with Indian tongues, this word should be Pah-mamar-roi, meaning literally "cottonwood grove by a water." Mr. Rees thinks that Robert Dempsey gave the stream this name. It was originally called Stinkingwater, and now appears on the map as Passamari. — ED.

By trading we had acquired a considerable number of beaver skins and other furs and as we needed powder and lead and percussion caps for our own use and some clothing and blankets and various other articles for trading with the Indians, Reece and I saddled up our horses and putting our furs and some bedding on pack horses, we started for a Hudson's Bay trading post on Crow creek not far from St. Ignatius Mission,[36] a little horseback ride of four hundred sixty miles altogether to do a little shopping.

We made the trip all right, but were greatly surprised to meet, on our return, James, Simmons, and Tabbabo, with all our stock at Camp creek, on the Big Hole river, moving to Deer Lodge valley. They told us that soon after we had left a large camp of Bannock Indians came into the valley and soon began to show an insolent semi-hostile disposition, and game being scarce, they killed one of our cattle. So to avoid serious trouble James packed up and started for Deer Lodge. We held a consultation and decided to go on to Gold creek and locate and work our gold prospect of 1858.

This insolent band of Indians was under a chief named Ar-ro-ka-kee, who was six feet, two inches tall and weighed two hundred and seventy-five pounds. Captain Grant and his retainers called him, "LeGran Coquin," which in French means "The Big Rogue," and our experience with him convinced us that they had rightly named him.

It was thought best that I should at once hasten on to Gold creek and locate a claim. I saddled up for a ride of sixty miles more, and putting a little food and bed-

---

[36] Fort Connah on Post creek or Crow creek. Built by Angus McDonald in 1847. One building of this fort still stands. — ED.

ding and our elk skin lodge on a pack horse, started, accompanied by Simmons and the young Indian.

At Cottonwood creek was camped Thomas Lavatta, Joseph Hill, and some others. Louis Simmons and Tabbabo remained there. I went down to Gold creek and begun cutting poles for a corral. Four days later Anderson and James arrived with the ox team, horses and cattle.

Settlement of Deer Lodge Valley

The winter of 1860 was more severe than either of the three preceding ones that we had spent in the Rocky mountains. Our cattle and horses were in good condition in the spring although they had no food except the native bunch grass which grows from twelve to thirteen inches high everywhere. They had no shelter except the willows along the streams and in some of the ravines. We spent the winter very pleasantly. Antelope, deer, and mountain sheep, were available most of the time, and although usually thin in flesh, the meat was good, for we had plenty of good army bacon to fry it with. We occasionally had visitors, as people passed coming from Fort Owen, in the Bitter Root valley, and from Hell Gate, three miles below where Missoula now is, and going on up to John Grant's at the mouth of Little Blackfoot creek, and sometimes on up to the little settlement on Cottonwood creek, where is now the beautiful town of Deer Lodge.

After a week or two they would come back on their return home and everybody always stopped over night with us and if it stormed they often stayed two or three days, and were hospitably entertained. In those days, nobody ever charged traveling visitors a cent for food and lodging, and this also extended to any scattering Indians that came along, but of course, we did not feed the villages of combined Nez Percés, Yakimas, Coeur d'Alenes, and Flatheads that passed every fall on their way to the plains of the Missouri and Yellowstone to spend the winter hunting buffalo. Those Indians did not hang around and beg, but had considerable self respect, and we usually asked the chiefs to dine with us when passing. We kept a small assortment of Indian trading goods and when passing they would buy what they needed. The Nez Percés often had money to pay for what they purchased, but the others seldom had any. If they did possess any and were asked where they got it the answer was, "We won it gambling with the Nez Percés."

We never refused any of these Indians credit for the few things they wanted, such as calico, red cloth for the ladies' leggings, calico shirts, vermillion paint, beads, knives, handkerchiefs, powder, lead, percussion caps, combs, and sometimes blankets. To their honor be it said, they always paid when they passed on their return from the buffalo range. We never lost a dollar through crediting them, for even if the purchaser was dead, or sick, the wife or husband or some relative, as the case might be, came and paid us in buffalo robes, dried meat, dried tongues, skins or something they had. If a white man came to an Indian's camp he was always welcome to the best he had without money.

In the fall of 1860, Frank L. Worden and Captain C. P. Higgins came up from Fort Walla Walla with a pack train of cayuse horses, loaded with a small stock of merchandise, and located on the north bank of the Hell Gate river, three miles below where is now the town of Missoula. Here they built a log store and a log cabin and named the place Hell Gate. They also brought up some garden seeds, and we determined to plant a garden and raise some vegetables as we had not had any for almost four years except for a short time while at Camp Floyd, south of Great Salt Lake City.

John Owen had among other things bought a plow at Fort Benton in the summer of 1860.[37] While camped on Greenhorn gulch just east of the summit of the Rocky mountains, the Blackfoot Indians stampeded the pack animals and got away with a number of the horses. This left them so short of pack animals that they left the plow there and we, hearing about it, bought it from Owen. We were mighty anxious to get at that garden, so early in April a young man by the name of John Seeber and I took a pack horse and went for the plow. We packed it with the greatest difficulty and in due time we arrived home.

We selected a place down in the damp river bottom and plowed up a piece of ground. After putting it in condition, we planted our seeds, expecting great things from this garden, but alas! our hopes in this direction were blasted. Frost visited this low land every month in the year, and no sooner did a vegetable poke its nose out of the ground than it was immediately frozen. Had we selected a spot on the bench east of the house, we could have watered it out of Gold creek and had a beautiful garden free from frost. As it was, we had nothing to speak of.

James and I were both great readers and we had been all winter without so much as an almanac to look at. We were famished for something to read when some Indians coming from the Bitter Root told us that a white man had come up from below, with a trunk full of books, and was camped with all that wealth, in Bitter

[37] Major John Owen had come to the Bitter Root in 1850 as an Indian trader. He purchased St. Mary's mission of the Jesuits and built a fort there which he named Fort Owen. Major Owen carried on extensive farming operations and built a sawmill and a grist mill. He also acted as Indian agent. Frank H. Woody, Sketch of the Early History of Western Montana written in 1876 in *Montana Historical Society Contributions*, 1896, vol. ii, pp. 91-92. *Fort Owen Journal.* – ED.

Root valley. On receipt of these glad tidings, we saddled our horses and putting our blankets, and some dried meat for food, on a pack horse, we started for those books, a hundred and fifty miles away, without a house, or anybody on the route, and with three big dangerous rivers to cross, the Big Blackfoot, the Hell Gate, and the Bitter Root. As the spring rise had not yet begun, by careful searching we found fords on these rivers, but they were dangerous, and at times we were almost swept away. Arriving in the Bitter Root valley we learned that the man who brought the books had gone back to the lower country, but he had left the precious trunk in charge of a man named Henry Brooks, whom we finally found living in a tepee, at a point on Sweathouse creek, near where the town of Victor now stands. We gradually and diplomatically approached the subject of books, and "our hearts were on the ground" when Brooks told us that Neil Mc-Arthur,[38] a Hudson's Bay Company trader, who left the books in his care, told him to keep them until he re-

---

[38] Henry Brooks came into the Bitter Root in 1855. He was the first justice of the peace of Missoula county. Woody, *opus citra*, pp. 93, 103. Neil McArthur had started, in 1846, the construction of the post on Crow creek which Angus MacDonald finished and named Fort Connah. After retiring from the Hudson's Bay Company employ, in 1856, McArthur came into the Bitter Root and later built a trading post at Hell Gate. *Ibid.*, p. 97.

McArthur and Louis R. Maillet became partners and they also established a trading post at Fort Colville. The business apparently prospered. In 1858 Maillet went on a trip to the "states and Canada to visit his family." During his absence of some two years he had no news from McArthur. On his return he found McArthur gone and with him their herd of stock. Apparently McArthur had gone to Fraser river. Maillet declared that the property when last valued by the two partners had amounted to $150,000, but Maillet now learned that his partner's bad management, debts, and numerous undertakings had lost everything. The last he ever heard of McArthur was a letter from him, in which he said that he was broke, had a bad horse, and was prospecting "so farewell." W. F. Wheeler, Historical Sketch of Louis R. Maillet in *Montana Historical Society Contributions*, vol. iv (Helena, 1903) p. 217. This sketch was written in part by Maillet and dictated in part to Mr. Wheeler. – ED.

turned.   He gave him no authority to sell any of them. We told him how long we had been without anything to read, and how we had ridden many days, seeking that trunk, and that we would take all the blame and would make good with McArthur when he returned. At last we won him over, and he agreed to let us have five books, for five dollars each, and if McArthur was not satisfied we were to pay him more.

How we feasted our eyes on those books. . We could hardly make up our minds which ones to choose, but we finally settled upon Shakespeare and Byron, both fine illustrated editions, Headley's *Napoleon and his Marshals*, a Bible in French, and Adam Smith's *Wealth of Nations*.   After paying for them we had just twenty-five dollars left, but then we had the blessed books, which we packed carefully in our blankets, and joyfully started on our return ride of a hundred and fifty miles.   Many were the happy hours we spent reading those books, and I have them yet, all except the *Wealth of Nations*, which being loose in the binding, has gradually disappeared, until only a few fragments remain.   McArthur never returned to the Bitter Root valley, and I do not know what became of the rest of the books, but I hope they gave as much pleasure to some others, as did the five to Brother James and myself.

In the summer of 1860, a mining enthusiast by the name of Henry Thomas (but who as his peculiarities became known I designated "Gold Tom," by which name he ever after went) came up from below by way of Pend d'Orielle lake and begun to prospect on Benetsee creek about one mile west of where the mining town of Pioneer now stands.   Some Frenchman told him where the creek was.

He started out to find the prospect hole that we had dug in 1858, when we made the discovery of gold. He had no difficulty in finding the place and began prospecting and got the same prospects that we did, ten cents to the pan of gravel. The place was full of enormous granite boulders and he saw at once that he could not dig there. He went out on the side of the creek some twenty-five or thirty yards from where we had sunk this hole and entirely unaided sunk a shaft twenty feet deep in the glacial detritus along the creek, getting a little gold all the way down.

He made a primitive windlass, and hewed out and pinned together with wooden pins and bound around with a picket rope, a bucket with which he hoisted the dirt while sinking the shaft. He would slide down the rope, fill the bucket with gravel, then climb up a notched pole aided by the windlass rope, and hoist the bucket of gravel. He encountered many boulders too large to go into the bucket. Around these he would put a rope and windlass them out. After we located at the crossing of Gold creek, I visited him several times and was amazed to see the amount of work he had done under exceedingly difficult conditions. He also hewed out boards eight inches wide and about seven feet long and made four little sluice boxes. He had no nails, but put them together with wooden pegs. He placed them near his shaft and then dug a ditch from the creek around to the sluice boxes, where he washed the gravel from his shaft and some of the surface dirt. He worked the summers of 1860 and 1861, but could not make more than one dollar and fifty cents a day and often less than that sum, owing to the great disadvantage under which he labored.

When I visited Gold creek in 1876, his windlass and

MISSOULA IN 1865 (LOOKING NORTH)
The settlement was then only a year old and was made up mostly of
former residents of Hell Gate
From an original pencil drawing made by Granville Stuart, December
25, 1865. [On the drawing is noted "sketched in twelve inches of
snow, thermometer 34° below zero"]

FRONT VIEW OF FORT BENTON, MONTANA (LOOKING NORTHEAST)
Fort Benton was the last great post of the American Fur Company in
Montana. It was at the head of steamboat navigation on the Missouri,
and the eastern terminus of the Mullan Road
From an original sketch made by Granville Stuart, June 10, 1866

four little sluice boxes hewed out with an axe pinned together with wooden pins were still there, but fast falling to decay. Alas! Poor Tom, I lost sight of him in 1864-5 and often wondered if he fell a victim to the *ignius fatus* [ignis fatuus] of Coeur d'Alene, Peace river, Stinkene, Cassiar, White Pine, Pioche, or Yellowstone, and last but not least the Black hills. Wherever he may be, may fortune smile upon him with a broader grin than fell to the lot of the pioneers at Gold creek in 1860-1-2.

He usually preferred to be alone, and would spend days and weeks in the mountains without other companions than his horses and trusty rifle. He was not at all misanthropic, and I never knew him to drink whiskey or to gamble.

As a pen picture of the life we led in Missoula county, Washington Territory,[39] which included all on the west side of the Rocky mountains of the present state of Montana, fifty years ago, I now copy from a daily journal kept by my brother James and myself alternately.

MAY 1, 1861. Finished sowing wheat and oats by two o'clock in the afternoon, will harrow them the last time tomorrow. Killed three large wolves last night with strychnine and probably more if they could be found. We went prospecting in the afternoon. Found tolerable good prospects. There is gold in all the ravines that we have tried. Weather warm and pleasant, strong west wind in the afternoon. Cloudy at dark.

---

[39] Missoula county was first organized by the legislature of Washington Territory, December 14, 1860. Its northern boundary was Canada, its eastern the main ridge of the Rockies, its southern the forty-sixth parallel and its western the one hundred-fifteenth meridian. Woody, *opus citra*, p. 99. – ED.

MAY 2. Finished harrowing the wheat and oats by twelve o'clock. Forenoon, weather calm and warm, but last night froze ice a quarter of an inch thick. In afternoon made hoe and axe handles. Green flies have been about to take possession of the ranch for the last week and some few mosquitoes. Antelope are tolerable plenty. Just now we have more meat than we can use before it spoils. Wish we had a barrel so we could salt some of it down. This had been the warmest day we have had this spring.

MAY 3. Morning calm and cloudy until about eleven o'clock when there was a shower of rain accompanied with a strong west wind. Planted some peas, onions, cabbage, and radishes. Afternoon planted some potatoes. Occasional showers of rain, and wind moderate.

MAY 6. Planted some corn in the forenoon. After dinner Granville went to Dempsey's camp six miles down the river, to try to get some beet seed, and gathered up the cattle as he came back.

MAY 7. Cold strong west wind, with occasional snow squalls, too cold to work. Caught a lovely trout that weighed four pounds, and Oh! but it tasted good, when nicely fried.

MAY 8. Chilly east wind this morning until ten o'clock. Froze ice one-half inch thick last night. In afternoon west wind with showers of rain and hail. Worked some today getting out timber for fence. Had a visitor. A Blackfoot Indian on his way from the Flathead country. Gave him his dinner and sent him on his way. Doubtless he will stay all night at Johnny Grant's at the mouth of Little Blackfoot creek, eight miles up the river and try to eat enough to do him to

Sun river, for there is no one living this side of there. Our settlement is now known as American Fork. Johnnie Grant's at the mouth of Little Blackfoot is Grantsville and the one above on Cottonwood creek is Cottonwood.[40] We are becoming somewhat civilized as we remain long enough in one spot to give it a name.

MAY 12. Worked on fence because we must get it done soon or cattle and horses will destroy our little crop. Froze ice a quarter of an inch thick last night. Light wind from the east in the morning and from the west the greater part of the day. Not so cold as it has been for several days past. F. H. Burr and Doctor Atkinson arrived today from the Missouri side of the mountains. They had bad stormy weather on the trip and say that vegetation is not as forward over there as it is on this side of the mountains.

MAY 15. Gathered up the cattle. Froze a little ice last night. Today east wind in the afternoon, with a little rain. Forenoon warm and pleasant. John F. Grant passed on his way home to mouth of Little Blackfoot creek, from Hell Gate where he visited with his father, Captain Richard Grant. With John, was Joe Piou, and an American with twenty gallons of whiskey on their way to trade with the Blackfoot Indians. They say that the Big Blackfoot and Hell Gate rivers are as low as they were in the winter. They have not commenced to rise because of the cold late spring.

MAY 17. Late yesterday evening John W. Powell and two other sports came here for a game of poker and we played all night. Powell lost $97.50, and one of the others lost $65.00. The other one and I were

---

[40] Later Deer Lodge. – ED.

the winners.   Occasional showers last night and in the forenoon.   Afternoon cloudy, east and north wind all day.   J. S.

MAY 18.   Granville built a corral.   I went hunting and killed one black-tailed deer, and three elk, all very poor.   Only brought the meat of one elk home with me.   I killed them with a Maynard breech-loading rifle, that uses a brass cartridge shell that can be re-loaded many times, and is water-proof.   The cartridge is fired by a tape cap, which is automatically put on the nipple, which enables the rifle to be fired very rapidly. J. S.

MAY 22.   Prospected some, found one and a half cent dirt to a pan of gravel.   Bercier and party passed on their way to Bitter Root valley.

MAY 23.   Froze a little last night.   Today warm, calm, and clear.   Prospected some, raised the color. I have been sick for about a week.   A stranger arrived from Fort Benton going to Coeur d'Alene Mission.[41] He is probably a lay brother.   He stayed all night.

MAY 24.   Prospected, Granville and I.   We found good gold prospects.   Received a letter from Bitter Root valley from Thomas Adams.   Brought here by Nine Pipes,[42] a Flathead Indian, a good reliable man. He says the weather is very cold and stormy down there.

MAY 25.   Nine Pipes and quite a number of Flat-heads passed on their way to hunt buffalo bulls on the Missouri.   (The Indians only kill the bulls at this time of the year because the cows already have calves or soon will have them.)   I went to Dempsey's [43] ranch today,

---

[41] Coeur d'Alene Mission was started by Father Pierre de Smet in 1842. H. M. Chittenden and A. T. Richardson, *opus citra*, vol. i, p. 372.

[42] His name is perpetuated in the Nine Pipes reservoir in the Flathead irrigation project. – ED.

[43] This ranch was up Dempsey creek south of the present Deer Lodge. – ED.

found everyone drunk and three strangers there with fifteen gallons of Minnie Rifle whiskey. Fortunately, Granville and I do not drink any kind of liquor. This kind is usually composed of one part alcohol and ten parts of water, with a considerable quantity of tobacco and cayenne pepper to strengthen it. These two men report that the crops in Bitter Root valley are damaged considerably by the frost. The season here is also very backward. The cottonwoods, alders, quaking-aspens, and willows are only commencing to leaf out.

MAY 26, SUNDAY. This has been a beautiful day. Warm, calm, and nearly clear. Thomas Pambrum and Oliver LeClaire arrived from Bear river, near Box Elder, Utah, Mormon settlement. They do not bring any news of any consequence. They went down there with Van Etten's [44] party to help drive a band of horses that Van traded from the Flatheads last winter. They all got through safely. Van's home is down near Salt Lake City. Gold Tom visited our ranch today. He had found some tolerable good prospects up the creek.

MAY 29. Planted beets, potatoes, muskmelons, pumpkins, and squashes. Froze ice a quarter of an inch thick last night. Also a very heavy frost.

MAY 30. Rained the greater part of last night and today. Bercier and party passed on their way home to Johnny Grant's from Bitter Root valley. They brought no news from any part of the world.

MAY 31. Went up to Little Blackfoot settlement and found the majority of the inhabitants on a drunk. Returned home in the evening. Little Blackfoot creek is high, nearly swimming.

---

[44] Van Etten was a Mormon trader who bought stock along the Emigrant trail and drove it to the Bitter Root to recuperate. In his employ at one time or another was a number of the settlers of the Bitter Root. Woody, *opus citra*, p. 98. – ED.

SUNDAY, JUNE 2, 1861. Frost last night. Forenoon warm, calm, and clear. Afternoon warm, nearly clear, very light breezes of wind from the east. Went to Grantsburg, returned in the evening. Gold Tom visited us today. Showed us several pieces of gold that weigh from ten to fifteen cents each.

JUNE 3. Hauled wood and made ready to start to Fort Benton to meet the steamboat that is expected there, intending to buy a good supply of food and mining tools. Going on horseback one hundred and ninety miles to get it. Surely this is a country of fine large distance and a great scarcity of inhabitants.

JUNE 4. James and Fred H. Burr,[45] wife and infant daughter, started for Fort Benton. Burr has a good elkskin lodge and the necessary poles with which to set it up, so they will be well sheltered. Forenoon, quite warm and calm. Afternoon, strong west wind and showers of rain. I went to Bercier's, his wife gave me a hen and a rooster, for which I thanked her most sincerely. Prospected a little, killed my daily ration, a duck. Tolman, Johnny Carr and Co., are on a drunk and as I never drink of course they had to come up and visit me. Oh! for a lodge in some vast wilderness where drunks could never come and where whiskey was unknown. Fat Jack went by, going to Bitter Root.

JUNE 7. Beautiful sunset. Washed my duds today. Gold Tom came down and stayed part of the day. He has abandoned his gold diggings in disgust. Did not look for my ration. The streams are falling a little today. It snowed upon the mountains south of here last night. Saw Indians after dark this evening, two

---

[45] Burr came into Montana in 1853 with Lieutenant Mullan's party. In 1856 he brought four hundred cattle into the Bitter Root and settled. Charles S. Warren, The Territory of Montana in *Montana Historical Society Contributions*, vol. i, pp. 62, 63. – ED.

on one horse, apparently somebody will have horses stolen or I will be surprised.

JUNE 8. Rained hard all last night and today. James Minesinger [46] came down from Grantsburg in the afternoon and stayed all night with me. I am glad to have someone come, as it is frightfully lonesome since James and Burr left. The frost night before last cut down the corn and potatoes, but did not hurt the peas, cabbage, onions, or radishes. It slayed my one melon. Ned Williamson's horse is missing. I fear those Indians took him.

JUNE 9. We have now nineteen young calves, four yearlings, thirty-three cows, fifteen oxen, two young steers, and three bulls. Frank Newell and Oliver Le-Claire came up from Bitter Root on their way to Grantsburg. They found the river ford, at the point of the hill, swimming and came back and stayed with me.

JUNE 10. Heavy frost last night. Forenoon, warm and pleasant. Afternoon one heavy shower. Three Flathead Indians passed in hot haste in the forenoon after some of their horses that were stolen from Camas prairie last night. Gave one of them some bullets and some percussion caps. The same Indians that stole their horses must have stolen Ned Williamson's horse. I have searched the country and cannot find him. The folks up at Cottonwood saw three Indians on Friday, one on foot and two on one horse, supposed to be Bannocks. Louis tried to catch them and turn them back but they hid and got away. It was they I saw on Friday night. I killed antelope with Adam's Maynard rifle, two hundred and forty yards, shot it off-hand. The bullet passed through the butt of its heart. Jack-

---

[46] Minesinger came in with Burr in 1856. *Ibid.* – ED.

son, Dempsey's friend, Oliver LeClaire, Tolman, and
Oliver left for a hunt up Flint creek. They took several milk cows intending to catch young moose calves
and have them suck the cows until they are old enough
to eat grass and willow twigs. I do not believe they
will catch moose calves enough to start any big herd.
Frank Newell and John Seeber start to the Bitter Root
tomorrow by way of the valley of Big Blackfoot river.
I saw a party on horseback passing along the foot of
the mountains south of here, and thought they were
probably those horse thieves. Oliver and I gave chase
and overtook them in six miles. They proved to be a
party of squaws from John Grant's on a root digging
expedition.

JUNE 11. Forenoon, cloudy and calm. I remod-
eled an old hat, making it look quite respectable. Afternoon cloudy, with one shower of rain and hail inter-
mixed. Those Flathead Indians returned this morning. They did not recover their horses, felt sorry for
them and gave them a piece of bread and an antelope
ham and sent them on their way rejoicing. Received
a call from Lady Catherine and Mrs. Powell, Indian
women, who are going from Grantsburg to visit Mrs.
Dempsey, a country woman of theirs. They told me
that the prowling Indian thieves stole one horse from
old Michael (a Nez Percé half breed) one from the
Frenchman Le Gris, one from Chas. DeLabreche, one
from Joe Piou, who was camped on Blackfoot creek a
few miles above Grant's, on his way to Fort Benton.
The river and creek are both falling considerable.

JUNE 12. Forenoon, clear with a strong east wind.
Found the horses in two bands this morning. They
are all in very ill humor. They fight each other like
devils. Afternoon, strong south wind with light fleecy

clouds. The women returned from Dempsey's going home. Seeber and Newell came back being afraid of the high water in all the streams here. The potatoes, corn, peas, and beets that were planted last are coming up fine. Began to enlarge my prospecting out in the ravine, looks good. This has been a beautiful day, smoky like Indian summer. Read "Byron" and indulged in many reveries while lying on the bank under the trees by the lovely creek and soothed by its gentle murmur. Woke up by having to return to earth and wash the dishes and roast some coffee. I am becoming very lonesome and long for brother James to return. Was bitten by several mosquitoes and saw the first horse fly of the season.

JUNE 15. Forenoon, calm clear and warm, but alas! A heavy frost last night. Dug some more, enlarging my cut in the ravine, got good prospects in beautiful gold. Joe, Powell's young Indian horse herder, came along and told me lots of news. He says that on the night of the eleventh there were stolen about ten head of Johnny Grant's horses, five of his mother-in-law's, (old squaw Giomman) three from Powell, one from Joe himself. I think they tried to catch some of ours and Burr's that same night as I found them split into two bands in the morning and very cross. Tied our best horses at the cabin door tonight and lay in the door with my rifle and revolver at my side. The three horses are Brooks, Old Fiend, and Cawhaw. Last night's frost does not show any effect in our garden yet. This day three years ago, we left Sheep rock, California, en route for the states and we have not gotten there yet. Today I received a visit from Johnny Carr and Frank Newell. They told me of a fierce single combat they had witnessed up at Dempsey's between Mrs. Dempsey and Charles Allen. Mrs. Dempsey was busy at the wood pile, chopping the day's supply, when Charlie, "half-shot" came along and begun to issue orders. Right there the fight began. Mrs. Dempsey landed away with the axe, but missed. Thereupon Charlie grabbed for the lady's hair. His aim was more certain and he got one hand full, whereupon the lady lit in with both hands and in two seconds Charlie's face looked like he had had an encounter with a wild cat. This desperate onslaught caused him to loose hold on her hair. She grabbed a stick of wood and used it with such good effect that she put the enemy to flight, but not until she had blacked both eyes, knocked out a tooth and scratched his face until his best friend would fail to recognize him. Mrs. Dempsey is known in these parts to be a lady of uncertain temper, but "more power to her elbow," say we all, for who could put up with the gang of drunken loafers that hang around Dempsey's without losing their temper.

JUNE 17. Clear and warm light west wind. I made a quick trip up to Johnny Grant's settlement and back to hear what was on up there. Those thieves who have lately been stealing horses were Blackfoot Indians. They came suddenly on a camp of Flatheads over the other side of the mountains. The Flathead camp outnumbered them and as they could not get away with all the stolen horses they took a few of the best and fled, leaving most of the stolen horses behind. The Flatheads (honest fellows) brought them over the mountains to Johnny Grant's and delivered them to their owners. Eight to Johnny, Jim Minesinger one, Johnny's young Indian one, and another stray returned with Johnny's. Twelve in all recovered. The Blackfoot thieves got away with Old Michael's one, and La

Breche's one, Joe Piou's one, Johnny's mother-in-law's five! Eight whose owners are known, but it is estimated that there are about forty missing from the Indians and whites from this side of the mountains. Lucky Williamson (the Indians did steal his horse as I thought) the good Flatheads recovered him and brought him back. River and creek rising a little. Some of the corn and melons that were planted on May 6, are just coming up. Plenty of mosquitoes at dark. Tied up our three best horses tonight as usual.

JUNE 18. Nearly clear, with a strong west wind cool and pleasant. Hoed corn and cleaned up around the house. Old Michael found four horses a few days ago, supposed to have been lost by the Nez Percés, and last night they were stolen from him, it is thought, by the Flatheads. Truly our horses have fallen among perilous times. The trees and bushes have just finished leafing out, river and creek rising a little. The snow is going fast upon the mountains. Too cool for mosquitoes at dark. Tied up our four [three] best horses tonight as usual.

JUNE 20. Another deadly black frost last night. Froze ice one-eighth of an inch thick. It cut down the wheat and oats and killed many of the wild flowers. All kinds of vegetation show the effect of it today, looking somewhat wilted. Went hunting, saw a cinnamon bear, two little white tailed deer, four antelope and did not get a shot, all very wild. River and creek falling a little. The Flathead war party that passed going south on the sixteenth, came back on the other side of the river this morning. They had ten loose horses and halted on the hill and sang me a war song and waved something on a pole that they wanted me to consider a scalp. I was quite willing to so consider it and glad to have the number of horse thieves that infest this neighborhood reduced by one.   Tied up the three horses again tonight and watched them.

JUNE 21.   Went hunting, killed a bull moose, saw one white tailed deer and five antelope.   Two Flatheads passed going after two horses that the war party left somewhere tired out.   They say that all eleven recovered their horses except one, and that they killed one Bannock (guess that was a scalp sure enough). One Flathead had a lock of hair cut off the back of his head by a bullet.   Fred's bay filly got her skin cut somehow and is lame.   River and creek falling a little. Can see many bare spots on the south mountains where the snow has lately gone off.   Many mosquitoes and a few horse flies.   Tied up the three horses and slept with one eye and both ears open.   The entire band of horses was stolen last night with the exception of the three I had at the cabin door.   Fred H. Burr lost eight good mares and six colts, and we lost six good mares and three colts.   While I was gone looking for the trail which I found, leading southeast towards Deer Lodge valley, one of our mares and colt, and Fred's little lame bay filly came back.   They were the least valuable and contrary to drive so the Indians left them on the road. Last night just at dark I saw two Indians, one on foot run out of the first ravine south of the house and to the brush south of the creek.   My first impulse was to jump on my horse and dash across the creek and try to find the horses somewhere on the bench west of the creek before the Indians got to them.   Then came the thought that some of the party of Indians were in all probability hidden in the brush along the creek just below the house, watching for a chance to get the three horses tied at the door which were worth as much as all our six on the bench. Oh! how I wish brother James were here with me for we would have sprung on two of the horses and the third one would have followed us and each of us armed with rifles and revolvers, we could have overtaken any Indians that might be driving off the horses. These eleven Flatheads overtook the thieves and the horses at Moose creek on Big Hole river, and killed two of them. There were four Bannocks in the party. They had the horses belonging to LeGris's party and had four horses packed with meat. They have probably been in the vicinity for a long time. The Flatheads said they could have killed the other two Bannocks, but let them go as a warning to the rest of their tribe. Only one of them offered to fight. San Pablo (St. Paul) took his bow away from him and told him to "go" and he went. O! mercy, ill bestowed, for I am sure that it was those Bannocks who stole our horses. It was evident that at first these Indians did not want to steal from the whites, for they had passed by the same horses twice before without molesting them, but after their misfortune at the hands of the Flatheads they ceased to be respectors of person. This is the Indian's ethics anyhow. In the evening James Minesinger came down from Grant's and stayed all night with me. How unfortunate he did not come last night, for if he had done so he and I would have saved our horses and very likely have killed the two thieves, for the horses that I tied were faster than others. A Frenchman named Decoteau, who lived forty miles south from here at Warm Springs saw the two Indians pass at sunrise the morning of the twenty-third driving about twenty horses. Kept our three horses tied at the door as usual.

JUNE 28. Rained all day, with the exception of a

little while about noon. Took some ammunition down
to Dempsey's for Tolman to take to Tom Adams at
Fort Owen in Bitter Root valley. Tolman and Jackson start for that place in the morning and Frank
Newell and John Seeber start to Walla Walla, four
hundred and twenty-five miles west. The wind blew
from all points of the compass today, coming from the
west at night. River and creek falling a little and the
water getting clear. Tolman, Jackson, and Oliver got
back from their hunt day before yesterday and they did
not catch any moose. I would have been greatly surprised if they had. I gave Jackson an order on Mc-
Donald for three bushels of wheat and Tolman an order
for two bushels. The wild flax and bitter-root are in
full bloom now and very beautiful. Kept the horses
staked out all day, and tied them up at night at the
cabin door.

JUNE 29. Rained all the forepart of last night.
Weather today very cloudy, warm, and sprinkling rain
occasionally. River and creek rising fast, and are up
to their highest mark again. I found a ripe strawberry and a rose in bloom, the first of the season. The
potatoes are coming up again. They are certainly
bound to win out in spite of their hard luck. Jim
Minesinger came down and stayed all night. I found
a new species of flower today. Kept the horses staked
out within gunshot all day and tied them at the door
at night.

JULY 1. Saw a huge comet last night in the northwest. Its tail reached half across the heavens. It has
probably been visible for sometime, but as it has been
cloudy lately I had not observed it before. The cottonwood trees are in full bloom. It is the first time I have
ever seen them in blossom. Nine Pipes, a Flathead,

came to get a nipple put in his yager rifle, but I had none that would fit it.   Sorry, for he is a good Indian.

JULY 2.   Plenty of mosquitoes, horse flies, gnats, and deer flies.   River and creek are falling a very little. Kept the horses staked out in the daytime, and tied them at night.   Saw the comet again.   It is not the one we saw in October, 1858, or at least it does not have the same appearance.   That party of Flatheads passed today, returning home after their buffalo hunt.   They had three buffalo calves, which they had caught over about the Three forks of the Missouri.   I traded three plew [47] of beaver skins and four buffalo tongues for them.   Four hills of melon seeds that we planted are just now coming up, having been in the ground fifty-six days.   Never saw the like before.

JULY 11.   Insect pests very bad.   We have now twenty-one calves, thirteen females, and eight males. Took a short hunt, found no game.   River and creek are now quite low.   Doctor Atkinson passed en route for Bitter Root.   Brother James arrived home to my great relief and joy for I have had a trying time during his long absence and have been very lonesome.   He was absent thirty-eight days.   He now keeps the journal.

---

[47] Plew or pluie is a French-Canadian word meaning pelt, probably derived from the French word *poil*.   It generally referred to beaver. – ED.

Life in Early Montana

I arrived home at ten o'clock today (July 11, 1861) and I have ridden ninety miles since the sun was two hours high yesterday morning. I have had a very disagreeable trip. The American Fur Company's steamboat burned and blew up at the mouth of Milk river. Cargo total loss, no lives lost. Higgins and Worden of Hell Gate lost a big stock of goods, no full particulars have reached Fort Benton as yet, except that the fire was caused by a deckhand who went down into the hold to steal some alcohol, of which there were several barrels. There were also several of whiskey. The d— fool had a lighted candle and when he bored a large gimlet hole in a barrel to fill his jug the fumes of the alcohol took fire and spread instantly and here is a failure of the retributive justice, for the cause of this great misfortune escaped with some slight burns. As it was known that there were twenty-five kegs of gunpowder on board, the steamer was run to the shore as quickly as possible and everybody ran ashore and out into the woods some distance and almost immediately the steamer blew up with a terrific report and sank. The greater part of the time I have been absent I had neither tea, coffee, sugar, nor bread. Only poor buffalo bull meat and water to live on. It reminded me of our experience here in 1858. There were no supplies of food at the fort, all having been eaten up and everybody waiting for the arrival of that steamboat to procure more. Now it is destroyed and those people, as well as ourselves, will have to get food supplies from Salt Lake City, five hundred miles away. While I was at Fort Benton the Crow Indians killed ten Blackfeet, and Little Dog, head chief of the Blackfeet, killed two of his own tribe and wounded one other very badly. It will probably be the cause of civil war among the Blackfeet for those killed were all sub-chiefs. The night of the fifteenth of June, I camped at the great falls of the Missouri river. Sun river was not fordable then.

JULY 12. F. H. Burr and Ned Williamson arrived this evening from Fort Benton. Gold Tom, who was with the party left at Prickly Pear creek to hunt on the Missouri river. Horse flies and mosquitoes are very bad here and torture me plenty. Clear, warm and strong west wind in the afternoon. Granville went hunting, but the flies were so bad in the pines that he had to come home without meat.

JULY 13. Clear and warm. Granville went hunting and killed a black-tailed deer. It was fat enough to be very good eating and we just needed it too. I cut out and made a raw-hide rope today. Jim Minesinger came down on a visit. Fat Jack passed here on his way to Walla Walla.

JULY 15. Wash day in camp. Granville and Burr went to Dempsey's ranch after two of Burr's cows. They borrowed a small fragment of a newspaper that Tolman and Jackson brought from Fort Owen in Bitter Root valley. Bad news from the states. The North and South are fighting. Tom Adams, John Grant, John W. Powell and party arrived from Benton.

JULY 16. Forenoon clear and warm. Ned Williamson returned from Grant's ranch accompanied by Michel Le Claire. I hoed potatoes. Afternoon, light

wind, cloudy and cool. Killed time by discussing the
outbreak of war in the states.

JULY 22. Frank L. Worden and party passed here
at sunrise this morning on their way to Hell Gate.
Michel returned about noon. Adams killed an antelope. Worked leveling ditch. John Grant, John W.
Powell, Thomas Pambrum, Louis Simmons and others
passed en route for the Hudson's Bay trading post near
the St. Ignatius Mission. Paid John F. Grant twenty-
eight pluie of beaver skins. War parties of Bannocks
have the mountains on fire in all directions. Somebody
will probably lose some more horses.

JULY 24. Afternoon, Michel and I went hunting.
Michel killed an antelope. Adams returned, only
went as far as Flint creek divide. Frank Goodwin
returned from Hell Gate. Nez Percés gold mines are
paying from five to fifty dollars per day per man. Eight
thousand miners there. I think that number should
be cut down to about two thousand.[48]

JULY 27. F. Goodwin came and got Pambrum's
gun. Party passed returning home from Hudson Bay
post. I went with them to Grant's and stayed all night.
Insects very bad.

JULY 29. Warm, clear. Gentle west wind. Tried
to stop a fire at the foot of the mountain from coming
down the creek to our ranch. From here to Flint creek,
about thirteen miles the land on the south side of the
river has been all burned over along the face of the
mountains, we do not know whether it was started by
whites, Indians, or lightning. The fire is still going
south towards Deer Lodge valley. Michel returned
home today. Powell came on a visit. Afternoon, very

[48] This refers to the district around Florence, Idaho.

warm. Cloudy with strong south-west wind. Laid foundation for calf corral.

JULY 31. Warm, clear, nearly calm. Fire still coming down the creek. Worked on corral for calves. Insect nuisance visibly on the decrease for which we are truly thankful. Doubtless our live stock is equally so, as the poor things have been the greatest sufferers for over six weeks. Last Sunday Granville lent Dempsey's employees a mowing scythe. I sent Michel after it last evening and instead of giving it to him they sent word that "they were using it and could not do without it for a few days yet." Now the weather is hot, but by jings, that is cool enough to bring on a heavy frost.

AUGUST 3, 1861. Very warm, clear and nearly calm. Three miners from the Nez Percé passed here today on their way to the states. They report plenty of people in those mines and some of them are doing very well. Worked on milk house and mowed. Insects bad.

AUGUST 5. Thomas Pambrum passed here going to Walla Walla. I wrote a letter to Clinton Bozarth, a cousin in Iowa, and sent it by Pambrum. Walla Walla is four hundred and twenty-five miles west, being our nearest postoffice. Johnny Grant's Indian wife was with Pambrum. She is going to stop at Hell Gate cañon below Flint creek and gather service berries.

AUGUST 10. Forenoon, calm, clear and warm. Cut and put up hay. Oliver went home. We had Mrs. Catherine and Mrs. Pambrum for dinner with us. Both well behaved Snake Indian women.

AUGUST 11. We had green peas of our own raising for dinner, but how they ever survived the many frosts beats me. Mosquitoes and flies are not so bad as they have been. Gnats are seemingly worse. Cuss a gnat anyhow, or anytime. We have had plenty of wild goose-berries for about ten days and now the rasp-berries are ripe. High living these days.

AUGUST 14. Clear, warm, and nearly calm, very smoky. Heavy frost last night. It came very near ruining our farm and garden and probably has done so, but we can't tell for certain for two or three days yet. Fires still burning on the mountains. Went prospecting, washed seven pans of dirt and got six cents, not quite a cent per pan. Gnats very bad, a few horse-flies and mosquitoes. Margaret, Thos. Pambrum's Indian wife, passed here from Grantsburg on her way to Dempsey's ranch. Adams and Michel escorted her down there. She had a fight with her relatives at Johnny Grant's and left them in disgust, which strikes us "out of the frying pan into the fire."

AUGUST 16. Prospected, washed six pans of dirt and got ten cents which is better than usual. Adams and Michel went to Pete Martin's today.

AUGUST 17. Prospected, washed seven pans of dirt and got six cents. Adams returned from above. He saw two men from the Nez Percé mines en route for the states. They are planning on going down the Missouri in a boat from Fort Benton. We feel certain they will perish if they start, for two men are too few to protect themselves from the Indians.

AUGUST 22. Capt. Richard Grant and Thomas Pambrum arrived from Hell Gate, and stayed all night with us. It is the first time we have seen the Captain since the winter of 1859. His rheumatism is much better than it has been. He is going on a visit to his son John. He brought us four letters from the states that were brought from Walla Walla by Bachelder's Express to Hell Gate, to Worden and Higgin's store. One letter was from our mother, one from Uncle

Valentine Bozarth, one from Cousin Sallie Bozarth, and one from brother Samuel. Great was our rejoicing at their arrival.

AUGUST 29. I returned home this evening. A Mr. Paris from Sun river government farm, arrived here this evening, en route to Bitter Root valley. Stayed all night.

SEPTEMBER 5, 1861. Warm and smoky. Frank Goodwin came down to see us. He contracted to build a log house for F. H. Burr for two horses and fifty pounds of flour.

SEPTEMBER 6. Rained hard last night and until ten o'clock today. I hope it will put a stop to all the fires in the mountains. Went fishing, caught twenty lovely trout, one very large one, over four pounds. Did not see the sun today.

SEPTEMBER 7. Rained a little. Very cold for this season of the year. The mountains are covered with snow almost down to the edges of the valleys. Robert Pelky and party of three wagons arrived from the states en route to Bitter Root valley and passed here in the afternoon. I went up to John Grant's.

SEPTEMBER 9. Frank Goodwin moved down from above with his camp, consisting of his Nez Percé wife, an elk skin lodge, and several horses. Last night Jack Collins and Ned Williamson arrived from Hell Gate en route for Fort Benton with whiskey for Indian trade.

SEPTEMBER 21. The Flathead Indians are camped in the bottom below here on their trip to the buffalo range for their usual winter hunt, and there are plenty of drunken Indians passing from Grantsville to their camp. I wish those whiskey traders would go on to the Blackfoot country or to Hades. Michel went to Grantsville.

SEPTEMBER 23. The Flathead camp passed on their way to hunt buffalo all winter. Am glad they are gone because of the d—d whiskey.

SUNDAY, SEPTEMBER 29. Warm cloudy. Jacobs [50] and Gwin had a shooting match for one and two dollars a shot. It was a standoff, for both quit even. Frank Goodwin went up to John Grant's and got into a drunken row and shot Michel LeClaire twice, with a navy Colt's revolver, wounding him (it is supposed) mortally. Poor little Michel he was under middle size but active and strong and only twenty years old. Goodwin was much larger, weighing about one hundred and sixty-five pounds and could have handled poor Michel without shooting him. It is a shame. This is the effect of bringing whiskey into a peaceful quiet community. I have expected that some of the Indians would kill each other while drunk, but so far have not heard of any fatalities among them. James returned from Grantsville this evening having been absent six days. He won four hundred and twenty-five dollars from a man named McCulloch playing poker.

OCTOBER 1, 1861. Four men from New York state passed en route for Walla Walla. A Frenchman named Le Gris who lives with his Assiniboine wife at Grantsville, and McCullough passed going to Bitter Root and Ned Williamson with them. Ned Collins has sold all of his whiskey and is going below for more.

OCTOBER 2. James, Powell, and Louis Maillet went to Hell Gate and Bitter Root valley. I bought a sore backed horse from Goodwin for ten dollars, and bought a small lot of gunsmith's tools from him for twenty-five dollars in ammunition. Bought two picks and shovels

---

[50] John M. Jacobs and John M. Bozeman constructed the Bozeman road. – ED.

and a pair of gold scales from him for cutting out his gun. Goodwin and Gwin have left this vicinity.

OCTOBER 5. Smith camped just above here with John Owen's pack train. They are packing hard bread from Fort Benton for the Flathead Indian agency on the Jocko river.

OCTOBER 9. Cold and stormy with west wind. I banked earth up against the house, preparing for cold weather. Dempsey's and Joe Blodget's wagons passed, loaded with flour and other goods, which were bought in Salt Lake City, five hundred miles away, but there is no food any nearer except at Fort Walla Walla, four hundred and twenty-five miles west, over a nearly impassable road for wagons. Two emigrant teams were with Dempsey and Blodget. Brother James and F. H. Burr arrived home.

OCTOBER 10. Nearly clear, and quite pleasant. I helped Jacobs haul house logs and fire wood. Powell, L. R. Maillet, and Jimmy Grant passed. James bought a steel rifle, light and handy about thirty-five calibre, made by Fisk of New York, for which he paid twenty dollars. It is entirely new and a bargain, but I would not exchange my trusty Maynard breech-loading brass cartridge rifle, which I bought from Thomas Adams for forty dollars for three like the Fisk rifles. Peter McDonald gave Brother James his double barreled Mortimer shot gun. James sold our wheat crop to Henry Brooks of Bitter Root valley for four dollars a bushel.

SUNDAY, OCTOBER 13. I went down to Dempseys. Jack Collins and A. K. Gurd, arrived from the Bitter Root valley with a wagon load of vegetables. One hundred and forty miles is a long haul to get to market, but they will make a good profit selling to the folks at Grantsville and Cottonwood, who are all hungry for vegetables.

OCTOBER 14. I churned five pounds of fine quality butter. Put handles in the picks and sharpened the shovels, and got ready to dig on our mining ditch. These tools were brought up for us from Walla Walla by Worden and Higgin's pack train. James Minesinger abandoned Grantsville and moved down to our pleasant little village.

OCTOBER 25. Clear, calm, and warm. Finished building dam. John Grant and his wife, a Bannock woman, passed en route for Bitter Root valley. Doctor Atkinson and Major William Graham arrived from Fort Owen in Bitter Root valley.

NOVEMBER 11, 1861. Snowed nearly all day. Meeks and party arrived from above. John Grant and Burr arrived from Hell Gate. They brought us a letter from Rezin Anderson. He wrote that he was going to enlist in the Federal Army. We hope he won't. Anderson is now visiting in Iowa.

NOVEMBER 12. All the Frenchmen from Cottonwood and Warm Springs passed here today, going to Hell Gate.

NOVEMBER 22. Calm, cloudy, and cold. Thawed a little about noon. "Old Sport Allen" went home. Allen is a peculiar character. He is continually after some of us to teach him to play poker. As he looses every time he gets into a game we have rather discouraged him in his ambition to become a real sport. Gold Tom and Jacobs hauled puncheons for Burr's floor.

DECEMBER 2, 1861. Cloudy and warm. A strong southwest wind, known as a Chinook, began about sundown, and in twenty minutes the water was running off the roofs and the warm wind caused the snow to settle

down very fast and this morning it was all gone. The
ground was covered with water. It looks good to see
the bare ground again, after having been covered with
snow so long, and so early in the fall. A camp of Pend
d'Oreilles of eight lodges passed here. They are going
over the mountains to hunt on the Missouri side during
the winter. They will, no doubt, be joined by a much
larger camp of Nez Percés, Yakimas, Spokanes, Flatheads, and Kootenais.

When Thomas Adams returned from Fort Benton
he brought Granville a new breech-loading fifty caliber
Maynard carbine rifle taking reloading brass cartridges
intended to contain forty grains of black powder. This
was the first gun of its kind seen out here and Granville
being an excellent shot had an idea that he could beat
anything or anybody shooting with that particular gun.
The first lot of cartridges that he loaded he had used
his powder flask and measured the powder exact, and
he had been doing some remarkable shooting on his
recent hunting trips and we had all been bragging a
good deal on the gun and his markmanship.

John Grant had a brother-in-law, an old Indian
named Pushigan. He had a long, heavy muzzle loading rifle of about forty calibre on which he had a sight
made of hoop iron. With this old gun and the hoop
iron sights, this Indian had been doing some fine shooting himself. John Grant had been bragging about
what his brother-in-law could do so one Sunday morning Sterne Blake, Powell, Bud McAdow, Jim Minesinger, Tom Adams, Granville and I went up to
Grantsville for a shooting match.

John Grant, James Grant, Chas. Jackson, Bob
Dempsey, and Tendoy (the old Snake Indian chief, a

brother-in-law of John Grant) were there ready to back Pushigan.

We took the end gate out of John Grant's wagon for a target and in the center marked a bulls-eye. Pushigan fired the first shot and made the bulls-eye. Granville stepped up to the mark, took deliberate aim, and missed the target entirely, and each one on our side was out one dollar. The match went on and the distance had been increased from one hundred yards to five hundred yards Pushigan having decidedly the best of it. Up to this point only light bets had been made. Granville was considerably crestfallen. He couldn't account for the inaccuracy of his little Maynard. At six hundred yards Pushigan made a bad score and Granville made a bulls-eye. Confidence was at once restored and Powell bet two horses to one. Our joy was short lived. Old Pushigan began carefully manipulating his hoop iron sights and made a bulls-eye at every crack of the rifle, while Granville made but one good score. By this time our side was flat broke and afoot. I offered to bet my trusty long range rifle with old Tendoy for a good little roan horse, but the old fellow refused so I suppose I lost my chance of handing my gun over to the wily old chief.

We all hoofed it back to camp arriving late in the evening, tired, cold, and hungry. Granville had little to say about that gun and only remarked that, "He never did believe in gambling," to which remark Powell made answer, "Too bad you didn't bet that gun and lose it."

Next day Granville was busily engaged loading brass cartridges. He carefully measured the powder putting in exactly forty grains to the cartridge and then taking his Maynard out back of the house he set up a target and found that he could make a bulls-eye almost every crack of the gun at two, three, five and six hundred yards. The trouble the day before was that he had loaded his shells by guess and there was too much powder in some, and in others not enough, which accounted for the bad shooting on Sunday.

DECEMBER 25, 1861. We went up to Cottonwood to Pete's grand ball. Had a fine supper and then danced all night till sunrise. There were a few students of toxicology occasionally, but they were well behaved and gave the rest of us no trouble. Snowed a little last night. Tom Campbell arrived from Sun river yesterday.

DECEMBER 26. I returned home. Had a visit from Pierre Ish Tab-ba-bo and his wife, a good young couple. He had married a Snake girl. Bud (P. W. McAdow) started to Salt Lake. I fear he will have a very hard, cold trip. Let Powell have the Arkansas steer to butcher for beef.

DECEMBER 27. Very cold and disagreeable. Stayed in the house all day. Roland and another man passed with Jack Williams, prisoner for stealing horses (first [49] arrest for this offense here). They passed last night. Kiplinger and Eaton went above today.

DECEMBER 30. Very cold. Caught my cream colored horse, that I bought from Frank Goodwin, and doctored his sore back. Dempsey and Major Graham got back from their Indian trading expedition. They traded for eighteen horses and about six hundred skins from the Sheep Eaters, and Digger Snakes. It snowed considerably today.

[49] I cannot recall what became of this horse thief; he was not hung and he had no trial. There were not at this time any courts nearer than Walla Walla.

JANUARY 1, 1862. Snowed in the forenoon. Very cold in afternoon. Raw east wind. Everybody went to grand ball given by John Grant at Grantsville and a severe blizzard blew up and raged all night. We danced all night, no outside storm could dampen the festivities.

JANUARY 2. Still blowing a gale this morning. Forty below zero and the air filled with driving, drifting snow. No one ventured to even try to go home (we lived eight miles below and many couples lived ten to fifteen miles up in Deer Lodge valley). Johnny Grant, good hospitable soul, invited everyone to stay until the storm should cease. We accepted his invitation without a dissenting voice. After breakfast we laid down on the floor of the several rooms, on buffalo robes that Johnny furnished, all dressed as we were and slept until about two o'clock in the afternoon, when we arose, ate a fine dinner that Johnny's wife, assisted by the other women, had prepared, then resumed dancing which we kept up with unabated pleasure until about nine in the evening, when we paused long enough to eat an excellent supper. We then began where we left off and danced until sunrise.

JANUARY 3. The blizzard ceased about daylight, but it was very cold with about fourteen inches of snow badly drifted in places and the ground bare in spots. We estimated the cold at about thirty-five below, but fortunately there was but little wind. After breakfast all the visitors left for home, men, women, and children, all on horseback. Everyone got home without frost bites.

The music for these dances was two violins; and the dance most popular, was the old-fashioned quadrille. The floors were all of puncheon hence not smooth or

waxed. Some men called the figures. The women
were Indian or half-breed and there were never enough
to go around. A man with a handkerchief tied around
his arm supplied the place of a woman in some of the
sets. There was as much rivalry among the women of
those days, as to their finery, as there is now among
their white sisters. At these balls they wore their
brightest calicoes with new scarlet leggings and handsomely beaded moccasins with gay plaid blankets and
ornaments of feathers, shells, silver money, beads, and
a generous supply of vermillion paint. The children
were also gotten up in the most elaborate beaded cos-
tumes that their mothers could supply. It was no uncommon thing for an Indian woman to spend all of her
spare time for six months, preparing a suit beaded and
embroidered with colored porcupine quills, for her
young son to wear to these festivities. Nor were the
men without vanity. We always wore our best flannel
shirt, a highly ornamented buckskin suit, and best
moccasins and trimmed our hair and beards. I kept
my handsomely beaded buckskin suit with its decora-
tions of fringe until 1880 when it was stolen from my
cabin on the cattle range.

JANUARY 17. All the women in this part of the
country have been at John Grant's, having I suppose an
Indian Dorcas Society something after the manner of
their white sisters, and like them it has broken up in a
row. All the women have left for home. That is,
they have joined their own people, leaving a goodly
number of widowers. Next thing the aforesaid widowers will have to hunt up their absconding wives and the
chances are most of them will have to yield up a number of good blankets or horse or two to father-in-law
to persuade the lady to return.

JANUARY 18. It is a little warmer today. Cloudy,
and nearly calm. Snowed a little. It has been bitter
cold every day since the first of the month and the snow
constantly becoming deeper. It is now about twenty
inches deep with a pretty strong crust on top and another one about eight inches below the surface. The
river is frozen over solid for miles, not a single air-hole
anywhere and many of the cattle are walking up and
down on the ice seeking water. At first we thought
that they would have to have water or die, but fortunately Granville and I remembered that when we were
wintering on Henry's fork of Green river in 1858-59,
Majeau, the French mountaineer trader, told us that
when a severe winter came the Ute Indians, who often
wintered on Green river, below Brown's Hole (a warm
sheltered little valley) would put their horses out
among the cedar hills where there was good bunch
grass, and good wind shelter among the cedar groves,
and would not let them have any water while the cold
and deep snow lasted, saying that if the horses were
allowed to drink the ice cold water they would become
chilled and rapidly lose flesh and many freeze to death.
Out in the hills they could not bite the grass without
getting enough snow to moisten it sufficiently, and they
stayed fat all winter. So we gathered our cattle and
drove them up into a deep little cañon on the north side
of the river just opposite our houses. There was no
water in it, but plenty of big willows also a great deal
of tall rye grass and the cañon extended north and
south and as the wind almost always blew from the
west it blew across it and did not get down into it at all.
We took our horses and broke paths through the snow
up the east side of the cañon to the bench land above.
We then drove all the cattle up these paths to the top

of the bench and left them there with our horses. The horses pawed the snow off the grass so they could get it and the cattle at once learned to stay with the horses and help eat the abundant bunch grass that they exposed.

JANUARY 19. Cloudy, and a little milder and calm. Today we put the remainder of the cattle across the river with the first lot and we noticed that just before dark they all came down the paths into the cañon where there was no wind at all and slept among the willows and tall rye grass.

FEBRUARY 1, 1862. Clear, cold, and nearly calm. Hauled two loads of fire wood. Danced last night. Oh! joy. It is not often that we have a fiddler and when we do have one, we try to keep him in practice by having a dance every evening.

FEBRUARY 2. Danced again last night.

FEBRUARY 4. Calm, clear, not quite so cold. Powell and I went to Grantsville. A party of Flatheads passed here with some Bannock horses that they had stolen from the camp at Beaverhead valley. Danced last night.   J. S.

FEBRUARY 5. Clear and cold. Light west wind. Last night about nine o'clock a party of Bannocks passed here. They were following those Flatheads. This morning they returned with two Flathead scalps and a band of horses. Danced last night.

FEBRUARY 13. Little Aeneas, the Flathead, or rather the Iroquois, adopted into the Flathead tribe, camped here with his lodge and family on his return home from hunting buffalo. Killed many and dried the meat. Another family joined him this evening. It is Narcisses and family. Tom Gold Digger came down from Grantsville and stayed all night. He says

that Dave Contois, Louis Descheneau, and Jake Meek
have left their ranches up in the valley and moved
down to Cottonwood creek village. Too many Indians
prowling about.

FEBRUARY 25. Snowed ten inches last night. Oh!
oh! Aeneas, and Narcisses, the Flathead, went up to
Cottonwood last night and found a Snake Indian
named Peed-ge-gee camped near there. They killed
him and took his lodge and camp fixtures and one of his
wives. He had eight horses. This has been a horrible
day, snowing and blowing furiously. About three
inches of snow fell.

FEBRUARY 26. Snowed one inch in the night and is
still at it this morning. Narcisses came down from
Cottonwood with the captured woman. Powell and I
[J. S.] ransomed the captive woman, thinking it just as
well not to allow Narcisses to take her down to the
Flathead country. It is usual when they take a captive
to turn her over to the women of their tribe and they
promptly make a slave of her; imposing all of the drudgery of the camp on her, and making her life anything
but a bed of roses. This woman is fair with red cheeks
and brown hair and eyes and is evidently half white.
The two other women of Peed-ge-gee made their escape
the night of the murder and made their way to the
white settlement on Cottonwood where they were cared
for by some Bannock women until they had a chance to
join their own tribe the following summer. Powell
killed the black Wiley ox for beef. He was fat, which
speaks well for the nutritive quality of the bunch grass,
for this has been a very severe winter. Snowed slowly
all day but melted nearly as fast as it fell.

FEBRUARY 27. Put two more weak cows up in the
calf corral to feed, making four now being fed. We

think our small haystack will last them from now until snow goes off. We could not begin feeding sooner as we only have a limited supply of hay, and cattle after being taken up and fed will not return to the range and "rustle" feed but will stand around until they starve hoping to be fed. No news from the states. I suppose Bachelder's Express from Walla Walla to Hell Gate and Cantonment Wright is snowed under. Thos. Adams took unto himself a wife last night. The bride is Louise, Lone-penny's step-daughter, a Flathead damsel.

MARCH 1, 1862. Cold, nearly clear. Snow is drifting very bad. I brought with me the Indian woman ransomed from Narcisses, the Flathead. Powell's wife objected to having her and as we have no cook it seems to fall to my lot to take her and take care of her at least until we can turn her over to some of her own people, should she wish to go. I might do worse. She is neat and rather good looking and seems to be of a good disposition. So, I find myself a married man. Granville says "Marrying is rapidly becoming an epidemic in our little village." J. S.

MARCH 3. Adams's wife left him today. They dissolved partnership by mutual agreement.

MARCH 20. Cloudy and calm. Thawed a little. Worden gives Burr ten dollars a day to take him and Baptiste to Sun river. We played poker last night. I won forty dollars. Worden was the loser. Powell and I came home today.

Sterne Blake comes with a good story of doings down at Hell Gate. Hell Gate is putting on "States Airs," and has a justice of the peace, and has held court and tried one of the distinguished citizens of that section for killing a neighbor's horse.

The trial was held in Bolt's saloon, a log building near Worden and Higgins' store. Suit was brought by "Tin Cup Joe" against Baron O'Keefe for killing a horse. Henry Brooks was judge; Bob Pelkey, constable; Frank Woody, prosecuting attorney; Sterne Blake was one of the twelve jurors and Bud McAdow was an onlooker. Baron O'Keefe conducted his own defense. (Anyone knowing the Baron would feel confident that he was well able to look out for himself.)

"Tin Cup Joe" accused the Baron of injuring one of his horses so seriously as to cause its death. The Baron denied the charge of malicious mischief and said that the horses had been in the habit of breaking down fences around hay stacks, that he put up for his own stock and that he had warned "Tin Cup Joe" to keep them away, a thing he had failed to do.

Frank Woody began for the prosecution and he had not proceeded far before some of his remarks about "Good Citizenship," were taken to be personal by O'Keefe. The Baron straightened up with eyes flashing and snorting like a war horse yelled, "Who are you, what kind of a court is this anyhow?" Then addressing himself to the Bench began, "Say Old Brooks, who in hell made you judge? You are an old fraud. You are no judge; you are a squaw man, you have two squaws now. Your business is to populate the country with half breeds. You —— —— ——." The Baron made a lunge at the person nearest him and in an instant the fight became general. Everybody took a hand, and as both sides had about an equal number of sympathizers, when the dust of battle cleared away it was considered to be a draw. But judge, jurors, constable, and prosecuting attorney, had disappeared and the fiery Baron held the center of the room declaring that "no Frenchman's horses can nibble hay from one of my stacks without suffering the consequences."

Quiet was finally restored, the judge and jury returned and the trial proceeded without further interruption. The jury brought in a verdict for "Tin Cup Joe" and awarded him forty dollars damages, but I do not know that anyone ever tried to collect the money from Baron O'Keefe. I do know that I would not have cared for the job. Such was the very first trial by court in what is now the state of Montana.[51]

The winter of 1861-2 was one of unprecedented severity. Severe cold set in about December 1. The snow was two feet deep and the thermometer registered above zero only four times in three months. The game was scarce and toward spring deadly poor. The Indians that were over in the buffalo country suffered terribly. They lost most of their horses and were unable to kill many buffalo, consequently, they were without meat and were in a starving condition.

Captain Grant lost many cattle and horses. We escaped loss by not allowing our stock to get cold and by keeping them in a sheltered coulees and by keeping horses and cattle together. The horses would paw snow and uncover the grass for the cattle. For sixty days our stock was without water to drink and only had the snow that they ate with the bunch grass. In the spring they were all in good condition, the young ones being fat.

The latter part of March a Chinook struck the country and in less than twenty-four hours the ice was breaking up in the streams, all the creeks and river were out of their banks. There were snow slides on all the steep

<hr>

[51] F. H. Woody denied that he ran away from the fight. Mr. Woody states also that O'Keefe paid the judgment. *Opus citra*, p. 101. – ED.

mountains. It was impossible to travel any distance. The smallest creek became a raging torrent. There were so few settlers in the country that there was not much loss from the floods. There was a big ice gorge in the river above Bold creek and the water and ice covered all of the river bottom below there. Large cakes of ice scattered over the bottoms and laid there until June before they melted.[52]

MARCH 29, 1862. Cold and stormy with west wind. John Jacobs, Brown, and Smith came down from above, on their way to the Bitter Root. The river is just barely fordable. Jacobs told us lots of news. Frank Goodwin arrived at Cottonwood, from Fort Benton (he had gone there accompanied by Gwin when they left here so suddenly after he shot poor little Michel LeClaire). The Gros Ventre Indians came on him near Fort Benton and killed his Nez Percé wife and robbed him of all he had in the world. It is a pity that they did not kill him and let the unfortunate woman escape. Tom Campbell and Jack Collins also arrived from Fort Benton. They did not make anything trading with the Indians, very probably because they were their own best customers. William Kiplinger, Eaton, and John Seeber also arrived from Fort Benton. They, likewise, made nothing trading with the Indians. Great excitement at Benton about reported gold mines at Chief mountains near the British line (a humbug). There is a war on between the Gros Ventres, and Piegan Blackfeet. Seven Nez Percés

---

[52] Judge F. H. Woody wrote, "Prior to this time stock raisers had never made any preparation to feed their stock, consequently no feed had been put up. . . In February, 1862, a thaw came, and while the snow was soft it turned cold and the snow was frozen perfectly solid rendering it impossible for stock to move or get feed and the result was that hundreds of cattle died as did many horses." *Ibid.*, p. 100. – ED.

went to Beaverhead valley to steal horses from Bannock Indians wintering there. They found four lodges of Bannocks and tried to take their horses, but the Bannocks overtook them and killed two of them. The other five got away, with one horse belonging to Tendoy, Grant's brother-in-law. Johnny saw the horse as they passed by Cottonwood and succeeded in getting it away from them.

MARCH 31. Snowed four inches last night, rather raw and cold today, but it thawed a little in the afternoon. Thomas Adams, John M. Jacobs, and party left for Hell Gate. The Nez Percés are moving camp down the river past here today. To-losh-to-nau, a Flathead, camped opposite here on the other side of the river. He told us that he went to drink in a creek over the mountains when he saw several pieces of yellow metal (the old story) lying on the bottom of the stream and that he picked one piece up, about the size of this thumb (what a whopper, and why didn't he pick up all those pieces of yellow metal) and that he had it yet, over at his lodge. We told him to bring it over and let us see it and we would tell him whether it was gold or not. He went, but did not come back today. Good lie that.

APRIL 1, 1862. Cloudy and cold. Sprinkling snow. That "Siwash" came over today and said that some of his friends told him that that piece of yellow metal was not gold and he gave it to his child to play with. Now if we should go over to his lodge to see it he would doubtless say that his child had lost it. Nez Percés still moving camp by here. Pierre Ish, Little Wolf, and company gave us a call. Rather drunk. Traded two buffalo tongues and a little dried meat from two squaws. River falling.

APRIL 5. Cloudy and cold. Nearly calm and snows a little nearly every night. Many Flatheads, Spokanes, and Pend d'Oreilles are passing on their return from buffalo hunting. Powell has been catching a few fish for about a week.

APRIL 6. Granville went to Cottonwood. Nine Pipes came to Victor's camp to hear the news. The Nez Percés have been lying about Johnny Grant, and Victor,[53] the Flathead chief, wanted to hear what we had to say about it. Fred Burr, who speaks the Flathead language fluently, made matters all right with him. I sold a mare (the Jacobs mare) to a Spokane Indian for eighty dollars in gold. Old Allen (Old Sport) came down here yesterday and returned home today. Tried to trade some furs from him but he asked too much.

APRIL 7. Victor's camp passed here today. We had a long talk with him about our Indian affairs. He thinks it is very probable that we will have trouble with the Pend d'Oreilles after awhile on account of our Snake and Bannock women. Maillet came from Cottonwood today to see Victor. Victor is much dissatisfied with John Grant's conduct this winter and is on his way to see Grant and try to have some settlement with him. He says Grant has Snake and Bannock wives and plenty of Indians (Snakes and Bannocks) coming to visit him and when they leave they steal horses from the Flatheads. He says Grant will have to keep the Snake and Bannocks away from his place,

---

[53] Victor was the "great chief" of the Flatheads. He was a Christian and a friend of the whites. It was with him, in 1855, that Governor Stevens negotiated the treaty at Council Grove near the mouth of the Bitter Root river that purported to surrender the Bitter Root valley to the whites. Father De Smet and Lieutenant John Mullan regarded him affectionately. Chittenden and Richardson, *opus citra*, vol. iv, pp. 1337-1341.

etc. As Deer Lodge valley and the valleys of the Big Hole, Beaverhead, and Jefferson have been, from times immemorial, a neutral ground for the Snakes, Bannocks, Nez Percés, Pend d'Oreilles, Flatheads, Spokanes, Coeur d'Alenes, and Kootenais, it looks like the old chief is too arbitrary in insisting that the Snakes and Bannocks should be forbidden to spend the winter and hunt there the same as all others, because of little squabbles common to all tribes. Maillet returned home today very much disgusted with Indians in general, and Victor in particular. Maillet also speaks Salish or Flathead. Tom Campbell and party started for Fort Benton yesterday.

APRIL 10. Many Indians still passing. Granville returned from Cottonwood. Jake Meek and several others are going to start to the Emigrant road in about eight days to spend the summer trading there. Some of the Fort Benton men camped on the other side of the river. They have a pack train loaded with supplies and clothing for Lieutenant Mullan's cantonment at the mouth of Big Blackfoot river.[54]

---

[54] This was Cantonment Wright built by Mullan in the fall of 1861 for winter quarters. It was named for General Wright. Captain John Mullan, *Report on the Construction of a Military Road from Fort Walla-Walla to Fort Benton.* (Washington, 1863) pp. 32, 33.

Gold Mining in Deer Lodge Valley

Our little settlement at American Fork has begun to take on the lively bustling appearance of a new placer camp.[55] Several parties were out prospecting with fair results. We have succeeded in getting one thousand feet of lumber, at ten cents per foot, whipsawed for sluice boxes. P. W. McAdow and A. Sterne Blake have been washing dirt in a short gulch on Gold creek and have taken out three dollars in nice clean gold dust from one hundred pans of dirt.

APRIL 30. Burr went down to Lieutenant Mullan's camp to deliver his two American horses (Old John and his bay stallion) that he sold to Mullan for three hundred dollars, when he was down there. McAdow came down and got his horses, he is going to move camp up the creek as the water has failed in his gulch. Johnny Grant sent Pierre Ish down to tell us that "Tom Gold Digger" and Tom Campbell had arrived from Fort Benton and say that there is a war party of Blackfeet on the road over to steal horses from this side of the mountains. Baptiste Quesnelle and Paul Michel came down and stayed all night. Napoleon went back. Tied up our best horses tonight. Powell killed an antelope and saw a band of elk.

[55] "In the fall of 1861 A. S. Blake came here [to Hell Gate] with the intention of prospecting and in the spring of 1862 in company with "Bud" McAdow, W. B. S. Higgins, Doctor Atkinson, C. P. Higgins, and E. D. Dukes went to Gold creek and commenced operations." F. H. Woody, *opus citra* 101. See also letter of McAdow of August 4, 1908, in Montana Historical Library. – ED.

MAY 2, 1862. Granville was married today to Aubony, a Snake Indian girl, a sister of Fred Burr's wife.
She had been living with Burr's family, is a fairly good
cook, of an amiable disposition, and with few relatives.[56]   Clear and warm.   Minesinger and I went up
to the mountains after lumber with the wagon and
three yoke of oxen.   We brought down about seven
hundred and fifty feet.   Martineau and Sam Hugo
moved down.   Old man Hugo started to Hell Gate to
see about building a bridge for Lieutenant Mullan.
Doctor Atkinson, Higgins, Blake, and company all
moved to Gold Tom's old place on the creek to try it
for diggings.   Tom Campbell came down and stayed all
night.   He says that "Tom Gold Digger" and Brown
are prospecting up on Cottonwood creek.   The Bannocks left Cottonwood today on foot.   They said they
were going to the Flathead country to steal horses, but
I think they will steal any horses they can, whether
they belong to white men or Indians.   F. H. Burr returned from Hell Gate.   He brought a lot of late
papers.

Doctor Atkinson is a most original character.   He
is always traveling about the country with a pack horse
and one or more companions, prospecting.   He carries
a large pair of field glasses, rides up the cañons keeping
along on the ridges when possible, from points of vantage he will take out his field glasses, take a look at the
surrounding country and declare that, "There, the
country does not look good."   Then putting away his
field glasses he will ride on.   I never knew of his dig-

---

[56] Aubony or Ellen became the mother of nine children of whom three,
Charlie, Sam, and Mary (Mrs. E. C. Abbott, wife of "Teddy Blue" of Gilt
Edge, Montana) still live. She also adopted two sons of James Stuart.
One of these, Robert, is still living. Aubony died in 1887 at Maiden,
Montana. This information is from the son, Sam. – ED.

ging a hole or of panning a pan of dirt. He does buy into claims occasionally and then resells them. On the whole he was about as lucky as some of us who dig many holes and wash innumerable pans of gravel and succeed in "just missing the pay streak."

MAY 5, 1862. Cloudy and cold with some rain. Jim and I hauled a log and put it across the creek for the dam to rest against at the head of the ditch. Cossette and Joe dug six rods of ditch. James and Tony made some of the sluice boxes, these being the first ever made in the Rocky mountains north of Pikes peak. They also made some of the horses to set the sluice boxes on. Those Bannocks tried to cut down the corral gate last night and we repaired it this afternoon. Oh! yes, certainly, they only wanted Flathead horses, d— them!

MAY 6. Cloudy with rain, Joe, Cossette, and I dug fifteen and three quarters rods of ditch. Finished the sluices and horses, and hauled them up to the ravine. Adams, Blake, and Creighton arrived from the Bitter Root. McAdow, Blake, and Higgins are finding good prospects in a small creek up at the foot of the mountains, five miles above here. Adams commenced boarding with us today.

MAY 7. Clear and warm and strong west wind. Finished the dam today and turned the water into the ditch. It broke away at the steep hill side by the three pines. Hauled up lumber and repaired the break by putting three joints of flume. Then we set our flume boxes ready to begin washing. Tony, Joe, and I dug several rods of ditch. Tebow came down and got two yoke of oxen and the wagon to haul Higgins's sluice lumber to his camp. Powell killed an antelope. L. L. Blake and Creighton went above.

MAY 8. Clear and warm. Adams, Brother James,

Jim Minesinger and I began to wash gravel with the sluices, but the ditch soon broke on the hillside, which was composed of soft clay shale. Repaired it and worked until nearly night when it broke again. Tony Cossette and Joe dug ten rods of ditch. Jimmy Grant and David Pattee arrived from Hell Gate. Nothing new down there. Tom Campbell and Joe Hill came down from above and report that those Bannocks stole about twenty-five horses from Johnny Grant. Gold Tom, Brown, Ish, Chas. DeLabreche and several others are in pursuit of them and I surely hope they may overtake them and return home loaded with Bannock scalps. They also report that Jack Collins and Frank Goodwin started to Fort Benton.[57]

MAY 11. Blake, Creighton, La Breche, and Napoleon, came down from above. Creighton bought five head of cattle. He and Napoleon went on down to Dempsey's. Napoleon is on his way to Walla Walla. McAdow came down from his diggings and showed a prospect of twenty cents to the pan of dirt. Martineau and Ball hauled down another load of logs for Pete Martin. Gold Tom came down from above. He says they overtook those Bannock horse thieves, but did not get their horses, because the Indians "bluffed" them off. I suppose there were six or seven whites and but ten Indians. They should have gotten those horses.

MAY 13. Tony, Joe, and Cossette dug on ditch.

[57] While in Benton Frank Goodwin became involved in a quarrel with a Greek over a gambling game and beat him over the head with his revolver inflicting severe injuries. Goodwin then left the fort and remained away until he thought the incident had been forgotten and then returned. The Greek was appraised of Goodwin's return and taking his rifle posted himself in a room upstairs, on watch for Goodwin who was in a store across the street. When Goodwin came out into the street he stepped to the window and shot him dead. There was no civil law and those at the fort thought the Greek was justified in killing Goodwin, nothing was done in the case. Thus was poor little Michel Le Claire's unprovoked murder avenged.

James, Jim, and I washed with the sluices in the fore-noon. In the afternoon they dug a hole to look for the pay streak. I killed a two year old beef, assisted by Pete Martin. Powell, Burr, and Adams also dug a hole looking for the pay streak, which I regret to state none of them found. LaBreche returned with Little Jake, who came to hire to Adams. Gold Tom and Brown moved their camp up to the upper diggings today. River and creek on a stand, but still high.

MAY 14. James, Jim, and Adams set the sluices in another place and washed all day. Powell went hunting and killed nothing. Burr and I went up to the diggings now called "Dixie," to take a look at them. Rather liked their appearance and took up three claims just below Blake's and McAdow's on Pioneer gulch. I took up a hundred and fifteen pounds of beef to them and salted down half a barrel of beef, with salt that we brought from Salt river in 1860. Leon Quesnelle and DeMars came down from Cottonwood to look at the diggings and stayed all night.

MAY 20. Working at ditch and sluices. Burr, Powell, and I went to Dixie, found everyone hard at work. Blake and McAdow made ten dollars yesterday and nine dollars today. Higgins worked about three hours on bed rock and made three dollars and a half. Doctor Atkinson and Gold Tom are digging tail races to their claims. We sponged on Blake and McAdow for our grub. We had rice, etc., for dinner; beans, etc., for supper. Blake was the cook, enjoyed our visit very much. They are a jovial set of miners and we had much fun at one another's expense in the way of jokes. I like the appearance of the diggings better than I thought I would. There is plenty of hard work, but I think there is good pay doing it. Maillet came down this evening on a collecting tour. Also Jim Grant and Pattee. They are on their way to Hell Gate. Peter Martin went to Cottonwood.

MAY 21. Dempsey and Jackson came to see us at work mining. Cleaned up the sluices and only had twelve dollars, most of it being in one nugget. This is the first nugget found here and there may be quartz ledges in this vicinity.[58]

MAY 27. F. H. Burr started for Fort Benton with Mullan's party. Cleaned up the sluices and had four dollars and twenty-five cents for two days' work. We have concluded to quit here for the present and all go up to the Dixie diggings.

MAY 28. A party of Flatheads and Pend d'Oreilles passed on the creek above us with twelve horses that they had stolen from the Bannocks. I am glad that those Bannocks are having to take some of their own medicine.

JUNE 4, 1862. Tony came down from Dixie today. They have gone down eleven feet in our tail race and no sign of bed rock. They sunk a hole about sixty yards up-stream above the end of the race, and found bed rock at nine feet with one inch of gravel that prospects one cent per pan of dirt. "BAD EGG."

JUNE 17. David Pattee arrived here en route for Salmon river mines, with a band of cattle for John Grant. Bill Hamilton moved down here today. I wish he had gone somewhere else. Granville and crew made seventeen dollars and sixty cents today. J. S.

JUNE 24. I went to Dixie. Granville's crew made seven dollars and twenty cents. Prospected Higgins's claim (the one he bought from Doctor Atkinson).

---

[58] This was the first gold nugget found in what is now Montana and I still have it in my possession, September 8, 1916.

Doctor Mullan and the Lieutenant's messenger passed
en route to meet Lieutenant Mullan at Fort Benton.
Arrived here today a party of sixteen from Colorado.
Acquaintances of our brother Thomas Stuart. Thomas
expected to come with this party, but was detained
and will come later with another party.[59] They have
gone up on Pioneer creek to prospect. Word came
that Captain Richard Grant is seriously ill at Walla
Walla, and his sons, John and Jimmie have gone to see
him. The doctors say he cannot live long. This has
cast a gloom over the entire settlement. Captain Grant
was a jovial kind hearted gentleman and very popular
with the mountaineers.[60]

JUNE 25. Barcier and others arrived from Fort
Benton. They say three steamboats have arrived there
loaded with emigrants, provisions, and mining tools
and supplies. Now everybody talks of going to Fort
Benton.

JUNE 29. Mr. Louthan, S. T. Hauser, John Ault,
Doctor McKellops, and Jake Mauttie arrived here
from St. Louis, having come up the river on one of the
steamboats. They are en route for Salmon river gold
mines, never having heard of this place.[61]

JULY 4, 1862. Five emigrants arrived last night and
twelve or fifteen today. All from Benton. Came up
the river on those four [three] steamboats. I [J. S.]
made arrangements about going into partnership with
Frank H. Woody.

[59] Among these was James M. Bozeman, who discovered the Bozeman
pass. He was murdered by the Indians on the Yellowstone in 1877. G. S.
See also Grace M. Hebard and E. A. Brininstool. *The Bozeman Trail* (2
vols., Cleveland, 1922). Vol. i, p. 214. Doctor Mullan was a brother of the
builder of the Mullan road. — ED.

[60] Captain Grant did not recover from this illness. His descendants are
now scattered over the Northwest. – ED.

[61] Speaking of the early days in the rich and almost inaccessible mining

JULY 5.   There are about forty-five emigrants in the mines at this time.   C. P. Higgins arrived from Walla Walla this evening.   He brought some letters for us from folks at home.

JULY 6.   Capt. C. P. Higgins went to meet his teams coming from Fort Benton.   We received one letter from Brother Samuel and one from Cousin Sallie Bozarth, both living in Iowa.   The Colorado party are finding some good prospects in a gulch about two miles north of Pioneer.[62]   We call the place "Pikes Peak." [63]

JULY 10.   Returned from Cottonwood.   That whiskey enabled Powell to buy nine cows and a yearling

---

camp of Florence. A bill of goods bought there in the spring of 1862, by one of my friends, who later came to Bannack. Here it is verbatim:

100 lbs. beans	@ 1.25	$125.00
300 lbs. flour	1.00	300.00
11 lbs. coffee	1.25	13.75
300 lbs. beef	.25	75.00
9 lbs. beans	1.00	9.00
3 sacks salt, 5 lbs. each		
1 lb. bar soap		3.00
6 lbs. nails	1.00	6.00
10 lbs. sugar	1.50	15.00
25 lbs. bacon	1.25	31.25
1 paper salaratus		6.00

$596.50

[62] Pioneer: a small fork of Gold creek where the Stuarts mined in 1862, named by Lieut. John Mullan. – ED.

[63] Stuart in *Montana As It Is*, pp. 8, 9, describes the naming of Pike's Peak. After telling of the settlement at Gold creek in 1861 he continued, "We succeeded during the following summer in finding prospects that we considered very good, upon which we began to make preparations to take it out 'big,' and wrote to our brother Thomas, who was at 'Pike's Peak,' as Colorado was then called, to come out and join us, as we thought this a better country than the 'peak.' How events have fulfilled this prediction will be seen hereafter. Thomas showed our letters to quite a number of his friends, and they became quite excited over them, and in the spring of 1862 many of them started out to find us, but became lost, and went to Old Fort Limhi, on Salmon river, and from there they scattered all over the country, a few of them reaching us about the first of July. We were then mining on

for beef. Adams, Burr, and Major Graham arrived from Benton today. I bought two hundred pounds of flour at twenty dollars a hundred and thirty-six pounds of salt at twenty-five cents per pound from Dave Contois. How I wish we had that spring on Salt river.

JULY 11. I visited Dixie.[64] Worden arrived from the states via Missouri river. Many emigrants arriving every day now. J. S.

JULY 12. With the emigrants today is a Mr. B. B. Burchett with his family, consisting of his wife, two very handsome daughters, one a blonde and the other a brunette, and two little tow-headed boys. It looks like home to see little blonde children playing about and to see white women. Miss Sallie Burchett is sixteen years old and a very beautiful girl. Every man in camp has shaved and changed his shirt since this family arrived. We are all trying to appear like civilized men.

JULY 13. Many emigrants arriving some going back to the states and some adventurous spirits are going to Salmon river, others to Walla Walla.

JULY 14. Clear, calm, and warm. This place here before known as American fork, has been re-christened

Pioneer creek, a small fork of Gold creek, without making more than a living, although some adjacent claims paid good wages.

"About this time quite a number of people arrived who had come up the Missouri river, intending to go to the mines at Florence and Oro Fino; but not liking the news from that region, when they arrived in Deer Lodge, a part of them went no farther, but scattered out and began to prospect, and most of them are still in Montana with a 'pocket full of rocks,' and stout and robust as grizzly bears, although some of them are suffering from a severe attack of an epidemic known as 'quartz on the brain,' which is now raging furiously all over Montana. It seldom proves fatal, however; the victim generally recovering after being bled freely in the pocket. The 'Pike's-peakers,' soon after their arrival, struck some good pay on a small branch of Gold creek, now known as 'Pike's Peak gulch.' The diggings of this region did not, as a general thing, pay very well that summer, and they have not been much worked or prospected since from the following cause." – ED.

[64] Dixie, a mining camp nearby. – ED.

Gold creek and so it is now called. We held an election today. Great excitement, but nobody was hurt except with an overdose of whiskey.[65]

JULY 17. Cool, with west wind. Woody and Worden arrived from Hell Gate. Fred Burr and Jack Mendenhall started for the old Mormon fort on Salmon river to get the things hid there by Jack and his party.

JULY 18. James Stuart played poker with Worden, Hamilton, and Woody and lost forty dollars. Powell has been above since yesterday morning.

JULY 20. Worden and Higgins's wagon arrived from Fort Benton loaded with merchandise for their store at Hell Gate. Our mining claims at Dixie are not paying expenses. The emigrants are still leaving for Salmon river mines and some are returning to the states.

JULY 22. John Grant's team arrived from Benton. Louthan and Hauser returned from their trip in Salmon river mountains. They started out for the Elk City mines, but as Salmon river flows for many miles

---

[65] This was the second election in what is now Montana, it being Missoula county, Washington territory. Polls were opened at Gold creek, Fort Owen, and Hell Gate. The following persons were elected: Representative to the Washington territorial legislature, L. L. Blake, with thirty votes; for county commissioners, Granville Stuart, and Thomas Harris, both with thirty votes. F. L. Worden, treasurer with thirty votes; for justice of the peace, Charles Allen, with thirty votes; for coroner, John W. Powell with twenty-nine votes. There were no party lines drawn in this election and only one ticket except that C. P. Higgins and L. L. Blake both ran for representative. Blake won, he receiving twenty-four votes and Higgins six. Names of those voting are as follows: John Franks, John J. Hall, J. W. Powell, James Conlin, Ed. Hibbard, Henry Thomas (Gold Tom) David Brown, John Carr, Louis Mat, Peter Martin, James Spence, Edwin Dikes, James Stuart, Thomas Adams, W. B. Higgins, James Minesinger, Thomas W. Hamilton, Granville Stuart, F. H. Burr, P. W. McAdow, and Major William Graham.

through an impassable box cañon, and there was no well defined trail over the mountains, and they had no guide, they became lost in the mountains.   After wandering about, suffering untold hardships and almost starving to death, they finally gave up and returned to Gold creek.

JULY 23.   Arrived at our town to-day a fine violin player accompanied by his handsome, seventeen year old wife.   His name is J. B. Caven.[66]   We purchased a good violin sometime ago, so we have the Cavens over often and enjoy the society of an intellectual white woman and good music.   Certainly we are approaching civilization or rather civilization is coming to us. All the men are shaving nowadays and most of them indulge in an occasional hair cut.   The blue flannel shirt with a black necktie has taken the place of the elaborately beaded buckskin one.   The white men wear shoes instead of moccasins and most of us have selected some other day than Sunday for wash day.

JULY 24.   There is plenty of whiskey in camp now and rows are of frequent occurrence.   To-day a drunken Salmon river chap became insulting to Worden who walked into him with a pick handle.   Captain Higgins took a hand at the finish or Worden would have been worsted in the fight.

JULY 25.   Very warm.   Whiskey business very dull. Tony Cosgrove and I started to Cottonwood for a horse thief.   J. S.

JULY 26.   Clear warm.   Stayed all night at Dave Contois'.   Started on the road to Benton after our man and overtook him at sundown.   Camped all night with him on a branch of little Prickly Pear creek.   J. S.

---

[66] J. B. Caven was sheriff of the Fairweather mining district for a few weeks in 1863, but resigned to be succeeded by Henry Plummer. – ED.

JULY 27. Very warm. Arrested our man at daylight and arrived home with him at sundown. J. S.

JULY 28. Cloudy and warm. We called a miners' meeting, tried him and found him guilty. In consideration of his age and contrition, his sentence was only to refund all of the stolen property that he had and to leave the country within twelve hours. As he was utterly destitute, the court, which embraced nearly all in the camp, gave him fifteen dollars and some provisions. He then departed from Hell Gate river toward Walla Walla and was seen no more.[67] J. S.

JULY 29. Worden and Higgins concluded to start a branch store in our village and leave a portion of their goods here and to-day I began helping them put up a log store. G. S.

JULY 31. Cool, and nearly calm. John M. Jacobs arrived from Soda springs with a train of forty wagons en route for Walla Walla. He reports many more behind. Some emigrants and Dempsey are on a spree to-day.

AUGUST 1, 1862. The grocery is doing a flourishing business. Several gambling houses started.

AUGUST 2. Monte tables going every day. The bank is ahead. We gave a company of emigrants permission to work our upper claims.

AUGUST 4. Many emigrants arriving from Pikes Peak. I bought two wagons and the harness with them for eighty dollars. The grocery is doing a fine business.

AUGUST 5. Dr. H. J. McKellops, dentist, pulled a tooth for me.

AUGUST 7. Worden and Higgins started for Benton after their goods. Captain Higgins went to Hell Gate.

---

[67] Hubert H. Bancroft, History of Montana (*Works*, vol. xxxi, San Francisco, 1890) p. 619, tells this story.

Powell arrived from prospecting and reports finding good prospects, east of the Rocky mountains on Boulder creek.

AUGUST 9. Louis Maillett started for Fort Benton. He left his blacksmith tools and other things with me. Powell has been on a big spree since he arrived here.

AUGUST 10. The little village is all astir today. There is a general stampede over the mountains to Powell's new discovery. Some are buying horses, some trading, everybody packing grub and mining tools, each one in a hurry to get out ahead of the rest.

AUGUST 15. Rezin Anderson arrived from the states (he having gone down the Missouri river from Fort Benton with Worden on the Fur Company's Mackinaw boat on March 25, 1861). We talked nearly all night and then could not relate all that had happened since we parted. He brought letters and news from home. It makes Granville and me homesick, although we enjoy getting all the news and meeting Reece again. We thought he had joined the army.

AUGUST 16. More emigrants arriving en route for Walla Walla. Rezin Anderson's train arrived here.

AUGUST 17. Powell sold his house to Terry's man and started to Deer Lodge valley with his family. Dempsey sold his ranch a few days ago and is now moving up to Deer Lodge valley.

AUGUST 19. Woody arrived from Hell Gate with a load of vegetables and thirteen chickens. He reports that there has been a good placer gold prospect found in Big Hole valley as much as two dollars and a half to pan of gravel.[68]

[68] These were the mines discovered by Mortimer H. Lott. G. S. For account of Lott and his discoveries see Thomas J. Dimsdale, *opus citra* (third edition) pp. 216-221. – ED.

AUGUST 20. Considerable excitement about the news that Woody brought about new placer discoveries.

AUGUST 21. Cloudy with a little rain. A number of persons are preparing to go to Big Hole valley to examine the reported new placer mines there. On the fourteenth inst., three men arrived at Gold creek from the lower country. They had six good horses, but very little in the shape of a traveling outfit. One of them, B. F. Jermagin, had no saddle on the horse he rode, but only some folded blankets strapped on the horse's back in lieu of a saddle. The other two men showed that they were on the gamble and one of them William Arnett, kept his belt and revolver on and rather posed as being a "bad man." The third, C. W. Spillman, was a rather quiet reserved pleasant young man, of about twenty-five years, he being the youngest of the three.

AUGUST 22. Woody, Burr, and several others started for Big Hole on a prospecting tour.

AUGUST 23. I have lost three hundred dollars staking a man to deal monte for me in the past three days. Think I will take Granville's advice and quit gambling. J. S.

AUGUST 24. Our monte sharps are about to take the town. Getting decidedly obstreperous in their conduct. J. S.

AUGUST 25. Our stranger monte sharps opened a two hundred dollar monte bank and I broke it in about twenty minutes. About four o'clock in the afternoon two men arrived here from Elk City in the Clearwater mountains.[69] They were in pursuit of our monte sharps for stealing the horses they rode from that place. One of the arrivals was armed with a double barreled shot

---

[69] The gold fields of Idaho.

gun heavily loaded with buckshot and a Colt's navy
revolver. Their names were Fox and Bull. Bull had
the gun. They slipped quietly into town in the dusk
of the evening and meeting me inquired if the three
men above described were there. Upon being informed
that they were, they stated that they were in pursuit
of them for stealing the horses on which they had come
from the vicinity of Elk City. They requested the
coöperation of the citizens in arresting them. I assured them that they should have all the assistance
necessary and went with them to look for their men.
They found Spillman in Worden and Company's store
and bringing their shot gun to bear on him, ordered
him to surrender, which he did without a word. They
left him under guard and went after the other two, who
had just opened a monte game in a saloon. Arnett was
dealing and Jermagin was "lookout" for him. They
stepped inside of the door and ordered them to "throw
up their hands." Arnett, who kept his Colt's navy revolver lying in his lap ready for business, instantly
grabbed it, but before he could raise it, Bull shot him
through the breast with a heavy charge of buckshot,
killing him instantly. Jermagin ran into a corner of
the room, exclaiming, "Don't shoot, don't shoot, I give
up." He and Spillman were then tied and placed
under guard till morning. J. S.

AUGUST 26. Proceedings commenced by burying
Arnett who had died with the monte cards clenched so
tightly in his left hand and his revolver in the right
that they could not be wrenched from his grasp, so were
buried with him. Jermagin plead that the other two
overtook him on the trail and gave him a horse to ride
and that he had no knowledge of the horses being
stolen, and what saved him, was Spillman saying that

he and Arnett had found him on the trail packing his blankets and a little food on his back and that they gave him a horse to ride on which he strapped his blankets. On this testimony Jermagin was acquitted and given six hours to leave the country and it is needless to say he left a little ahead of time. Spillman who was a large, fine looking man was found guilty and sentenced to be hung in a half hour. He made no defense and seemed to take little interest in the proceedings. When I asked him if he had any request to make he said he "would like to write a letter." He was furnished with writing material and wrote a letter to his father stating that he was to be hung in half an hour; that keeping bad company had brought him to it, begged his father's forgiveness for bringing disgrace upon his family and concluded by hoping that his fate would be a warning to all to avoid evil associates.

He wrote and addressed the letter with a hand that never trembled and when asked if there was anything else he wished to do said "No." Although the time was not up he said he was ready and walked to his death with a step as firm and countenance as unchanged as if he had been the nearest spectator instead of the principal actor in the tragedy. It was evident that he was not a hardened criminal and there was no reckless bravado in his calmness. It was the firmness of a brave man, who saw that death was inevitable, and nerved himself to meet it. He was hung at twenty-two minutes past two o'clock August 26, 1862. He was buried by the side of Arnett in the river bottom just below town.[70] J. S.

AUGUST 27. My birthday. I am twenty-eight years

---

[70] This was the first execution in what is now Montana and it caused

old. Weather very warm. Everything very quiet in town. Fox and Bull started back to Elk City with the six horses. No news from the states. The grocery is doing a very poor business. Michel Ogden, Major Graham,[71] and a stranger arrived from Hell Gate. G. S.

AUGUST 29. I won fifteen dollars bucking at monte, last night and forty dollars to-day playing poker with Louthan, Parker, and Pete Martin. J. S.

AUGUST 30. Very warm. Dull times in town. Burr and party returned from Big Hole, did not find anything that would pay to work. J. S.

AUGUST 31. Granville quit mining and moved down here. Rezin Anderson hauled some coal and is now ready to go to work blacksmithing. J. S.

SEPTEMBER 5, 1862. Jim Brown had an extra gun and some clothing that he wished to dispose of for a good price and decided to raffle them. As almost ev-

the little town of Gold creek to be put down as "Hangtown," on some of the western maps for some years after. It was never known by that name in this vicinity.

Justice was swift and sure in those days. There was no moving for a new trial or any of the thousand other clogs upon the wheels of justice, which but too often render the execution of the law a mockery. It may be claimed that the punishment was severe beyond all proportion to the crime, but it must be remembered that there was no recognized court in the country and the nearest jail was at Walla Walla, four hundred and twenty-five miles distant, over rugged mountains. The communities were too small and too poor to indulge in costly criminal prosecutions and hence it was advisable to inflict such punishment as would strike terror to the minds of the evil doers, and exercise a restraining influence over them. I have always regretted that Spillman did not plead for his life, because if he had, I think he could have made such a good showing that the death penalty would have been commuted to banishment. I now think that he was so stunned by the fearful calamity that had overtaken him, that despair seized him and he thought it useless to try to escape death. As to the letter he wrote I have an indistinct impression that Brother James destroyed it for, of course, we would not send such a letter to anyone's father.

[71] Michael Ogden was in charge of Fort Connah. Major Graham was a guest of Major John Owen. – ED.

erybody is on the gamble it did not take long to gather a crowd. The raffle was held in the saloon and the contestants threw dice at one dollar a throw. Clark won the gun, Burr the clothing, and Worden the gum boots, which were the first ever seen here. J. S.

SEPTEMBER 9. Cool and windy. Played poker and won a little. J. S.

SEPTEMBER 10. Granville and Woody started to Hell Gate to try and organize our county government, Granville having been elected county commissioner at our election last July, and Frank Woody having been elected auditor. I gave bonds and took the oath of office, having been elected sheriff of Missoula county, Washington Territory. J. S.

SEPTEMBER 12. Powell came down on a visit. We had a social game of poker. Fred Burr won some little. J. S.

SEPTEMBER 13. Cold and cloudy. Powell and I went up to some new placer mines on the head of Pioneer creek. Saw some men take out one piece that would weigh one dollar or more. They are working with rockers. Sunday went with a party of comrades to Blackfoot. As there are no churches around here to attend and not even a Sunday school, we passed the time playing poker. Funny how often our little testament gets lost, but we can always dig up a deck of cards any place or anywhere. I lost twenty-three dollars. J. S.

SEPTEMBER 14. Balanced accounts with Worden and Co. Are four hundred and fifty dollars in debt. J. S.

SEPTEMBER 18. Woody and Granville arrived from Hell Gate accompanied by two lower country-men.

We played poker last night. Worden was winner.
I lost twenty-two dollars. J. S.[72]

SEPTEMBER 20. Played poker, lost eighteen dollars.
Granville and Reece Anderson mended Plummer's
double barreled shot gun, which he had broken off at
the grip, coming through the timber from Elk City.
Reece forged four strips of iron about five-eighths in.
wide and three and one-half in. long and Granville set
them into the gunstock on top and bottom of the grip,
and screwed them down solid so that the gun stock was
stronger than before it was broken. J. S.

SEPTEMBER 21. Woody and York started to the gold
placer mines near Beaverhead. Plummer and Reeves
went with them. I played poker and won one hundred
fifty-two dollars. Ed. and Freeman House were the
victims. Granville found the out crop of coal in Pikes
Peak gulch. J. S.

SEPTEMBER 22. Mrs. Burchett and family dined
with us and will remain here with us while Mr. Burchett, Ed. and Freeman House go over to look at the
Beaverhead mines.

SEPTEMBER 25. James went to Dempsey's. Bob
Nelson and I begun hauling hay. Bought Charlie
Allen's colt. Mailette, John Grant, Thos. Pamburm
stayed all night en route from Hell Gate. Minesinger

---

[72] On our way to Hell Gate at Beaver Dam hill we met two fine looking
young men. One of them said his name was Henry Plummer, the other
was Charles Reeves. Woody and I told them who we were. They were
from Elk City on Clearwater, and enquired about the mines at Gold creek
and at Beaverhead. They rode two good horses and had another packed
with their blankets and provisions. We liked their looks and told them that
we were only going down to Hell Gate and would return to Gold creek
in a few days and asked them to return to Hell Gate with us and then we
could all go up the cañon together. They accepted our invitation and in a
few days we all went up to Gold creek together. These men proved to be
notorious road agents and were hanged later.

and Jimmy busy hauling logs for Woody and Stuart's grocery. Burr went hunting. The boys up at the head of Pioneer creek making good wages working with rockers. Reece and I have made fifty-eight dollars in the shop in the past few days. G. S.

SEPTEMBER 26. Rained slowly most of the day. Mountains white with snow. Captain James Fisk,[73] who lately arrived with a large emigrant train that he brought across the plains from St. Paul, Minnesota, and a small party passed and camped just below here. He is inspecting Captain John Mullan's military wagon road from Fort Benton to Walla Walla. He has a brass mountain howitzer with him. Fred Burr killed four black-tail deer this evening. Reece and I did eleven dollars worth of work in the blacksmith shop.

SEPTEMBER 27. Raw and cold. James returned from above. Bob Nelson hauled a load of charcoal. Reece and I did twenty-two dollars worth of work in the shop.

SEPTEMBER 28. Sunday. Decidedly cold, I dined with Captain Fisk and had a splendid dinner. He was considerably "high" in the evening. The boys had lots of fun with him. Sullivan and P. C. Wood tried to get up a party to take the Captain's howitzer, but they failed. Jack Mendenhall started for Salt Lake.

SEPTEMBER 29. Captain Fisk started below. Several parties quite drunk. Reece and Granville busy in the shop. P. C. Woods and "Buzz" Caven moved here from Little Blackfoot. We are glad to have Caven for we will enjoy some good music and like to

---

[73] This was the first of Fisk's expeditions to Montana. Fisk's *Journals* are in the library of the Minnesota Historical Society. Bancroft, *Montana*, pp. 622, 634-637, describes briefly the expeditions. – ED.

have his white wife about. We have had no white women in camp since Mrs. Burchett and family went to Beaverhead mines. J. S.

SEPTEMBER 30. Woody returned from Beaverhead mines. He reports that nearly everybody is making money over there. Everybody excited.

OCTOBER 5, 1862. York and Irvine came from Beaverhead mines yesterday. They report two hundred Pah-Ute Indians over there when they left, under the old chief Winnemucca and as these Indians are an insolent treacherous band it is feared that they will make trouble so a party of us are going to start over there to help if it becomes necessary.

OCTOBER 22. We went to the Beaverhead mines, so called although they are not on that stream at all, but on a small creek that comes into the Beaverhead from the west a little below the junction of it and Red Rock creek.[74] We had fine weather during the ten days that

---

[74] These were the Bannack mines on Grasshopper or Willard creek discovered by John White in July, 1862. He was one of the Pike's peakers whom Stuart described in 1864 as follows: "Many of the 'Pike's peakers' became rather lost and bewildered in their attempts to reach Deer Lodge and were scattered all about through the mountains; this, though a source of infinite vexation to them at the time, proved of great ultimate benefit to the country, for one small party of them discovered some gulch mines at the head of Big Hole prairie that paid tolerable well during the summer of 1862, but they seem to have been exhausted, as they have not been worked since that time. I have been told by men who worked there, that they worked across a vein of good coal thirty feet wide in the bed of the gulch, and that they put some of it on the fire and it burned brilliantly. If this is the case, this locality will become valuable in a short time.

Another party happening to camp on Willard's creek, began to prospect and found very rich diggings, where a great many men made fortunes during that summer and winter. This attracted almost every man in the country to the spot, and the mines at Gold creek were deserted for the richer ones at "Bannack City," as a small town that had sprung up at the head of the cañon of Willard's creek was called, and have virtually remained so ever since, for about the time that the Bannack mines began to decline a little and people began to think of branching out again, a party of six who had

we were gone. We found everybody making money
and well satisfied. There are about four hundred men
there. We have decided to move over. Woody remained to look after things, until I can get back with a
load of goods. We hired Butler to build us a log
building twenty feet square for which we are to pay
$140.00. There was no Indian trouble. The Pah-
Utes have gone over to the Yellowstone to hunt buffalo
and there were only a few Digger Indians there when
we arrived. They are always very peaceable. Hired
William Babcock to haul about a ton of freight over
for us.

OCTOBER 23. Hugh Bratton, an old friend of ours
from California, arrived yesterday.

OCTOBER 25. Below zero. A severe change in the
weather. James, Hugh Bratton, Bob Nelson, and
James Collins started for the Beaverhead mines with
the "Old Steamboat" wagon full of goods. Lots of
Flathead Indians in town to-day. Snow twelve inches
deep – awful!

OCTOBER 27. Gathered up all of our cattle, and
Reece and I did some work in the shop for Indians.

started to the Yellowstone country, on a prospecting tour, and had been
driven back by the Crow Indians, who robbed them of nearly everything
they had, camped, as they were returning, on a small branch of Stinkingwater river, afterwards called Alder creek, because of the heavy growth
of that wood along it, not a single tree of which is now to be seen, the
wants of the miners having used them up long ago, and the banks and
bed of the stream are dug up and piled about in a most extraordinary
manner, considering the short time that has elapsed since its discovery.
But to return to the discoveries. They camped on the creek about half a
mile above where the city of Virginia now stands, and on washing a few
pans of dirt they "struck it big," getting as high as four dollars to the pan.
They staked off their claims and went to Bannack City to get a supply of
provisions, and to tell their friends to return with them and take claims,
which they did. The creek proved almost fabulously rich. Thousands of
men having made fortunes in it, and still it is not half worked out. *Montana As It is*, pp. 9, 10.

They did not move to-day. The town women folks are doing a big business trading for dried service berries, camas, bitter root, etc. I bought a hair rope for one dollar.

OCTOBER 28. Indian village moved to-day. Everybody trading for Indian horses. Reece busy in blacksmith shop. Thomas Adams captured his little boy from the Indians. The boy's mother left Adams; going back to her tribe and Adams had not seen the child before, but when he found him with the village he took him. The little fellow cannot speak English and is weeping bitterly for his Indian relatives.

OCTOBER 29. Daubed part of the walls of our house with mud mortar. Kiplinger and Knuckols arrived from Beaverhead mines and said everybody is taking out big wages in placer gold.

OCTOBER 30. Adams's little boy wept all night and we persuaded him to let the child join his Indian mother. He has finally consented and handed the boy over to a couple of Flatheads, who will join the village tomorrow. The child is once more happy. Sold Kiplinger eight head of cows for beef at $60.00 a head. He paid me $164.50 and is to pay the balance, $315.50 when he returns from the mines. I paid Worden and Co. $280.00 in clean gold dust at $16.00 per oz.

NOVEMBER 1, 1862. Reece and I went up to Pioneer creek and hauled down the rest of the charcoal and sixteen sluice boxes as we need the lumber.

NOVEMBER 3. Worden and Peter Martin started to Beaverhead mines.

NOVEMBER 4. Sold Worden and Co. 54 lb. of tea @ $2.00, $108. Got the sorrel stallion "Brooks" back.

NOVEMBER 5. I made one bunk to sleep in. Our puncheon floor was rather solid, while a bunk built against the wall and filled with hay is so restful that we hate to get up of mornings. Reece, while hunting our horses, saw an Indian driving off one of Jack Gunn's oxen late this evening.

NOVEMBER 6. Reece, Burr, Purple, Bill Fairweather,[75] and I went after the Indians that took Gunn's ox and overtook them in Hell Gate cañon, twenty miles below here. We found the ox in their possession and they said they had traded for him with a white man at Charlie Allen's place. We brought him back with us to have him point out to us the man that traded with him. It was dark before we reached home. I think he is lying about any white man having traded that ox.

NOVEMBER 7. Burr had the Indian locked up in his one room log house last night, but he concluded that he did not want to help us hunt up the white man that he traded with for the ox, so in the night he let himself out and fled leaving his pishamore, a buffalo skin rug used under his saddle, horse leggins, and knife behind him. A southern gentleman, named Captain Simms, who had sojourned in our little town since he lodged here sometime last summer, and who was usually engaged in reducing the visible supply of whiskey around town, which he always paid for, however, took possession of the Indian's horse and contemplated keeping him.

NOVEMBER 8. A brilliant day. I felt the *dolce far niente* common name "laziness," pretty strong, but I struggled valiantly against it and succeeded in building another bunk and then went after our cattle to Flint creek, but did not find them. Reece worked in the shop. A crowd of women and men left here for Cottonwood to attend a ball given by Thomas Lavatta's

---

[75] Bill Fairweather later discovered Alder gulch. – ED.

folks. Everybody in town nearly sick. Cause, tight houses.

Two Coeur d'Alene Indians passed intending to overtake the Flathead village beyond the mountains somewhere. I gave them something to eat and sent them on their way rejoicing.

SUNDAY 9. All the Indian women went up to Johnny Grant's today. Maillett and Tom Lavatta came down and stayed awhile.

NOVEMBER 10. Sent three men from Pikes Peak gulch down into the cañon below the mouth of Flint creek to prospect for gold. It looks like the famous Beaverhead diggings down there. I think rich placers will be found in that vicinity.[76]

NOVEMBER 11. Worden and Pete Martin got back from Beaverhead mines. Brother James and the ox team will stay at Cottonwood tonight. Blake and Higgins had their horses stolen at the spring six miles this side of Beaverhead. Supposed that Snake Indians took them. I sent two yoke of oxen to meet Jim Minesinger in the cañon. He is coming with a wagon load of goods and but one yoke of oxen. They have entirely played out.

NOVEMBER 14. Had a big dance in Minesinger's house tonight.

NOVEMBER 15. Major John Owens, Major William Graham, and C. C. O'Keefe arrived from Fort Benton.

---

[76] The Pike's Peak men did not find the placers, nor was I one of the discoverers, but four years later, in 1866, my predictions were verified by the discovery of the very rich mines of Bear gulch.

Bannack and Pike's Peak

NOVEMBER 18, 1862. I have concluded to go to the Beaverhead mines with James and open a butcher shop during the winter. Woody will run the grocery outfit.

NOVEMBER 19. Started for the mines with the ox teams loaded with goods and supplies of all kinds. James and I rode horseback and Bratton drove the wagon. Reece Anderson will remain in charge of the property left at the little town of American Fork.

NOVEMBER 22. We arrived at the mines and at once moved into our log cabin. The village is now called Bannack. We have fixed up our cabin quite cozy and home like. There is a fire place in one corner, two bunks against the wall, a couple of shelves and a calico curtain does service for a cupboard, another shelf holds our five books and James's tobacco pouch and pipe. The table and some stools complete the outfit.

NOVEMBER 23. The building which we contracted for the butcher shop is also finished and we will begin business at once. Most of Fisk's train is located here and quite a number of others among them, Henry Plummer, Charlie Reeves, Louis Cossette, the Burchett family, and "Buz" Caven, and his charming wife.

A number of the men of the Fisk train who had wagons and mules or oxen turned their attention to freighting, going to Salt Lake and returning with supplies. There was so little snow on the divides that these freighters crossed all winter without difficulty. This was most fortunate for there were so many people in the country and no supplies whatever that had the winter been severe with deep snow many must have perished from starvation. It would have been utterly impossible to have furnished game for so many people.

The Bannack mines were very easily worked; being mostly bars of gold bearing gravel on the banks of the creek, lying at from ten to twelve feet above the water in the stream. At the edge of these bars there was but a thin layer of rich gravel on the underlying limestone bed rock and I, several times saw the miners pull up the small sagebrush that grew on the edge of the bars and shaking off the sand and fine gravel, that adhered to the roots, into a pan which they carried to the creek and obtained from twenty-five cents to one dollar to the pan, in small pieces of beautiful gold. This caused the saying at Bannack that "we could pan gold out of the sagebrush."

Bannack City, during this winter gradually drew to itself the greater part of the people then scattered over the region round about, and by spring, mining was assuming large proportions. Many gamblers and desperate characters drifted in, lured by the prospect of acquiring gold dust without digging for it. It became the custom to go armed all the time.

The miners of Bannack met and established a miners' court. B. B. Burchett was elected judge and Henry Crawford, sheriff. A mining claim was one hundred feet up or down the creek and as far out on each side as the pay dirt extended, they were numbered 1, 2, etc., above or below discovery as the case might be. Title to a claim was established by staking it and posting a notice and then taking it to the recorder and having it recorded. The claimant was then obliged to work his claim every day when water was available. An absence of three days constituted a forfeiture and the claim could then be jumped. In case of sickness the claim was protected until such time as the owner was able to resume work. The laws laid down by a miners' court were very simple and absolutely just. There was no appeal from the court's decision. These early day miners were men of unquestionable honesty and integrity and there was little disposition to infringe upon the rights of others, consequently the law was followed to the letter. Neither James nor I did any mining at Bannack.

There were two good fiddlers in camp, "Buz" Caven and Lou P. Smith, and something over thirty white women. Seven were unmarried, but did not remain so very long. We had a number of fine balls attended by all the respectable people and enjoyed by young and old alike. Best suits packed in the bottom of our "war bags" and long forgotten, were dragged out, aired and pressed, as best we could, and made ready for these festive occasions. A very few of the men who had their wives with them, sported white shirts with stiffly starched bosoms, but the majority wore flannel shirts with soft collars and neckties. These dances were very orderly; no man that was drinking was allowed in the hall. The young people danced the waltz, schottish, varsoviane, and polka, but the older ones stuck to the Virginia-reel and quadrille. There were usually about ten men to every woman at these balls so the women danced every dance. These gatherings were very informal and very enjoyable. Tickets were $5.oo gold and there was no supper served.

"Buz" Caven possessed considerable dramatic talent

and he and his wife gave several entertainments consisting of songs, dancing, and recitations. So passed the winter of 1862 at Bannack City, Dakota territory.

About the fifteenth of March, 1863, I made a trip to Gold creek to get a load of goods from Worden and Company's store. In this load were two dozen long-handled shovels, which I sold quickly at Bannack for ten dollars each. I also had fifteen pounds of chewing tobacco for which I received fifteen dollars a pound. I was certainly glad that I did not use tobacco.

On April 10, 1863, James Stuart, with a party of fifteen started for the Yellowstone valley to prospect for gold.[77]

After selling my goods I closed up the business at Bannack; selling everything but two town lots and two houses. I had collected all together about three thousand dollars and on April 24, started for Gold creek with that gold dust in my cantinas at my saddle bow.

I had a distinct recollection of the fate of Charlie Guy and George Edwards,[78] and that their murderers

---

[77] James Stuart was in command of this expedition. His Journal of the Yellowstone Expedition of 1863, is published in the *Montana Historical Society Contributions*. (Helena, Mont., 1876) vol. i, pp. 132-205. – ED.

[78] The rich "diggings" of Grasshopper creek attracted many undesirable characters and I believe there were more desperadoes and lawless characters in Bannack the winter of 1862-3 than ever infested any other mining camp of its size. Murders, robberies, and shooting scrapes were of frequent occurrence.

In November, 1862, Charles Guy, who had some money and a good team of horses and a wagon, started to Salt Lake for supplies and was found murdered and robbed, and his horses gone, on Red Rock creek. No trace was ever found of his murderers, but it was supposed afterwards that some of those later known as "road agents," had followed and murdered him. He had no relatives at the mines.

The second murder this winter was perpetrated in January, 1863. A young man named George Edwards went to look for some horses that were on the range and failed to return. After a few days his friends became were still in town, so I was very careful not to let any one know that I had the money or that I intended leaving town. I had my horse brought into town the evening before so that I could get an early start next morning. I arose very early, ate a hurried breakfast, and left town just at sunrise. I saw nobody stirring and passing along a back street took the road to Deer Lodge valley. I was armed with my short breech-loading rifle, with plenty of cartridges and I knew that there was not another breech-loader in town, and in my belt I carried a tried and true Colt's navy revolver and handled both as quickly as any of the robbers.

I had just begun to congratulate myself on getting away without being seen, when I heard horses coming behind me and knew that I was being pursued. In a few minutes three men on horseback came in sight around a bend in the road. They were Charlie Reeves, William Graves [79] and a man whom I did not know,

---

anxious and went to look for him. Some snow had fallen and they were unable to find his tracks on the range, but quite by accident found his blood-stained clothing stuffed into a badger hole, but the body was never found.

Edwards had several hundred dollars on his person when he left town and this must have become known to some of the bad characters that infested Bannack that winter. The murderers stripped the body for two reasons, first to make sure that they had all the money and second to hide the clothes to prevent identification of the body if found. Edwards had no relatives in the country and I do not think any effort was made to find the body after the snow melted in the spring.

His murderers were never apprehended. I have always suspected that Charlie Reeves and William Graves (Whiskey Bill) committed this murder. At this time there was no law or courts, save the miner's court and no steps were taken to do more than to regulate affairs relating strictly to mining matters. Every man was expected to take care of himself. G. S. Stuart's manuscript contains a chapter on "Undesirable Citizens" that closely parallels the account in Langford, *opus citra* and is omitted. – ED.

[79] Reeves was banished in 1863 but later returned. He later fled when the vigilantes became active. Graves, alias, Whiskey Bill was hanged by the vigilantes at Fort Owen January 26, 1864. Dimsdale, *opus citra*, p. 22. – ED.

but I did know that Reeves and Graves were tough characters.

The road followed up a ravine to the top of the mountain about a mile. I did not think they would attack me so near town, but determined to give them no chance and when they drew near I dismounted and pretended to be cinching my saddle, being careful to keep my horse between me and them. I did not take my eyes off them; intending if they made a move toward their revolvers to shoot with my rifle, which was hung on a shoulder strap and ready for action. They saw that I was watching them and that my rifle was conveniently near. As they rode up Reeves called to me asking where I was going and volunteered the information that they were going to Deer Lodge and rode on. Just at this minute to my dismay I saw another horseman coming up the ravine. I thought I might possibly stand off three, but it would be about impossible to escape from four. I remained by the side of my horse and when the horseman drew near, you may imagine my relief when I discovered him to be my friend, Edwin R. Purple, and that he too was armed with a navy revolver.

As soon as he came up to me I explained the situation to him and we decided to travel together to Deer Lodge. We knew that our safety depended upon our not allowing them to get behind us. It was not long before we overtook them and several times during the day they halted ostensibly to tighten their saddle cinches. We both immediately did the same, always stopping behind them. They were very anxious to do the agreeable, but we kept close together and always a short distance in the rear.

It was sundown when we reached Divide creek,

where it issues from the mountains near the summit of Deer Lodge pass. Here Purple and I decided to camp for the night hoping the others would go on, but they too decided to camp. We allowed them to select their camp first and then we chose ours a spot about fifty yards below them on the little stream. We ate our lunch and then sat down by our camp fire in a position where we could watch their camp. Purple smoked his pipe and then spreading down our saddle blankets for a bed and our saddles for pillows we lay down. We agreed to keep watch all night. I took the first watch for two hours. Our neighbors also retired, but I had no desire to sleep with those three men only fifty yards away; I was only anxious that they remain just where they were.

The night seemed very long, but we all arose at sunrise and eating our breakfast resumed our journey. All morning our unwelcome companions tried to get behind us, but this we prevented by stopping every time they did. When we passed Warm springs they spurred their horses into a gallop and left us, reaching Deer Lodge an hour ahead of us. We spent the night at Deer Lodge and went on down to Gold creek next day, but our three companions remained in Deer Lodge.

These were dark days in Bannack; there was no safety for life or property only so far as each individual could, with his trusty rifle, protect his own. The respectable citizens far outnumbered the desperadoes, but having come from all corners of the earth, they were unacquainted and did not know whom to trust. On the other hand the "Roughs" were organized and under the able leadership of that accomplished villain, Henry Plummer. At times it would seem that they had the upper hand and would run affairs to suit them-

selves. The law abiding citizens were beginning to get
better acquainted and although the few attempts made
to administer justice had failed they believed that the
time would come and that at no distant day, when the
community would rid themselves of this undesirable
element.

During my brother James's absence I decided to
remain at Gold creek, as I was anxious to do some
prospecting down the river, at a place some fifteen
miles below the mouth of Flint creek.   Reece Anderson had remained at Gold creek to look after the cattle
and blacksmith shop while we were in Bannack.

APRIL 17, 1863.   Killed a young steer for beef and
hauled a load of wood.   Four Flatheads came along
on foot followed by three on horseback.   They said
they had had nothing to eat for several days and from
the way they made beef disappear, I am inclined to
believe them.   They say the Flathead village will be
here in four days.

APRIL 18.   Hauled all the lumber we had down out
of the mountain; gathered up our cattle.   I brought in
two milch cows, determined to have some milk and
butter.   Decided to enlarge our house and am putting
in spare time on that.

APRIL 19.   Traded four gallon of pure spirits to J.
M. Morgan for a good new horse.   This would seem
to be a rather high price for spirits, but Morgan will
add a few pounds of plug tobacco, a quantity of cayenne
pepper, some mountain sage tea, and rain water enough
to fill a barrel.   This will enable him to start in the
whiskey trade in first class shape.

APRIL 20.   Hugh Bratton and I went "gold hunting" down the river to about fifteen miles below the
mouth of Flint creek, where there is a belt of rotten

limestone resembling that around Bannack. We prospected all around there, but could hardly find a "color" of gold so returned.[80]

MAY 5, 1863. Two pack trains arrived from Walla Walla. Bought from them the following:

52	lbs.	Tobacco	@	$4.00	$208.00
168	lbs.	Bacon	@	.40	67.20
241	lbs.	Sugar	@	.60	144.60
17½	lbs.	Soap	@	.50	8.75

$428.55

The pack trains brought us our mail, some letters from the states and some San Francisco papers sent to us from Hell Gate by Worden.

The letters from Iowa came by way of the Isthmus of Panama to San Francisco, then to Portland and the Dalles, and then overland to Walla Walla, and on by Frush and Sherwood's Express to Hell Gate, then up here by any reliable person coming this way. We pay $1.00 express on each letter received and 75c on each sent out, but letters from home are welcome at that price.

MAY 9. Worden and Company's teams stopped over night with us. They are on the way to Fort Benton after goods which are being brought up the Missouri river by steamboat. There is a good deal of travel past here now and Anderson and I are kept busy in the blacksmith shop shoeing horses, mending wagons, and repairing fire arms. Took in $62.30 today.

MAY 15. Maillette, Pattee, Eaton, and Peou, left

[80] We were on the right track even if we were not lucky enough to make a discovery. Three years later the rich Bear gulch diggings was discovered near where we prospected.

for Cottonwood en route to Fort Benton. Reece Anderson and I hauled wood for a coal pit and while he set up the pit, I tried to fix the meat-house so it would be fly proof. We have been much annoyed by these pests and suffered no small loss by their blowing meat for us. Higgins left a fine black dog skin overcoat hanging in our cabin and when he came for it some weeks later it was white all over with fly blows and they could not be brushed off, but had to remain until the sun came out warm enough to hatch the darned things. This was quite awhile and at a time when Higgins needed his coat. These flies have the ingenuity of the Devil and up to the present time we have been unable to keep them out of the meat-house. We have carefully tacked mosquito netting over our windows and closed every crack, yet they keep getting in. Sunday I took a day off to watch for them and to try to discover how they got in and to my surprise I saw them poke their front feet into the mesh of the mosquito netting and pull it apart enough to get their heads through and then by wiggling and squirming they got the rest of their body in and the hole would close behind them. They seem to have eternal life, for as cold weather sets in they crawl behind loose bark on dead trees or any crack or crevice that will afford a hiding place and then freeze solid. As soon as a Chinook wind comes and it begins to thaw a little, out they come, lively as ever and begin their work. They will repeat this performance as often as thaws come, and freeze again every time it freezes.

MAY 20. James Grant arrived from Hell Gate and reports many men on their way here from "below." We bought four fine Hudson's Bay shirts from him @

$3.00 each.[81]   These shirts are far ahead of our American things called "hickory."

MAY 21. Rainy and cold. We opened our coal pit and had about twenty bushels of charcoal. Eight men arrived from Clearwater this morning. They are going to stop and prospect up the creek for awhile. These new arrivals got up a shooting match. We have heard nothing but what fine shots they were and how one of them was "barred out" at a shooting match "below" because he won so many chickens. We think we are "some shots" here so it didn't require much hunting to get up a team. We set up a board five feet long and eight inches wide at one hundred yards distance. We did not do any remarkable shooting, but managed to rake in most of their loose coin. Only one in their party hit the board at all. I suppose the change of climate affected their marksmanship.

MAY 22. A man, by the name of Townsend, has been busy making a lot of saddles, which he intends to take to Benton to sell to emigrants coming up on the steamboats. We made a lot of rings for him.

Fourteen Pend d'Oreille Indians came along well mounted. They said they were going to steal horses from the Crows. They unsaddled and showed a disposition to stay all day and night too, but we were not very cordial, and they left in the afternoon. I burned three warts off my left hand with nitric acid.

MAY 23. Worked in the blacksmith shop and caught cold in my hand where I burned the warts off. My hand and arm are much swollen and very painful. I could not sleep last night for the pain. Worden and Company's store has a bottle labeled, "Merchants

---

[81] Grant was a trader for the Hudson's Bay Company. – ED.

Gargling Oil, a liniment good for man and beast," and this morning I went for it and wrapping my hand in several folds of cotton cloth kept them soaked in it. It felt better and toward evening the pain is less severe. My whole arm is badly swollen and inflamed.

One of the priests passed going to St. Ignatius Mission.[82]

MAY 25. Word came that two Pend d'Oreille Indians had killed a white man in Hell Gate cañon, somewhere near the Beaver Dam hill, and had taken his horses and pack and joined the Flatheads. A party of men left here to go after the Indian and punish him. Reece Anderson joined the party, but my hand was in such bad shape that I could not go.

MAY 26. The priests' wagon from St. Peters Mission[83] passed here today taking a sick man to St. Ignatius. A very remarkable looking man was driving two yoke of oxen to this wagon. His mouth was all on one side and looked as though it had been broken into three pieces and badly put together. His eyes did not match and looked in all directions; one could not tell whether he was looking at you or away from you. I cannot think where he came from, but the Fathers do pick up some queer specimens of humanity. I sent some letters by him to Hell Gate to be mailed; also all the tin pans in Worden and Company's store to Captain Higgins, who wanted them.

---

[82] St. Ignatius Mission was first established on Lake Pend' Oreille in 1844 by Father De Smet. In 1854 a new location was selected by Father Adrian Hoeken south of Flathead lake and west of the Mission mountains where the mission remains today. Chittenden and Richardson, *opus citra*, vol. ii, p. 474, vol. iv, p. 1234. – ED.

[83] St. Peters Mission was founded in February, 1863, by Fathers Giorda and Imoda for work among the Blackfeet Indians. It was located on the Missouri not far from the mouth of the Sun river. Lawrence B. Palladino s. j., *Indian and White in the Northwest* (Lancaster, Pennsylvania, 1922) p. 194.

St. Ignatius Mission, 1866

St. Ignatius was, and still remains, the center of Jesuit missionary work with the Indians of western Montana From an original drawing by Peter Tofft. Tofft was an artist of real ability and made a number of excellent drawings of early Montana

A man from Prickly Pear stopped with us over night.
He reports about fifteen men getting ready to mine
there; bringing in a ditch about a mile and a half long.
They get small prospects for eighteen feet down and
then come to a strata of gravel (thickness as yet unknown) that prospects forty-five cents to the pan of
dirt.[84]   I churned about three pounds of good butter
this evening.   My hand is improving, thanks to the
Gargling Oil.   The priest thought I had blood poison
and had it not been for the oil I suppose I would be
dead now.

MAY 27.   Van Court, the man from Prickly Pear
mines, left for home.   Charles Frush and G. J. Sherwood arrived and took dinner, then went on to Fort
Benton.   They brought states [papers] dates to April
18th.   From the war news it would seem the South
is getting rather the best of it.

Our mail to Hell Gate has fizzled out; as it would
not pay to carry it for so great a distance.   Louis Mullan, a brother of the Lieutenant, had the contract and
lost money on it.

MAY 28.   Baptiste Quesnell came down from Cottonwood (La Barge City now).   La Barge, a trader
from St. Louis, promised to build a store and put in a
stock of goods; hence the change of name.   Charlie
Allen came from Bannack and reported that old Johnson had been killed up near Bird Tail rock by four men
and robbed of eight hundred dollars.

MAY 30.   The men returned from Hell Gate.   They
went to the Flatheads and demanded the surrender of
the Indian, who had murdered the white.   At first the
chief refused to give him up saying, that the culprit

---

[84] In this neighborhood was discovered Last Chance Gulch the next
year. – ED.

was not of his tribe, but as he was with them the whites insisted that he be given up and after some parley he was brought forward and turnéd over to them. As there was no question as to his guilt he was sentenced to death and hung at Hell Gate.

MAY 31. The Flathead village arrived here today. The chief rode out into a spot that suited him and dismounting stuck his spear into the ground and sat down beside it. The squaws came up, unsaddled his horse and led it away, while others undid their packs and set up the lodge over his head. Some style about that fellow! These Indians are on the way to hunt buffalo bulls. At this time of year the cows are calving and the bulls go in herds by themselves and are very fat and fine eating. They do not hunt the cows or disturb them, if they can help it, but leave them and the calves until fall when they are fat and the robes fine.

Captain Felix Burton and another man arrived from Three Forks of the Missouri, where is a small settlement called Gallatin City, and took dinner with us. Six Pend d'Oreille Indians came along going on a war party after the Snakes. One of them had a paper from the priest, stating who he was and where he was going and requesting that no one molest him. We told him "all right, but do not get too near any of our horses." I start to Bannack with my wife tomorrow to try and finish collecting some outstanding debts. We go on horseback, a nice little ride of one hundred and ten miles.

JULY 3, 1863. Left our ranch on Gold creek on May 31 and returned today. When we reached the top of the mountain about a mile from Bannack we met a big stampede from town. I inquired what it was all about and learned that six men had come into town a couple of days before to get some provisions, and under promise of strict secrecy had told a few of their friends that they had found a rich gulch and would take them to it. Of course enough leaked out to create a great excitement, and everybody got ready to follow. So here they were, about seventy men. I asked who made the discoveries and they replied, "We only know one of them and his name is Bill Fairweather, and he and the other discoverers are all in front of the crowd." They were strung out for a quarter of a mile, some were on foot carrying a blanket and a few pounds of food on their backs, others were leading pack horses, others horseback leading pack animals. The packs had been hurriedly placed and some had come loose and the frightened animals running about with blankets flying and pots and pans rattling, had frightened others and the hillside was strewn with camp outfits and grub. My wife and I assisted some to round up their animals and collect and re-adjust the packs; soon they were all on their way again hurrying and scurrying lest they get left behind.[85]

This party (Bill Fairweather's) had intended to join James Stuart's Yellowstone expedition but were detained by not having horses. They went to La Barge City to intercept a Flathead village and purchase horses. After securing the horses they started for the mouth of the Stinkingwater, where they expected to join the Stuart party, but found they were too late and

[85] This stampede was on its way to the famous Alder gulch. The discovery was made by Bill Fairweather, Henry Edgar, Bill Sweeny, Tom Cover, Henry Rogers, and Bainey Hughes. G. S. Another account by one of the party of this expedition is the Journal of Henry Edgar, 1863, in *Montana Historical Society Contributions*, vol. iii (Helena, Montana, 1900) pp. 124-142. In the same volume pp. 143-153 is another account of the discovery of Alder gulch by Peter Ronan, who came into Alder gulch with the first rush. – ED.

that the main party had passed. Taking the trail, they followed on expecting to overtake them. Before they did so they were captured by a large band of Crow Indians and led prisoners to the Crow village.[86]

I remained in Bannack all of June and collected about three hundred dollars and rented the store building to a baker, for forty dollars a month, rent in advance. Bannack was almost deserted on account of the new diggings on Stinkingwater. James, my wife and I, returned to our home at Gold creek; found our old California friend, Hugh Bratton, living with Anderson and laid up with a sprained back and hip. Everybody, but two Frenchmen, have abandoned Pioneer gulch and moved over to Pikes Peak gulch, where they have found good placer diggings.

JULY 4. Rested after our journey and talked matters over. James and Clabber, our Indian horse herder, caught twenty-five large trout and we celebrated the national day by having a fine dinner with trout as the principal dish.

JULY 5. Reece and I went up to the upper sink of the stream in Pikes Peak gulch cañon to see if we can bring the stream on down past the sink in a ditch. At the upper sink a stream two thirds the size of Gold creek runs into a hole in the marble limestone bed rock and forever disappears. This water is much needed for the new placer discoveries in Pikes Peak gulch. We think it practicable to bring the water from just above the sink around in a ditch, but the cost will be great. Killed a beef today.

JULY 6. Everybody came down from the mines today, to get their weekly supply of provisions. They

---

[86] Here Granville Stuart inserts the Edgar Journal noted above which the editor omits.

are all anxious to get the water and agree to pay for it, if we will convey the water to their mines. I caught thirty-five trout, using grasshoppers for bait.

JULY 7. James and I went up and made a survey of a ditch to bring the water into the Pikes peak gulch placers. It can be done, but at a high cost, and just now we haven't that much money.

JULY 8. James went to La Barge City with a four horse wagon, after flour and other things. Bratton, Cook, and Bob Nelson bought out Parker Ball and Company, in the old Discovery claim in Pikes Peak gulch for one horse and $120.00 cash. We advanced the cash.

JULY 9. James and I made another survey of that ditch, but there will have to be so much fluming and at the high cost of lumber we think it impracticable. Clabber quit herding for us. We paid him $25.00. This boy has been one of Captain Grant's retainers and this $25.00 is the first wages he ever had. He is a good faithful Indian.

Several men from Walla Walla passed on their way to Bannack. Peter Martin and family returned from Fort Benton yesterday greatly disgusted. No steamboat arrived this season and everybody over there in a semi-starving condition. One steamboat came as far as Dauphins rapids; ninety miles below Fort Benton and had to stop, the river being very low. There are three other boats behind somewhere. Powell and Worden are on them and we are all much concerned about them, and are afraid something may have happened to them. These boats pass through the Sioux country, and when the water is low, as it is this season, they are often stuck on sand bars for days; exposed to hostile attacks from the Indians.

JULY 11. Strong east wind, cool and pleasant; very smoky for several days past, caused presumably by forest fires west of us. James and I went hunting; he taking the north side, I the south. He only saw one black-tailed deer; shot it with his Sharps rifle, the trusty gun that he carried on his Yellowstone expedition. I had worse luck; saw one white-tailed doe and shot and killed her off hand at seventy-five yards with my Maynard breech-loading rifle. I could only see her head and neck; broke the latter and when I came up to her found she had young ones. I would have given anything to have restored the poor thing to life and to have allowed her to go free with her children.

JULY 12. Frush and Sherwood's express arrived from Walla Walla. They brought us states papers dates to June 16th. This being Sunday, all the miners are down for supplies; sold all the deer meat to them.

JULY 13. I went up to Rock creek to see if it was possible to make a ditch from it to Pikes Peak gulch; I found it possible, but at an enormous cost. I followed up the creek to a beautiful little lake about a mile and quarter long and half mile wide. It is surrounded by high mountains in the midst of a lovely forest. There were many trout in it and one lone duck floated on its placid waters. No doubt I was the first human being it had ever seen, for it had no fear of me, and probably thought I was just a new kind of a deer, and my horse only an elk.

I decided to join the duck in a swim in the water, which was as clear as a crystal; found it slightly warm on the surface to a depth of two feet, but below that so icy cold that I could not remain more than a few minutes and came out shivering in the hot July sun. It lies very high; the creek flowing out of it falls over one thousand feet in the first three-quarter mile. The lake has been formed by several land slides from the mountains which filled up the cañon about one thousand feet deep at the lower end of the lake, which must be that deep. This lake belongs to me, as I am probably the first white man who ever stood on its shores, and tried to bathe in its icy waters. Saw several deer, but not near enough to get a shot, and the horse flies tried to eat up "Old Fiend" my horse.

JULY 14. Reece and I began making a pair of spurs and found it no easy job. James and Peter Martin started to Bannack after a load of flour, and bacon.

JULY 16. Red and Mat Craft returned from Bannack last night; they bring news that Lee's army is within three miles of Washington, D. C., with terrible fighting going on. Charlie Allen started to Bannack to try to settle up the estate of George Carhart, his partner, who was accidentally killed in a saloon row.[87] Reece and I finished my steel spurs, they are noble, noisy ringers. Mat Craft and his wife (the only white woman in camp) moved up to James Minesinger's house. Johnny Grant passed on his way to Hell Gate.

JULY 17. Reece piled up the charcoal. Made shelves and put up the drugs and medicines. Bratton is still laid up with his lame hip and back, and his horse is sick and likely to die. A small band of Pend d'Oreilles passed; returning from a war party and don't look or act as though they had been very successful. They asked for whiskey, but did not get any and passed on.

JULY 19. Am glad I do not have to attend church

---

[87] Langford, *opus citra*, vol. i, p. 314, describes this shooting in detail.

and sit on a bench two hours listening to some fellow telling us how much hotter it would be somewhere else, and that we were headed for that particular spot. We may miss some of the good things of life by being out here, but we escape some mighty disagreeable experiences. All the miners (five now here) came down from Pikes peak gulch and had their tools fixed up. Red and George Craft started on a prospecting trip to the head of Flint creek, by the way of the head of Gold creek. We had a high old game of cribbage.

JULY 20. Sixteen Flatheads and Pend d'Orielles passed, returning from a horse stealing expedition against the Crows. We came near having a row with them, but by a friendly talk it blew over; and we traded with them for a mare and colt that they had stolen from the Crows. They had two horses belonging to Fred Burr, that the Crows had stolen from him at the crossing of the Big Hole river; Te-losh-ten-aw, a good Flathead, had these horses and returned them to Burr, he paying the Indian all that they were worth for his trouble.

JULY 21. I smoothed the interior of our shot gun. Thirteen men are here en route to Fort Benton. They are from the Florence mines: say that the soldiers had a fight with the Indians on Snake river, in which they killed eight hundred Indians and captured two thousand ponies; which is so big a story that we do not believe it.

They have twenty-five thousand dollars worth of gold dust with them in buckskin sacks; and intend building a boat at Benton, and going down the Missouri river to the states in it. We advised them not to do it; and also admonished them against exhibiting so much treasure, as there were some people in the country who were not particular as to how they came into possession of gold dust, just so they got it. They did not seem to pay much attention to our warning and went on their way.[88]

JULY 23. Rained all last night and until ten A. M. to-day, John Grant and Captain Higgins arrived from Hell Gate to-day, and Frush and Sherwood arrived from Bannack. Captain Higgins brought us one dozen fine Hudson's Bay shirts; price three dollars each. They are much better and, thank goodness, have much longer tails than the miserable "high water," hickory, American shirts that we are sometimes obliged to wear.

---

[88] Their fate was not known until several years later; when William Keyes spent the winter of 1871 on the Missouri river, below Rocky point, and there married an Indian woman. Seeing her husband with gold dust, she told him of a squaw who had some and related to him the story of how she came by it, which is as follows:—

A village of about one hundred lodges of Sioux Indians were camped on the bank of the river, and they saw a boat with white men coming down. The warriors at once began firing at them. The men in the boat had a small cannon, which they loaded and fired at the Indians; but so heavy was the recoil that it loosened a plank in the bottom of the boat and it began to sink. The men beached it on a sand bar, but on it there was no shelter and they were still within reach of the Indians' rifles. The white men had only the cannon and revolvers. They did not use the cannon after the first shot, and the Indians killed them all; then crossing over to the sand bar, they stripped them naked, scalped them, and cut them up in a most horrible way; and then proceeded to plunder the boat. Finding the buckskin bags filled with the gold dust, and not knowing what it was, they emptied it out on the sand and took the sacks, which they could use for many things. One squaw, out of curiosity, kept one bag of gold and put it in her parflash. Keyes's wife persuaded this squaw to show him the bag of dust; later she accompanied him to the scene of the massacre.

Keyes tried to find where they had emptied the gold. In the spring he and his wife came to Fort Benton and told their story to John Lepley, a wealthy cattle owner on the range between Shonkin and Arrow creek, whom they persuaded to go down the river with them to make further investigation. The sands of the bar had washed and were so changed that they found but little of the gold; but were convinced that the party murdered was the men from the Florence mines.

Eighty-five in the shade on the south side of the house, up under the eaves. If I put the thermometer on the north side, where I can not watch it the Indians will steal it. It would be of no use to them, but not understanding what it is, they think it is some sort of "medicine" and are very curious about it.

Virginia City

JULY 26, 1863. The new discovery at Stinkingwater is now attracting attention from everywhere. The mines are turning out big. People passing here every day on their way over. All the miners here are abandoning their diggings and going over and we have about decided to move also. James and Reece Anderson are going over tomorrow to see what best to do.

JULY 27. Brother James and Anderson started for Stinkingwater mines today. Solitary young man arrived from "below" on his way to the states via Fort Benton. He had a large boil on his cheek, was almost barefooted, poorly mounted, nearly naked, and not much money; but carried a double-barreled shot gun. He invested in $5.25 worth of "grub," shot, and fish lines. I told him that it would be utterly futile for him to try to make his way down the river alone in a boat. He would be murdered as soon as he struck the Sioux country. I advised him to go over to the mines, where he could get work and later return across the plains with some freight outfit. I think he will take my advice.

This evening, while Bratton and I were enjoying a quiet game of cribbage, we were suddenly interrupted by all the women in the village rushing in, headed by Mrs. Craft; all trying to talk at the same time: English, Flathead, Blackfoot, Snake, and Bannock; some were weeping, some, ready for a fight; a regular Tower of Babel performance. We finally learned that all the commotion was caused by Mrs. Craft's having accused Pierrot's squaw of stealing her "shimmy."

They appealed to me to settle the row; but what could one lone man do in a case of this kind? I was no Solomon. I asked Mrs. Craft what the thing looked like. She called me a "fool," and left with her nose in the air. Madam Pierrot denied vehemently ever having touched the thing. I called my wife in and after talking things over, discovered that a young Indian girl visiting with Madam Pierrot saw Mrs. Craft with a new fangled garment brought from the states; and not wishing to be behind with the styles, she had purchased some cloth and seeing the coveted garment on Mrs. Craft's clothes line had "borrowed" it for a model after which to construct her own; but before she had time to return it, Mrs. Craft had missed it, and so great was her wrath that the Indian girl became frightened and hid it instead of returning it.

JULY 30. Captain Higgins arrived today bringing states papers. It is said Vicksburg has been taken and that a mighty battle is in progress on the Potomac.

AUGUST 7, 1863. U. S. Marshal of Idaho Territory, D. S. Payne, arrived en route to Bannack City, Stinkingwater mines, and Boise. His business is to estimate population, resources, etc.; and to establish election precincts through this part of the country, which is now Idaho Territory.[89]

Mrs. Craft, good woman, is introducing many new innovations into society here. She has decided we should wear starched shirts. I have been called upon to make a "bosom board;" which I did, and she has starched front, neck, and wristbands of our shirts; and is busy every day explaining the process of ironing shirts to the "native Americans."

---

[89] Idaho Territory was established by act of Congress in March, 1863, out of parts of Dakota Territory and of Washington Territory. – ED.

AUGUST 13. James and Reece Anderson returned from Stinkingwater mines and reported everything "booming" over there. The mines are turning out very rich and are quite extensive. James hired a man to build a log blacksmith shop for $150.00; we will soon move over bag and baggage.

AUGUST 17. James took a load of lumber to Cottonwood. (It is Cottonwood once more. Captain La Barge failed to start his store there and the inhabitants went back to the old name.) Worden, Powell, Mailette, Louis Demars, and Al. Clark arrived today from Fort Benton. Worden is accompanied by his sister. They all came up the Missouri river on the delayed steamboat. We have made Miss Worden as comfortable as possible. This must seem a strange country to a young lady from the states, but she seems to be very well contented.

AUGUST 21. We have brought all of our cattle over to Robert Dempsey, who is camped at the crossing of the wagon trail from Bannack city to Stinkingwater; and will leave them with him to be wintered.

AUGUST 26. Arrived at the new diggings and camped in Daylight gulch. The new town is called Virginia City, the district Alder Gulch. Our blacksmith shop is almost finished. James bought two thousand pounds of flour at ten dollars per cwt.; and one hundred and fifty pounds of bacon at thirty cents a pound, and stored it in Bannack when he was over before. We have hauled that over here; also all of our things from Gold creek including lumber. James and W. B. Dance formed a partnership and will open a general store as soon as a building can be erected.

AUGUST 30. Reece and I went to work in the blacksmith shop; lots of work. In two weeks we cleared three hundred dollars; and then took in Frank McConnell as a partner and ran two fires, I acting as sledge hammer man for both fires; which was a heavy job as the weather was very warm.

SEPTEMBER 18, 1863. We have a large lot of boots, shoes, harness, saddlery, and leather coming up the Missouri river. One lot of 1290 lbs. arrived and I paid $348.30 freight on it, being 27c per pound.

OCTOBER 15, 1863. Today we moved into our log house down town. James bought a Charter Oak cooking stove No. 8; it and utensils for it cost $150.00; also a heating stove for the store cost $35.00. Frank McConnell, Reece, and I are very busy in the blacksmith shop.

OCTOBER 27. Unusual excitement in town today news has just arrived that the coach that left here for Bannack on the twenty-fifth was held up by highwaymen and the passengers robbed. That morning the driver was ill and as a furious storm was raging no one could be found willing to make the trip. Finally Billy Rumsey who is a good driver consented to take the coach over to Bannack. There were three passengers and as they were several hours late Rumsey made the best time possible to Stinkingwater station. Here another delay. There was no stock ready. Men were sent out in a hurry to bring in the horses but after being gone for some time the stock herder returned with only a portion of the stock. Rumsey ordered them to hitch up what they had and he started out on a run.

At Dempsey's they were again delayed because of the stock not being ready. Daniel McFadden, better known by the sobriquet of "Bummer Dan," and the discoverer of Bummer Dan's bar; one of the richest bars in Alder gulch who had been spending a few days here, took passage on the coach.

At Coplands everything was ready and the horses were quickly changed and all possible speed made to the Rattlesnake ranch but in spite of the best efforts it was almost dark before they arrived, and only to find that the stock had all been turned loose; the excuse given was that it was so late they had ceased to expect them.

Rumsey ordered the herder out to bring in the horses; he went but came back without them. It was impossible to proceed further without fresh stock so there was nothing to do but remain all night where they were. William Bunton who was in charge of the ranch showed himself to be the soul of hospitality being especially liberal with his whiskey. The "crowd" was repeatedly called to the bar and treated. Rumsey would not drink with them, but most of the hangers-on spent the night drinking and gambling. At daybreak Rumsey went himself with the herder to look for the missing horses, but they could not be found and he was obliged to hitch up the jaded team that he had driven in the night before and proceed on his journey. When all was ready he shouted "All aboard for Bannack." Matteson, Percival, and McFadden took seats in the coach, Wilkinson announced that he was going to accompany Bob Zachary and ride one of his horses. Bill Bunton came out with a bottle and glass, and offered everybody a drink; and announcing his intentions of going also, mounted the seat beside the driver.

It was cold and stormy and the passengers inside let down the curtains to the coach. The horses were traveling along at a fairly good gate; Bunton doing the whipping and Rumsey the driving, but as the team was played out before they started they soon settled down to a slow trot.   Bunton complained of being cold and left the seat beside the driver for one inside the coach beside Bummer Dan; Percival and Matteson were on the front seat with their backs to the driver.   They had not gone more than a mile when Rumsey saw two men wrapped in blankets with hoods over their heads and a gun apiece and knew in a flash that they were road agents.   He shouted to the passengers to get their guns; but all were too much surprised to move.   The robbers were coming on a run for the coach and were down on them in an instant.   "Throw up your hands" was the preemptory order.   Rumsey drew up his team and complied.   Bunton began to beg and plead for his life; repeating over and over, "For God's sake, don't shoot. Take what I have, but don't kill me!   For God's sake, spare my life!"   This was all for effect and to distract the others for Bunton was a member of the road agent band.   The driver was ordered down and the passengers out.   Rumsey objected saying he was afraid that the team would get away.   Bunton offered to hold the horses which he did.

Rumsey was next ordered to take the arms from the passengers and throw them in a pile on the ground, and after that to take their valuables and deposit them in the same place.   McFadden handed out two small purses and Rumsey took them and threw them on the ground as directed; whereupon the spokesman shouted to him with the most terrible oath to unload his dust and to be quick about it or he would perforate him with lead.   Dan lost no time in getting off a belt and handing over two more purses of dust.

These preliminaries over, all were ordered back in the coach and Rumsey was told to drive like hell and

never to open his mouth or they would kill him sure.
The order was obeyed in so far as getting out of that
neighborhood in the shortest possible time and the
coach proceeded on its way to Bannack where they
reported the robbery. Bummer Dan lost $2500.00 and
the others about $500.00 between them. So far as I
can learn no steps have been taken to discover who the
robbers are or to punish them.

NOVEMBER 10, 1863. Have been ill with typhoid.
Miss Matilda Dalton, whom I named "Desdemona"
in Bannack last winter, because she was beautiful and
so good, is also very ill of typhoid.

James and W. B. Dance have opened the store. Virginia City is a very lively place and reminds us of the
placer days in California.

NOVEMBER 13. Sam T. Hauser and N. P. Langford [90] started for St. Louis today overland via Salt
Lake City. The departure of these dear friends has
cast a gloom over us. Before them lies a long perilous
journey of eighteen hundred miles; through cold and
storm and be-set on all sides by hostile Indians and road
agents. It will take six weeks to make the trip. "God
be with them."

NOVEMBER 29. Gillette's wagon train arrived from
Fort Benton bringing six hundred pairs of heavy
leather boots for Dance and Stuart. The freight from
St. Louis here has cost thirty-five cents a pound. The
boots are not what are liked here by the miners and I
see that we will not make any money on these goods.
Two men killed and one severely wounded here the
past month in drunken rows.

---

[90] Hauser was territorial governor of Montana from 1885 to 1887 and for
many years thereafter was a leading Democratic politician in the state.
Langford became noted as a writer and for many years was connected with
the Minnesota Historical Library. – ED.

NOVEMBER 30. A man murdered twenty miles below here. I did not learn the particulars, but I sur-
mise robbery was the motive. There has been several
robberies on the road between here and Bannack seventy miles away and few are people living between the
two camps. There is certainly an organized band of
highway men about here and something will have to be
done soon to protect life and property.

Louis Maillett and DeMars arrived from Salt Lake
with loads of flour. Flour is now selling for $28.00
cwt. It has been as high as $40.00, but a quantity
arriving from Salt Lake made it fall to $28.00. Fresh
beef sells at 15, 20 and 25 cents a pound according to
cuts; beef tallow 30c a pound; sausage, made from
beef scraps, 30c lb.; bacon, 40c; sugar, 60c; coffee, 90c;
table salt, 50c; keg butter, $1.50 lb.; eggs, $1.50 per
doz. (very scarce); turnips, 25c lb.; potatoes, 40c lb.;
candy, $1.50 lb.; raisins, $1.00 lb.; board from $16.00
to $18.00 per week.

News of the discovery of gold in Alder gulch spread
with incredible rapidity and as soon as claims were
staked attention was turned to building a town. The
first stampede reached the gulch on June 6, 1863. The
stream was marked on either side by a dense growth of
beautiful dark green alders and willows and it was
because of the presence of the growth that Henry Edgar
named the district "Alder Gulch."

Campers, at the upper end of the gulch, accidentally
set fire to the dry grass and, as a high wind was blowing,
the fire was soon beyond control; sweeping down the
creek with such rapidity that many who were camped
along the creek and in the brush, had no time to remove
their belongings and lost everything they had. This
was indeed a serious calamity as there were no supplies

to be had in the camp. Those who escaped the fire divided with those who lost everything and, by so doing, managed to get along without serious discomfort until supplies arrived.

On the sixteenth of June the Varina Townsite Company recorded a claim to three hundred and twenty acres of land. A town was laid out, and named Varina, in honor of Mrs. Jefferson Davis. The name was soon changed to Virginia by Judge Bissel, who bluntly refused to use the name of Jeff Davis's wife on any document that he prepared and accordingly as he named it so it remained. The change of name caused us no little inconvenience for several years; when a U. S. mail route was established. There was already a Virginia City, Nevada, and letters and papers intended for us were sent there and their mail found its way to Virginia City, Montana.

People flocked to the new camp from every direction; all the other settlements in the country were deserted. There were no houses to live in and not much in the way of material to construct houses. Every sort of shelter was resorted to, some constructed brush wakiups; some made dug-outs, some utilized a convenient sheltering rock, and by placing brush and blankets around it constructed a living place; others spread their blankets under a pine tree and had no shelter other than that furnished by the green boughs overhead. The nearest sawmill was seventy-five miles away on the creek above Bannack, but the nearby mountains furnished an abundance of house logs and the ring of the axe was a familiar sound and soon log houses made their appearance on all sides. The first building was erected by T. L. Luce, on Cover street and was occupied by a baker, but Henry Morier was soon in the field and had his building up and a saloon started. I think this is about the first time in the history of founding a mining camp where the bakery got ahead of the saloon. Frederick Root and Nathaniel J. Davis were the first to complete their store building, but R. S. Hamilton brought in the first stock of merchandise. John Lyons built and occupied the first residence, but before cold weather set in there were houses all up and down the gulch and most of the families were housed in comfortable log cabins; although windows were not as numerous as they might have been. Sash and glass had to be brought from Salt Lake and there were no panes of glass larger than eight by ten; most being six by eight, and the cost $1.00 per pane. The first lumber brought over from Bannack sold readily for $250.00 gold per thousand feet. P. W. McAdow and Thos. Cover succeeded in getting a sawmill in operation on Granite creek in February, 1864, but the price of lumber did not decrease for some months as the demand exceeded the output about ten to one.

A. J. Oliver and Company started a stage line from Virginia City to Bannack and Salt Lake City in August, 1863. We were rejoiced to pay $1.00 each for any paper or letter received and 75c for all letters despatched. There was no government mail route until November, 1864. George B. Parker was the first postmaster. The first newspaper published in Montana was the *Montana Post*, printed by John Buchanan and issued on my birthday, August 27, 1864.

The winter of 1863-64 was a mild one, building and mining operations were carried on with but little interruption all winter and before spring every branch of business was represented. Gold was coming out in

large quantities. The district extended from the foot
of Old Baldy to twelve miles down the creek. The
bed of the creek and the bars on both sides were uni-
formly rich; the bed rock being literally paved with
gold. The Alder gulch diggings were the richest gold
placer diggings ever discovered in the world.

Freight teams from Salt Lake arrived until late in
the fall, bringing in supplies; and while we were not
provided with luxuries there was no suffering from
food shortage. Molasses was considered by us, a great
delicacy and it was both scarce and dear. Sam Hauser
hit upon a plan all his own whereby he kept the only
one gallon of molasses in our mess all to himself. Returning home one evening tired and hungry, we found
Sam sitting at the table holding a mouse suspended by
the tail: the little animal had every appearance of
having been drowned in the molasses. Sam didn't say
that he had taken the mouse from the molasses, we just
reached that conclusion by inference and immediately
lost our fondness for molasses – not so with Hauser – he
continued to spread molasses on his bread every meal
until it was all gone. One day, in an inquiring mood,
he asked us why we all quit on molasses. James replied that he liked molasses but not well enough to eat
it after a mouse had drowned in it: whereupon Hauser
informed us that he had killed the mouse and smeared
it with molasses later just to see how we would take it.

There was a great number of saloons and each dispenser of liquid refreshments had the formula for making "tanglefoot:" – a quantity of boiled mountain sage,
two plugs tobacco steeped in water, box cayenne pepper, one gallon water; so if any one got low in whiskey
he promptly manufactured more. Saloons, gambling
houses, public dance halls (hurdy gurdies) ran wide

open and here, as in California, gold dust flowed in a yellow stream from the buckskin bags of the miners into the coffers of the saloons, dance halls, and gambling dens.   Gold dust was the sole medium of exchange and it was reckoned at $18.00 an ounce.   Every business house had gold scales for weighing the dust. If a man was under the influence of liquor, the bar keepers were not averse to helping themselves liberally to the man's dust, when paying himself for drinks and he more often took $1.00 for a drink than the going price of twenty-five cents.   A dance at one of the hurdy gurdies cost one dollar and as each dance wound up with an invitation to visit the bar where drinks for self and partner were expected, the cost of a waltz, schottische, or quadrille was usually $1.50.   Dances kept up all night long but were usually orderly.   If a man was found to be getting too much under the influence of liquor, some obliging friend would expel him from the hall.   Every sort of gambling game was indulged in and it was no uncommon thing to see one thousand dollars staked on the turn of a monte card.   The miner who indulged in gambling usually worked six days, then cleaned up his dust; and placing it in a buckskin sack hied himself to the nearest gambling house where he remained until he had transferred the contents of the sack to the professional gambler.   If he played in luck he could usually stay in the game twenty-four hours. He would then return to his "diggins" without money and often with little grub; a sadder but no wiser man, for he would repeat the same thing over and over as long as his claim lasted and would then start out, blankets on his back, in search of new "diggins."

There was a hotel and several restaurants in Virginia City, but most of the miners built themselves cabins and did their own cooking. Some of these cabins were the pink of neatness, while others were not so well kept but cleanliness was the rule.

Open-hearted generosity was met with on all sides. There was quite a number of families in Virginia City at this time. All the ladies did their own house work and in case of sickness helped nurse and care for their neighbors. There was quite an epidemic of typhoid fever during the fall and early winter and some people were very ill, but there were no deaths. The women were particularly kind and helpful, leaving their own work to nurse and care for those who were ill. No appeal for assistance ever went unanswered. A subscription paper setting forth its purpose would be circulated up and down the gulch; two or more responsible citizens taking it, was all that was required to get sufficient money to relieve any case of distress. Everybody would contribute a sum of gold dust.

During the winter Prof. Thomas J. Dimsdale [91] opened a private school; all of the children of school age attended. The fee charged was $2.00 per week for each pupil – a very modest sum for those days. The school was a good one.

There were many dances and social gatherings where all the families in town attended, bringing the children with them. There was usually a bed or two provided in some adjoining room and all the little ones were put

[91] Thomas J. Dimsdale was an Englishman, at one time a student at Oxford University and a man of fine culture and character. He taught a private school for a time and was appointed the first territorial superintendent of instruction. He was also the first newspaper editor in Montana and as such wrote the articles in the *Vigilantes of Montana* published first in the *Montana Post* and published in book form in 1865. It has gone through several editions. There is a brief life of Dimsdale imprinted from the *Rocky Mountain Gazette* of March, 1901, in the third edition of the *Vigilantes of Montana* (Helena, Montana, 1915). – ED.

to bed and the folks took turns looking after them. It was no uncommon thing for a man and wife to appear at a ball carrying a clothes basket between them in which was snugly deposited the baby. These parties were very informal and most enjoyable. Dancing would be kept up until an early hour in the morning. A fine supper was usually served at midnight and the tickets cost $5.00 each. J. B. Caven and wife gave several theatrical entertainments and the tickets were $3.00.

Rev. A. M. Torbett [92] arrived early in 1864 and was the first protestant minister in Montana. He started a little church on Idaho street and I think all the protestants of every denomination attended and supported the minister and the church.

Although there was no court except the miners' court there was a number of lawyers in camp: Samuel McLean, G. W. Stapleton, and J. P. A. Smith being the first to arrive. Dr. J. S. Glick, a skilled physician and surgeon, arrived in 1863 and begun the practice of medicine.

In order to make clear how debts were collected in days before courts of law were established, I will here give a notice of a miner's meeting called to settle a question of a debt between two citizens. Copied from the *Montana Post* of November 5, 1865.

"At a meeting of miners of Brown's District, Bevins Gulch, Madison County, Territory of Montana; held at J. H. Hughes' saloon in Bagdad City, October 30, 1864, for the purpose of settling a dispute between W. P. Allen and Company and Caleb Perry.

"Willa Huffaker was called to the chair and N. T.

---

[92] Mr. Torbett did not remain long in Virginia City. He had left before July 18, 1867. Daniel Tuttle, *Reminiscences of a Missionary Bishop*, p. 125.

Headley appointed secretary. On motion, the Chair appointed Clitus Barbour, O. C. Stanley, W. S. Ferris, W. L. Britton, S. McKee, and G. G. Ford, a committee to try the case and render a decision according to the evidence and testimony advanced before them. The committee brought in the following verdict: – 'That we find Allen and Company entitled to receive from Perry the sum of one hundred dollars.' Mr. Perry then declared he would pay nothing. The following resolutions were then offered and adopted.

"Whereas it is a notorious fact that Caleb Perry will pay no debts unless forced to do so; and whereas after having agreed to abide by the decision of a jury of six men, appointed to make such decision, and then disputing the right of such jury to try the case, and refusing to make any settlement.

"Resolved: That the miners of the district put Mr. Allen in possession of the claims of Caleb Perry and assist and protect him in working the same until he shall take out one hundred dollars clear of expenses. On motion, C. Farnham and S. Jeff Perkins were appointed a committee to wait upon Mr. Perry and to notify him that unless he complied within twenty minutes with the decision as rendered by the jury selected to try the dispute between Allen and Perry that Mr. Allen should be put in possession of his (Perry's) claims on the following day.

"The Committee appointed to wait upon Mr. Perry reported that he (Perry) refused to comply with the decision of the meeting.

"On motion the Chair appointed the following committee to put Mr. Allen in possession of Perry's claims:

Bishop Tuttle quotes from some newspaper notices of Torbett in Montana *Historical Society Contributions* (1904) vol. v, p. 292.

James Hunter, C. Farnum, S. Jeff Perkins, Michael
Hughes, and Joseph Woodward."

The Perry claims were accordingly turned over to
Allen and Company, who worked them until they had
taken out one hundred dollars over and above cost of
working and then the claims were turned back to Caleb
Perry.

About the middle of January, 1864, a regular stampede craze struck Virginia City. The weather had
been quite cold and work in the mines was temporarily
suspended. A large number of idle men were about
town and it required no more than one man with an
imaginative mind to start half the population off on a
wild goose chase. Somebody would say that somebody
said, that somebody had found a good thing and without further inquiry a hundred or more men would
start out for the reported diggings.

One report of a discovery on Gallatin river started a
large party out in that direction. Every horse that
could be found fit to ride was made ready. We had
some horses on a ranch near town and brought them in
and in less than an hour we had sold them all for about
twice what they would have sold for at any other time.
Four hundred men left town in mid-winter, with the
ground covered with snow, for some place on the Gallatin river; no one seemed to know exactly where they
were going, but most of them brought up at Gallatin
City. Many, who could not get horses, started on foot.
The first night out brought them to a realization of the
futility of such a trip and they turned back.

Late in the evening on January 22, a rumor started
that a big discovery had been made on Wisconsin creek,
a distance of thirty miles from Virginia City. The
report said that as much as one hundred dollars to the

pan had been found; and away the people flew all anxious to be first on the ground, where they could "just shovel up gold." Virginia City was almost deserted: men did not stop for horses, blankets, or provisions, the sole aim was to get there first and begin to shovel it out at the rate of one hundred to the pan. Fortunately the distance was not great and the weather was mild. Robert Dempsey had a ranch nearby and the stampeders got a supply of beef from him to last them back to town. It is needless to say that they found no diggings and all returned to Virginia in a few days.

The next great excitement was caused by a rumor of new rich discoveries on Boulder creek, a branch of the Jefferson. We sold every horse that we would spare at about three times its real value. Reece Anderson was among those taken with the fever and he joined the expedition. He had a good saddle and pack horses and plenty of food and blankets. There were so many in this stampede who started with little or nothing that those who had good outfits were obliged to share food with those who had none to keep them from starving and in the long run those with good outfits did not fare much better than those who started with none. Our friend, Reece Anderson, returned in about two weeks without having found any big thing in the way of gold mines, but he had accumulated quite a valuable stock of experience and got his nose, ears, and fingers badly frost-bitten.

The next big excitement started right in town. Somebody reported a "find" at the edge of town and in the morning claims were being staked off the main streets and on the rear of all of our lots. One enthusiastic man began to sink a hole in the street, just above the store and it began to look like we would be dug up and washed out without ceremony.   Of course there was no gold found and mining operations in the streets and back yards was soon suspended.

A grand stampede to the Prickley Pear valley in which more than six hundred people took part was the last of the season.   Away they went, crossing the hills into Boulder valley.   They found the snow very deep, but fortunately not cold.   Some good mines had been discovered on one bar about six hundred feet long, but all good ground had been taken when the stampeders arrived.   The little army of disappointed men turned around and returned home once more.

Pioneering in Montana

The Making of a State, 1864–1887

CARROL OR ROCKY POINT, MONTANA, IN 1881

This was a rendezvous of horse thieves and cattle rustlers, and here some of them were hanged by vigilantes

From a photograph by F. J. Haynes of St. Paul

Contents

Illustrations

First Years of Montana Territory[93]

In February, 1864, my brother James started with a second expedition to the Yellowstone. A place on the Gallatin river about twenty-five miles below Gallatin City was selected as the place of rendezvous. A company of seventy-five joined him and on February 27, they started on their expedition.

This was a cold late spring, snow lay on the ground so that they could not get up into the mountains to prospect. They found Lieutenant Menadier's camp on the Stinking river fork of the Big Horn, where he reported his party had found gold in paying quantities in 1858. They prospected thoroughly, but could not find more than a color. The formation was sandstone and it is certain that Lieutenant Menadier was duped by some of his men for there never was gold there or near there.

At this place the entire party split up. James decided to return to Deer Lodge and about twenty-five men accompanied him. The others scattered about over the country; some intending to prospect more thoroughly when the snow was gone. On this trip they did not see either Sioux or Crow Indians. James and his following reached Virginia City on the eighteenth of May. The rest of the party returned during July and August: they went to the Sweetwater river and then split up into small parties and straggled back,

[93] Here Mr. Stuart has two chapters; one called *The Knights of the Road*, the other *The Vigilantes*. Both closely parallel Langford, *opus citra*, and are omitted. – ED.

some by the Emigrant road, and some through the mountains. None of them succeeded in finding any diggings that would pay.

Soon after James left them two men went out hunting; a sudden snow storm came up and lasted three days. They became bewildered and separated; one finally turned and tried to overtake those who were returning with James, but fell in with a small camp of Crow Indians on the Rosebud (a branch of the Yellowstone) who robbed him of all he had and compelled him to stay with them for a couple of weeks. At the end of that time he persuaded them to go with him to the Gallatin valley; telling them that they could get a good trade with the white people there. After much persuasion the Indians consented to go. The Crows were always a hard lot of Indians to trade with and they did not succeed in making any trade, but Indian Dick by this ruse succeeded in getting back among his friends and took one of their best horses to reimburse himself for the things they had robbed him of. This, however, did not profit him much for the horse soon took sick and died, and thereupon he came to me and borrowed twenty dollars to buy himself some clothes as he was almost naked. Which twenty dollars he still owes in this year 1916.

The other man's body was found during the summer of 1865, lying in the willows on the Stinking river near where he left the party when he started hunting on that ill-fated morning. He had been shot, as was supposed by Indians and had run into the brush and died there. The Indians had not dared to follow him, as his gun, clothes, etc., were all there, but his horse was found among the Crows a year later.

So ended my brother's second Yellowstone expedi-

tion. These two expeditions had cost us two thousand
dollars in money and loss of much valuable time and
many precious lives. It was our last attempt to open
up the Yellowstone country.

Jim Bridger and John Jacobs made a road from the
Red Buttes on North Platte to Virginia City via Wind-
river, Stinking river, Pryors fork, Clarks fork and the
Yellowstone river and a large number of wagons came
by that route.[94] Some of them turned and went up the
Yellowstone above the first cañon and prospected for
gold and found some diggings and called the place
Emigrant gulch. First among these miners was my
old friend, D. B. Weaver. There was a grand stampede from Virginia City to Emigrant gulch, but as the
mines there were not extensive most of them returned.[95]

Our partner, W. B. Dance, had been in St. Louis
for some time purchasing goods for the firm. Early in
April he left St. Louis, on the "Welcome" for Fort
Benton. The trip was a tedious one, the water being
very high and the swift current carried much drift
wood and logs that greatly hindered the old side-
wheeler boats then used on the Missouri. There was
no fuel provided for the boats on the upper river and
they were obliged to stop and allow the crew to cut
sufficient cord wood to last until another landing could
be made.

At the mouth of the Yellowstone, Judge Dance got

---

[94] For further account of the Bridger trail see Grace R. Hebard and E. A.
Brininstool, *The Bozeman Trail*, vol. ii, p. 119, n. and index. Jacobs was
connected with Bozeman instead of Bridger. The *Fort Owen Journals* contain probably the earliest description of the Bridger road. – ED.

[95] Mr. D. B. Weaver of Saxton, Pennsylvania was one of the party that
discovered Emigrant gulch. He has written a splendid description of that
event, in the *History of the Yellowstone Valley*, published by the Western
Historical Publishing Co., Spokane, Washington. G. S. Mr. Weaver is still
living in Saxton, Pennsylvania (1924). – ED.

off the steamer to lay off a town site which he called
"Oraopolis." While thus engaged the boat pulled out
and left him. Securing a horse from Fort Union he
started out and tried to overtake the boat, but the horse
was a poor traveler and gave out and Dance was obliged
to leave him below the mouth of Milk river and proceed on foot. His situation was now desperate: He
was without food or blankets, in the midst of a hostile
Indian country. After traveling for two days without
food, he managed to reach Fort Galpin [96] where he
remained until another boat came along and took him
on to Fort Benton and later he arrived in Virginia
City without further mishap.

Early in June, 1864, we formed a partnership with
Frank Worden and opened a store in Deer Lodge and
brother James went over there to live; leaving me in
the store at Virginia City.

The autumn of 1864 was beautiful and there was no
severe weather until about the tenth of December, when
a sudden storm came on: the thermometer fell to thirty-seven degrees below zero and a foot of snow fell in
the valleys. Chinook winds refused to blow, the first
snow lay on the ground and daily storms added to it
until there were two feet of snow in the valleys and
from five to six feet on the divides.

On September 24, 1864, a party of twenty-five men
furnished with the necessary implements, started for
the Yellowstone to build boats for a journey east down
the river. They were to build twelve boats large
enough to accommodate twelve passengers each. One
hundred twenty men had signed to go on this trip.
The boats were to be completed October first. William

---

[96] Fort Galpin was a small post about fifteen miles west of the mouth
of the Milk river. – ED.

Young with a company of ninety-four men left Virginia
City late in September on foot, with their luggage
hauled in ox wagons.

On their arrival at the boat yard, a point on the
Yellowstone near where the town of Livingston now
is, they expected to find the boats ready to start but to
their surprise and chagrin they found but two boats just
begun. Some of the party became disgusted and returned to Virginia City with the ox wagons; but about
seventy-five turned in and helped finish the boats which
were little better than rafts, and on the seventh day, all
being ready, the start was made. The river was low
and full of sand bars; in many places the current was
swift and the boats unwieldy, they were no sooner off
one sand bar than they were caught on another. The
provisions were getting low and they were obliged to
hunt game for food and the game was scarce along the
river at that season of the year. A severe storm came
on, nine inches of snow fell and the river filled with
mush ice.

The ammunition was getting low and the captain
took charge of all on board. Six of the best hunters
were selected to do the hunting, no shots were fired only
when necessary to get food. The party was on half
rations most of the time and suffered severely with the
cold.

When twenty miles above Fort Union the boats froze
in; the party was obliged to abandon them with most
of their luggage and make it to Fort Union on foot.
Thirty days had been spent on the Yellowstone, during
which time they had suffered everything but death.
Twenty-five of the party gave up the trip and remained
at Fort Union. Forty-eight kept on to Fort Berthold,
there twenty more of the party elected to stay until

spring, and tried to persuade their companions to do likewise but some were homesick and the desire to meet their friends and families urged them to go forward.

On December 3 thirty of the party left Berthold on foot; they were well supplied with ammunition and good firearms, but little else. The first night out it begun to snow and continued to do so for three days. The little army of travelers lost their way and after wandering about until exhausted they lay down on the storm-swept plains without fires until the storm abated. Twenty-three of the party returned to Fort Berthold, but Young with six companions continued the journey. The weather had cleared up and the little party was making good time: no difficulty had been experienced in getting what game was required.

One evening while camped on the river bottom, preparing their evening meal they were surprised by a band of Indians who took them prisoners. Three of the party had been hunting and had deposited their guns and some ammunition beside a log just outside of camp, where they had been dressing an antelope. The Indians marched them all off to their village, some three miles further down the river. There were about fifty lodges and three hundred Indians, men, women, and children. The prisoners were taken to a lodge near the center of the village and while the Indians had not shown any disposition to hurt them, still they were not particularly friendly and had taken possession of all the firearms in sight and all the blankets. The prisoners were not bound but they felt certain that they were so carefully guarded that it would be useless to try to escape. After all the Indian men in the lodge had been fed, a squaw brought some roasted buffalo meat and gave it to the captives. The meat was dry and hard and without salt, but it was eaten with relish just the same. After eating their meat they were assigned a place in the lodge where they could lay down and sleep. The lodge was warm and comfortable but they were given no robes or blankets to lie upon and were too anxious to learn their ultimate fate to sleep very much.

Early next morning they were awakened by a group of young Indians who drove them out of camp and ordered them to go – pointing down the river. The ground was covered with snow and it was bitter cold, but the captives were glad to escape on any terms.

When they were out of sight, they circled around and made for their camp of the day before and to their great joy found the guns and ammunition and one hunting knife where they had left them. Securing the guns they lost no time in getting out of that neighborhood and traveled forty miles that day. The weather grew colder and a nipping north-east wind chilled them to the bone. Most of the party had frozen their hands and feet and traveling next day was slow and painful and they only made fifteen miles.

Finding a sheltered nook in a deep ravine near a timbered bottom, they made camp. Young and Burton went for wood and carrying it to camp on their shoulders, Burton dropped his end of the log and broke Young's collar bone. The situation had been bad enough but this last calamity made it critical. Burton refused to leave Young, so it was at last decided that they remain in camp while the others pushed on to Fort Rice where they could get a team to send back for the injured man.

That same evening three families of friendly Indians came along and seeing the camp fire paid a call. These

Indians were on their way to Fort Rice. From them they learned that the fort was fifty miles distant. The Indians offered to take the men to the fort. One of the squaws, exercising much ingenuity in fixing up a travois, made the injured man comfortable. Eight miles from Fort Rice they met the team and turned it back. The little company spent two weeks at Fort Rice waiting for Young's recovery and then joined an ox train bound for Sioux City, Iowa. The trip was made in four weeks.

At Sioux City the company divided; Young went by stage to Tella and from there by rail to Tonlon, Stark county, Illinois, by rail.[97] He spent the remainder of the winter in Illinois, but was again in Virginia City, Montana the next summer, having returned by the way of Salt Lake City.

In September, Virginia City was incorporated and we put on regular city airs. There were about ten thousand people in the district and the greater part of them lived in Virginia City.

During the summer of 1864 Stuart and Hauser purchased six silver quartz claims on Rattlesnake creek in Beaverhead county and started development work in them. In addition to looking after the store in Virginia City, I kept the books for the Deer Lodge store and the mining camps and had to attend to getting the goods for the stores freighted from Fort Benton to Deer Lodge and Virginia City.

The new year saw marvelous changes in Montana: from a primeval wilderness, inhabited by a few roving bands of Indians and an occasional trader or trapper, we had emerged into a full fledged territory, with a

---

[97] Young gave the details of this story in a letter from Illinois to Reece Anderson.

population of fourteen thousand eight hundred seventeen souls. Many new and important gold discoveries had been made at Prickley Pear, Last Chance, Silver Bow, and Ophir.[98] Thriving villages had sprung up at all of these places.

The first territorial legislature was in session at Bannack, enacting laws for better government.[99] Emigrants were thronging into all the principal valleys and many fine ranches were being improved. Virginia City was an incorporated town: law now reigned supreme, offenders were promptly arrested and tried by authority of judge and jury. Good public schools were provided wherever six or more children could be assembled. Professor Dimsdale conducted a singing school where lovers of good music met once a week for instructions and practice.

There was also a lyceum where lectures were given by men of undoubted talent and knowledge. Two large and commodious churches were built and crowded congregations listened with reverence and attention to the sermons. Two Sabbath schools were in successful operation. The Reverend Father Giorda, a missionary father, ministered to the spiritual needs of Catholics; celebrating mass each Sunday.

The Montana Historical Society was organized with Wilbur F. Sanders as president, Judge H. L. Hosmer, historian, and Granville Stuart, secretary. There was a strong Masonic lodge in Virginia City and during the summer the organization built a handsome Masonic hall.

---

[98] Last Chance was discovered by John Cowan in 1864 and later became Helena. Prickley Pear and Ophir are near there. Silver Bow is near Butte. – ED.

[99] Montana was organized as a territory from northeastern Idaho, May 26, 1864. – ED.

A daily mail and stage service was in operation between Virginia City, Bannack, and Salt Lake City and a weekly stage from Virginia to other towns in the territory carried mail and passengers. A great number of steamboats made regular trips from St. Louis, Missouri, to Fort Benton and each one was loaded to capacity with freight and passengers.

Early in the spring six dromedaries were brought up from Arizona and it was proposed to start a pack train from Virginia City to Fort Benton. The claim was made that the dromedaries could travel much faster, carry a greater load and that as the Indians were afraid of them, the trains would escape raids from the aborigines. Circulars were distributed about Virginia City advertising exhibitions to take place on the street, where would be demonstrated how a dromedary would carry ten children or one thousand pounds of freight, that they would kneel and raise at the word of command, etc.

An exhibition was given in front of the Gibson House on Idaho street and it was easily shown that the dromedaries could carry ten or more children. Every youngster was on hand for a trial ride. One young lady of sixteen summers perched comfortably on one of the kneeling animals, but when the awkward beast attempted to regain its feet she was wholly unprepared for the sudden dip forward and was pitched head first into the street, but fortunately escaped serious injury. This mishap brought the exhibition to a close and as the strange animals frightened every horse that came in sight of them, causing serious runaways, the owner was ordered to take them out of town.

They were removed to the valley in the neighborhood of Snow Shoe gulch, where they remained for

sometime. One day a hunter spied an animal brows-
ing in a clump of willows and taking aim fired, the
animal dropped and thinking he had killed an elk, he
ran up to secure his game; what was his astonishment
to find a camel instead of an elk. Not having heard
of the dromedary train, he was much puzzled to know
where the animal came from, but was soon enlightened
by the appearance of the owner on the scene, who informed him in a very pointed and energetic manner
that the camel was his. "Well Mister," replied the
Nimrod, "you can have the camel if it is yours." The
dromedary train proved a failure and the remaining
five animals were taken to Utah and Montana saw them
no more.

Early in the year Mr. A. M. Smith arrived in Virginia City with a camera and photographic supplies
and opened a gallery over "Con" Orem's saloon. The
place was crowded with people every day, all anxious
to have likenesses taken to send home. Most of us had
a tintype taken and then this enterprising man, Smith,
would place it in a little black case lined with red
velvet, call it a "daugerrotype" and charge us $5.00
for the same. The photograph gallery was as profitable as a "claim" in the bed of Alder gulch.

There was also a "hair dressing parlor" opened by
Thomas White, where one could not only have his hair
cut and combed, but could also have it colored, the
proprietor even going so far as to guarantee that the
shade would be a beautiful glossy black or brown.

The hardest fought prize fight on record was called
for January 1, 1865, at Virginia City: between John
Condel Orem and Hugh O'Neil for one thousand a
side. That date falling on Sunday, Professor Dimsdale appealed to both contestants to change the date

to Monday, January 2, to which they cheerfully consented.

The ring was pitched at the lower end of the Leviathan hall, on the north side of Jackson street. Precisely at fifteen minutes past one o'clock Hugh O'Neil shied his sombrero into the ring followed by one hundred ninety pounds of as good bone and sinew as one could expect to look upon. "Con" Orem instantly reciprocated and deposited his castor over the ropes introducing one hundred thirty-eight pounds of as tough humanity as ever crossed the Rocky mountains or any other mountains for that matter. "Con" Orem was thirty years of age, stood five feet six and a half inches and was a model of symmetry, form, wiry and healthy, with a boxer's eye. Scarcely could an improvement be suggested. His training had been perfect and he showed it throughout the fight. Hugh O'Neil was thirty-two years of age and had the advantage of fifty-two pounds weight and two inches in height, being altogether the larger and more powerful man; thick set, cool, of unflinching nerve, and great bodily strength. The betting was altogether in his favor as it seemed impossible to hope that a man of Orem's size could contest the fight with him successfully. Hugh was not so firm of flesh as Orem, and had dissipated to some extent while Orem had never taken a drink of intoxicating liquor or used tobacco.

At twenty minutes to two o'clock, time was called and quickly each man toed the mark and the battle begun and lasted three hours and five minutes, in which one hundred eighty-five rounds were fought. At this junction a sudden feeling seemed to animate the backers of both men. The referee was called on by both parties to stop the fight. (The men themselves were still game and ready to go.) This was accordingly done to the satisfaction of most people present. Bets were declared off and the ring money was divided evenly.

During the winter of 1864 a company of St. Paul men organized the Idaho Steam Packet Company and purchased two steamers, the "Chippeway Falls" and the "Cutter." Their object was to establish a route from Minnesota to the gold mines at the headwaters of the Missouri (as all the great northwestern country was then called). The company advertised to take passengers to the newly discovered mines in ninety days. Both boats were outfitted and started from La Crosse on April 18, 1865, with two hundred and fifty passengers on board and quite an amount of freight. The boats proceeded without trouble, making excellent time, until they reached Fort Randal.

The government had sent General Sully against the Sioux and he was seriously handicapped for lack of means of transportation and on May 10 impressed the "Chippeway Falls" to carry supplies for his expedition. All the passengers and freight were transferred to the "Cutter" and, although overloaded and most uncomfortably crowded, she made her way to Fort Benton and discharged her passengers and freight. Here she was deserted by crew and engineers, who ran off to the mines, and the boat was tied up for the rest of the summer.

The "Chippeway Falls" was ordered down the river to "light off" a steamer loaded with expeditionary stores, which was on its way up to General Sully, and join him at Fort Randal. Sully moved on the east side of the Missouri, the "Chippeway Falls" following near him along the river until the expedition reached a

point near the Cannon Ball river. Here the "Chippeway" ferried the troops across and then started for a
point, designated by General Sully, on the Yellowstone
river, where was one of Manuel Lisa's old trading
posts.

The "Chippeway Falls" was to carry provisions and
forage to this point in company with a steamer called
the "Alone." General Sully started back with an Indian guide and as they could not carry with them many
rations or much forage it was of utmost importance
that the boat reach the point named on time.

Captain Hutchinson with sixty-five thousand rations
and accompanied by the "Alone," started on up the
Missouri and soon reached Fort Union at the mouth of
the Yellowstone. Here he left the "Alone" and his
cargo and started up the Yellowstone on an exploring
expedition.

Captain Hutchinson ran up only about fifty miles on
this trip, but finding about four feet of water pro-
nounced navigation on the Yellowstone practicable and
returned for his consort and freight. Leading again,
the "Chippeway Falls" attended by the "Alone" started
up the Yellowstone. This time they ascended to the
old trading post at the mouth of the Big Horn,[100] where
they waited for the troops six days. The "Alone"
grounded six miles below the post and could go no
further.

Sully's troops had been on half rations for several
days and were rejoiced to see the boats. The animals
were also starving; many had been abandoned and
killed. After having recruited their strength, Captain

---

[100] This post was first established by Manuel Lisa about 1807 and was
known as Fort Lisa. Later it was renamed Fort Benton. Chittenden,
American Fur Trade, vol. i, p. 150 n. After 1850 it was known as the Big
Horn post. – ED.

Hutchinson ferried them across the Yellowstone and descended to Fort Union.

The expedition finally went down the river to Fort Berthold,[101] here Captain Hutchinson was released from government service and took the "Chippeway Falls" to St. Joseph, Missouri. So it was that, the "Chippeway Falls," which drew about thirteen inches of water when light, commanded by Capt. Abraham Hutchinson, was the first steamer whose paddles ever stirred the waters of the Yellowstone.

Early in the spring of 1865 an attempt was made to build a town on the Missouri at the mouth of the Marias, where steamboats could land and discharge their freight and thus save twenty miles of shallow and difficult navigation between there and Fort Benton. The Ophir Townsite Company surveyed a town and offered lots for sale. A steam sawmill was purchased and men sent down to get out logs, preparatory to building a town. On May 25, while at work in the timber three miles from the landing, ten men were surprised by a band of one hundred Blackfoot Indians and all were massacred. Four of the men were scalped. The Indians made a hasty retreat and crossed the line into British territory before they could be overtaken and punished.

In 1865 the sole medium of exchange in Montana was gold dust. The few greenbacks and treasury notes brought into the country by emigrants were a commodity, and bought and sold at market price. Mer-

---

[101] Old Fort Berthold was built by the American Fur Company about 1845. In 1862 it was moved to a nearby location on the Missouri river near the present Fort Berthold Indian reservation. In 1864 government troops were stationed there and it was important in the Sioux war. It was abandoned in 1867. *South Dakota Historical Collections*, vol. i (1902) p. 134.—ED.

chants usually made one trip east during the year; taking with them the year's accumulation of gold dust with which to pay their obligations and to purchase additional goods.

During the winter of 1865 a number of trains from Salt Lake, loaded with flour were snowed in in Beaver cañon and all the oxen perished in the storm. Provisions of every kind became scarce. Potatoes sold for 65c per pound, bacon $1.00 per pound, sugar 85c, tea $3.00, butter $1.75, candles 90c per pound, beans 40c, soap 50c, hominy 75c and flour $27.00 per cwt. On the twentieth of February there was a big raise in the price of flour from $27.00 to $40.00 and up and up until it had reached $150.00 per cwt. Most people, especially those with families, were unable to purchase flour at that price and as all provisions were scarce, many were reduced to a diet of meat straight. Beef was quite plentiful and sold for fifteen cents per pound. It was evident that a corner was held on flour. Groups of people collected on the streets and the all absorbing topic of conversation was the price of flour.

On April 18 word came that a large body of men armed and well organized were marching up from Nevada with the avowed determination to take possession of all the flour in town and divide it among the citizens at a reasonable and fair price. This information was soon verified by the appearance of five hundred men marching in file, all armed with revolvers and rifles. This force was under a leader on horseback, carrying an empty sack nailed to a staff as a banner. The men were divided into six companies each commanded by a captain and moved in military fashion. There was no doubt of their intentions: within five minutes after their arrival they commenced at the foot of Wallace street and searched every store and place where flour could be concealed. About one hundred twenty-five sacks were found and safely stored away in Leviathan hall. The search was orderly but very thorough and disclosed sundry lots of flour concealed under coats, in boxes and barrels and under hay stacks. An armed force determined to have all the flour that could be found in stores or the property of dealers wherever hidden and yet going through the matter as quietly as if it were a seizure by order of the court.

The men took no notice of people on the streets or of remarks addressed to them but followed after their captain; halted, fronted, and stood like a provost guard while the leader made known his business and detailed a party for the search. This being completed, if flour was found it was packed off without ceremony; an account being kept and a promise to pay for all at the rate of $27.00 per cwt. for Salt Lake flour and $36.00 for states flour. A notice was handed in to the *Montana Post* ordering all flour to be sold from $27.00 to $30.00 for the future.

A meeting was held in Leviathan hall in the evening: representation having been made of three cases in one of which flour had been taken from a boarding-house keeper and another in which a baker's stock had been confiscated and in a third where flour had been taken from a family. The complaints were investigated and the flour returned next day. A number of dissatisfied citizens and flour dealers held a meeting in the court room in the evening, but no action was taken.

On Wednesday the distribution of the flour was begun: twelve pounds were issued to a man who was willing to affirm that he had no flour and was unable to procure any; a double ration was given to a married man, and more in case there were children. A barrier guarded by armed men was placed at the door of the flour depot. The men were admitted to the hall in squads of ten. At the instance of Mayor Pfouts the committee promised that any flour brought in by pack train from Snake river or Salt Lake City should be sold at a price not to exceed fifty dollars per cwt. unless proof of its costing more be made.

Some of the citizens became much annoyed by the vigor of the search but upon the whole there was but little ill-feeling. On Thursday the committee paid for all the flour that they had taken, at the rate of $27.00 per cwt. George Mann, J. T. Sullivan, Joseph Marion, John Creighton, Ming and North, and Kercheval and Company were the principal holders of flour. After the flour was distributed the members of the committee returned to their homes.

During the winter (1866-67) Governor Smith inaugurated the custom of holding weekly levees in the council chamber, at Virginia City. Governor Smith assisted by Mr. Thomas Frances Meagher received the guests. These were the first exclusive gatherings in the territory. Guests were admitted by invitation cards only.

On September 22, 1866, occurred the death of our beloved friend Professor Dimsdale. This gentle, kind-hearted, Christian man came among us in the summer of 1863. A man of culture and refinement he drew to himself all that was best of society at that time in Virginia City. He organized and taught the first school in the territory, was the first superintendent of public instruction and edited the first newspaper published in the territory. He published *The Vigilantes* an absolutely correct narrative of the operations of that society.

Of an extremely delicate constitution the arduous duties and close confinement attendant on managing and editing a newspaper undermined his health, and he died at the early age of thirty-five, mourned by all who knew him.

While in Benton on August 29, 1866, a freight wagon drawn by four mules and escorted by a company of miners, arrived. The wagon was loaded with two and one-half tons of gold dust, valued at one million five hundred thousand dollars. The gold was all from Confederate gulch and was shipped down the river by steamboat. This was the first and only time that I ever saw a wagon load of gold dust at one time.

This same year a tanning mill was located on Mill creek about twenty-five miles from Virginia City. The bark was ground by water power and they were able to tan about two thousand cow hides during the summer. This mill was in successful operation for about five years and turned out an excellent quality of leather.

In 1866 a telegraph line was completed from Salt Lake City to Virginia City, Montana.

In the fall of 1867 I sold the business in Virginia City to F. E. W. Patten and took up my permanent residence in Deer Lodge.

Quartz Mining and Railroads

The next few years were busy ones for me. We were engaged in mining at Argenta and Philipsburg, had a store and lumber yard at Deer Lodge and a store in Philipsburg. The quartz mill at Philipsburg was completed and put in operation on October 2, 1867. We had spent large sums of money and two years of time on this enterprise and had employed meteorologists and chemists of national reputation, but when the mill was put in operation it would not save the values in the ores. My brother James again spent the winter in St. Louis purchasing additional machinery, and the following summer made another trial but without success and we were obliged to abandon the enterprise.

In the spring of 1870 James was appointed post trader at Fort Browning [102] and went over into eastern Montana and I was left alone to look after the business in Deer Lodge which consisted of various mining enterprises, a ranch with a limited number of horses and cattle, a lumber yard and a mercantile establishment.

In addition to our private business I was county commissioner and school trustee and devoted no little time to county and school affairs.

From 1865 to 1870 was an era of great prosperity in Deer Lodge county. During this period the placer

[102] Fort Browning was a government fort in northeastern Montana, the agency post for the Assiniboine and Upper Sioux. Abandoned in 1873 when the Assiniboine agency was moved to Fort Belknap sixty miles above on the Milk river and the Sioux agency was moved to Fort Peck. – ED.

mines produced more than $20,000,000 in gold dust
from gulches as follows:

Gold creek	$2000000
Ophir	5000000
McClellan	1600000
Lincoln	1200000
French gulch	1000000
German gulch	3000000
Nevada	
Jefferson	
Washington	1500000
Bear gulch	2600000
Scattering	2000000

The valleys were well settled with prosperous ranchers.
The town of Deer Lodge was the center of education
and refinement for the territory. Many families moved
to town and built beautiful homes because of the
superior educational advantages offered for their children. Every branch of business was represented by
large and substantial establishments.

In August, 1870, L. E. Graham and J. B. Taylor
arrived in Deer Lodge valley with four hundred and
fifty heifers and five bulls of pure Durham blood. The
cattle were purchased at Omaha, Nebraska, shipped to
Ogden, Utah, and from there driven north. This was
the first herd of thoroughbred cattle brought to Montana. During the summer of 1870 many wagons
loaded with melons, tomatoes, cucumbers, green corn,
and apples were hauled from the Bitter Root valley
and sold in Deer Lodge.

In May, 1869, Miss Guine Evans, daughter of Morgan Evans, filed on one hundred and sixty acres of land
on Warm Spring creek. This was the first homestead

entry made by a woman in Montana. Miss Evans lived on her homestead and proved up on it and was granted a government patent to the land.

Virginia City was not what could be called a quiet town at this particular time. In addition to the members of the legislature there were numerous lobbies from various sections of the territory, the strongest one being the one in the interest of the railroad subsidy bill. These gentlemen were liberal entertainers and liquid refreshments flowed across the hotel bars as freely as the waters over Alder gulch. These revels were kept up all night long and after the legislature was in session it was no uncommon thing for the sergeant at arms to be sent through the legislative halls to arouse the drowsy members when a vote was being taken on some important bill.

Governor Potts and secretary, James E. Calloway were appointed by President Grant and were both Republicans while the legislature was solidly Democratic but the session passed without the friction between the executive and legislative branches that had marred previous sessions.

The question of the permanent location of the capitol arose. Deer Lodge was a strong candidate for that honor. There was much bitter feeling between the contending towns. Cartooning came into vogue for the first time in Montana. James M. Cavanaugh, our one time delegate in Congress, in a speech sarcastically referred to our splendid city of Deer Lodge as "the little village on the trail to Bear" and to this day (1915) the appellation has stuck.

From 1866 up to 1872 every legislature had passed laws voting extra compensation to United States and territorial officers out of the territorial treasury.

$282976.00 had been so expended and the financial condition of the territory had been badly involved, the indebtedness being over $500000.

The railroad subsidy bill was not favored by the governor and it did not pass although its friends kept up a bitter fight throughout the entire session. No sooner had the legislature adjourned than the railroad subsidy ring begun clamoring for an extra session, the nominal excuse being the imperfection of laws passed by the regular session. The real reason was the determination of the railroad subsidy crowd to pledge the territory to an exceedingly heavy subsidy to build a north and south railroad. Deer Lodge county strongly opposed the calling of an extra session. In March, 1873, Governor Potts did call an extra session to convene on April 14, 1873.

From 1870 to 1880 was a period of financial depression in Montana. Until 1870 placer mining was the all important industry in the territory: but from that time gold production decreased rapidly from all the old placers and there were no important new discoveries. Many of our leading citizens thought it time to abandon the country to the Indians and buffalo and not a few did leave for the states and for the new gold discoveries of the Black hills.

The Cheyenne, Arapaho, and Sioux Indians driven north and west from Kansas and Minnesota united under the able leadership of the great chief Red Cloud, harrassed the Missouri river transportation and emigrant trains to Montana and raided our ranches at will. For a time it did look as though the Indians would take possession whether we were willing or not.

Important discoveries of quartz ledges of gold, silver, and copper had been made and we had vast coal

beds. Carefully kept weather records and considerable experimentation had proven that agriculture could
be carried on successfully in all of our valleys but none
of these resources could be developed without cheaper
and better transportation facilities; a railroad into the
territory became a necessity.   How to get one at a cost
that would not bankrupt the new and sparsely settled
territory engaged the minds of the thoughtful citizens.

There were three possible chances to be considered.
A north and south line to connect with the Union
Pacific, an extension of the Utah Northern narrow
gauge north from Snake river, Idaho, or the Northern
Pacific transcontinental line across the territory east
and west.   This latter route was most feasible and to
it we pinned our faith until the panic of 1873 carrying
Jay Cooke and Company to the wall shattered our
hopes in that direction.

All of the railroad subsidy bills introduced in the
earlier legislatures called for sums of money sufficient
to construct the proposed roads without other assistance and were entirely beyond what the territory should
be expected to pay.   Governor Potts who was an able
lawyer held that the legislature had no legal power to
bond the territory to subsidize a railroad and for that
reason strongly opposed any act in that direction.

Meetings were held in different counties and com-
mittees appointed to solicit propositions from the Utah
Northern and the Union Pacific looking to their early
entrance into Montana.

John Young, a son of Brigham Young of Utah, was
constructing a narrow gauge road northward into Idaho
and offered to extend the line, three hundred miles to
the mouth of the Big Hole river in Montana, the same
to be completed in three years, for a consideration of

$5000 per mile. When the ninth session of the territorial legislature convened on January 3, 1876, a law was passed authorizing an election whereby qualified voters could pass on issuing $1500000, of territorial bonds to contribute toward the construction of a railroad from Franklyn, Idaho, to Big Hole river in Montana.

Another act authorizing counties to be benefited thereby, to submit to the voters the proposition of issuing bonds to aid a railroad and still another act allowing counties through which the Northern Pacific railroad would pass to call elections whereby voters could decide on bonding the said counties to aid that road was passed.

At the election, bonds for a railway subsidy failed to carry and in April, 1877, Sidney Dillon, president of the Utah Northern made a proposition to the Governor of Montana, to extend the line into Montana and Governor Potts called an extra session of the legislature to consider the proposition. Before a special election to vote on bonds could be held the road crossed the Montana border and was being pushed northward as rapidly as possible. The Utah Northern narrow gauge was completed to Silver Bow in 1880 and a branch extended to Garrison in 1881.

Life and Customs of the Indians

The first years of my residence in Montana were spent west of the Rocky mountains and the Indians I came in contact with were the Shoshones, Bannocks, Flatheads, Kalispells, Kootenais, Spokanes, and Nez Percés. Their life and habits became to me an interesting study and as all of these tribes were friendly and constantly camped near us I had a good opportunity to study them.

Each tribe had a head chief and several sub chiefs. The head chieftainship was sometimes hereditary, but more often he was elected by the council. His authority was almost despotic, although when questions of unusual importance arose the head chief called a council of all the sub chiefs, and head men of the tribe. Much attention is given to the advice of old men of the tribe.

The war chiefs were elected because of some unusual feat of bravery or daring. Any young man of a tribe could become war chief if he possessed the requisite qualifications. The war chief was often selected for a season but held his place so long as he excelled all others of the tribe in waging successful war against their enemies and in bringing home the greatest number of stolen ponies.

After each successful battle there would be a war dance. A fire would be built in the open and all the warriors present assembled. The scalps taken were placed on a long pole and stuck up near the fire. The women and young boys formed an outer circle and were spectators but never took any part in the dance. The war chief opened the dance by standing up and reciting the deeds of bravery, then all the warriors would form in a sort of promenade around the fire chanting their war songs. Then another brave would recount his exploits and so on until each one had been heard or until they were all exhausted. On occasions when there had been a big fight and many scalps taken and few lives lost on their side, the war dance would be kept up for three or four nights.

Indians believed implicitly in magic. Each tribe had its medicine man. He occupied a tent by himself and spent much time in solitude, conjuring up magical powers to bring success to the tribe, to keep away evil spirits, to prevent misfortune and to heal the sick. He usually had a highly ornamental parflash, in which he kept one or more fetishes. Sometimes it was a small bush or herb and again it was a queer-shaped stone, a piece of hair or a bear's claw. No one excepting the medicine man dared to go near or touch the sacred parflash.

The medicine man was always consulted before the tribe engaged in an enterprise of any magnitude. If he was successful the medicine was considered strong and the medicine man rose in tribal favor, but if unsuccessful the medicine was considered weak and the dispenser thereof must get to work and improve his brand or he would soon be discarded altogether. Most of the medicine men were sagacious old fellows and managed to keep their positions unless the tribe had a very hard run of luck. Some of them like old Winnemucca and Sitting Bull gained an influence that transcended that of head chief.

These tribes also had sort of shrines usually a tree or some peculiarly shaped rock on which they placed gifts to the Great Spirit. There was one large pine tree on top of the hill just west of McCary's bridge in Hell Gate cañon, on which the Indians hung small articles of bead work, bear claws, strips of red cloth, queer-shaped stones, bunches of white sage, pieces of buffalo scalp, small pieces of bone, etc. There was another such tree in the Bitter Root valley fifty miles above Stevensville. The objects were hung on these trees as the Indians passed on their way out to the hunting grounds and were placed there to invoke the aid of the Great Spirit to make game plentiful and to make them successful in their enterprises.

In the big bend of Milk river thirty miles east of Fort Belknap is a big gray granite rock resembling a buffalo lying down. This rock was greatly reverenced by the Blackfeet and River Crows and in passing they always placed on it some talisman. Many of them made long pilgrimages to this sacred rock for the sole purpose of making offerings.

Another sacred rock was a huge red sandstone boulder on the side of a grassy bluff on the northwest of Fort Benton. This huge rock once rested on the top of the bluff but as the rains and snows washed the soft gravely earth from around it, it gradually slipped down the hillside. Indians are very observing and as they noticed the changed position of the huge rock on the hillside they attributed it to something supernatural and it became a sacred shrine to them. In addition to placing objects on these rocks, they often carved or painted figures or characters on the rocks.

The sun dance was the great annual reunion of the tribe and was the most important ceremony of the

plains' Indians. It was held late in the summer or
autumn, first before the big or fall buffalo hunt. The
head chief decided the time and place for this meeting
and every member of the tribe was present.

The great village was arranged in a semi-circle with
the opening toward east. The head chief directed the
placing of the tepees but they were arranged with
reference to the rank and influence of the families in
the tribe. At one side and some little distance from
the outskirts of the village were placed three or four
tepees for the exclusive use of the medicine men. These
tepees were sacred and no one but the occupants must
go near them.

As soon as the tribe had gathered the medicine men
retired to these tepees and remained there fasting and
in meditation and in preparing talismans and in the
performance of secret rites. This finished, preparations for the erection of the big lodge are begun. This
lodge is always placed in the center of the semi-circle
but the exact spots where the center pole and altar is
to be placed is selected and consecrated by the big
medicine man of the tribe, with much ceremony.

The center pole is selected and prepared by young
men, members of a secret society and no one else must
touch the sacred pole. Around this center pole is
placed a roofless lodge one hundred feet in diameter
and about eight feet high with the opening toward
the east. As soon as the big lodge is up the medicine
men and those who are to dance go inside and spend
the night fasting, meditating, and in dedicating the
lodge.

On the following morning the altar is prepared at
the west side of the lodge. An oval-shaped hole is
scraped out about six inches deep and in this is placed

braided wisps of sweetgrass, sage, willows, or juniper and around it about four inches apart is set a row of brilliantly-colored willow sticks; behind this is placed an elaborate arrangement of buffalo skulls, elk and deer horns.

This finished the medicine men begin to paint and adorn the naked bodies of the dancers by smearing them with grease paint and placing wisps of willow and sage about their heads, necks, arms, waists, and ankles.

Those who are candidates for warriors have slits cut in their flesh underneath the shoulder blades and through this is passed a rawhide rope or thong to the ends of which is attached three or four buffalo skulls that drag on the ground behind the dancer until the flesh gives way and he is released.

At the south end of the lodge six or seven musicians sit around a large drum and when all is ready the musicians begin beating the drum and chanting, the dancers form a circle and the dancing begins, all blowing on a whistle made from the quill of an eagle's wing. The dancing and the noise is kept up for hours or until all the buffalo skulls have torn loose from the flesh. It is considered a piece of great cowardice to be released in any other way, and the one who can endure the greatest torture for the longest period of time ranks highest as a warrior.

These dances are not only for tests of valor but they are for the purpose of calling up Chinook winds, driving away evil spirits, making game plentiful, averting lightning and pestilences, and to give luck to the warriors, gamblers, and horse thieves. At the conclusion of this dance the participants take an emetic and then go to the sweat house.

After this comes the feast of commemoration for the dead. The men who have lost relatives or friends during the year, dance and chant death songs. If a head chief has died or been killed the whole tribe joins in the ceremony. His son recites his deeds of valor before the dancing begins. When this is finished the big council starts. The head chief presides. The rank of chiefs and warriors is decided, tribal differences settled, and new policies inaugurated.

At the close of the big council there are banquets among the chief's relatives and friends and the social dance in which both men and women take part and there is always a number of weddings.

The duration of the social festivities is determined largely by the condition of the commissary. If pemmican, fat dogs, smoked buffalo tongue, and like delicacies were plentiful they lasted a week or until they were all eaten up, then the families all pack up and leave to follow their every day pursuits.

The center pole and the altar are always left standing. They are considered sacred and must not be disturbed.

The tepee always belongs to the Indian man, but it is the woman who provides it and forever looks after it. Constructing an Indian lodge was no small undertaking.

First of all there is the skin covering to prepare. In 1858 the most used covering was made from the elk skin. The squaw skinned the animal, then folding it carefully, carried it, with the meat to the camp. The man's work began and ended with the killing of the animal. If horses were plentiful the woman was allowed a pack horse to bring in the meat and hide, but if scarce she carried it in on her back. The skin was then stretched out and pinned securely to the ground with wooden pegs and then with a piece of elk horn sharpened much like a chisel she would go over every particle of the hide scraping and removing any particle of flesh that adhered to it. Then turning it over and hanging it over a pole which was placed slanting against a tree, she took a buffalo rib and scraped all the hair and scriffin from the other side. This was a long tedious operation as they had only a little strip about three inches wide and a foot long to work on when the skin would have to be shifted. It would often require weeks to get the hair off of one hide. After both sides of a skin was thus prepared, the next thing was to go all over it with a cobble rock split in two; with the sharp edge of this rock they rubbed and pounded and worked the skin until it was soft. It was again stretched on the ground, the brains were melted and poured over it and thoroughly rubbed in. It was then left in the sun until the brain substance was absorbed. It was again taken up and washed in warm water until it was thoroughly clean and white, then wrung out and rubbed and stretched and pounded until it was perfectly dry. Four skins were then fastened together like a square box. A hole was dug in the ground and filled with pieces of bark or dead wood and set on fire. This would make little heat, but a dense smoke. Over the hole they would place a tripod and inside of that were hung the skins spread out well over the hole so that the smoke would reach every part of them. When skins were well smoked they were a beautiful light brown, soft as cloth and would never after become hard when wet. Elk, deer, antelope, and mountain sheep skins were dressed in this way.

It required from ten to twelve elk skins to make a

lodge and these had to be cut and sewed together with sinew; all the little holes for the sinew were punched with an awl.

Next was the preparing of the frame work. This required from twelve to fourteen poles, twelve or sixteen feet long and three inches in diameter at the bottom, tapering somewhat toward the top. It is some trouble to get exactly the right kind of lodge poles so the camp usually make a trip to some well-known spot where the right kind of poles could be found. Here they camp and allow the squaws to get and prepare a quantity sufficient to do all hands for some time. The poles are carefully peeled and laid out straight to dry. Then a hole is burned in each one about twenty inches from the top. This is to enable them to tie them together in bunches of six or seven so they can be fastened, one bunch on either side of the saddle with the other end dragging along the ground. In this way they are moved when the camp is traveling.

The men ride ahead and select camping places. When there is a large village the chief directs the placing of the tepees. The women then erect three poles which are fastened together with leather thongs. The top of the skin covering is fastened to the tops of these poles and then raised and stood up like a tripod, the other poles are next placed in the crotches of these three poles and when all are placed and the elk skin covering drawn around them a squaw enters the lodge and pushes the bottom of the poles out in a circle until the skin is stretched perfectly tight over the poles; they then fasten it securely around the bottom with wooden pegs. These pegs are carried with them and there is always a supply on hand. The only openings to the lodge are at the top where the poles project, and a small opening about three feet square cut in one side of the lodge about one foot from the ground, used for an entrance and over this opening is hung a deer skin stretched on a wood frame. This is kept shut in cold weather, but is always open when warm.

The fire is built in the center of the lodge and the smoke escapes through the small opening at the top. Two poles six inches in diameter are placed three feet apart from the door to the fire. This is the entrance.

To the right of the door and occupying one-fourth of the lodge is the woman's department; here are the small children and whatever cooking utensils and sewing materials the lodge affords. No visitor ever trespasses in this part of the lodge. The floor of the rest of the space is covered with rye grass or willow twigs. All around the circle is placed the tanned robes, and parflashes containing the dried meats, pemmican, dried roots, and berries, dressed skins and in fact everything belonging to the family. The family spread their robes on the rye grass and sleep in a circle with their feet to the fire.

A lodge the size of the one described will accommodate a family of ten. Girls remain in their parents' lodge until married, sleeping on the same side of the circle with the mother, but the boys leave the home lodge early and live apart five or six in one lodge. Brothers often remain together, but sometimes a lodge is made up of cousins or friends. The mother and sisters provide the lodges, move, and set up these bachelor apartments.

Some of the lodges were painted and decorated with colored drawings; these drawings represented victorious battles or horse-stealing raids and some of them were very cleverly executed. The coloring was always harmonious and pleasing. When an Indian possessed one of these decorated lodges he would not sell it. I doubt if there is one of them in existence today.

A good elk skin lodge is a very comfortable thing to live in. The opening in the top, while very small, would let in no rain or snow, and was a perfect ventilator, letting out all smoke and bad air. A very little fire kept it warm and in summer time it is raised up about two feet all around the bottom. This allows the air to pass and keeps it perfectly cool. All the cooking is done outside, unless the weather is very bad. I do not remember of ever having a cold while living in an elk skin lodge.

The women do all of the work even to saddling and unsaddling the horses for their lords and masters. Girls are taught to do all the work which falls to the mother's lot, when they are very young. When game was plentiful hundreds of animals, deer, sheep, elk, and buffalo, were killed and the women dressed all the skins and dried all the meat beside the regular routine work of camp life.

The moving of an Indian village is an interesting sight. The herders bring in all the ponies; each one selects his own and the saddling up begins. Some of the men saddle their own ponies, but more often the women do it for them. Next the lodges are dismantled, parflashes, and robes, and extra baggage are packed on pack horses. The lodge poles are tied in bundles of from four to six each, and a bunch tied on either side of the saddle, the other end dragging on the ground. On these poles and about two feet from the ground is piled the lodge covering, cooking utensils and robes or skins or dried meat. These things are all lashed on securely and ride along as easily as though they were in a wagon. This is called a travois. In this way one pony will drag one hundred fifty to two hundred pounds.

The parflash is a box made of rawhide in which is carried dried roots, sugar or salt, if the village had any, and any small articles like red paint, beads, elk teeth, porcupine quills, or things likely to get lost or be injured by getting wet. These parflashes are usually packed on pack horses, and often small children are packed on with them. Boys and girls old enough to ride have their own ponies, two or three children ride on one pony. The infants are strapped to a papoose board and this board hung over the pommel of the mother's saddle, from where the little thing dangles during the long marches.

When all is ready the cavalcade advances, first the chiefs and braves, then the younger members of the village, then pack horses and travois, children, and last the squaws and dogs. Not that the dogs rank with the squaws! A dog is a valuable asset in an Indian village, he is night watch and then his flesh is considered a dish of great delicacy. He travels with the squaws from choice, he knows that the nearer he is to the squaws, the nearer to the commissary.

When I first came among these Indians they had plenty of good horses, clean new blankets, much red cloth, and gay-hued calicoes. The chiefs sported the most gorgeous war bonnets, highly embroidered and beaded buckskin suits, and moccasins. A moving village was a most entertaining and picturesque sight.

When streams were high they constructed boats by making a round basket shaped frame work of willows and then stretching buffalo hides tightly over that they had a fairly good boat in which two could paddle themselves across nicely. They also spread out the lodge skins and packing everything inside drew the skin up tight and tied it. This made a large balloon shaped bundle and with a rawhide rope attached to the top, was then placed in the stream and a woman and two or three small children would be perched on top clinging to the rope. An Indian with a pony, that was a good swimmer, would take hold of the end of the rope and start out across the stream. The queer-looking bundle would bob and bounce around in the swift current, but the pony would finally make the shore and land everybody safely and comparatively dry. Whole villages would cross the largest, swiftest, streams during flood waters and I do not remember of ever hearing of one drowning, although many white men lost their lives in attempting to cross the same streams.

An Indian could have as many wives as he wished and many of them had three, but seldom did they have more than five. Usually the chief took the captives, but if the captive was a woman she was turned over to the women of the tribe to be tortured to death or made a slave and compelled to do the drudgery of the camp.

Wherever there is an Indian village there is a number of sweat houses. These are constructed out of willow bushes made round about seven feet in diameter and four feet high. Over this they spread robes or blankets and inside build a fire and heat a pile of cobble rocks. When the rocks are red hot they scratch out the fire and provide themselves with a bucket of cold water, strip and crawl into this small wickiup and pour the cold water over the hot rocks. This creates a dense steam and makes it suffocatingly hot. The occupant remains here as long as he can stand it, then he comes out takes a run to the nearest stream and plunges into icy water. The sweat house is the Indian remedy for all illnesses. When smallpox first appeared among them, many lost their lives by using this treatment.

The Catholic missionaries had come among these Indians before I arrived and most of them had embraced that faith. This was especially true of the Flatheads but before that they were sun worshippers. When an Indian tried to convince you, he invariably pointed to the sun and said "The Great Spirit, the sun knows I do not lie." Through all their legends the sun is the Great Spirit and is given power over all other spirits.

The tribes of western Montana were hospitable, truthful, and scrupulously honest, until the whites taught them otherwise. Horse stealing was a legitimate game among all the tribes and a clever horse thief ranked with a sub chief.

The women of some tribes were virtuous, in others the men traded wives as readily as they traded horses and virtue was unknown. The Nez Percé were the highest type of Indian that I met with and the Crows the lowest. I have found little in the Crows to commend.

Among all the tribes the women were sold. The young people more or less made their choice, but when a man takes an Indian girl he is expected to leave a good horse, some blankets, and trinkets at her father's lodge when he takes her away. If she is a particularly attractive girl he will leave two or more horses.

I have had letters from eastern people asking me if I could furnish them copies of Indian love songs – I have read of Indian love songs but never heard any such songs among the Montana tribes. The only songs I ever heard them sing were their war songs, and a pecu-

liar chant which they kept up while gambling, for the
purpose of making them lucky at the game. Should
the strains of a war song reach the ear of an Indian
maiden she generally climbed a tree or crawled into a
convenient hole until the warbler drifted out of her
neighborhood. A war song is one of the most ear-
splitting, blood-curdling howls that ever reached my
ear and they are only indulged in when a battle is being
waged.

If a "brave" wishes to attract the attention of some
particular Indian maiden he usually dresses up and
does some fancy riding stunts, on his best pony, in the
vicinity of her father's tepee, or kills an unusual lot of
game, or drives his share of stolen ponies past her door,
or displays some fresh scalps on his con stick. I have
seen young couples sauntering around on the outskirts
of a village looking as silly as white couples do, but not
often.

At a very early age the Indian boy is taught the art
of war, the chase, and horse stealing. He can use a
bow and arrow almost as soon as he can walk. He
practices all sorts of fights to cultivate bravery and
cunning. His standing in the tribe depends upon his
acts of bravery and his cunning at capturing horses belonging to an enemy. The young men usually follow
the advice of old men of the tribe but it is not difficult
for him to become a sub chief if he is a clever hunter,
skilled horseman, and brave in the face of danger.

The little girls play with dolls and make pets of the
puppies, often binding the little fellows on a papoose
board and carrying them on their back in imitation of
their mothers carrying the baby. At a very early age
the girls are instructed in all the arts of their home life,
sewing, bead work, dressing skins, etc.

A young girl's entrance into womanhood was attended with much ceremony. A place was selected in a dense thicket or grove near a stream, and some distance from the village. Here a small tepee would be erected. The mother of the maiden would then instruct her in a code of ethics, which would affect her whole after-life. She must sit erect in the center of the tepee lest she become lazy, she must fast lest she become gluttonous. She must not speak lest she become garrulous. Her meditations must be on obedience to her parents, speaking the truth, kindness and gentleness and being a dutiful wife and a good mother.

With these instructions she retires to the tepee and there remains in solitude for four or five days. During this time she does much bathing and before leaving the tepee she is given wisps of sweetgrass, white sage or pine needles with which she builds a smudge, then leaning over it allows the smoke to envelop her then standing erect in the smoke she faces the sun and extending her arms above her head chants a sort of prayer. Her mother then brings her new clothing and when dressed she would leave the tepee and return to her home.

In every Indian village there is one very old man who will tell stories to the children and at this tepee the children love to gather and they are as anxious for the legends as are the white children for the fairy tales told them when gathered about the open grate at home.

There is one legend told, with some few variations, by almost every tribe of Indians in Montana. It was given to me by a Nez Percé boy and here it is just as he told it to me.

It appears there was at one time a great giant who lived in the valley of Kamiah (Kam-yaph) Idaho.

This valley has been settled by the Nez Percé tribe of Indians so far back no one knows. The giant's head extended as far up as where the town of Kooskia now stands (or Indian name Tu-ku-pa). This clear water valley in the vicinity of Kamiah (Kam-yaph) Kooskia (or Tu-ku-pa) is the Garden of Eden of north Idaho. This giant was eight miles long and use to swallow every living thing that came in his way, and the coyote heard about it and he planned a scheme to kill this great giant. The coyote was just in the prime of life and was very popular and a great man among all the living beings at that time. It appears all the living creatures or animals at that time were supposed to be human beings and this coyote prophecied that the time was coming and this time was very short when new and more superior human beings would take their place, meaning the present human race. As stated above, coyote determined to kill the great giant, so he went to work and made him a rope from hemp, willow bark, etc., to tie himself and fasten these ropes to high mountains, such as Pilot Knob, Seven Devils, and other high mountains, and then he [coyote] stationed himself on top of the Whitebird hill, between Camas prairie and the Whitebird cañon, made a crown out of bunch grass so the giant could not see him or detect him. Then the coyote challenged the great giant to swallow him, but the giant could not see him. This giant had heard about the coyote being a very popular and a very hard man to be beaten.

The great giant challenged the coyote to swallow him [giant] first, but coyote insisted that the giant swallow him, so finally the great giant drew his breath and the coyote came jumping into the mouth of the great giant. Before the coyote allowed himself to be swallowed he secured a bunch of fir pitch and also secreted five flint spears or knives in his person. After coyote being swallowed first thing he came to was a rattlesnake and the snake wanted to bite him, made all kinds of hissing noise. Coyote stamped on the snake's head and flattened it, coyote said to snake if you were so brave and so dangerous why did you allow yourself to be swallowed by this giant and not do anything to save yourself and all that have been swallowed by this monster and allow him to rule over you. Coyote went further and the grizzly bear met him and growled at him and showed fight. Coyote treated him [grizzly] the same way as he did with the snake, kicked the grizzly in the nose, that turned grizzly's nose up, etc.

Coyote finally arrived at the giant's heart, first thing coyote did was to see that all living things got out of the giant and he kicked all the bones out, then he went to cutting the giant's heart, and built a fire with the fir pitch he brought with him. The giant began to feel the pain and begged coyote to let him alone and that he [giant] would allow him to go free, but coyote said, "No you swallowed men, and now you got to take the consequences." Coyote broke all his flint knives, but one with which he finished cutting in the heart. Before the giant died, coyote managed to get out. After the giant died, coyote took his last flint knife and cut the giant up and distributed different parts of the great giant's body all over North America and commanded that out of this giant's body shall be made different tribes of Indians.

When he had finished his partner, fox, said to him in his usual quiet way, "Coyote, you have forgotten this part of the country, and have not left any part of giant's flesh."

Coyote turned to fox and said, "You are always stupid, why did you not tell me before?" So coyote told fox to bring some water, for his hands were bloody. Coyote took the water and dipped his bloody hands and sprinkled the bloody water on the ground and commanded that out of said bloody water the Nez Percé tribe of Indians should come forth. Though the Nez Percé tribe may be a small tribe, they will be the most intelligent, bravest, and greatest fighters of any tribe in North America.

The Nez Percé name for the giant the coyote killed is "Iltz-wa-we-tsih."

About the only difference in the story is in the location of the valley. With the Nez Percé it is the valley of the Kamiah; with the Crows it is the valley of the Big Horn; with the Flatheads, it is the Mission valley.

Niñumbee is another very singular fairy tale told among the Snakes and Bannocks. It runs about as follows: In the Salmon River mountains there lives in caves among the rocks, a race of fairies, about two feet high, who, with bow in hand and arrow-case slung on their backs, go out and hunt and kill sheep, deer, elk, and antelope which they carry home on their backs; they eat the flesh, and their wives dress the skins, from which they make themselves clothes while the men go entirely naked.

Now whenever the Indians are in their vicinity, and a woman goes out after wood or for any other purpose, and happens to lay her infant down and gets out of sight of it, one of these fairies immediately devours it and taking its place, begins to cry at a terrible rate; the woman hearing her child, as she supposes, crying, returns, and taking it up gives it to suck to pacify it, when it instantly seizes her by the breast and commences devouring it.

Now these fairies are a kind of human "monitor" being perfectly proof against knives, axes, stones, clubs, or firearms, so the poor woman cannot get rid of him, and her screams being heard by her husband or friends, they rush to the spot, when the little devil takes to flight, leaving her in a dying condition. She always dies before morning. If they leave her to go after more help the fairy instantly returns and finishes the job by eating her up altogether.

When these fairies see little children playing together a little way out of camp, one of them will take his tail in his hand and gives it a wind around his body to conceal it, will approach the children and want to play with them. Sometimes they discover the tail and take to flight and "save their bacon" but at other times they do not notice it and let him come among them, when first thing they known he "gobbles up" some little "image of his dad," clasps him astride of his tail and runs off with him, and that is the last that is ever seen or heard of that unfortunate child.

Their cannibalistic propensities, however, do not appear to extend to Indian men, for whenever they happen to meet one near their dwelling, they invite him in and give him something to eat and insist on his staying all night, but he invariably refuses; saying that he has killed some game and must go and take it home or the wolves will eat it. The general opinion, however, is, that he is afraid to stay, but he scorns the imputation.

The fairies often gather together of an evening on high rocks and cliffs and sing most boisterously, and are supposed to be having a good time generally. They are seldom seen except in the evening.

There is also another kind of these fairies that live in streams, and are called "pah-o-nah" which means, "water infants." They devour women and children in the same manner as the land fairies, and are malignant "little cusses."

Indian Wars of the Northwest

The summer of 1864 was the beginning of our trouble with hostile Indians. With the exception of the Blackfeet, the native Indians of Montana were not hostile and this tribe had confined their depredations to horse stealing and murdering an occasional lone trapper or prospector.

The Crows, the most treacherous and insolent of all the native tribes, professed friendship for the whites but never lost an opportunity to steal horses or murder white men if they got a chance. They were friendly only because it enabled them to trade for guns and ammunition and furnished them a powerful ally against their hereditary enemy, the Sioux.

In 1863 the Sioux, driven from Minnesota and Dakota, took refuge west of the Missouri and along the Yellowstone. Just at this period when the United States was in the throes of a civil war the British subjects, if not the government, along our northern border gave much aid and comfort to hostile Indians on both sides of the line; trading them quantities of arms and ammunition and furnishing a safe refuge for the hostile bands that fled north across the line whenever pursued by the whites. Most of the arms and ammunition in the hands of the hostile Sioux came from the British and half-breed traders across the line.

The brutal and entirely unjustifiable massacre of a village of five hundred friendly Arapahoes in Colorado

by Col. John M. Chivington [103] drove the entire tribe
of Arapahoes and Cheyennes to the war path. The
campaign against them in Nebraska and Colorado
sent those tribes to the southern tributaries of the Yellowstone. As the Indians were driven north and west
so were the buffalo and other large game and this section of country became a veritable Indian paradise.

Red Cloud, as brave a warrior and able a diplomat
as ever guided the destinies of the redmen, made his
headquarters on Powder river and lost no time in taking advantage of the situation, but set about forming a
confederation of all the Indian tribes east of the Rocky
mountains and north of the Arkansas river. At this
time he was twenty-six years old, an eloquent and im-
passioned orator and a natural-born leader. He was
fully six feet tall, muscular, and active as a panther and
as fine a horseman as the world could produce. His
emissaries were to be found wherever there were Indians. They were in the camps of the Chippeways,
with the Crows and Blackfeet; south among the Cheyennes and Arapahoes; west with the Shoshones. There
was no tribe of Indians too small or too weak or too
insignificant to escape the attention of this wily chief,
whose purpose was to form a confederation of all the
tribes and sweep the white man from the face of the
earth. His was to be a war of extermination. At one
time he had twenty thousand warriors in his confederation and at least ten thousand under his personal
command.

Up to this time Red Cloud had refused to sign any
treaties but had kept up a relentless war, murdering
settlers, burning ranches, stealing stock, and falling

---

[103] The Chivington massacre is described in detail in Paxson, *Last American Frontier*, pp. 259-261. – ED.

upon outlying posts. The Sioux were particularly aggressive along the route of the Bozeman-Bridger road to Montana. Scarcely an emigrant train passed without being attacked and most of them were compelled to fight all the way from Laramie, Wyoming, to Virginia City, Montana.

In the spring of 1864, the government planned a campaign on an extensive scale against them, the object being to pursue and conquer them and to forever put a stop to their depredations. Early in July the expedition consisting of the 5th and 6th regiments of Iowa cavalry, the 30th Wisconsin infantry, the 8th Minnesota infantry mounted, six companies of 2nd cavalry, two sections of artillery, and a company of white and Indian scouts with Gen. Alfred Sully, an old and experienced Indian fighter, in command, crossed the Missouri river at the point where Fort Rice now is and began the construction of that fort. Accompanying the command was a supply train of three hundred government teams and three hundred beef steers. Fifteen steamboats were loaded and started up the Missouri to distribute supplies and assist the troops along the course of the Missouri and Yellowstone rivers. An emigrant train of one hundred sixty teams and two hundred fifty people, men, women, and children bound for Montana, joined the expedition at Fort Rice.

At two o'clock on the afternoon of the twenty-eighth the scouts reported that they had located an extensive camp in the foot-hills of a low range of mountains along Knife river. They reported fifteen hundred lodges not three miles distant. The Indians discovered the advancing army about the same time that the scouts discovered them. Both sides began preparations for battle. General Sully dismounted the infantry and threw out a skirmish line with a reserve of cavalry to cover the flanks.   The artillery was placed within supporting distance of the battle line.

The Indians showed no excitement but appeared to rather court a battle and seemed confident of being able to defeat the soldiers.   They stripped for battle, mounted their war ponies and rode out to meet the foe. A few Indians rode up to almost within a gun shot, waving their war clubs and shouting defiance to the troops.   At last the whole body mounted and came on a run directly at the battle line and discharging guns and arrows, wheeled and ran back to reload.   The troops answered with a volley all along the line and the battle was on.   The Indians repeated their charges again and again and fought with great bravery, but their guns were not as long ranged as the troops' and many of them were armed with nothing but bows and arrows.   The battle lasted until sundown, when the artillery was brought into action and the troops moved forward, advancing toward the camp.   So confident had the Indians been of success that not until this time had they made any attempt to save their camp.   The first shell thrown into camp created the greatest confusion; women, children, and dogs swarmed from the tepees. The women rushed about midst bursting shells, tearing down lodges and removing contents.   The voice of the war chief, rallying his braves sounded clear, above the cries of the women and children and the barking of the dogs.   It was no use; the Indians were completely routed and their camp with most of their supplies was captured.

On the twenty-first of April, 1867, Thomas W. Cover returned to Bozeman bringing the intelligence of the murder of John M. Bozeman on April 16.   Cover and

Bozeman had started for Forts C. F. Smith and Phil Kearney. They reached the Yellowstone without incident and had supper at Nelson Storey's cattle camp near Benson's landing. While there, five Indians drove off quite a bunch of horses, but Mitch Buoyer followed them and recovered all but one pony. Next morning Bozeman and Cover crossed the Yellowstone and followed down stream; camped for dinner on a little creek a few miles below the old Crow agency. While cooking their dinner they saw five Indians approaching camp on foot leading a pony. Both men picked up their rifles, Cover went over to the horses and Bozeman advanced toward the visitors. When they were within a hundred feet Bozeman said, "They are Crows, I know one of them." Cover was not so certain and began saddling his horse, Bozeman shook hands with the visitors and at that instant Cover saw one of the Indians move as though to bring his gun to play and called to Bozeman to shoot. The warning came too late. The Indians fired two balls striking Bozeman, one passing through him, and he fell dead. Cover fired and brought down one Indian but received a wound in the shoulder. He then took refuge in some choke-cherry bushes near camp, firing on the Indians as he retreated, but as his gun was not working well he missed his targets. Two of the Indians began saddling the horses while the other two kept firing at Cover concealed in the brush but they did not come close enough to hit him or to be in danger of his rifle. When the horses were ready the whole party mounted and rode away carrying their dead companion with them. Cover returned to camp to make certain that poor Bozeman was beyond all earthly help. The Indians did not scalp him or take his watch. Cover then made his way to Storey's

camp where he was furnished a horse and taken to
Bozeman.   Nelson Storey and another man went to the
scene of the disaster and buried Bozeman where he lay.
These Indians were found later to be some renegade
Blackfeet who had been expelled from their tribe and
had taken refuge with the Crows.

The news of recent murders together with the report
from a Bannock chief that the Bloods, Blackfeet, and
Piegans had sent their squaws and children across the
British line and were prepared to attack the Gallatin
valley created the wildest excitement.   Scouts were
sent out to guard the passes and couriers to bring in all
the women and children from the ranches.   Everything pertaining to the militia was hurried forward.
Several companies were enrolled at Bozeman at once
and were ready to march under Colonel Thoroughman
on receipt of orders.   Virginia City sent out a company
of cavalry and twenty-five special scouts.   Helena
boasted that Captain Lyons's company were in saddle
and ready to march by May 14.

Early in May, 1867, Governor Meagher [104] appealed
to the government for permission to muster in eight
hundred citizens as a territorial battalion.   General
Sherman granted the request conditionally.   Under it
the work of preparation was carried forward rapidly
and a military department organized.

About the middle of May, Mitch Buoyer and John
Poiner, both half-breeds, arrived at Bozeman from
Fort C. F. Smith and reported an alliance being

[104] General Meagher was appointed secretary of Montana Territory by
President Johnson in 1865. He was never governor but in the frequent absence of the governor he was acting governor. Correspondence of Meagher
in Bureau of Rolls and Library, Washington. Eulogy of Meagher by Martin Maginnis in *Montana Historical Society Contributions*, vol. vi. (Helena,
1907) pp. 102-118. Account of his death in *Ibid*, vol. viii (Helena, 1917) p.
131. – ED.

formed between the Sioux, Arapahoes, Cheyennes, and Gros Ventres; that they were holding sun dances on Powder river and would be on the war path about June first. They reported that the Indians claimed that there would be twenty thousand warriors in the field.

These men also brought word that there were but two hundred men at Fort Smith, that all of their horses had been killed or driven off by the Indians and that they were without provisions save a small quantity of corn which they boiled for food. The message stated that if they did not receive help immediately they would all perish.

Captain Hynson called for volunteers to go to the relief of Fort Smith and every man of his company stepped forward. An expedition was at once planned. Forty-two men, well-armed and equipped with ten wagons loaded with supplies, under command of Colonel De Lacey left Camp Elizabeth Meagher for Fort C. F. Smith. Mitch Buoyer and John Reeshaw, both half-breeds acted as scouts. The streams were very high, the roads almost impassable because of mud and late snow. They did not reach Fort C. F. Smith until June 10. Numerous small parties of Sioux and Crows were seen on the road but the train was not attacked. This can be accounted for, because at this time most of the Sioux were on Powder river holding sun dances and the small bands that were hanging about Fort Smith were there for the purpose of trading with the Crows for arms and ammunition, which those Indians were getting regularly from the traders north, and from Fort C. F. Smith. They did not feel strong enough to attack so large a party and were laying low preparing for the grand raid when they expected to completely

annihilate the white race.   Reeshaw and Buoyer kept
in the lead and had various talks with the Sioux which
partly accounts for their keeping at a distance.   Blackfoot, a Crow chief, joined the expedition on the Yellowstone and proceeded with them to Fort Smith, but
he left the greater portion of his band at Clark's fork.

In the midst of all these military preparations General Meagher, the leading spirit, fell from a steamboat
at Fort Benton and was drowned on July 1, 1867.

Early in July a party of Flathead Indians camped
within a few miles of Camp Meagher and stole some
horses from a nearby ranch.   Captain Campbell with
a squad went to the camp and recovered the horses and
demanded the thief.   The first night the Indian could
not be found but arrived in camp next day and the chief
at once surrendered him to the captain, who declared
his intention of hanging him; but told the chief that he
would reprieve him if he said so.   The chief said he
was a very bad Indian who gave much trouble and that
he wished him to die: so he was hung in the presence
of the camp.

Shortly after this, a party of one hundred Crows
came to the Gallatin on a horse-stealing raid.   Captain
Nelson and a companion on their way from Bozeman
to the camp were advised of the matter.   Captain
Nelson with his company, immediately started in pursuit and after a hot race for more than thirty miles they
overhauled the Indians at the ferry of the Yellowstone,
killed two and recovered the stolen stock.   The first
one killed at the ferry had braided in his hair a long
strand of light brown hair, evidently from the scalp of
some white woman recently murdered, yet these Crows
were supposed to be friendly Indians.   This Indian's

scalp was taken together with the lock of long brown hair and sent to Bozeman as a souvenir.

On October 23, 1867, the Montana militia was mustered out. The cost of the campaign was $1,100,000.00. Col. Neil Howie and Col. Chas. D. Curtis paid the Helena men in full out of their own pockets and were never reimbursed. Colonel Black of Bozeman furnished supplies generously, all of which were never paid for. Merchants and ranch men all over the state furnished horses and supplies generously, taking vouchers for pay. The legislature of 1868-69 adopted resolutions setting forth the claims of the citizens for services rendered the government during the Indian wars. These claims were considered by the general government as being excessive and no appropriation was made to pay them. In 1872, General Hardee was sent to the territory to investigate the claims and after his report Congress made an appropriation of the sum of $515,325.00 to pay the vouchers, but by this time most of the vouchers had been sold to speculators for little or nothing and the people who rendered the services as a rule received little or no remuneration.

From a very early period, if not from its beginning, our management of Indian affairs has presented a most astounding and humiliating spectacle; being a mixture of stupidity, foolish sentimentalism, utter mismanagement, and hypocritical rascality, which later came into full bloom with the advent of Grant's so called "Quaker policy," and thrived luxuriantly for many years thereafter. The Indians became wards of the government. Large areas of land (about one fourth of Montana, consisting of the choicest agriculture land in the territory) was set aside for their exclusive use and benefit. They were to be provided with schools and churches and were to be educated and taught the arts of civilization. Rations, clothing, and' farming utensils were to be issued quarterly, and they were to receive large sums of money as indemnity for lands relinquished to the government. The white man was not to be allowed to come on the Indian reservation unless by permission of the agent. This all looked well on paper, but let us take a review and see how it worked out in practice.

The Indian was told that he *must* remain on his reservation, but there was no provision made to compel him to do so or to compel Congress to appropriate money to pay them for their relinquished lands. There possibly were not more than a dozen men in Congress at that time who had ever seen an Indian and not one who knew a thing about the minds or customs of the Indians of the great plains. Men from the far east were usually selected for Indian agents.

The Indians east of the Rocky mountains were fully alive to the advantages and disadvantages of treaties. Their fathers and grandfathers had made treaties with the whites. Some of the old chiefs had medals presented to them as far back as President Madison's time.

They might get the money for their relinquished lands but the chances were that they would not, and they governed themselves accordingly. Commissions composed of high dignitaries from Washington journeyed out to the Bad Lands of Dakota and Montana to make treaties with these savages. A description of one of these councils, which my brother James attended at Fort Sully, is a fair sample of all of them, and I will give it here.

In October, 1865, a commission, whose members were

Gov. George N. Edwards of Dakota, Rev. H. W. Reed, Gen. H. H. Sibley, Gen. Samuel R. Curtis, Col. E. B. Taylor, and O. Guernsey came up the river in the steamer "Calypso" ladened with goods and trinkets to be delivered in the form of presents to those who were willing to treat. This body of dignified gentlemen, representatives of our great government, waited about the fort ten days before any of the Indians appeared and then but a few bands of Sioux came in. The Cheyennes and Arapahoes refused to make any treaty whatsoever. The councils were held inside the stockades at Fort Sully and the beginning of the pow-wow was attended by much ceremony. The Indians conducted their part with much dignity.

The Indians were camped on the plains below the fort. The chiefs rode up, accompanied by an escort of young warriors mounted on their best horses and themselves and ponies decked out in all of their available savage finery with their faces and persons liberally daubed with vermilion paint. Only the chiefs and head tribesmen were allowed inside the stockade. At the gate they dismounted and strode across the open space with heads erect, never deigning to glance to right or left until they reached the council tent.

The members of the commission occupied a place at the end of the tent; behind them was the shield of the United States draped with bunting and the stars and stripes. In front of them and spread out around were the chiefs surrounded by their retinue, decked out in their robes of state which consisted of elaborately decorated feather head-dress and robes highly ornamented with beaded embroidery, quills, elk's teeth, and bits of scarlet cloth. One chief had ermine skins in number and quality to have done honor to the Czar of Russia.

The council opened by General Curtis presenting the terms of the treaty, which was for the opening of a road up the North Platte and Powder rivers along the base of the Big Horn mountains and over to the Yellowstone; the Indians were to retire to their reservation; receive rations; schools, churches, houses for their use were to be constructed, teachers, carpenters, blacksmiths and artisans were to be sent. They were to receive farm implements and be instructed in the art of farming. A large sum of money was to be paid them in ten annual payments. Emigration was to travel unmolested on this road and up the Missouri river by boat.

Iron Nation, head chief of the Brulé Sioux made answer. The Indian is a natural-born orator and Iron Nation possessed this racial trait in a very high degree. He made a speech of two hours' duration, enumerating with great force the reasons for their hostility to the white man. "You wish us to plant corn. God gave us the heavens and the earth, the buffalo and the arrows to kill them with. We kill the buffalo and our women and children have food and clothing, always we have done this; the buffalo are here always and always we have arrows. The buffalo are the Indian's cattle. God gave them to the Indians – the white man has another kind of cattle, they are not the buffalo. We do not want the white man to come with his rifles and kill our cattle. We have planted corn and the frosts kill it – we do not like to plant corn, we had rather hunt buffalo for that is sure. Our women and children are never hungry or cold when we hunt buffalo. We do not like your building forts on our land. The soldiers come with many guns, the white men trade fire water to our young men and then they have a bad heart they will not listen to the councils of the chiefs, they kill white men and then the soldiers come with the big guns and kill all – old men, women, and children – all. Can't you see? You know this. You lie when you say you do not. We will be at peace when you go away and leave us alone. You always come with lies. We show you our papers. They were given us by the big captain who swears, the white chief, with the gray beard (meaning General Harvey). You all tell lies. Tell your great chief these things." While he spoke some of the Indians showed restlessness and much animosity, but finally Iron Nation strode forward and signed the treaty, touching the pen six times one for each of the charges he had brought against the whites; then casting a withering glance at the commission he turned and left the tent.

Medicine Ball, a young chief of the Lower Brulés, was a magnificent looking fellow. When he rose to speak he stood six feet two inches in his moccasins, he was naked to the waist and presented a perfect picture of muscle and manly beauty. A highly ornamented robe was thrown carelessly over one shoulder and an unusually large number of scalps dangled from handle of a war club worn at his side, emblems of his prowess at war. He was extremely bitter in his denunciations of the whites. "What are you here for? We did not send for you, we do not want the white men to come. You say you wish to make a treaty. We are here to listen but what we shall do is another thing." This about expressed the sentiments of most of the young Indians.

White Hawk, a very old chief of the Yanktons, wore a silver medal presented to him at a treaty during President Madison's administration. He held up the silver medal and asked, "Why do you come here? You come for our land, you come always begging. The land is ours. We have given you land before."

White Hawk had parchments of four other treaties that he had signed all of which had been broken by our government. These he presented one at a time to General Sibley asking each time, "Who broke this? Who lied, white man or Indian? You speak with two tongues. Your agents are thieves. We do not want your presents. White men sell fire water to our young men that gives them bad hearts. Go! We will not plant corn, we will hunt buffalo and the deer. We will listen but our hearts are sad. My people do not want the roads built. We do not want the white man to come." For several days White Hawk refused to sign but finally came forward and touched the pen.

One old chief came forward and said, "Who is afraid to sign this paper? I will sign it with my feet and hands." And suiting the action to the word he touched the pen first with each foot and then with each hand. This was considered a very significant ceremony as the ground upon which they stand is considered by an Indian as an emblem of eternity. Doubtless the old chief intended it to mean that it was the last treaty he proposed to sign.

The council lasted two weeks when finally all the chiefs present had signed, then the peace pipe, a large pipe carved from red sandstone, on the stem of which were cut many notches, records of other treaties, was passed. This ended the pow-wow but for the next week all hands at Sully were busy distributing rations and presents to the waiting throng of Indians who seemed highly pleased with this part of the program.

The haughty young Brulé and disdainful White

Hawk were promptly on hand to receive their share of the spoils. Many thousands of dollars worth of presents were handed out to them, including ammunition and guns. The Indians took their presents and decamped. So ended this treaty, but what the result!

The rations issued to the Indians consisted of flour, beans, rice, dried fruits, syrup, sugar, coffee, and tobacco. As they had subsisted on an almost exclusive meat diet for generations, the gorging themselves with unaccustomed food made them very ill; in fact some of the children who had eaten large quantities of uncooked dried apples and had drunk syrup from the can like water, died from the effects. The Indians attributed this to poisoning and of course had an added grievance against the whites. Treaties were forgotten; guns and ammunition brought forth, tomahawk and scalping knife sharpened and as soon as the grass was green and the weather warm they again took the war path; stealing, plundering, murdering, and destroying all property within reach.

Another treaty was called, and these same Indians with scalps of women and children, victims of recent atrocities, dangling from their belts, appeared at the council. More speeches were made – more promises – more presents – more guns and ammunition issued to red-handed murderers, and all was ready for fresh outrages on defenseless settlers and unprotected travelers.

In April, 1868, another commission came to Fort Laramie to make another treaty. This Laramie treaty was the most atrocious of them all and was responsible for the continuous Indian wars and massacres which lasted until 1881. At this time Chiefs Sitting Bull and Gaul, with their bands, surrendered at Fort Yates and were sent to Standing Rock agency; there to live at the expense of the government, in ease and luxury. This treaty gave to the Indians, for their exclusive use and benefit, the territory commencing on the Missouri river at forty-six N. latitude down east to a point opposite to the northern line of Nebraska, then along this line to longitude one hundred four degrees west, thence north on a meridian line to a point where the forty-sixth parallel intersects the same, and east along parallel forty-six to the point at its crossing of the Missouri; together with existing reservations on the east bank of the Missouri. They were also to have all the country north of the North Platte and east of the summit of the Big Horn mountains. It further provided for the closing of the Bozeman road to Montana, and the removal of all military posts in this ceded territory, and further stipulated that the government should punish white men or other Indians who perpetrated a wrong on the tribe and to punish wrong doers among the tribe. They received presents of food, clothing, ammunition, firearms, knives, tomahawks, beads, paint, and trinkets. For all this they gave nothing but their promise to be good.

There was no possible excuse for such a treaty with these Indians. They were not being driven from their homes or ceding large tracts of territory to the whites. To the contrary they were themselves interlopers. They were Sioux who had been driven out of Minnesota in 1863 for the atrocities committed by them on the whites; and as a reward were receiving a section of country rich in agricultural and mining resources, as large as the present state of Montana and were promised the protection of the United States government against invasion from without or any internal disturbance among themselves. They were furthermore to be provided with arms and ammunition, food and clothing that they might be the better prepared for their marauding parties against the white settlers and their Indian neighbors.

The forts must be abandoned that there might be nothing to interfere with their pleasant diversion of butchering defenseless white settlers and plundering and destroying their property. And this is exactly what they did.

The chiefs who were at the council and signed the treaty were on the war path in less than a fortnight and murdered the settlers with the guns and ammunition furnished them by the government. They scalped defenseless women and children with their new sharp knives and tomahawks presented to them at the conclusion of the treaty.

Now we will turn once more to the agencies. The treaties established the boundaries of the lands apportioned, to each tribe and an agent (who was usually a man from the east without any knowledge whatever of Indians) sent to look after their affairs.

Schools were established and usually presided over by the wife, sister, or daughter of the agent who sat in front of empty desks and their labors consisted chiefly in making out elaborate reports and sending them to Washington. The farming machinery was hauled about to different places on the reservation and left to fall to pieces. The farming done was limited to a small garden patch grown for the exclusive use of the agent and his family and instead of the Indian being instructed in gardening he was rigidly excluded from the place by a high picket fence placed around it to keep him from stealing the vegetables when grown.

Instead of remaining near the agency the Indian kept as far away as possible. He had no intention of sending his children to school or of himself learning to farm. Indeed it would be nothing short of a miracle had he had any such an inclination. Nothing in his experience had ever caused him to feel the need of an education or of cultivating the soil. The chase supplied his every need; and horse-stealing raids and war parties to neighboring tribes furnished diversion. He had no intention of changing his happy mode of existence for one contrary to his nature and wholly distasteful to him, and there was no one to compel him to keep the treaties which he signed.

True there were armies sent out for the purpose of protecting the settlers who came in to occupy the lands thrown open for settlement; but so bound up with red tape that they were worse than useless. The inactivities of these armies only the more fully impressed the Indians with the idea that the whites were afraid of them. If an army officer took things into his own hands and attempted to punish them, as they deserved to be, for their unprovoked massacres he would at once be called to Washington and severely reprimanded if not dismissed from the service.

Whiskey traders there were in numbers who infested the reservations. Selling whiskey to the Indians was a crime attended by severe punishment if caught, but owing to the unsettled country and great distances they plied their trade in comparative safety. A goodly share of the money paid the Indian for lands found its way into the pockets of these bootleggers.

There was also the Indian ring. Many persons made huge fortunes furnishing supplies to the government for the Indians and the armies in the country. It was

CAPTURE OF WHISKEY TRADERS

From an original water-color drawing made by an old wolfer,
Andy McGown

FORT CAMPBELL IN 1865

Fort Campbell was an adobe structure built as a fur-trading post
about 1846. It was soon sold to the American Fur Company, and abandoned for Fort Benton nearby. The Jesuits used it for a time as a
mission. In 1865 it was occupied by a detachment of soldiers to protect the white settlers from the Indians. Their protection was so
feeble that William Fisk Saunders told them that if they would bring
over their arms, the settlers would protect them

From an original pencil drawing by Granville Stuart

owing largely to the influence of these unscrupulous persons that Indian affairs were conducted as they were.

A good story went the rounds in the early seventies in which there was more truth than poetry. Three gentlemen arrived in Montana from the Humboldt river country and shortly thereafter one of the trio was elected delegate to Congress and secured for his friend an Indian agency and the other member of the trio was engaged as clerk of the agency. He being a man of genius proposed a scheme for the enrichment of himself and his principal. He collected straggling Indians from different bands and tribes and founded the "Teton Sioux." The name was derived from the three beautiful mountain peaks at the head of Snake river near which the new tribe was colonized. They were represented by the agent as being the most blood-thirsty savages, who had declared a war of extermination against the whites, their number was estimated at eleven thousand. These reports properly substantiated were sent to Washington and through the instrumentality of the congressman, Mr. S—— was appointed "special agent" for the new tribe. He was supposed to have had an interview with the head chief at the risk of his life. The result of the "big talk" was sent to Washington. The Tetons were represented as being hostile and about to take the war path, but hopes were entertained that presents would keep them quiet and bring about friendly relations between them and the whites. A modest appropriation of five hundred thousand dollars was asked for this purpose. The eloquent delegate from the territory pressed the matter at Washington and a bill appropriating five hundred thousand dollars for the "Teton Sioux" became a law.

After a goodly portion of the money had been expended, not on the Indians but among the members of the ring, rumors reached Washington that the "Teton Sioux" really did not exist, the agent started with a few Indians, kept up by the ring for the purpose of making annual visits to the national capital, and arrived there in due time. The presence of the agent and his plumed and blanketed warriors at Washington was enough to satisfy the most skeptical and the agent was granted an additional ten thousand dollars to defray the expenses of himself and charges to Washington and return.

In 1874 Major Maginnis (our then delegate to Congress) explained to an Indian commission why it was that the Indian appropriations were increasing at the rate of a million dollars a year and yet the Indians were dissatisfied and continually on the war path. He said that he had personal knowledge of the operations of the Indian bureau and Indian agents.

"They will take a barrel of sugar to an Indian tribe and get a receipt for ten barrels. For a sack of flour the Indians sign a receipt for fifty sacks. The agent will march three hundred head of cattle four times through a corral, get a receipt for twelve hundred head, give a part of them to the Indians, sell part to a white man, and steal as many back as possible."

Mr. Maginnis strongly recommended placing the Indian affairs in the hands of army officers who would treat the Indians with justice and firmness, and who have no relish for Indian wars, as they entail much hardship and bring no glory.

In 1868 Fort Shaw was built on Sun river about five miles above the town and four companies of the 13th infantry were stationed there to protect the settlers and the Benton road. So frequently had the Wells, Fargo

Company coaches been fired upon and the stations raided and stock driven off by Indians that a company of mounted cavalry was ordered from Fort Shaw to patrol the road between Kennedy's ranch and Tingley's.

Early in April, 1868, the Blackfeet made their appearance in the Gallatin valley and along the Benton-Virginia City road. A party stole a bunch of stock from Nelson Storey, but was pursued and all the stolen stock recovered. Three of the animals died later from arrow wounds.

On the twenty-seventh of April, taking advantage of a dark rainy night, they entered the town of Bozeman and stole fifteen head of horses. An expedition of citizens outfitted in the morning and started out in pursuit. They were gone several days but as the Indians had several hours the start they made good their escape and the pursuers found neither Indians nor stock.

On the return to town the party found the body of Peter Cahill, on the road near Aults' mill. He had been to the coal mine for coal and was overtaken by the Blackfeet and killed and scalped. The wagon was left standing in the road but they had cut the harness into small bits and scattered it along the road. The four fine mules accompanied the Indians.

Word came to Fort Shaw that a band of Bloods was camped on the Teton and had in their possession much stolen stock. Sixty troopers under Lieutenants Newman and Stafford set out in pursuit of them. The Indians not feeling secure, hastened north and crossed the British line with their plunder. The soldiers scouted around for twelve days until their provisions were exhausted and then returned to Fort Shaw.

On May 20, 1868, a party of five Indians came down from the bluff opposite the boat landing on the Yellowstone and drove off eleven horses belonging to a Frenchman. Soon after word reached Colonel Broadwater that the camp of J. J. Rowe, eight miles below Benton, had been attacked, the horses and mules driven away and the camp plundered by a large band of Bloods. Broadwater, accompanied by thirty-five well-armed men, was soon in the saddle in pursuit of the marauders. They not only rescued their own stock but recovered a band of cattle belonging to I. G. Baker and Company.

Six days later forty Blackfeet raided the Missouri valley and drove off two hundred head of horses and mules. Six ranchmen and an Indian boy, who had been raised by a white family, started in pursuit and overtook them on Duck creek. A skirmish ensued but the Indians so outnumbered the whites that they were obliged to retreat. The Indian boy became separated from his companions and was taken prisoner. The ranchmen returned to the settlements for reinforcements. There were plenty of men who volunteered and there were guns and ammunition but all of the horses in the vicinity had been stolen and mounts could not be procured for the volunteers. The Indians crossed the Missouri river and appeared in the Deep creek country and drove off thirty-five head of horses; with this booty they crossed the Belt range and were well out of reach of any but a large and well-organized party.

On the morning of May 27 a party of seven Indians arrived at Ivan Johnson's ranch just below Lincoln gulch. Johnson and a hired man were in bed asleep when their self-invited guests arrived. They opened the door and entered without ceremony and awakened the sleeping men and ordered them to get up and prepare breakfast. As they were taken wholly by surprise there was nothing left for them to do but to comply. The Indians examined the contents of the cupboard, ordered the food cooked that was to their liking. While some of the party amused themselves in this way, the others took possession of the bed, there to take a smoke while awaiting the products of the frying pan. When all was ready they fell to and devoured every morsel of food in sight. They helped themselves to all the tobacco and left, taking all the horses with them. The outraged ranchers started for Lincoln gulch and twenty-five volunteers were soon in pursuit of the Indians but they were well mounted and had too much the start and so made good their escape.

A few days later a party of Piegans appeared at Confederate gulch, drove off all the horses and fired a parting shot at some miners working in a gulch just below town. These Piegans were on their return from the Missouri valley where they had committed many depredations. They had stolen horses that were picketed at the doors of houses in which families were living.

The appearance of Indians in Confederate gulch created intense excitement in Diamond City. A meeting of citizens was held and eighty men volunteered to fight Indians. A considerable sum of money and ten days provision were contributed. The women and children from the ranches were brought into Diamond City. The next day the expedition started. One division starting out in the direction of Benton, for the purpose of intercepting their retreat, while the others followed directly on their trail. This latter division came upon the Indians at the divide between the Missouri river and the Musselshell where they had a sharp skirmish. The whites were poorly armed and had but a limited

amount of ammunition and were compelled to give up
the fight and return to Diamond City.

The steamer "Alabama" did not leave St. Louis until
the tenth of September, 1868, and her progress up
stream was very slow. On the twenty-fifth of October
she reached Fort Peck and, finding that she could go
no farther on account of low water, discharged her
cargo and tied up for the winter. X. Biedler [105] was
placed in charge of the freight and a sorry time he had
of it.

A large village of River Crows was camped just
below the landing and they hung about; begging, stealing, and making a nuisance of themselves in general.
When they were refused presents they became insolent
and knocking the chinking out of the stockade amused
themselves by shooting arrows at the cattle inside.
There were but ten white men at Fort Peck and they
were anxious to avoid trouble if possible. A wagon
train was on its way from Virginia City to get the
freight, and the men at the fort knew that if they had
any difficulty with the Indians that they would waylay
the wagon train and possibly massacre the whole party,
so there was nothing to do but keep inside the stockade
and put up with the annoyance until relief came, which
did but from an entirely unexpected source.

On the second of November a war party of fifty
Sioux put in an appearance. The Crows numbered
two hundred fifty warriors and they lost no time in
raiding the Sioux camp. The Sioux took refuge on a
little bar on the river which was covered with a willow

---

[105] J. X. Beidler was a famous vigilante, before the establishment of
courts in Montana, and after became an efficient deputy United States marshal. Judge Lyman E. Munsen in *Montana Historical Society Contributions*,
vol. v (Helena, 1904) p. 210. *Ibid*, p. 283. – ED.

growth and drift wood, with a high bank in front.
From this place of vantage they put up a stiff fight
which lasted three days. The Crows succeeded in
getting five Sioux scalps but lost one brave, whereupon
they gave up the battle and returned to the fort and
held a war dance just outside the stockade. The Sioux
took this to be a sign that the whites had abetted the
Crows and after gathering reinforcements to the number of two hundred they returned.

In the meantime, the Crows knowing that the Sioux
would not be long in seeking revenge packed up and
started in haste for their own country. The Sioux
overtook the Crows on the Musselshell. In the encounter the Sioux lost fifteen warriors but succeeded in
killing twenty-two Crows and capturing three hundred
head of horses. They then returned to Fort Peck surrounded it and kept up a fight with the whites for six
hours but as the men in the fort had longer range guns
than the Indians they succeeded in keeping them at a
safe distance.

Edgar Sears, a trapper who had been out for a couple
of months, was murdered and scalped a short distance
from the fort. The Sioux were led by Chief Sitting
Bull who did a lot of fancy riding mounted on a
splendid black horse and wearing a most gorgeous war
bonnet; but was careful to keep well out of range of
the rifles. The arrival of Garrison and Baird's ox
train escorted by cavalry under Lieutenants Newman
and Townsend put a stop to the performance. The
Indians left in haste for the winter camp.

The Indian campaign of 1869 was opened when a
band of ten Blackfoot Indians entered the Gallatin valley by way of the old Flathead pass, about twelve miles

northwest of Fort Ellis and proceeded to a ranch on Dry creek where they drove off all the cattle and horses. The alarm was given and a small party of ranchmen went in pursuit, but fearing the Indians would soon join a large camp and, not having sufficient ammunition to attack a strong war party, they returned to Bozeman for assistance.

News of the marauding party had preceded them and forty mounted infantry men under command of Captain Clift, accompanied by fifteen citizens had started out on April 5 to intercept and capture them if possible. On the third day the advance guard overtook the Indians, twelve in number, about noon. They were on the North fork of Sixteen Mile creek, about seventy-five miles from Bozeman. From signs discovered there were doubtless other bands of Indians in the vicinity scattered in different directions.

On the approach of the pursuers the Indians fled to the top of a very rough mountain, upon which was a fortification, formed by nature, almost impregnable. Here they imagined they were safe from the attacks of a host, and from this point commenced shaking their blankets at the men and making other demonstrations of hostilities daring them to come on, cussing and swearing in very plain English.

Captain Clift divided his forces sending Lieutenant Thompson around the mountain upon the east. Then came the ascent and a raking fire from the Indians. The summit was reached at last and from the crags and roughness of the surface they were enabled to obtain positions that completely surrounded the Indians and from which they could fire with safety. Nearer and nearer the men began to close in, creeping from point

to point and firing whenever an Indian raised a gun or
made a movement. At this junction the Indians saw
that they were trapped and that there was no hope of
escape, and began singing their death song. Nearly
half of their number were killed or disabled. The
firing had been going on about two hours and the sun
was getting low; fearing that darkness would overtake
them and that the Indians would yet make their escape,
Captain Clift called for volunteers from those nearest
the fortifications to make a charge. A dozen men responded, revolver in hand and were met with fire from
the Indians. Private Conry was killed and King severely wounded but the last Indian was killed.

Such was the situation east of the Rocky mountains
and now we turn to the Indians on the other side of the
range.

That section of the country lying west of the Rocky
mountains and east of the Bitter Root range was the
home of the Salish,[106] a once numerous and powerful
tribe who had always been friendly to the whites, but
were wholly neglected by the government.

Although living west of the mountains they claimed
the headwaters of the Missouri river as their hunting
grounds and the entire tribe annually crossed the range
to hunt buffalo; only the very old people and young

[106] The Salish, or more generally speaking, the Flatheads were one of
the more important tribes of the Salishan family which included the Coeur
d'Alenes, the Pend' Oreille, the Kalispell, the Kootenai, the Nez Percé, and
probably the Okanogans, and other Indian tribes on the upper Columbia.
The name Salish means "we the people" and the sign was to strike the head
with the flat of the hand. Thus from this sign they apparently acquired the
name of Flathead. Father Pierre DeSmet and Father Lawrence Palladino
lived among them for many years and both express high opinions of their
character as did also Mullan and Stevens. Chittenden and Richardson
opus citra, vol. iv, pp. 1263-1265 and index. Palladino, *Indian and White
in the Northwest* pp. 1-6. – ED.

children remained at home. Their old trails across the mountains were worn deeper and had been traveled more and longer than any other Indian trails in Montana.

These hunting grounds were disputed, being claimed by the Blackfeet and from time immemorial bitter war raged between the tribes. In the earlier period of their history the Salish with their ally, the Nez Percé a small but superior tribe that lived on the upper Columbia were more than a match for the Blackfeet and hunted wherever they chose. The advent of the Hudson's Bay Company among the Blackfeet enabled that tribe to procure firearms at a much earlier period than the Salish could. This gave them such superior advantages that they not only drove the Salish from the hunting grounds but followed them across the range carrying the war into their own country and threatened to annihilate that tribe.

The Salish were not a warlike people but they wanted firearms that they might stand an equal chance in their encounters with their enemies. Firearms could only be procured from the white men, so from the first they welcomed the few trappers and traders that found their way into the Salish country.

In 1853 Isaac I. Stevens [107] on his way from St. Paul to the coast with a surveying party looking out a route for the Northern Pacific railroad came into their country and was welcomed by the chiefs and head men of the tribe. Stevens did not promise them firearms but held out the prospects of making a treaty with the

---

[107] Isaac Ingalls Stevens became governor of Washington Territory and superintendent of Indian affairs. He also had a leading part in the construction of the Mullan road. His life is by his son Hazard Stevens (New York, 1900, 2 vols). – ED.

Blackfeet so that both the whites and Indians could dwell in peace. This was a welcome piece of intelligence to the Salish for they were heartily tired of the never-ending wars in which they were continually worsted.

In 1855 Governor Stevens returned to the country to make a treaty with them and was accorded a hearty welcome. More than one thousand warriors arrayed in all their savage splendor rode forth to meet him. The council [108] was opened by Governor Stevens setting forth the terms offered by the government. The Indians were asked to cede extensive tracts of land, practically all that they had, and to retire to a reservation. In return they were to receive certain annuities, cattle, farming implements, seed grain; and schools were to be provided for their children. Teachers, farmers, carpenters, and blacksmiths would be sent to teach them to till the soil and to build houses.

The Indians were willing to cede the land and they did not object to the reservation plan but the location of the reservation was the stumbling block. They were in reality one tribe, the Salish but there were three branches, each inhabiting a particular section of country to which they were strongly attached. Chief Michael lived with the Kootenais on the headwaters of the Columbia and north of Flathead lake, Alexander with the Pend d'Oreilles were south of the lake and in the Jocko valley while Victor, chief of the Flatheads and hereditary chief over all, claimed for his home the beautiful valley of the Bitter Root and neither chief

---

[108] Council grove near the junction of the Bitter Root and Clark's fork rivers. This is an excellent account of the council. The text of the treaty is in Charles J. Kappler, editor, *Indian Affairs, Laws and Treaties* (Washington, 1903) pp. 542-545. – ED.

was willing to leave his home. The council dragged along for days without reaching an agreement and then the treaty was finally signed without settling the question of the location of the reservation.

A few presents of red paint, beads, bright calico, knives, and blankets were distributed and Governor Stevens departed. Years passed and nothing more was heard of the treaty. No cattle, farming implements, or seed grain arrived, nor farmers to teach the Indians how to till the soil.

The Salish crossed the range and hunted buffalo for their living and carried on the same old wars with the Blackfeet, and their children had no school other than those furnished by the Jesuit Fathers and Sisters of Charity that were among them when Stevens came. White people came and were welcomed and given land by the Indians until the Bitter Root valley was quite well settled and there were two good-sized towns, Stevensville and Corvallis. The old chiefs were dead and their sons reigned instead.

The white settlers begun to clamor for government titles to their lands and they wanted roads and bridges and schools. In 1871 like a bolt of thunder from a clear sky, came an order from the President to remove the Flathead Indians from the Bitter Root valley to the valley of the Jocko.

Without a shadow of right or justice and without warning or provocation these kindly peaceable Indians were to be driven from the home that had been theirs since the beginning of time. Charlot, their head chief, refused to go. In 1872 General Garfield was sent out to make a treaty with them and to try to induce them to go to the Jocko. Charlot, head chief, and Arlee and

Adolph, sub chiefs met at the council. Charlot spoke for the Indians. He remembered the treaty and he also remembered that the white men had not kept their word and the Indians could not keep theirs. He pointed out that the white people's farms were all over the Indian's hunting grounds and that the Salish still crossed the mountains and fought with the Blackfeet in order to get food and shelter and clothing. The white men or their fields had never been hurt by the Flathead Indians.

Victor, his father, said they would remain in the land of their fathers and Charlot would not go.[109]   He left the council. Later Adolph and Arlee signed the treaty. Gov. B. F. Potts, Congressman William H. Claggett, Wilbur F. Sanders, J. S. Vial, and D. J. Swain signed as witnesses. General Garfield returned to Washington and the treaty was published as having been signed by all the Indians and at the same time Arlee was recognized by the government as head chief of the Flatheads. In reality Arlee was only a half-blood Flathead his father being a Nez Percé. Preparations were hurried forward for the removal of the Indians to the Jocko.

Chief Charlot was a Christian, having embraced the Catholic faith and was honest, just, and truthful in all of his dealings with the whites and had many staunch friends among the settlers in the valley. When he learned of these outrages his indignation knew no bounds, every vestige of confidence that he had had in the white race vanished, his sense of honor and justice was outraged. He declared that he would never leave the Bitter Root valley alive.

---

[109] Major John Owen in his Journals expressed the opinion that the Flatheads would never leave the Bitter Root unless forced to do so. – Ed.

Arlee and his following moved but Charlot and his people remained. Those that went to the Jocko received something in the way of annuities but they had, to say the least, inefficient agents and but little was done to better their condition and they fared but little better than those that remained in the Bitter Root and received nothing from the government. They all continued to go to the buffalo country to hunt in order to live.

In 1877 Major Peter Ronan a man who was conversant with Indian customs and habits and of fine executive ability as well as of unimpeachable integrity was appointed agent for the Flatheads, and immediately set to work to straighten out the tangled affairs. Honest and just in all of his dealings with them he soon won their confidence and remained until his death their trusted friend and adviser. Major Ronan was familiar with the Stevens treaty and with the subsequent proceedings. His sympathies were with Charlot but he could see the futility of further resistance and used all of his powers of persuasion to induce the old chief to reconsider his decision. Charlot would not listen, his confidence in government officials was gone.

Settlers continued to pour into the valley and settled on the land. The buffalo were fast disappearing on the ranges and there was but little game in the Bitter Root and the condition of the Indians became desperate; the matter was finally taken to Congress and Senator George Vest of Missouri and Major Maginnis, our delegate in Congress, were appointed to investigate the matter. The investigation brought to light a long story of injustice, ingratitude, duplicity, and an utter disregard of treaty pledges on the part of the govern-

ment agents in dealing with these Indians and their
report to Washington was to that effect.   General Garfield was forced to acknowledge that Charlot had not
signed the treaty.

In January, 1884, Major Ronan received instructions
to bring Charlot and his head men to Washington for
a conference; the object being to try to secure Charlot's
consent to remove with his band to the Jocko reservation.

Nearly a month was spent in Washington and several
interviews held with the Secretary of the Interior but
no offer of pecuniary reward or persuasion of the secretary could shake Charlot's resolution to remain in the
Bitter Root valley.   He treated with disdain and dis-
trust any person connected with the United States
government and refused all offers of assistance from
the government.   He asked only the poor privilege of
remaining in the valley where he was born.   In March,
1884, Major Ronan held another council at Stevensville with the Indians at which he promised: first – a
choice of one hundred and sixty acres, unoccupied land
on the Jocko reservation; second – assistance in erecting
a substantial house; third – assistance in fencing and
ploughing a field of ten acres; fourth – the following
gifts; two cows to each family, a wagon and harness and
necessary agricultural implements, seed for the first
year and provisions until the first year's harvest.
Twenty-one families accepted this offer and went to the
Jocko.

The department kept its part of this contract and
also authorized the construction of an irrigation ditch
to cover the land settled upon.   So well did this plan
work that in a year, other Indians, witnessing the pros-

perous condition of their friends and relatives also determined to go to the Jocko and eleven more families moved down. But alas! The red tape was in full operation again. Although Major Ronan wrote and urged and explained and finally went to Washington at his own expense to try to get the necessary funds to supply these eleven families with the things given the first twenty it was all to no purpose. The excuse given was no appropriation at that time. Later orders came to issue supplies to Charlot and those at Stevensville and again the eleven families were left out as they were not at Stevensville. Major Ronan issued them supplies assuming the responsibility himself.

Food, seed grain, and a limited amount of farming implements were issued to Charlot's little band at Stevensville; but the Indians were not farmers and they were too far away to receive instructions and supervision necessary to make their efforts a success. The young men were fast becoming addicted to the use of whiskey and the women and children were starving.

In 1891 General Carrington was sent out to see if he could make some sort of treaty whereby the Indians would remove to the Jocko. Charlot was ready to go. He said, "I do not want your land, You are liars. I do not believe you. My young men have no place to hunt, they get whiskey, they are bad. My women and children are hungry: I will go." Into exile went this truly noble Indian.

During all these years of the treating and wrangling with the Flathead Indians, the settlers in the Bitter Root valley were kept in suspense as to the titles to their lands. There was no incentive to make improvements as they did not know whether they might remain and get title or be ordered off to seek homes in some other locality.

Such was the peace policy of the government which was in operation for so many years, during which time the Indians were almost exterminated, the lives of hundreds of white people sacrificed, expensive Indian campaigns carried on, and much valuable property destroyed. A number of Indian agents and traders made fortunes, hied themselves to their eastern homes and spread stories about the murderous capacity of the white settlers who encroached upon the Indians.

Looking for a Cattle Range

In 1850 Capt. Richard Grant with his sons John and James Grant begun trading along the Emigrant road in Utah for footsore and worn-out cattle and horses. This stock was usually of good quality and only needed rest and a little care to make them fine animals.

The Grants spent the summers along the Emigrant road between Bridger and Salt Lake, and in the fall drove their stock up into what is now Montana.

In 1856 Robert Dempsey, John M. Jacobs, Robert Hereford, and Jacob Meek begun trading along the Emigrant road and drove six hundred head of cattle and horses up into Montana and they, together with the Grants, wintered on the Stinkingwater.

When we came to Montana in 1858 the Grants and Jacobs had herds of several hundred cattle and horses. These cattle fattened on the native grasses, without shelter other than that afforded by the willows, alders, and tall rye grass along the streams. In the spring they were fat and fit for beef and were driven back to the Emigrant road and traded for more footsore and worn-out animals which in turn were driven back to winter range in Montana, the favorite places being the Beaverhead, Stinkingwater, and Deer Lodge valleys.

In the fall of 1860 we drove in sixty head of cattle and Robert Hereford brought in seventy-five head from the Emigrant road. At this time there was a small herd at St. Ignatius, a few at Fort Owen, and about two hundred head in and near Fort Benton.

These herds all increased rapidly and when gold was struck at Alder gulch every emigrant train brought in a few cattle, ranches were established and by 1863 cattle growing had become an industry of considerable importance.

In 1864 a bill was introduced in the legislature regulating marks and brands. The act concerning marks and brands became a law Jan. 31, 1865.

Nelson Storey of Bozeman drove the first herd of Texas cattle into Montana in the spring of 1866. Storey purchased six hundred head of cattle at Dallas, Texas, and started north with them, arriving in the Gallatin valley on December 3 and camped where Fort Ellis was later located.

In 1878 D. S. G. Flowerree purchased one thousand head of stock cattle in Oregon and placed them on the Sun river range and then begun the stocking of ranges on a large scale.

The first beef cattle driven out of Montana was a small herd belonging to D. J. Hagan of Sun river. Hagan sold them to Ornstein and Popper and delivered them at Salt Lake City in the fall of 1866. That same fall Jerry Mann drove one hundred and thirty head of steers and fat dry cows to Ogden and sold them.

In May, 1874, James Forbis purchased three hundred head of fat beef steers from Conrad Kohrs and drove them to Ogden and from there shipped them to Omaha by rail. Later in the summer Allen drove five hundred choice steers from the Madison valley to Granger on the Union Pacific and shipped them by rail to Chicago. In the summer of 1876 Kohrs drove three hundred head of choice steers to Cheyenne, Wyoming and shipped them to Davenport, Iowa.

During the summer of 1879 a co-partnership was entered into between A. J. Davis of Butte, Erwin Davis of New York City, Samuel A. Hauser, and Granville Stuart of Helena, Montana, for the purpose of engaging in the business of cattle raising. The capital stock of the firm was one hundred fifty thousand dollars. The brand was "H." The firm name Davis, Hauser and Co. The interests were divided into thirds; the Davis Brothers one-third, Hauser one-third, and Stuart one-third. I was elected superintendent and general manager and directed to begin at once to look about for stock cattle that could be purchased at a satisfactory price.

By the first of January I had contracts for about two thousand head that could be purchased in Montana and Oregon. The price paid ranged from $14 to $17 per head according to the number of steers in the bunch. The young calves were thrown in with the mothers. By the first of March I had contracted an additional two thousand head of Oregon cattle.

SUNDAY, April 11, 1880. Left Helena for a trip to the Yellowstone country to look for a good cattle range. The first part of the journey was by stage coach.

Morning bright and pleasant, thermometer at 7 A. M. 42°, gentle breeze, Bar. 25.825. Pretty good grass on Spokane creek and on Beaver creek divide, road muddy and bad from Half-way house to Beaver creek, and then that infernal rocky road extending nearly to Bedford shook us up horribly. That is the rockiest road on this earth. Had a good dinner at Bedford and was all shaken down so that I enjoyed it.

Saw the abandoned mining town of "Hog Em" in the distance and reached Radersburg about 4 P. M.

Very little grass from Beaver creek on but in the red shale hills there are immense quantities of Mexican bayonet.

12th.   Left Radersburg at 7 A. M. for Bozeman, fine range to Galen's but badly eaten out and no water obtainable for irrigation although it is all fine farming land.   Good grass from near Galen's to near the Jefferson river but no water obtainable or it would be eaten out.   Very strong wind today.   Took dinner at West Gallatin; here saw the first faint tinge of green in the little sage along the road.   Plenty of snow drifts along the fences and banks as we neared Bozeman and the mud was deep and sticky, making progress slow.   The foot-hills full of big snow drifts clear down into the valley and edge of town.   A different soil here extending across the mountains and down the other side to near the Yellowstone river.   Black loam over hills and all and a much damper climate.

13th.   Left Bozeman at 4 A. M. in a snow storm with high cold wind, when partly up the range it turned to a regular old-fashioned state's sleet, the first I ever saw in Montana.   Coated twigs and grass with ice one-eighth inch thick and our clothing also.   The stage was a little open spring wagon and one played-out team. We had to walk, most of the way to keep from freezing. The team mired in the snow in the sage and had to be dug out, wagon unloaded and pulled out by hitching a long rope to the tongue and then all hands pull.   There were fortunately no women in the party so we all helped the stage driver to swear.   Each time we mired down we all got wet to our hips and our trousers froze stiff so that we could hardly walk.   Crossed the summit at an altitude of six thousand two hundred and six feet.

The sleet turned to snow when we reached the Yellowstone with a bitter N. E. wind that nearly "peeled the bark" all the rest of the day and all night. At Sweet Grass creek we changed horses and had a better team but the driver missed the road and we wandered around on an old wood road half the night tired and wet and half frozen.

It quit snowing about sunrise when we were between White Beaver and Stillwater. Confound night traveling – don't let me see but about half the country. What little I could see of White Beaver basin after it came daylight, showed that it was a pretty grass country surrounded on all sides except the N., with rocky hills covered with yellow pine woods. It lies at a considerable elevation above the Yellowstone river and about six miles from it, with a high pine ridge between, through which it breaks near the S. E. side of the basin. Plenty of old snow drifts in it and the storm has put about two and one-half inches of new snow all over it. It would be a good range for a few thousand cattle. Saw a few cattle and they looked well, as was also the case on the Yellowstone bottom to Stillwater. River runs in quite a cañon five or six hundred feet below the general level of the country on each side with small bottom on either side alternately. Nice little bottom at Keiser creek, but the prettiest that I saw, albeit it was small, was at Henslup, a short distance above Young's point where begins the famous Clark's fork bottom on the N. side of the river and the largest on the whole river.

This bottom consists of a low bottom from one to three miles wide along the river and then a bench some twenty-five or thirty feet above it which extends back to the bluffs which are ten to twelve miles back and thinly timbered. Saw some considerable gravel patches along the road on the lower bottom but was told that most of the valley was good soil if water was only obtainable for irrigation. It is well grassed. Laid over here to sleep and rest and had to wait until next coach came along at 4 P. M. of the fifteenth. Have seen no country yet where I would like to trust more than a few thousand cattle.

At Coulson I met my old friend P. W. McAdow who was with us at Gold creek in 1862. We had a great old visit and enjoyed reminiscing over old times. Coulson is a tough little town. They tell me that there are sixteen graves on the hill above town and every one of the occupants met a violent death.

Left Coulson at 4:15 P. M. on the fifteenth in a big open dead axle wagon. Went down ten miles to Huntley and crossed the river on a wire ferry and took to the high prairie about dark, for Fort Custer forty-five miles distant. Crossed Pryors' creek soon after starting and then over high rolling prairies all night. The driver said it was a good grass and stock region. I was obliged to take his word for it, for it was as dark as Ebras.

Reached Fort Custer at sunrise on the sixteenth. It is situated on the high point between the Big and Little Horn rivers, and about one hundred feet above them. Elevation opposite Fort Custer 3260 feet. No settlements here, nothing but the fort because it is a part of the Crow Indian reservation.

The valley on west side of Big Horn river is from three to five miles wide, well grassed and with grassy bluffs back but no water at all except in the river.

Generally good soil, very little valley land on east side of Big Horn, from Custer down to the mouth some forty miles. Green grass about two inches high from Stillwater to Huntley and about three inches high here. Had to keep to the big dead axle wagon down to Terry's landing on the Yellowstone about four or five miles above the mouth of Big Horn. Here we changed for a covered jirky.

Not a very inviting country about Terry's landing, greasewood bottoms and bluffs on north side of river runs in close to the river. Pease's bottom begins on the N. side about two miles below the mouth of Big Horn river, is rather narrow, from one-half to one and one-half miles wide and about three miles long, is bounded on N. by high cliffy bluffs. It is very fertile, sheltered from all winds and is nicely timbered with cottonwoods and some cedars and pines on the bluffs. I like it better for farming than any place that I have seen over here. Night set in before we left it and when daylight came we were just below Big Porcupine creek and in sight of Porcupine Butte, a square tower of rock on top of a conical hill some miles back from the river.

Crossed Little Porcupine in the forenoon. Both these streams have very deep beds of good size with only a small stream now but the drift wood shows that at times they overflow the bottoms on either side and become impassable torrents for days at a time. Breakfasted at Short creek if one could call boiled beans and Worcestershire sauce breakfast. Provisions all out here. Elevation 2736 feet.

We had dinner at Bull creek, a fine dinner, bread, buffalo tongue, and coffee. Arrived in Miles City about 5 P. M. April 17.

From the Porcupine clear to Miles City the bottoms
are liberally sprinkled with the carcasses of dead
buffalo.   In many places they lie thick on the ground,
fat and the meat not yet spoiled, all murdered for their
hides which are piled like cord wood all along the way.
'Tis an awful sight.   Such a waste of the finest meat in
the world!   Probably ten thousand buffalo have been
killed in this vicinity this winter.   Slaughtering the
buffalo is a government measure to subjugate the
Indians.

Passed the mouth of Rosebud river (which comes
into the Yellowstone on the south side) just after crossing Little Porcupine creek.   The country around the
mouth of the Rosebud is low and looks better grassed
than any that I have seen since I left White Beaver
basin but after passing it the country soon begins to put
on a sterile brown bad land appearance which grows
more desolate looking all the way to Miles City (forty
miles).

Tongue river is considerably larger than Sun river
but is muddy like the Missouri as are all the streams
here, including the Yellowstone, which is here about
one hundred seventy-five yards wide now and has just
become unfordable.   It is about three hundred yards
wide when high.

Miles City stands on the east bank of Tongue river
and in a grove of big cottonwood trees of which a great
many have the bark torn from the upper side of them
for several feet above the ground by an ice gorge here
apparently about twelve or fifteen years ago, perhaps
longer: so some day the town will likely be destroyed
by another gorge – bad location.

There is a wire rope ferry across the Yellowstone
river about two miles above Miles City and it takes the

soldiers a long time to get a boat across.   There is also a wire rope ferry across Tongue river at Miles City, but both rivers are unfordable, which is very unusual at this time of the year.

I put up with my old friend Thomas H. Irvine and we boarded at the jail with Sheriff W. H. Bullard and deputy Jack Johnson and jailor Wash Kelly.   Mr. Creighton was the cook.   The hotel accommodations in Miles City in 1880 were not first class, in fact I do not think there were any hotel accommodations.   The people that frequented Miles City in those days usually came to town to stay up nights and see the sights.   They did not feel the necessity for a bed or much to eat. They were just thirsty.

At Miles City I outfitted with saddle horses.   Bought two little plugs of horses for $50 each, a saddle for $35.00, bridle $3.50, three halters $1.50 each, four saddle blankets $12.

Thomas Irvine had a good saddle horse and a pack mule with two pack saddles.   I induced him to accompany me on the trip.

Waited until the twenty-second for Captain Baldwin to return from Fort Custer as he was desirous of going with us on the trip but the Cheyenne Indians started a racket and he could not go.   He loaned us a good army tent.

Left Miles City on the twenty-second at 11 A. M. and went up the river twenty-three miles to Anderson's ranch where we fell in with Yellowstone Kelley (Luther S. Kelley) Phillips, Eugene Lamphere, a nephew of Captain Baldwin, an L. A. Huffman, a young photographer [110] from Fort Keogh.   They were

[110] Mr. Huffman is still living at Miles City.   He has photographed much of the life of the country around. – ED.

looking for timber fit for lumber and for a small cattle range.

It sprinkled rain all day and looked very threatening. We did not put up our tent but all slept in the cabin on the hardest dirt floor that I ever laid down on.

APRIL 23. Packed up at 7 A. M. and started in a drizzling rain. Tom Irvine's pony objected and lit in to buck and frightened the pack mule and he lit out across the hills with the entire party in pursuit. Rounded him up and brought him back to the road. By this time it was raining hard and continued so until about 11 A. M. when it turned into a snow storm which fell fast with a high wind. We kept on to Smith's ranch, three miles below the mouth of the Rosebud and camped with George Johnson and Ed Maguire who we found there storm bound. They were short of provisions but we had a good supply and the cabin was large enough to hold us all. There was a big fireplace and plenty of wood. We each took turns cooking. Smith had just built a large new house which he was using temporarily as a stable and into which we put most of our horses and fed them hay. It snowed furiously all afternoon and all night and was bitter cold.

Plenty of big scrubby ash trees in the breaks along the dry creeks and bluffs and also many short ravines full of rather nice cedar trees. Excellent grass everywhere but it is rotten now. Green grass is about three to four inches high. Saw many antelope and the boys shot at them several times. Kelley finally bagged one and we had fresh meat for supper. Traveled but fifteen miles this day.

APRIL 24. Snowed all night and still snowing and

badly drifted, and bitter cold. Laid up in Smith's cabin all day. Only nine of us in one small cabin. This is a horrible spell of weather, kept our horses in the house and fed them hay. A flock of black birds are in a tree and some of them singing.

APRIL 25. As it seemed to have cleared up we packed up and started. There were six inches of snow on the level and drifts two and one-half feet deep. Traveled three miles up the Rosebud and here lived a solitary man, Joe McGee. At this point we separated. "Yellowstone" Kelley and Phillips went across the hills west of the Rosebud to look for pine timber and we kept on up the Rosebud twenty-two miles, having much trouble getting through the snow drifts on the edge of coulees. Killed a buck antelope but the meat was not good. From this up it is a sage country with some good grass but badly broken bad lands. Poor range and no water except in the rivers and it is a detestable mean stream to water stock. Deep narrow channel, with steep muddy banks, water very muddy and deep with miry bottom. Came near swimming and miring to get across it and there are very few places where it is possible to cross at all. The roads are very muddy and traveling slow and laborious and hard on the horses. We camped in a muddy bottom where the buffalo had eaten off most of the grass. From the bluff the Little and Big Wolf mountains are both in sight far to the south. Traveled twenty-five miles this day.

APRIL 26. Started from camp at 7:30 A. M., traveled thirteen miles and camped just above the Cone butte at the end of Little Wolf mountains on the east side of Rosebud. Fine bottom land well grassed, a good deal of black ash and box elder along the river but it is the same muddy miry stream as below. At this point the country opens out into more of a valley. Hills are low and grassy, with many cañons and beautiful buttes with scattering yellow pine timber. This open grassy valley is about one mile wide and probably eighteen miles long with little grassy vales running far back among picturesque buttes. The Big Wolf mountains are heavily timbered and perfectly white with this last snow.

If there was any other water (which there is not permanently) than in the Rosebud or if it were a different kind of stream this would be a good range for one thousand to fifteen hundred cattle but as it is it wouldn't do at all for they would all mire in the Rosebud.

Just before camping time I discovered a band of buffalo bulls up a little draw to the south and Huffman and I went and killed one. We took the tongue, the tenderloin, and the "fries." Huffman considered them a great delicacy. I preferred the loin fried in a separate pan with strips of bacon. The others of the party going to camp killed a white-tailed deer. There was a band of buffalo, about fifty in number, across the river from camp but we did not trouble them.

Traveled twenty-eight miles this day, roads muddy in places but the snow nearly all gone in the low lands.

APRIL 27. Had to mend a broken pack saddle which kept us in camp until nine o'clock. Buffalo all around us. Huffman and Eugene couldn't resist the temptation to have a run so they crossed the Rosebud and went for a bunch that was grazing along the edge of a ridge and after a lively chase across the bench land killed one. Only took the tongue as we had all the fresh meat that we could use.

The country is very beautiful although the valley is narrow. We are passing through what is called the cañon where the Rosebud cuts through the Big Wolf mountains, but it is not much of a cañon, being never less than one mile wide and with beautiful little grassy vales extending back among the picturesque castilated red buttes which have considerable nice yellow pine scattered over them. Went twelve miles and camped for noon, rested until 2 P. M. and then traveled on ten miles and camped at 5 P. M. because it looked like rain. During this ten miles we passed two nice creeks coming in from the southeast with beautiful little valleys along them, extending back as far as we could see but they were mud bottomed and steep miry banks, although their waters are almost clear, while Rosebud is still thick with mud and has a yellowish brick dust color and deposits a thick layer of mud in the buckets of water left standing a few minutes.

The scenery these ten miles is very beautiful, buttes and bastioned fortresses of all shapes and sizes capped and often landed with broad belts of vivid red scoviacious shelly rock, crowned with beautiful clumps of yellow pine trees and in many of the glades and sags are fine groves which add much to the beauty of the scene and where burned off, the hills are green with new grass. It is all a scene of beauty and only the river is vile. This day's travel was through a good grazing country where plenty of hay could be cut all along, but there is no accessible water and therefore it won't do for cattle. Hundreds of buffalo in sight all the time. We had lots of fun running them but had to forego much of the pleasure as the sport is too much for our horses.

Traveled twenty-two miles this day. The bottoms

were heavily timbered with good black ash and box
elder, till the last five miles, when the timber began to
run out.   Valley along here about one-half mile wide
with little lateral valleys extending back into hills
which are becoming more grassy on their sides and
summits.   Passed several streams coming in from
northwest side which looked as though they might be
permanent ones, and camped opposite one of considerable size.   Put up our tent for the first time and just at
dark it began to rain slowly.

WEDNESDAY, April 28.   Rained hard in the early
part of the night and was very lowering and threatening this morning with light showers of rain and snow.
Waited to see if it would clear up so did not leave camp
until 11 A. M.   It was still cloudy with a cold northwest wind.   Traveled up the Rosebud six miles.
Country all burned over last fall but it is a fine grass
region, much resembling some parts of high prairies in
Iowa, with small groves of ash and box elder in ravines
and along little creeks which are mostly dry now, and
have mud beds.   The valley of the Rosebud here opens
out into a sort of basin; hills low and grassed all over –
high snowy hills to the southwest in the fork of the
creek.   The whole country is black with buffalo.
Eugene killed one.   Being a boy he couldn't resist killing just one, although we did not need the meat.   He
took the tongue.   Came to a dry creek which came in
from the S. E. and as a very large and old trail went up
it I knew that it must be the Indian trail crossing over
to Tongue river so we followed it for about ten miles
to the top of the divide and then a couple of miles further where we camped on a beautiful clear little creek
with fish in it, which proved to be a tributary of

Tongue river.   Some ash and box elders even up here
(elevation 4056 feet).   The country is now all broken
up into low grassy hills and mounds.   No timber but
splendid grass everywhere and buffalo in every direction.   This high region is about one-third covered
with hugh snow drifts left by the storms of the twenty-
third and twenty-fourth.   It froze ice one-half inch
thick in this camp.   We all went fishing and caught
about a dozen small ones that we fried for supper.   Altitude at camp 4056 feet.   Traveled sixteen miles this
day.

APRIL 29.   Traveled southeast a few miles and
struck another small tributary of Tongue river through
a good grass region though broken.   Some nice pine
timber in clumps and many scattering yellow pines.
Run out of snow banks some time before reaching the
river.   Saw four black-tailed deer, first on the trip.
Small bands of buffalo in sight all the way down to
Tongue river, which we struck in the cañon at upper
edge of Wolf mountains.   River quite muddy here.
Curious firey red cliffs, bluffs, and buttes, evidently
caused by the burning out of great beds of lignite and
oily shales which once underlaid all this region.   There
are indications of petroleum all along from the Porcupine to here.   Tongue river is about the size of Sun
river and is quite low and can be forded on any riffle.

After we rested and had dinner, Eugene Lamphere
and L. A. Huffman packed up and started down the
river on their return to Fort Keogh and Tom and I are
left alone.   We miss our friends sadly.   Eugene has
all the enthusiasm of a boy of twenty-one, in a country
where everything is new and wonderful to him, and
Huffman is one of the most companionable men I ever

traveled with. Tom Irvine is the best reconteur on earth and we have had some great old times on this trip. This morning Irvine's little roan objected to being saddled in the cold and wet and bucked into the campfire, scattering coffee-pot and frying pans, consequently we had plenty of ashes for relish.

APRIL 30, 1880. Started at 7 A. M. and traveled up Tongue river. Saw ten white-tailed deer soon after we left camp but did not get a shot. The white-tailed deer is the hardest game in America to get a shot at. Both hearing and scent are peculiarly sensitive. An old Indian friend of mine sizes up the situation in this way:

"Wild turkey hard to kill. Indian break some stick, turkey stop one second, say maybe Injin, Injin be good hunter he get shot. White-tailed deer, he hear some little noise way off – say Injin by God! W-u-zz he gone, Injin no get one shot."

That is about the way it is. White-tailed deer hear or scent a hunter before he gets in gunshot and they are off in an instant.

We followed up Tongue river twenty-four miles and crossed the river twenty times, it being the crookedest stream in Montana, with long high spurs or points of mountains putting down into every bend with considerable bottom-land which was well grassed but often mixed with tall young sage. Only tolerable grass on spurs and hills. At about eighteen miles we emerged from the upper end of the cañon into a high rolling country, pretty well grassed with a good deal of sage on bottoms and on hills, and many high rather rocky buttes in sight and scattered about, with a few pines and plenty of big black ash and box elder and some small

groves of cottonwood. Not a very inviting looking
country, has a sombre red and brown appearance and
is not a good stock region. Too rocky and too much
sage which holds the snow and does not allow it to
drift or blow away. Irvine killed a goose, flying, with
his Winchester this A. M. Dense growth of scrub cedar
on most of the mountain sides, with a few yellow pines
in the cañons. Elevation here 3356 feet. Traveled
twenty-four miles this day.

MAY 1, 1880. Traveled thirteen miles and camped
at the mouth of Prairie Dog creek. Elevation 3356
feet. This creek is about fifteen to twenty feet wide
and a good swift current and is very muddy. It comes
in from the south. Country not so good. Since the
first five miles too much sage and rocky hills and burnt
looking country and no water, excepting in Tongue
river and Prairie Dog creek. Here we found a nice
little white and dun spotted horse, doubtless dropped
by Sioux Indians as they came through here to steal
horses from the Crows.

We only traveled eight miles in the afternoon and
camped across the river from two new hewed log
houses that had been built last winter. Nobody at the
houses. Large good grassed bottom along here but a
good deal of sage among it and much short sage on the
rusty looking hills. Mired our pack mule down in
crossing a coulee near river, but after two hours of hard
work we got him out and our stuff carried out on the
dry ground. All the coulees are miry near the mouth
and so is the river and deep when still, but fordable on
all ripples. Quite a creek comes in here from the west,
very muddy with deep cut banks and could not cross it.
Had to cross the river below its mouth. Hardly a pine

or a cedar along route today. I killed a fine fat goose today, and we roasted it on a spit over our camp fire.

MAY 2. Traveled twelve miles and camped for noon about one and one-half miles above the mouth of Goose creek which comes in from the southeast. It is nearly clear and is about two-thirds as large as Tongue river above the junction, the latter still quite muddy. Plenty of black ash and box elder all along the river and some nice small cottonwood groves. Very heavy growth of grass on bottoms which are not very large, but not very good on brown rocky burnt hills. Too much sage on both bottoms and hills. No old big sage but a young slim tall growth. No good country so far for stock. Found a bench where the grass had been burned off and where the young grass was very forward, being about three to four inches high. We let our poor horses fill up well on this grass at noon.

Saw many white-tailed deer today but they are all wild. Irvine killed a yearling just before we camped. Took the hams which are nice and tender. Saw five black-tailed deer on a hill. One buck had beautiful antlers but we did not have time to go after them. Passed several creeks on the north side of the river that have plenty of timber on them and camped on a clear rocky-bottomed creek, about a mile below an unoccupied cabin near which was a bay horse. A few miles before camping the sage ran out and the hills and valley are covered with a good growth of buffalo and gramma grass. This grassy belt is only about six to eight miles wide from foot of mountains out and then runs into the brown burnt somber-tinted hills and bluffs covered with short sage among which is some good bunch grass and the country rather rough and rocky.

The greatest objection to this for a cattle country is that nearly all the streams have steep-cut banks and deep channels and it is very hard to find a place where they can be crossed and especially where a place to get down and out is found, the bottom of the stream and both edges are usually miry and the coulees are miry when the snow is going off and after rains.

Elevation five miles below the Bozeman road 3906 feet and at the Bozeman road 4000 feet. Traveled twenty-five miles this day.

MAY 3. Started at 7:30 A. M. went up Tongue river three miles and came to the stage station of the mail route from the U. P. R. R. at Rock creek to Fort Custer [111] via Reno and Fort McKinney. At this point were three men trying to plow in the bottom with two mules and two horses all abreast. Asked them some questions about snow fall, etc. The chap that stammered and choked made himself spokesman much to our annoyance. He said there was a foot of snow and it went off and came on again and went off and sometimes they had snow and sometimes not any and it was warm winds in spells and then the wind was cold and then there was more snow and a warm wind and "you know how it is around here pretty much all the time." They had a herd of one hundred thirty cattle and nine of them died.

Elevation at this point 4000 feet. Here were several

[111] Fort Custer was established in 1877 on the Big Horn river not far from the battle ground of Custer's last fight to hold the Crow Indians in check. Its establishment came as a result of the Custer battle. Hubert Howe Bancroft, History of Montana in *Works*, vol. xxxi (San Francisco, 1890) p. 719. Fort Reno on Powder river was built in 1865 to protect the Bozeman trail. It was abandoned in 1868 as a result of the Fetterman massacre. For history see Hebard and Brininstool *opus citra*, vol. ii, pp. 122-135. Fort McKinney was on Piney fork of Powder river near the present site of Buffalo, Wyoming. *Ibid.*, vol. i, p. 255 – ED.

cabins and a bridge across the river and a woman with five very small children. They must have been twins and triplets they were all so near one size. They also had some hogs and chickens.

Went up to the foot of the mountains and took the old Bozeman road but before we reached it we came to a creek with very muddy water and utterly impassable steep banks. Could get neither in nor out and had to go two miles below where there was an abandoned ranch. Someone had dug down the banks and made a crossing. These steep-banked miry streams would be bad for cattle.

The Big Horn mountains have upheaved the strata which all slope down toward the plains and this grassy belt from six to eight miles wide along the base is evidently owing to the erosion of a vast quantity of these tilted strata which were softer and which has given to the country along the foot of the mountains a smooth and rounded look with a more fertile soil generally.

Cloud peak which has been in full view since we crossed the divide coming from Rosebud is really a very lofty point. It is a sort of jagged ridge or crest with a number of craggy peaks on it, and from it, west, for more than forty miles the top of the range is above timber line. From there west it gradually slopes down till just west of the Big Horn cañon it is quite low.

These mountains are very steep all along this side and are poorly timbered with scrubby trees – at least until high up on them where it may be better. There is no timber in the foot hills. Camped for noon on first branch of the Little Horn river. There is a settlement here which consists of eight or ten cabins scattered on river and creek in vicinity.

Traveled ten miles in the afternoon over a nice grassy country and only a few small snow drifts. Camped on second branch of Little Horn river. Grass much more forward in this valley. Used dead branches from wild plum trees for wood. There are many wild plum thickets along the streams and in the coulees but they seem to be dying out and the bear break them down and many are destroyed by the prairie fires, as are also the cherry bushes which are very numerous. Plenty of box elder and a little ash timber on these two creeks and they have rocky bottoms and stock can drink from them and cross them almost anywhere without danger of miring. It is a fine stock region. Saw many white-tailed deer today and yesterday but did not kill any as we did not need the meat.

Our horses are getting played out especially Bessie, the pack mule. I must buy some fresh ones as soon as I get a chance.

MAY 4. Broke camp at 7:30. Grass was good at this camp and our horses had all that they could eat and rested up. Plenty of green grass about three inches high everywhere. Traveled four miles over rolling grassy hills to Little Horn river. Charming country. Stream about the size of Flint creek and heavily timbered with ash, box elder and cottonwood and more willows than usual. Stream swift flowing over gravely bed with low banks and clear water. Stock can get in and out any where and there is a beautiful low bench on west side of the creek about one mile wide and eight miles long. Lots of deer here. Went eight miles over a high grassy ridge with water in all the ravines to Grass Lodge creek which is also a clear stream with low banks and rocky bottom. Considerable ash and box elder with a wide belt of willows along the stream;

more than we have seen anywhere on the trip. The valley is not so wide as that of the Little Horn but there are beautiful low grassy hills on either side.

Crossed a small creek in about three miles and in three more came to Rotten Grass creek, clear and with low banks and rocky bottom. In two miles more we crossed Soap creek and then camped for the night. Finest grass all over a rather hilly country which has all been burned off last fall clear to the Big Horn river. A constant succession of plum thickets on this stream. There are plum bushes in every sag and ravine and they are just beginning to blossom. The air is filled with their sweet fragrance. The timber along here is box elder and large willows. Deer and antelope in sight all the time and a great number of prairie chickens everywhere. 'Tis very pleasant to hear the larks, flickers, black birds, and curlews all singing every morning early. The frogs croak all the time day and night. Traveled twenty-two miles this day. Elevation 4000 feet.

MAY 5. Started at 7:40 A. M. and crossed a high grassy ridge to a little creek that empties into the Big Horn river just below the ruins of old Fort C. F. Smith.[112] Went down the creek to the fort. The ruins of the fort are of red adobe. It was once quite extensive and very well built. It stands on a high bench about sixty feet above the Big Horn river and about three hundred feet from it. What a shame for the government to allow the hostile Sioux to burn it down. Visited the cemetery which is on a high part of the bench four hundred yards southwest. There is

---

[112] Fort C. F. Smith was built in 1866 on the Big Horn to protect the Bozeman road. It was abandoned in 1868 after the Fetterman massacre. For history see *Ibid.*, pp. 135-146. – ED.

a nice monument of white marble but the Indians have shot it in several places knocking off some of the corners but it is still in fair condition. Most of the head boards have rotted down but most of the names are on the monument. Just above this graveyard a little creek comes in from the south and right at the mouth of this creek on the river bank is where the Crows fired into my brother James's party on the night of May 12, 1863, killing two and wounding seven.

Elevation of [Fort] C. F. Smith 3700 feet. Went down ten miles further to the mouth of Rotten Grass creek and camped. A furious wind was blowing that raised clouds of sand from the bars on Big Horn. We could hardly get our tent up. It began to rain at dark. The grass along here is four inches high. There is an abundance of fine hay land all along and fine grass on hills and benches. Traveled twenty-three miles this day.

MAY 6. Traveled down Big Horn river ten miles and then turned east to go over to Little Horn river distance about fifteen miles over some high bad land hills but generally well grassed but with considerable sage however. Went and visited the place where Reno fortified himself on the hill at the time of the Custer massacre.

Picked up some mementoes of the fight and camped for the night on the Little Horn about two miles below or half way between Reno hill and where Custer and his men were killed. Their monument is in sight on the point of the ridge where they fell. The river is about fifty or sixty yards wide and about thirty-eight inches deep on an average and very swift. Considerable timber in clumps but not much underbrush. There is some very good ash and box elder and fine grass.

The green grass is six inches high. Long slopes and ridges on west side of Little Horn between it and the Big Horn river well grassed and somewhat broken country on east side extending back to Rosebud mountains only tolerably grassed and with much short stunted sage and short-cut bank coulees extending back a short distance from the river. Cloud peak and most of Big Horn mountains visible from this camp. Elevation 3200 feet. Traveled thirty miles this day.

MAY 7. In the morning we went up to the battle field and walked all over it. Saw just where the men and horses fell. The bodies were placed in shallow graves and covered with loose earth. I made some sketches of the battle and picked up some shells. Cut some ash canes at the place where Custer tried to cross the river and was driven back and from there we returned to camp and packed up, came back, and followed the route taken by them which was marked by bones of horses and graves of men marked by a stake at their head. The first stand was made by a few in a little sag near the top of the ridge where were the bones of several horses and the graves of several men. This was about a quarter of a mile from the river and from there they curved to the left along the crest of the ridge for about five hundred yards further where Custer and the last of his men fell. Keogh and his men were killed in a sag on the north side of this ridge. Custer and others at the west end of the ridge. Bones of men and horses are scattered all along between. On the point where Custer fell is built up a sort of pyramid of cord wood with a ditch around it and inside filled with bones of horses. I found two battered bullets and many empty shells. This ridge is not steep and is covered with short grass and low stunted sage and a person can

gallop a horse over nearly any part of it. The ground
rises steep about thirty feet in a sort of bench and then
slopes back gradually to the fatal ridge. There are
some small sags and ravines running back to it also.
The field is a ghastly sight.

Went down to Fort Custer and bought some provisions and had some of the horses shod and was ferried
over the Big Horn and camped on the west bank.
Elevation 3100 feet. Traveled sixteen miles this day.

MAY 8. Rained in the night and is raining and
snowing a little this morning with a high west wind
and very raw and cold. The bluffs on both sides of the
river are white with snow. We concluded to wait a
little for it to clear up.

Fort Keogh [113] is on a high point of bluff at the junction of Big and Little Horn rivers about one hundred
feet above the river and has a fine view of Big Horn
mountains and all the rest of the country and catches
all the wind that is going. Little Horn river is gravelly
banks and bottom clear to its mouth and can be crossed
anywhere.

About noon it cleared up and we traveled down the
river eighteen miles to the Half Way ranch, which is
a beautiful place where the bluffs run down close to the
river and are more or less timbered with nice yellow
pine trees and castle rocks in places. They run back
ten or twelve miles and are beautiful in form and have
lots of game in them. The Big Horn river is heavily
timbered with good cottonwood and some ash. The
bluffs on west side of the river are distant six or eight
miles from where they begin, which is a little above
Fort Custer and gradually narrow in until they reach

---

[113] Fort Keogh was built by General Nelson A. Miles in 1877 as the
principal fort in eastern Montana. Bancroft, *Montana*, p. 719. – ED.

the river at the Half Way ranch.   They are quite high
and level on top (to the west) and are well timbered
and form a beautiful back ground to the view.   The
land is all good.   There is but little water but it can
be brought from the river.   This would be an ideal
cattle range but it is on the Crow Indian reservation
consequently out of the question.   Big Horn and Pryor
mountains visible from Half Way house.   Elevation
2990 feet.   Traveled eighteen miles this day.

SUNDAY, MAY 9, 1880.   Went down the river twelve
miles and camped at noon in the forks of the Yellowstone and Big Horn rivers for the purpose of looking
for my brother James's name, which with date he
carved in the sandstone cliff between the rivers, when
on the Yellowstone expedition 1863.[114]

Many portions of the cliffs (which are a soft sandstone which weathers badly) have fallen and my
brother's name I could not find.   I found some of his
comrades' names.   First cut in bold capitals is "D.
Underwood, May 6, 1863;" next, "W. Roach, May 6,
1863;" and then "G. Ives;" and between these last
some Indian has scratched a crude picture of an Indian
with a war bonnet on and a "coup" stick in his hand
seated on a horse.   This was the best drawn horse I
ever saw drawn by an Indian, and about twenty-five
yards to the west is faintly scratched "S. T. Laust" and
near it is "W. R." and close to this is "H," and the
water has run down and washed away the rest of the
name, but below is "May 6 18" and nearby to the right
is "G X Ives 1863."   This is very well executed and
to the right of it is "A S Blake May 6th 1863," and I
could find no more.   Went about two miles up the
Yellowstone river to Terry's landing where we ferried

<hr>

[114] See note 77. – ED.

to the north side and put our horses in stable.   Tracks
of six Sioux Indians (on foot) were found a few miles
back of the landing and most of the inhabitants are out
with their guns tracking them up.   They tracked them
into a thick bottom full of brush about three miles above
town and set fire to it in the hope of burning them out
but only a portion would burn and so they had to give
them up.   There is a telegraph and post office here.
Elevation 2930 feet.   Got $250.00 from a gambler, B.
F. Williams.   Gave him a check on First National
bank of Helena for same.   Only man in town with any
money.

MAY 10, 1880.   Hired John Roberts with rifle horse
and pack horse for $50.00, to go with us the rest of the
trip.   The Crow Indians tell us that the country between here and Flat Willow is swarming with Sioux
in parties from ten to ninety strong.   The Crows keep
pretty close tab on the Sioux but they lie so one can put
no dependence in what they say.   We will keep watch
and with four fine Winchesters and two revolvers and
plenty of ammunition we will be able to take care of
ourselves.   Left Terry's landing at 2 P. M. and traveled
seventeen miles where we found a spring in a coulee
and camped for the night.   The first few miles was
through rough broken bad lands with plenty of pine
timber and some good grass and a little sage.   Some
clumps of cottonwood in coulees where the water stands
in holes and is quite strong of alkali.   There has been
a large herd of buffalo across here lately and they have
eaten the grass off close.   Saw a herd of buffalo running across the hills east of our camp.   Indians after
them of course.   Kept all our horses tied at the tent
and stood guard.   The Crows may be right and we may
run into some Sioux yet.   Killed an antelope this after-

noon and saw some black-tailed deer but did not get a shot. Traveled seventeen miles this day.

MAY 11, 1880. Breakfasted at 5:30 A. M. and left camp at 6:30 and traveled twenty-two miles and camped at noon on Alkali creek about five miles from the Musselshell river. Water strong of alkali and salty besides, although it runs a small stream with big pools along its course. Large bands of antelope and hundreds of buffalo in every direction. I killed one at camp. High rolling prairie country most of the way after the first six miles from the Yellowstone to top of divide, when there comes in some nice yellow pine groves and the country breaks up into bad land bluffs which extend to the Musselshell which is about six or seven miles from the summit of divide.

After dinner we went five miles to Musselshell where the country is black with buffalo and crossed and camped one-half mile below at cabin of Jack Allen and Bush, which is deserted. In the cabin was a fry pan, coffee-pot, gold pan, and a case knife and outside about a gallon of coal oil in a five gallon can. Dead buffalo, dead wolves, and dead dogs are thick around the cabin and the smell is not that of attar of roses, and there is a lot of it such as it is.

The country, both bottom and hills, is all covered with stunted sage and greasewood and but little grass. There are petroleum indications all through here and some day Montana will produce oil but it is worthless now. The myriads of buffalo have eaten out what little grass there is so our poor horses will fare badly here. The river water is cold and pleasant to drink and less strong of alkali than the holes out of which we have been drinking. Saw pony tracks (17) not very fresh. We think they are about ten days old, doubtless Sioux

Indians. Harry Wormsley and John Roberts stood guard tonight. Had to run out and shake our blankets to frighten the buffalo away from camp and to prevent their stampeding our horses.

MAY 12. Started at 7 A. M. over a rough country broken by ridges and coulees and all covered with stunted sage and greasewood and very little grass and ten thousand buffalo busily engaged in eating up what little there is. Took a northwest course for Flat Willow creek, leaving the Little Snowy range a little to the west of our course. The Snowies at this distance (probably sixty miles) look like a large hump of a ridge white with snow on top and black with timber below, and running northeast and southwest and to right is other lower black-looking mountains and buttes not snow covered. Buffalo by the thousands in every direction. Could have killed many as we traveled along but we did not need the meat so did not molest them. Tom Irvine killed an antelope and we took the tenderloin and the hams and went on and camped at noon at a hole of rain water in a little dry creek. Had to use buffalo chips to cook with, for the first time on the trip. While in this camp a band of antelope lay down on a point on one side of our horses and two old buffalo bulls on the other side are standing guard for us. Antelope and buffalo are very tame here. Will hardly run from us.

I will here mention that whenever there is water in all this country where I have been, the frogs sing both day and night and the birds also, at least the larks do. Heard a thrush or mountain mocking bird at our camp in Eighteen Mile coulee. It sang beautifully.

In the bad land ridges soon after leaving Musselshell are great numbers of apparently fossil fragments

of fishes all of one kind, long and slim; picked up and
kept a few specimens. In the afternoon we started at
3:25 P. M. Scant sage and greasewood soon played out
and the hills and vales have here a rounded grassy appearance but it is mostly short curly buffalo grass and
extends from here to Flat Willow creek some twenty
miles and just before we halted for noon the bad land
nature changed to gravelly rounded hills and ridges
which extend to Flat Willow which is bounded on the
south side by high sandstone cliffs. When we passed
there were pools of rain water in many dry ravines and
flats remaining from the big storm of April 23 and 24.
Although this country has a well grassed appearance,
it is very thin in places and is about all buffalo
grass, short and curly. Feed is very poor since leaving
the Yellowstone so we kept on traveling until we
reached Flat Willow, although it took us until 8:30 P.
M. When we reached Flat Willow we found the
grass better than anywhere since we left the Big Horn
but it is not as good even now as we found it on the
Little Horn river and its tributaries and it is not so
good a looking country for stock down here but comes
next to it.

There are a few plum thickets and choke cherries and
plenty of box elder, but no ash, and but little cottonwood or under brush. Deep rich soil. "Pike" Landusky and Jo Hamilton planted corn, potatoes, and
turnips and they all grew. There is no doubt but that
tomatoes, squash, pumpkins and such can be grown
successfully here.

There are some yellow pines and cedar on the bluffs
but not much and it is about eighteen miles up to the
spur of the Snowies on the south side of the creek to
good pine poles and logs. Flat Willow is about thirty

to thirty-five feet wide with generally steep cut banks (muddy) but mostly gravel bottom. Water very muddy, like the Rosebud, and from three to four feet deep. Hard limestone water. Blue joint grass in the bottom but not usually thick enough for hay.

Landusky and Hamilton have three log cabins of one room each, dirt roof and dirt floor. They have a picket corral of box elder logs about seven or eight feet high and sixty feet square where they corral their horses every night and put a boy, Harry Morgan, out to watch them day times. The Sioux Indians raid this country regularly.

They tell us that the snow did not get over six inches deep at any time last winter and did not lay on the ground long at any time. Traveled forty-three miles this day.

MAY 13, 1880. Laid over all day and let our tired horses rest, as the grass is good and we can put them in the corral nights and need not stand guard. We take our meals with Landusky. John Healy is stopping with him and they are trapping beaver. They caught two she ones while we were there, one had four kittens and the other two. They have them in a box. I do not believe they will live and have begged them to put the poor things back into the creek. They have a garden and Andy, the negro who had his feet and hands so badly frozen some years ago at Carroll, is cooking for them. Harry Morgan (son of John Morgan and about fifteen years old) is horse-guard day times and the horses are all put in the corral at night. Plenty of good hay land around here and picturesque cliffs coming on the south side.

MAY 14, 1880. Rained quite a shower in the night and is very cloudy and cold, with a high wind blowing and looks rather stormy. After waiting until 9 A. M. for it to clear up, we packed up and lit out and when we were about five miles on our way, it began to rain. We kept on for about three miles until we found a place where we could get tent poles and dry wood to kindle the fire and then we camped. The rain soon turned to slushy snow and rain and was decidedly disagreeable. We finally got the tent up and cooked our dinner. In the afternoon it cleared but left it muddy. Tom Irvine and Hank Wormwood walked out to the bench about a mile and killed an antelope and brought in the tenderloins and hams and then three big elk walked out of the brush on to a little ridge and "sassed" us plenty, but we had meat and so would not kill them. Grass very good and creek gravelly bottomed and easily crossed. Traveled ten miles this day.

MAY 15. Traveled about eighteen miles up Flat Willow creek to Brown's trading post. This is where Bill Hamilton wintered and said it was such a fine place for cattle. Brown tells me that the snow was never more than ten inches deep at any time all winter and that it did not lay on the ground long at any time. There is good grass in the bottoms and on the rolling hills with beautiful groves of yellow pine but so far no fir or lodge pole pine. Creek still muddy but not so thick as below.

Passed about forty lodges of Piegan and North Blackfoot Indians a few miles from Brown's. Elevation at Brown's 4000 feet. Kept on for about ten miles over a charming rolling grass country with water in all the ravines and small creeks. There are magnificent groves of tall straight yellow pine trees. Snow must fall very deep along here because there are snow drifts in many of the sags and bends of ravines. The world

FIRST ATTEMPT AT ROPING
From an old photograph among the Granville Stuart papers

INDIANS STALKING BUFFALO
From an old drawing in the Granville Stuart papers
The Indians would cover themselves with coyote skins and approach
the herd without arousing alarm. They could then shoot as many as
they chose with bow and arrow and thus save powder and shot

could not beat this for a summer range and it is very
very beautiful. Saw many elk and black-tailed deer
and bands of antelope. Since leaving Flat Willow,
all the little creeks are clear and much colder than any
water we have had on this trip.

The Little Snowie mountains loom up to the southwest quite grandly. They have a large quantity of
snow on them and the tops of them seem to be above
timber line. To the north are the Judith mountains
but they are not nearly so high or so well timbered as
the Little Snowies and have only a few snow drifts on
the south side. To the right of them a short distance,
standing at the beginning of the plain, on rather rolling
ridges of little height rises the "Black butte" which is a
beautiful curved top cone. It is very high and very
steep and can be seen a long distance and I presume is
a favorite roosting place for Sioux horse-stealing
parties.

Chamberlain's place is on McDonald creek. The
ranch was visited about ten days ago by a party of ten
Sioux Indians who stole all of Chamberlain's horses
and a lot of ponies from some Red river half-breeds
who were camped here. Strange we have not run into
some of these war parties but so far we have played in
luck and still have our horses and our scalps. Chamberlain says the snow was about twelve inches deep in
January but it did not lay long and then all went off and
but little more fell and that did not lay. Traveled
three miles down the creek below Chamberlain's and
camped for noon. Grass nice and green and about four
inches high. There are large patches of choke cherries
on the creek and quantities of bull berries and red haw-
thorn bushes.

Once in a while there is a very large old cottonwood

tree but no young growth of cottonwood at all. Went on down the creek about nine miles and camped for the night. Killed an elk and saw many more. Plenty of antelope, we see bands of them on all the ridges. There are lots of sage and prairie chickens all over the country but no ducks or geese. Shot the heads off of two prairie chickens with my Winchester and we had fried chicken for supper. The new grass is six inches high at our night camp. The box elder trees are getting quite green. Willows not so much so. There is a fine hay bottom about nine miles below Chamberlain's on the north side of the creek. It is about two miles long and from one-fourth to one-third miles wide.

Found Sioux tracks where a party of about six crossed the creek on foot. They are doubtless looking for horses and it won't be their fault if they travel far on foot. We will take no chances with our horses. There is timber on the bluffs on both sides of the creek sufficient for present use. Not very good but will do for building and for fence posts. No poles nearer than twenty miles or so.

The valley of McDonald creek is not wide only from one-half to three-fourths of a mile wide with the stream meandering from side to side. Bluffs not very high. Sometimes on the north side breaking down to sloping benches. There is good gramma and buffalo grass on the bottoms and benches, also some stunted sage among it along here and some greasewood, while up between Brown's & Chamberlain's there is a big growth of grass, some regular bunch grass and no sage. Up there on the foot-hills indications are that there is too much snow for cattle to stay all winter.

Camped in narrow bend of creek with good brush shelter and after supper we moved about a mile further down the creek and made our beds in the dense willow brush. Tied all of our horses up short to avoid standing guard. Our course was northeast a few miles and we crossed the ridge between McDonald and Ford creeks and from the top of it had a good look over the country. Saw two considerable lakes one on each side of Ford creek. Water in all these ravines and coulees but is probably not permanent. Good grass in broken good shelter ground until we got on Ford creek side when it became rather short and thin and mixed with stunted sage. Do not like the country north and east of McDonald creek. Too much sage.

Traveled up Ford creek about twelve miles when the sage played out on the north side and it looks smooth and grassy north to Black butte and west to Judith mountains probably twenty or twenty-five miles but so far (noon) the grass is short being mostly buffalo grass. After dinner we kept on up Ford creek five miles, killed a black-tailed deer out of a band of six. Took the meat and then crossed over through a pine forest of pretty fair timber and some good holes too, onto a branch of McDonald creek near the foot of divide between McDonald creek and Judith basin. Good grass at camp. Some splendid bunch grass on the benches between the creeks and along several little creeks and in the sage.

MAY 19. Started out at 7:45 A. M. and traveled six or seven miles up the head branches of McDonald creek to the top of the divide between it and Judith basin. Elevation of summit 4500 feet. During this morning's travel we passed through the most beautiful timber thinly scattered along the hillsides and ravines. Mostly straight yellow pines but some fine fir trees also and plenty of both fit for saw logs. No white pine for poles but many groves of quaking aspens along here. Saw some on the creek down near Chamberlain's and this is the only locality I have seen any at all since I struck the Yellowstone this side of Bozeman. Some yellow pines all along here and finest bunch and other grass all along. Went to twelve miles beyond the divide into the Judith basin and camped for noon between Juneau's fort and Bowles and Reeds place. Juneau has a little log stockade fort about 100x150 feet with two bastions at opposite corners, but the logs are so small that a bullet from any heavily charged gun such as a Sharps or Needle gun, would go right through them. It is neatly fixed up on the inside and the houses of the Red river half-breeds are in marked contrast to the posts of the white men through here. There is quite a settlement of Red river half-breeds here who are plowing and planting a crop. A war party of Sioux Indians came through here three nights ago and stole thirty head of their horses. If we had not been delayed by the storm we would have probably met them over near Black butte and would, in that case have had some fun.

From the top of the divide the view is grand. To the south loom up the Little Snowies, white to the foot. To the west rise the Belt mountains with some snowy peaks but not nearly so much snow as on the Little Snowies. To the northwest is the huge steep castillated-like mass of the Highwoods and to the north and near by are the Big Moccasin mountains, not very high or with much snow. To the northeast are the Judith mountains, rough but not very lofty and in the center of this grand panorama of mountains and at our feet lies the famous Judith basin. Now with the billowy hills covered with green grass it resembles an enormous lake. It is about sixty miles long and fifty wide. It has magnificent bunch grass but is too open and exposed for a cattle range and the snow too deep. The soil of the basin is very deep and fertile and it would be a splendid farming country if there was a market. Big Spring creek takes its rise in one big spring up at the base of the Little Snowies and here at Juneau's it is twenty-five yards wide and two feet deep and very rapid. A beautiful stream of clear cold water. There is no timber and but little brush in the basin here. The basin was all burned off last fall and the green grass is up so as to make good feed for our horses but it is three weeks behind the grass on the Big Horn. After dinner we took the old Carroll road and went up the valley across a high bench that runs down from the Little Snowies and after traveling nine miles camped on Beaver creek and used the remains of a squatter's abandoned shack for wood.

With the single exception of Cottonwood creek which we crossed two miles before we camped, there is not so much as a willow twig big enough to burn from Reed's ford clear over to Judith gap and on to Hopley hole a distance of sixty miles. There is water in every coulee at this time of the year and little creeks of permanent water every few miles. There is a cold northeast wind and storming on the mountains. This is a cold bleak region and there are snow drifts still under banks and in ravines.

MAY 20, 1880. Left camp at 8 A. M. cold raw southeast wind, traveled twenty-five miles and camped at 2:30 P. M. at a little shack on a small creek about five miles north of the divide. Not a twig of wood on the road or at camp so had to take some of the roof poles to cook with. Here is the turning off place to the Yogo mines. Mr. Barrows came along and reports six steamboats already arrived at Fort Benton and more expected daily. The Yogo mines are not paying anything yet and I fear they are a failure. Snow drifts quite plentiful as we near Judith gap and the wind is very cold. Elevation here 4650 feet.

MAY 21, 1880. It rained all night. Got up late and saw an antelope within gunshot from camp and a buffalo bull still closer behind the tent. Tom Irvine took a shot at the buffalo but did not give him a mortal wound, followed him a quarter of a mile and killed him. Took the tongue and tenderloin. The weather cleared and we struck camp about 9:30 A. M. and traveled twenty miles. Camped for noon at Hopley hole. No wood on the road and the grass thin and poor except at Severen's sheep ranch where there is a large bottom of hay land. This side so far is not nearly so good a country as east of the Snowies on McDonald and Flat Willow (for grass timber or shelter). Hopley hole is a deep narrow valley sunk down one hundred fifty feet below the level of the table land or high bench which extends from the base of the mountains down to the Musselshell river.

Our camp was in a ravine on the west side of Hopley's hole which has many huge snow drifts in it. Used buffalo chips for cooking our dinner. Let our horses feed until 4 o'clock and then went on to Daisy Dean creek which we reached at 7:45 P. M. Could find neither wood nor grass sooner. We had nothing but small willows for fuel and it was very cold. Daisy Dean creek is narrow, deep, and very muddy, and ice one-half inch thick froze in our water bucket. Traveled thirty-seven miles this day.

MAY 22, 1880. Packed up and left camp at 8 A. M. and traveled four miles to Martinsdale at forks of the Musselshell. This town consists of four or five houses scattered over a mile or so of ground. There are thirty soldiers stationed here, and it is a good safe place for them as there are some settlers below to keep the Indians off them and the big spring roundup of cattle is now commencing and there are fifty men camped here who will work down the river fifty or sixty miles, so the soldiers are reasonably well protected. Here I parted with my companions Thos. H. Irvine, Hank Wormwood, and John Roberts who return from here to the Yellowstone. Paid Irvine $125, Roberts $50, and Wormwood $40. They are good men and true.

My horses are about exhausted and I have them with W. D. Flowers until I come back this way and I will go on to Helena by stage. High wind and very cold. Traveled four miles this day.

SUNDAY, May 23, 1880. Had to spend the day here and so stopped at R. H. Glendenning hotel, store, and post office. Stage does not go until tomorrow. Snowed about one inch early this morning and is very cold with flying snow squalls on the mountains. It looks as though there would be no spring this year. North and South forks of the Musselshell are both very high. No grass here, eaten into the ground. I wonder that the cattle here did not all die last winter. There are big snow drifts in all the sags and ravines and under banks. No timber but a few little cottonwoods along the stream and some yellow pine and fir twelve miles off on steep mountains. All the streams along here are muddy. I certainly would not select this for a cattle range but I presume there are five thousand cattle in here now.

Four of the six houses that I mentioned are saloons

and the brand of whiskey must be bad for the inhabitants "whooped her up" all night and I cannot say that I passed a quiet, peaceful Sabbath.

MAY 24.   Started at 8:30 on the stage (big old open wagon) for Helena.   Ten miles above the North fork is a very picturesque cañon with good yellow pine timber.   A man by the name of Hall is building a sawmill here, so goodby to the lovely pines.   They will soon all be sawed into lumber.   Took dinner at Copperapolis, only three cabins and but one of them inhabited.   Arrived at White Sulphur Springs at 7 P. M.   A pretty valley here and rather agreeable broken grass country with groves of yellow pine and firs on the high hills on the way here.   Lots of big snow drifts that are hard frozen and bear up the stage and horses, to my surprise. Elevation at Copperapolis 5600 feet; at White Sulphur Springs 5000 feet.   There are some hot springs here strong of sulphur and said to be a sure cure for rheumatism.   Have no thermometer so cannot get temperature.   Had a bath in the water.   Very agreeable only for the sulphur smell.

MAY 25, 1880.   The coach left for Helena at 4 A. M. so we breakfasted at 3:30 A. M.   Good hot coffee and venison steak and flapjacks.   Raining cold and disagreeable and I was the only passenger.   Snowed very hard while crossing over the mountains into the head of Confederate gulch and then it turned to rain as we descended the mountain.   Had dinner at Diamond City, now a mere wreck of a once prosperous placer mining camp.

MAY 26-27-28, 1880.   Remained at home answering letters and meeting my co-partners in the cattle venture and giving in my report and then went over to Deer Lodge to arrange to start the cattle toward the range.

I have decided to locate on Little Big Horn if I can lease grazing land from the Crow Indians, if not then, I will locate somewhere in Flat Willow country. Telegraphed to B. F. White at the terminus of the Utah Northern R. R. to know if the Crow Indian delegation and agent had arrived on their way home from Washington and received answer that they had just arrived. I determined to intercept them at Bozeman and interview them as to getting a lease to graze our cattle on the Big and Little Horn rivers.

JUNE 2, 1880. Met· Agent Keller, two interpreters (Tom Stuart and A. M. Iurvey) and six Crow chiefs (Two Belly, Plenty Cow, Long Elk, Old Crow, Medicine Crow) at Gallatin and went with them to Bozeman where I was agreeably surprised to meet Colonel Pickett and Capt. Henry Belknap. The former hunts all the time and the latter has located a cattle range on Stinking river (fork of Big Horn). Agent Keller desired me to go to the agency before trying the Indians.

JUNE 6, 1880. Interviewed Agent Keller this morning. He is afraid to mention the matter to the Indians lest they should refuse to ratify the cession of the upper end of their reservation so I started on my return home at 10 A. M. in the usual rain storm. Remained in Helena until June 16 when I started for Sun River arriving there on the seventeenth. Remained in Sun River one day and sent one wagon and seven men to join Swett and go with him to Beaverhead to receive a small herd of cattle there. I took four men with me and started for Flat Willow creek via Fort Benton with a light wagon, two horses and six saddle horses. Country much cut up by ravines, and remnants of two ancient high benches are visible on foot of the mountains. Traveled sixteen miles this day.

MONDAY, June 20.   Struck camp at 6 A. M. and traveled fifteen miles to Alkali creek at the north foot of
Square butte, which should be called Table butte, for
it is not square at all but is level on top and very high.
Square (or Table) butte is evidently the point from
which a great outpouring of lava or basalt took place
and spreads over the adjacent country.   It rises about
two thousand feet above the plain at its foot and is very
steep.   Running down its sides in every direction are
tremendous basaltic or try-dykes which stand up in
narrow precipitious, jagged comb like ridges and about
half way up it is surrounded by a belt of jagged irreg-
ular pinacles of basalt or trychyte while its summit, a
plain about one-half to one and one-half miles long, is a
table of series columnor basalt, which is verticle in most
places from twenty-five to fifty feet.   Under a cliff
facing Arrow creek is quite a patch of seemingly good
fir timber.   This fork of Arrow creek is only in pools
full of cattails and is strongly alkaline.   Between
Shonkin and Arrow creeks is a number of small lakes
that seem permanent.   Fine grazing country all over
here.   There is quite a number of cattle in here now
and Henry McDonald has a band of two thousand
sheep on Arrow creek.   The Indians are also bad here
and are continually stealing these people's horses.
From Alkali creek we went ten miles down the fork to
Arrow creek which is deeply sunken down in Bad Land
bluffs.   Good grass here in abundance.   Ray Davenport and Kingsbury have about seventy-five head of
thoroughbred short-horned cattle here.   Met Mark
Ainslie's bull team of fifteen wagons hauling Brown's
and Allis' steam sawmill to Musselshell.

JUNE 22.   We started at 6 A. M. but it took us an
hour and a half to climb the fearful bad land hill on the

east side of Arrow creek. Once on top we found ourselves on a vast plain. To our right loomed up the
Square butte and Highwoods. Due south is Judith
gap and just to the left of it is the long snow capped
ridge of the Little Snowies. Away to the northeast
rises the blue and beautiful forms of the Bear Paw
mountains which are across the Missouri river. Found
water in all the ravines between Arrow creek and Wolf
creek a distance of twelve miles.

We camped for noon on Wolf creek and caught a
few small fish. After dinner we packed up and traveled fifteen miles to the forks of Sage creek which runs
but little water and looks as though it too went dry in
August. Grass fine all over this country, but no wood,
not even willows and no shelter for cattle. Saw quite
a herd of cattle (Power and Co.'s) on a small creek
before reaching Sage creek. Sage creek is so named
because there is not so much as one sage bush on it.

We overtook and camped with some pilgrims who
are going to the Musselshell. There was a small band
of antelope off on a ridge and I took my Winchester
and started after them. One of the pilgrims went with
me. He told me that he was a mighty hunter back in
Illinois. I let him have the first try at the antelope but
he missed and they ran off. I started back to camp
and he to follow the antelope. My hunter friend did
not come in and when it begun to be dark his companions got uneasy about him. Went out to the top of the
ridge and fired their guns several times and shouted.
No response. Our party went to bed but the other side
of camp was restless and moving about and shouting
most of the night. In the morning two of their party
were missing: the antelope hunter and another that
had gone to look for him. None of these young fellows

have ever been out of town before, know nothing of this country and haven't the slightest idea of direction and are completely lost as soon as they are off the road. I told them to remain where they were and we would endeavor to locate their companions. Started my men out after the missing men. Found one sitting on a knoll about two miles from camp. The other we found eighteen miles from camp near the junction of Ross fork and the Judith river, completely lost and without presence of mind enough to look to see that the sun rose in the east.

The Judith is high, swift, and quite muddy owing to the placer mines at Yogo being on one of the branches. This whole basin is fine grass country but poor shelter for stock. There is water in all the coulees at this time of year. This whole basin is underlaid by regular bad land strata of dark colored clay and shale in nearly horizontal layers but its bad land character only shows when cut by the streams. There are antelope in sight almost all the time but only four or five in a band and they are wild. Camped for the night on Cottonwood creek about three miles below the Carroll road.

JUNE 24, 1880. Started at 6:10 A. M. and went on past Bowle's fort and Juneau's fort and camped for noon at the foot of Judith mountains about four miles east of Juneau's fort. In the afternoon went about three miles beyond the divide and camped for the night on a branch of McDonald creek.

JUNE 25. Started for Chamberlain's place on Mc-Donald creek. On our way down overtook about fifty carts of Red river half-breeds who have just moved over here from Judith basin and are going to Flat Willow and beyond to hunt buffalo. They have carts with two very large wheels in which the families ride.

They made a peculiar "screaky" noise that can be heard for miles.

JUNE 26, 1880. Maillette, Grant, Cameron, and I traveled down McDonald creek about fifteen miles looking for hay land but did not find anything to suit. Saw two doe elk and four fawns. Grant Gorden wanted to kill one but I begged him not to do it as the does would be poor and the fawns too young to eat, so he finally put his rifle back in the sling and let the pretty wild things live. We crossed over to Good Luck creek about three miles and here found fifteen cow elk with some calves. The boys would run them and Cameron killed a fawn, which we took to camp. Did not find any good hay land on Good Luck creek and the water tasted like slough water because of so many old beaver dams. It is a pretty smooth grassy country here but there is no timber excepting box elder and willow. Rode forty miles today over a beautiful grassy country but with little wood and still less hay land. Returned to Chamberlain's. About forty more carts and half-breed families arrived. Came from toward Black butte. Joined these already here which now make quite a village of lodges and carts.

SUNDAY, June 28, 1880. This morning I went down to the half-breed village to inquire of them about hay land streams and the country in general. Sevire Hamlin, quite an intelligent one, tells me that he knows just the sort of place I am looking for. Hired him to take me to the place. At 9:30 Maillet, James Heilman, and I, with Sevire Hamlin as guide, started out for Judith mountains. Traveled slowly and camped at sundown at a spring in a patch of willows where we were sheltered from a disagreeable wind. In the morning we traveled about three miles to a creek on which were

some small groves of cottonwood. Stream of clear
cold water and here about two miles from the mountains we found a magnificent body of hay land with
cold springs all through it. This is the very place we
have been hunting for. The whole country clear to the
Yellowstone is good grass country with some sage and
all of this country for a hundred miles in every direction is well grassed, well watered, and good shelter.
There is an abundance of yellow pine and poles for all
fencing and building purposes at the foot of Judith
mountains. This is an ideal cattle range. They tell
me it does not snow deep and it cannot lay on the
ground because there is too much wind. Returned to
Chamberlain's, seeing some splendid range on the way.

JUNE 30, 1880. Spent the day looking around and
tried to buy Chamberlain out but he asked too much.
I offered him $250 for four tons of wild hay and his
two small cabins but he wanted $500, too much. In-
structed the three men Cameron, Heilman, and Grant
to lay foundation logs for seven claims. Two claims
above Chamberlain, two up the creek near his hay land
and three in three bottoms below. None of this land is
surveyed and the only way to hold it is by occupying it.
This meadow land I intend for a winter range station.
Maillet and I then started for the big hay meadow on
the head of Ford creek to lay three foundations there
for claims. I intend to make this the home ranch for
the outfit.

Life on the Cattle Range

As soon as I reached Helena I made our arrangements to start the various herds of cattle to the range and then hurried back to attend to locating the home ranch.

I selected a spot on Ford's creek near some nice cold springs, about three miles from the foot of Judith mountains, and began the construction of a log stable that would accommodate ten horses, a cabin for cowboys, and a blacksmith shop. These buildings formed two sides of a large corral.

We also built two log houses one for Reece Anderson's family and one for my own use. These houses formed two sides of an open square and as Indians were likely to be troublesome in that section of the country, the two houses were connected with a bastion like those used at the early trading posts. I located one thousand acres of hay land and later acquired title to about four hundred acres using soldiers' scrip principally. This land was fenced with barbed wire fences as soon as we could get the material.

In July, 1880, Fort Maginnis was established by Capt. Dangerfield Park. The location for the cantonment was on the upper end of the hay meadow that I had selected for my home ranch. In spite of my best efforts at persuasion they included more than half the meadow in their reservation. It was annoying to loose the hay land but the fort was a convenience as it furnished telegraphic communications, post office and a convenient place to purchase supplies.

By the first of October we had our buildings completed, some range cabins built, and five thousand head of cattle on the range and sixty head of horses.

Two companies of the Third Infantry were at Fort Maginnis. Mrs. Fitzgerald and three children, family of the post tailor was the first family to arrive. About the middle of October Mrs. John T. Athey, wife of the post trader, arrived. The first notice I had of her being there was when a sergeant appeared at my door with an empty bed tick under his arm and told me that Mr. Athey had sent him down to have it filled with "Montana feathers." We had cut some fragrant sweet grass in the meadow during the summer so I sent the tick down to the stack and had it filled with the sweet-smelling hay. Mrs. Athey told me afterward that it was the most luxurious bed she had ever rested on.

In the early spring a baby girl was born to the wife of Frederick France at the fort. This was the first white child born in this section of the country and we could no longer consider ourselves beyond the borders of civilization.

In November, 1880, all bids for furnishing beef to Fort Maginnis were rejected by the commander as being too high. They then purchased twenty-five head of beef steers on the Shonkin and sent a detachment of soldiers to drive them to the fort. The soldiers were entirely unfamiliar with the country and knew nothing about driving range cattle so had trouble with them from the start and by the time they reached the crossing of the Judith river, they had lost about one-half of the bunch, and here they encountered a storm. The cattle stampeded and the soldiers became lost and bewildered but finally struck a trapper who kindly piloted them to the fort.

After this mishap the commander appealed to us and I finally agreed to furnish them beef that is I sold them four fat old steers delivered at Fort Maginnis for $45.00 per head, and they butchered them themselves.

The following year all bids were again refused, although they were lower than the ranchers were receiving at the mining camp of Maiden nearby. None of the cattle outfits sent in bids to furnish beef to the fort because they were all new on the range and busy getting located and could not keep extra men to attend to small orders.

This time the commander purchased a few head of beef steers on Flat Willow about twenty miles from the fort and again sent a detachment of soldiers to drive them to the fort. An accidental discharge of a shotgun stampeded the cattle and they scattered and could not be found. For weeks detachments of soldiers rode over the range chasing and disturbing our cattle greatly to our annoyance and detriment. These troopers were mostly of foreign extraction and from the East. They knew absolutely nothing about range stock and could not read a brand ten paces from an animal and were as incapable of taking care of themselves when out of sight of the post as three-year-old children.

We protested to the commander against allowing the soldiers to ride the range and chase and scatter our cattle but I failed to make him see how the soldiers riding about among wild range cattle and running the fat off them, could injure us or how it could be that we did not like it. I finally sent some cowboys out; rounded up the lost cattle and delivered them to the fort at our expense. I then invited the commander to dinner at the ranch and in an after dinner chat took occasion to explain to him the natural antipathy that a cowboy had for a soldier and that if they persisted in disturbing our cattle it would be at their own risk. We had no further trouble from that source for some time but it fell to my lot to furnish them beef. This time we butchered them at the ranch and the soldiers came and got the carcasses.

Our next trouble came in shape of a roving band of Cree Indians from Canada. The range riders notified me that they were killing the cattle. Taking two cowboys with me, I started for their village. There were about fifty men, women, and children in the party headed by a white man who claimed to be a Catholic priest. They had no provisions and were depending solely on the game that they could kill for sustenance.

I called for their chief and an old Indian came out to meet me. Pointing to a frozen beef hide thrown across a pole I asked for an explanation. The chief said his people were starving and game was scarce, that my cattle being on the range made the buffalo go away; that the priest told him that he had a right to kill the white man's cattle when his people were hungry. I asked him if he did not know that his hunting grounds were in Canada and not south of the Missouri river? He acknowledged that he was not in his own country but said that they could find nothing to eat there either and that the priest told him that it was right to kill our cattle when their children were hungry. I called for the priest and after a time he reluctantly appeared. I asked him what right he had to come on our range and advise the killing of our cattle? His excuse was that the women and children were hungry. I discovered that they had killed three steers, one cow, and one yearling. I ordered the chief to round up their horse herd and then selected five ponies to reim-

burse me for the slaughtered cattle, then told the chief
to leave the range at once. Some of the young Indians
protested at my taking their ponies and became quite
ugly. I called for the priest[115] and in dealing with
him was rather more emphatic, promising to hang him
higher than Haman if he ever set foot on the range
again. He and the Indians lost no time in getting
north of the British line. Roving bands of Canadian
Indians continued to harass us all winter.

The winter of 1880-81 was one of unusual severity;
our cattle were new on the range and not feeling at
home drifted badly. We had to watch every pass and
were kept busy turning them back on the range when
they had gone too far. Quite a number of the horses
evaded us in spite of our vigilance and returned to their
old homes. We had range cabins and kept range
riders out all winter looking after the cattle.

On December 8 eighteen inches of snow fell and the
thermometer registered thirty-two degrees below zero.
The storm lasted four days and from that time on until
May 15 there was a series of storms with the thermometer from twenty-two to forty degrees below zero. The
snow lay deep and many of the buffalo died. On our
range the snow did not lay long on the ground. The
hillsides were bare most of the winter but the gullies
and coulees were drifted full. A snow storm set in on
the fourteenth of January and two feet of snow lay on
the ground. It turned cold and mercury fell to twenty-
eight degrees below. The range looked and felt like
the Arctic regions.

On the evening of the seventeenth, I noticed flat pan-
cake chinook clouds in the western sky. The wind
began to roar on the mountains and blew so hard that

---

[115] I afterwards learned that this man was not a priest at all.

it was almost impossible to stand against it. At midnight the thermometer was forty-eight degrees above, the snow had disappeared and the gulches and coulees filled with water to a depth that would swim a horse. On the other side of the range, in the Judith basin there were three feet of snow. The Chinook did not reach them and the snow lay on the ground until the first of April.

The first year on the range we had no neighbors and as we had watched the cattle closely but few had strayed from the range. We rounded up alone, beginning May 25. Our losses all told, this first year were thirteen per cent, five per cent from Indians, five per cent from predatory animals and three per cent from the storms. The small loss from the storms was because there were so few cattle on the range; that feed was unlimited; and the creeks, and brush, and tall rye grass furnished them dry beds and shelter equal to a good stable and our cattle were northern range stock.

The same summer an English company drove five thousand head of cattle from Texas and located their home ranch at the mouth of Otter creek in Custer county. The cattle did not reach Montana until late in the fall and they were thin and worn from the long drive. Practically the entire herd perished. The sheriff of Custer county could find but one hundred and thirty-five head in the spring to satisfy a judgment held by Charles Savage of Miles City for supplies. The cowboys with the outfit were never paid their wages.

At this time (1880-81) the management of our Indian affairs was about as bad as it could well be and it was idle for us to hope for relief from wrongs that would have made Henry Ward Beecher swear like a trooper.

Let me review this delectable system and how it worked. First the government sets apart for each tribe enough of the choicest land to make a state; larger in fact than many of the older states of the Union, upon which the white man in search of homes may not put his foot, or even allow his domestic animals to feed upon the grasses which there grow up and decay without benefit to anyone, but the Indian who makes no use of this vast domain is allowed to leave at his own sweet will, and to stay away as long as he pleases and this he does for the well-known purpose of stealing the white men's horses, eating his cattle, and robbing his cabin. Time has no value to an Indian and he has no business that will suffer from his absence or neglect. He conceals himself in the timber and brush on the mountains or along the streams, for weeks or months, if necessary, subsisting off cattle killed as his needs require. His ideal of a good living is not a lofty one, and he is willing to submit to severe privations for the chance of finally stealing a horse, for a clever horse thief ranks next to a chief in an Indian tribe.

At last he secures his prize and by the time the victim discovers his loss the thief is fifty, sixty, or seventy miles away, for all Indians are desperate riders, and their flight always up to the limit of the speed and endurance of the horses stolen, and in this country unless a considerable number of horses are taken it is extremely difficult to find and follow the trail, and the loser is confronted with the question of, which direction did they go? for we are surrounded by Indian reservations, which means thieves. If found and followed, the trail, of course leads to some reservation and we are strictly forbidden to enter upon the poor Indians' little patch of ground (usually about one hundred by a two hundred miles square) without first obtaining the consent of a resident autocrat known as an "Indian agent" who is the joint product of the "Indian ring" and some village in the eastern states, where a careful study of Cooper's novels and the equally truthful and rose-colored reports of former Indian agents have convinced the resident population that the western Indian is a Christian gentleman of aesthetic tastes, with a child-like and bland smile, and that the western pioneer is a border ruffian and a villain, whose chief aim and object is to steal the purse, good looks, and clean shirts of the noble red man, while he is attending church. First the reservation, next the "agent," who is selected with especial regard to his utter and absolute ignorance of the Indian language, mode of life, habits, character, and best methods of influencing and controlling the nation's wards. Then come the united efforts of the government and the agent to civilize and enlighten the Indian, by so far as possible, isolating and cutting him off from connection with civilization, as found and embodied in all well-ordered communities of white men, by wrapping his robe of savagery and barbarism more closely about his filthy form, by concentrating him on reservations far from the only known civilizing agencies, contact and constant communication with the superior race.

The system which herds the Indians together on remote reservations, allows them to be armed and mounted at all times and under the leadership of their chiefs insures the propagation of all their old prejudices, lawlessness, and habits of thought and life, will not civilize them in ten thousand years, for public opinion is as strong in an Indian village as in any white community.   Public opinion among Indians is to assign to women the lot of a slave.   She is considered a little better than his dog but not anywhere nearly so good as his horse.   To her he kindly assigns everything in the shape of work connected with the Indian *menage*, while his duties consist in wearing grease paint and feathers.   He also has a passion for going on the war path and stealing everything in sight within a radius of four hundred miles from his particular agency.

The annual appropriations of the government for several years has been ample to board everyone of the agency Indians, big and little at a first class hotel, yet somehow all of this money does not seem to fill a long felt want (or the Indians either) for he remains the same dirty poverty-stricken thief that he became when first placed on a reservation.   It is well-known that everything brought from the east shrinks most awfully in this high dry altitude, yet this scientific fact would hardly account for the portly and robust appropriations becoming so thin and emaciated, that when they do finally reach the Indians they are like the darkies' fish, "all swump up."   The Indian knows that he is being robbed and in turn becomes a thief.   So long as these conditions prevail the cattlemen and the homesteaders remain the victims of the "system" and their only salvation lies in their ability to protect their property and look out for their scalps.

First we appealed to the Indian agents at the various agencies, notifying them of the presence of the Indians on the range and of the depredations they were committing and requested them to keep their Indians on their reservations.   Some of our communications were an-

swered and some were not. Major Lincoln, of the Fort
Belknap reservation, kept the Gros Ventres at home
demonstrating that it could be done and very few depredations were committed by that tribe. From some of
the other agents we received fair promises but no action.
Added to the trouble with our own Indians was that
with the British Treaty Indians, the Crees, North As-
siniboines, Bloods, North Piegans, Sarcees, and Sioux,
all related to and speaking the language of our northern
tribes.

Each autumn after their annual payments at Forts
MacLeod and Walsh, these tribes swoop down upon us,
their number carrying strength. They defy the white
men, and the military pay no attention to them except
to report to headquarters, and then inspect their forts
and test their safety in case of an attack. Occasionally
a squad of ten men and a lieutenant are sent out to "order the Indians to return at once" at which the chief
would smile, grunt, ironically admire the brass buttons
on the blue coats, and pay not the least bit of attention
to the order. The Indians continued on their way robbing ranches, frightening women, stealing horses and
subsisting on our cattle.

Between the months of November, 1880, and April,
1881, three thousand head of cattle were wantonly
butchered by Indians in Choteau and Meagher
counties; there was therefore in six months a destruction
of $60,000.00 worth of property by the malice of In-
dians.

Losses of this magnitude from one source alone could
no longer be borne by the stockmen. We had also discovered that someone was furnishing whiskey to the
Indians which partially explained the inordinate desire

of the Indians to spend so much of his leisure on the range. An Indian would part with his last pony, dog, child or wife, or barter his blanket or last pound of flour, steal or commit murder in order to get whiskey. A sober plain Indian was bad enough but when crazed by the rot-gut whiskey peddled to him by the human ghouls that prowled around the border of the reservation, he became a raving savage maniac, a peril to everybody within his reach.

These whiskey peddling fiends were not allowed on the reservations and if caught they were severely punished but located at convenient places on the range masquerading as trappers or wood choppers they plied their nefarious trade in safety, as the Indians would never tell where they got their whiskey. These whiskey traders would visit an Indian village; sell or barter what whiskey they had and then clear out of that neighborhood as speedily as possible, leaving the Indians to consume the fire-water and then do whatever their savage instincts prompted them to do. A drunken orgy at one of these isolated villages, where crazed savages beat, abused and mutilated their women and children; cut, slashed, and shot each other, beggars description.

Horses were the most desirable property for trade so when the whiskey trader had all that the Indian had he simply "lit out" and stole more horses and traded them for more whiskey. These whiskey traders were well aware that most of the horses that they traded for were stolen property, for Indian ponies have no harness marks or shoes on them. They would drive them to places in the bad lands, where it was impossible to find them unless perchance one accidently stumbled on them, remove their shoes, if they had any, change the brands and hold them there until they could drive them east into Dakota or north across the British line and dispose of them.

Confronted with these enormous losses the young struggling stock-growing industry faced certain annihilation unless immediate steps should be taken to protect it.   M. E. Milner, secretary of the Shonkin Stock Association, called a meeting of the stock men of Choteau and Meagher counties at Fort Benton on August 15, 1881, for the purpose of organizing a stock protective association.   The meeting was well attended in spite of the fact that many of the stockmen were out on the roundup, I being one of that number.   We sent letters, which were read at the meeting, promising our hearty co-operation in any measure that gave promise of protection to our property.

At this meeting the executive committee appointed one stock man residing at Fort Benton, to accompany Sheriff John J. Healey on all expeditions taken in behalf of the Stock Protective Association, who was to be paid by the association.   A reward of $500 was offered by the association for the apprehension and conviction of any person or persons selling, bartering, or giving whiskey to Indians on the ranges of stockmen, members of that association.   A reward of $100 was offered by the association for the apprehension and conviction of any persons detected in selling or giving intoxicating drinks to half-breeds upon the range.   A reward of $500 was offered for the apprehension and conviction of any person or persons maliciously or carelessly setting out fires on the range.   A standing advertisement to the above effect stating the rewards offered was ordered inserted in the Fort Benton papers.

It was further decided that the association hire men

at its own expense to ride range and look after Indians. Canadian Indians were to be intercepted at the border, ordered back across the line; if they went peaceably, well and good, but if they persisted in coming through the range, they did so at their peril, and the final issue would be raised then and there. Our own Indians were to be treated in the same manner. Stealing horses and stealing cattle would no longer be tolerated.

Hon. Martin Maginnis, our delegate in Congress, was called upon to address the meeting. Mr. Maginnis said he coincided with the views expressed by members and approved of the movement they had set on foot. While he deprecated any action that would lead to a war with the Indians, he could not but sympathize with the stockmen in the present case. If the government refused to extend its strong arm for the protection of the citizens of northern Montana, there was no recourse left them but to protect their own property and it was natural that they should do so.

The Major stated that in the past he had done all in his power to obtain redress of wrongs suffered by stockmen, but without any good result. While claims presented were generally allowed by the proper officer, Congress would not appropriate money to meet these demands, already amounting to several millions. He promised at the coming session of Congress to put forth his best efforts to secure relief for the stockmen and to see to it if possible that the British Indians did not commit further depredations on American soil. As soon as the Stockgrowers Protective Association was organized and their proposed action made public, a great hue and cry went up over a threatened Indian war that the stockmen were about to precipitate. The whiskey peddlers were loudest and most active in spreading the alarm. They proclaimed from the house tops that homesteaders were being driven from their homes and their property confiscated by the cattle men. Much was said about the attitude of Great Britain and that she would not stand for any interference with her Treaty Indians and that an international clash was inevitable. Strange as it may seem, our leading newspapers published all of these lurid alarms with large headlines and on front pages. A call for more troops for the frontier was sent in. General Terry, then commander of the division of the Northwest, stationed at Fort Snelling, said that he could spare no more troops. Everything possible was published and sent broadcast that would lead the general public to believe that the cattle men were encroaching on the Indians as well as small ranchers or "nestors" as they were called. At the same time these whiskey traders were not producing a single dollar and were doing more to degrade and debase the Indian and to endanger the lives and property of white settlers than all the cattlemen in Christendom ever could do.

The stockmen took no little pains to track up and find the source of these stories about homesteaders being driven from their ranches by cowpunchers. Invariably they were traced to the whiskey traders. One story in particular had a wide circulation and created something of a sensation.

Mrs. Annie Boyd came driving into Bozeman with six small children in the wagon box and a baby in her arms. She told the authorities that her husband had located a ranch on the Yellowstone and that while he was absent from home working, cowboys had come to the ranch and ordered her to leave the place. She was ill in bed, having a baby but ten days old so she could not go, but remained in terror for ten days when they again appeared at the ranch, caught up the team and hitched it to the wagon, then throwing in some provisions and loading in the children they ordered her to drive on and not to stop on that range again.

I was eating my breakfast in the Leland hotel in Chicago, when a benevolent old gentleman, knowing that I was from Montana, handed me the *Chicago Times* with the story copied from a Bozeman paper. I knew that there was no truth in it but determined to track it and see if it had a foundation. That afternoon I purchased my ticket to Bozeman instead of Helena.

I found Mrs. Boyd in Bozeman where she was being nicely cared for by sympathizing citizens and heard her very graphic but "fishy" story. My next move was to visit the Crow agency and there I learned that Mrs. Boyd's very hard working husband had taken refuge across the British line where he had fled to escape arrest for selling whiskey to the Crow Indians. He had located on the Crow reservation and the agent had ordered this family to leave and when they failed to go, he had sent the agency police to eject them. The Boyds were not on the cattle range and no stockman or cowboy had ever seen or spoken to them.

When Congress convened, Delegate Maginnis sent a letter to the Secretary of the Interior in which he called attention to the grievances of the stockmen of northern Montana and the steps they had taken to prevent further depredations by Indians on the range. Major Maginnis called the attention of the department to the fact that losses sustained by citizens of Montana, heretofore had never been paid by the government, so that they seemed to have no recourse but to defend their property by force if necessary. He sought to impress the fact that a few collisions between the stockmen and Indians might result in a bloody and expensive war and asked that prompt action be taken to prevent impending conflicts. He also made it clear that there never was any excuse for permitting British Indians to cross the line and commit depredations on our people. He made it quite clear to the department that unless the Indians were kept on their ample reservations that trouble was sure to ensue.

The Secretary addressed the following letter to the Commissioner of Indian affairs and there the matter rested so far as they were concerned, until this good hour.

Department of Interior,
Washington, September 15, 1881.

To the Commissioner of Indian Affairs:

Sir: I am in receipt of a letter from the Hon. Martin Maginnis, Delegate in Congress from Montana Territory enclosing a letter from Hon. Granville Stuart, of Helena, M. T., relative to the threatened disturbances between the settlers and Indians upon the Blackfeet Reservation in said Territory.

The treaty of October 17, 1855, with the Blackfeet and other tribes of Indians mentioned therein (article 3) allows certain lands therein noted to be used and considered as common hunting ground for ninety-nine (99) years. These lands have been penetrated by stock raisers who represent very heavy interests in the Territory, and it is complained on their part that these Indians are in the habit of committing depredations upon them by wantonly killing and destroying their stock.

Article 7 of the said treaty (vol. ii, p. 958) allows citizens of the U. S. to live in and pass unmolested through the country.

Article 11 of said treaty provides that any property taken by the Indians, or injured or destroyed shall be paid for out of their annuities and article 12 provides that in case of violation of this treaty, their annuities may be withheld.

I have requested that you will communicate with the agent having control over the tribes of Indians above indicated upon the subject matter of the letter of Mr. Maginnis and its enclosure and instruct them in all cases where hunting permits are hereafter issued to Indians under their charge, a capable and efficient employee of the agency should accompany each party, to watch over the Indians and prevent any depredations on their part.

In the present temper of the settlers, slight provocation might precipitate a conflict between them and the Indians, the result of which would be deplorable and such difficulty should be avoided by every effort possible in the power of the Agents.

Very respectfully,

S. J. KIRKWOOD, Secretary.

Just as we expected all these documents were carefully pigeonholed in accordance with the best government usage and the stockmen left just where they were before and that was not to expect help from the government, but to work out their salvation in their own way.

We did not have to wait long before the opportunity to try our methods came to us. In August a band of Canadian Indians raided the Yellowstone, driving off twenty-five head of good American horses belonging to three ranchers, Brown, Harrison, and Murray. Immediately after the stockmen's meeting Sheriff Healey accompanied by his deputy and Mr. Harris started north to look for the horses, two of which they found on the Blackfeet reservation, right at the agency and directly under the eye of the agent. He also captured Bad Bull, a Blood Indian, belonging to the band of Bull-who-goes-'round and brought him back to Benton in irons. Bad Bull was an ugly customer and gave his captors no little trouble by resisting arrest and by his attempts to escape. He was held as hostage at Benton and word sent north to his friends and relatives that he would not be released until the stolen horses were recovered.

Failing to recover all the horses stolen, Mr. Harrison accompanied by the Piegan chief, White Calf, and seven warriors, continued the journey north to Fort McLeod with every assurance of finding them among the Bloods at the agency. When they reached the agency a search was instituted in a quiet way for the horses but none could be found. Thereupon Calf Shirt summoned the chief of the Bloods to conference with Mr. Harrison. He was told that all that was wanted was the stolen horses. The Blood chief went away and soon returned with a few head of horses, some of them Harrison's, all in a miserable condition. He reported that these were all that were in camp, but Harrison suspected, and the event proved it so, that the best horses had been sent for trade with the Kootenais and after buffalo. Thereupon application was made to Major James Crozier, commandant of Fort McLeod, for assistance. Major Crozier had been aware of a war party of thirty Indians having come back from across the line with white men's horses a few days before. He immediately sent out some mounted policemen and in a few hours they had brought in seven of the party – all that could be found, to the fort.

A jury of twelve citizens was impaneled and the trial held before Colonel McLeod. In less than two hours and a half, the seven Indians were found guilty. Sentence was suspended fearing that it might make the remainder of the party, for whom search was being made, get out of the country.

These forcible and summary measures had a good effect on the Indians; the first of which was the surrender of eighteen head of horses which had been stolen from time to time. All of these horses were turned over to Sheriff Healy who in turn restored them to their owners.

The first action taken by stockmen to protect their own property proved that the British government was as anxious to keep their Indians at home, as we were to have them and that if complaint was made to the authorities, that their methods of capturing and punishing the thieves and restoring stolen property was both expeditious and effective. The Indians were shown conclusively that they could no longer steal horses in the United States, drive them across the line and remain there with them in safety.

It was further proven that if the Indians were made to understand that they could no longer run about over the range, drink whiskey, kill cattle and steal horses, without paying the penalty then and there: that they would remain on their reservations and without the slightest danger of Indian war. An Indian's idea of war meant a big noise, a big bluff, lots of paint and feathers, and fancy riding; but when he finds that somebody is certain to be hurt and that there is neither bluff or noise he will calmly fold his blanket about him and retire to the friendly shelter of his reservation.

It was the custom of the British government to pay to their Treaty Indians the annual annuities in September, consequently some six thousand Indians assembled at Forts McLeod and Walsh at that time to receive their annuities, and as soon as they were paid would start for the cattle ranges where they would exchange their money for whiskey and there kill cattle and steal horses the rest of the winter. The Stock Protective Association was working without the law save that of self-protection from justly apprehended harm. For two years they took care of their Indian problems in this way and while it was not a complete success it was a step in the right direction. It put a check on cattle killing and horse stealing and partially rid the range of Indians. The Canadian mounted police at all times co-operated with us and rendered valuable assistance.

On the sixteenth day of September, 1881, a prairie fire started at Grass range and we sent a crew of men to put it out, when reports of fire on Crooked creek near Haystack butte were sent in and men hurried to that locality, then a disastrous fire near Black butte that threatened to destroy the horse ranch. Fires sprang up in all directions almost simultaneously and spread with alarming rapidity. The flames swept up McDonald creek at the rate of a mile a minute. Great columns of black smoke rolled up in every direction, filling the air with ashes and cinders. At night, lines of flame crept along the ridges, flinging a lurid glare against the sky line. For ten days every available man in the country, with wet gunny bags, fought the flames with desperation, some of them sinking in their tracks from exhaustion. In spite of almost superhuman efforts more then five hundred square miles of the finest grass land in eastern Montana lay a blackened waste.

We lost no fences or hay but the loss of much grass was a hardship as we had increased our herd by five thousand head of cattle and one hundred horses.

When we came to use our brand we found it blotched and was not plain so we changed it to "D-S" and the name of the company to Davis, Hauser, and Stuart. On the range an established cattle company was "an outfit" and everthing pertaining to it was known and called after the brand. From this time on, the ranch, cattle, horses, cowboys, and the owners were known as the "D-S" outfit.

We had had some ploughing done in the fall and in the early spring we planted forty acres of oats and a patch of potatoes. I set out an orchard of fifty fruit trees, apples and crab apples. The oats yielded one hundred bushels to the acre but the trees did not do well as there was a family of beaver in the creek just above where I planted the trees and they built a dam and flooded my orchard.

I did not want to kill the poor things and I did not want them to leave the ranch so I just tried to discourage them from building the dam at that particular place, by repeatedly tearing it out. It did no good for as often as I tore it out they rebuilt it in the self-same spot and I finally gave it up and let them have their dam and the trees all died with the exception of a few crab apple trees that stood out of the way of the flood. There were lots of wild strawberries in our meadows and gooseberries, choke cherries, and bull berries grow along the streams. We planted rhubarb, currants, and gooseberries, and all did well.

In the summer of 1881 James Fergus came to the range and located on Armell's creek. Kohrs and Bielenburg brought in three thousand cattle and turned them loose on Flat Willow. Power Brothers and Charles Belden brought two herds into the Judith basin, Robert Coburn and Henry Sieben had herds on Flat Willow. John Dovenspeck located on Elk creek. This spring the several outfits on the range "pooled," that is we all worked together as one outfit.

The first meeting was held at the D-S ranch on May 29, 1882, and the minutes of that meeting will give an idea of how we conducted the business. I acted as secretary of the meeting. Present, James Fergus, Andrew Fergus, N. J. Bielenburg, and N. J. Dovenspeck.

It was moved and carried that every stock owner have one vote for each rider furnished and employed by him on the range, and that all persons having one thousand or less cattle on the range be required to furnish one rider, or in lieu thereof pay the roundup fund $2.00 per head for branding and marking their calves, that being the price fixed for branding calves for those not attending. And that all owners having more than one thousand cattle on the range furnish one rider for each one thousand head or fraction of five hundred or over.

W. C. Burnett was nominated for Captain of the roundup and was unanimously elected, with pay at the rate of $2.50 per day from beginning to close of each roundup, to be paid out of roundup fund.

It was decided to send one man to the Musselshell to bring back any cattle from this range found there and to brand and mark all calves as found. It was decided that one man tally all calves branded and to see that there are turned out by their respective owners seven bull calves, to each one hundred heifer calves. N. J. Bielenburg was elected to attend to the same.

All mavericks were to be sold to the highest bidder at the corral, branded and marked and turned with the purchaser's herd. Only cattle owners on the range could purchase these calves. The money received from sale of mavericks shall be turned in to the roundup fund.

The spring roundup for 1882 is to begin on the north side of the range May 30. It was decided to begin the fall calf roundup Sept. 1 on the north side of the range, and the beef roundup to begin October 1 on the north side of the range.

It was decided to pay the day and night horse wranglers and the wood hauler out of the roundup funds. The men sent out to attend other roundups were also paid out of said fund.

On motion the meeting then adjourned.

GRANVILLE STUART, Sec.

In the fall we drove the beef to Fallon station on the Northern Pacific and shipped from there.

On this trip, while camped on the Porcupine, I found some peculiar round balls of very hard bad land clay about the size of a cocoanut, broke one open and inside was a mass of small fossil shells and the back bones of fish imprinted in the mud. I also noticed oil shale along the bad land cuts and extensive veins of coal along the Yellowstone. When the country settles these coal beds will be valuable.

In the fall I found that there were twelve children of school age within reach of the ranch so gave a room in the house for school purposes and organized a school district and had a six-months term of school. Miss Cecil Benda of St. Louis was our first teacher.

In the early range days the Texas system of everybody's placing his brand on every calf found unbranded on the range, without even trying to ascertain to whom the animal belonged, was in full vogue. From the first I took issue against this kind of business. It was only a step from "mavericking" to branding any calf without a brand and from that to changing brands. Cowboys permitted to brand promiscuously for a company soon found that they could as easily steal calves and brand for themselves. If we are to believe the stories that floated up from Texas to our range, a goodly number of big Texas outfits had their beginning without capital invested in anything save a branding iron. In the broad open country of the range a man's conscience is apt to become elastic. A strong stand against anything approaching cattle stealing must be taken if the industry was to thrive.

In spite of warnings and protests a goodly number of calves were being mavericked and many horses stolen. The thing of paramount importance to the stock growers was a strong association for the betterment of range conditions. In the fall of 1882 I was elected a member of the Thirteenth Legislative assembly and spent two months in Helena. The council was evenly divided politically and there was a contested seat, both parties claiming the member from Chouteau county. The council could not organize but after the usual amount of wrangling attending such an occasion I was selected as a compromise, and elected president of the council.

There were a number of cattlemen in the legislature and we made an attempt to pass some much needed laws to protect the rapidly growing range industry, and did succeed in getting a few measures through but some of the much needed ones failed to pass because of lack of information on the part of the members of the legislature and by the very hostile attitude of the newly appointed governor of the territory, John Schuyler Crosby.

Governor Crosby was from New York, a cultured gentleman, a delightful person to meet socially. He had spent most of his life on the staff of various generals of the army and in Europe but was entirely out of harmony with his surroundings in Montana and unfamiliar with the industries or the needs of the territory and he used his executive powers very freely, to veto legislative bills.

The centers of population were in the western part of the territory, and our chief industry had been mining, so it was not strange that but little attention had been given to the rapid changes taking place in the eastern part of the territory.

Failing to get the much needed laws passed to protect their property, the cattle men turned their attention to perfecting a strong organization among themselves

THE STEAMER "W. B. DANCE," OF THE FORT BENTON PACKET LINE
lying twelve miles above Nebraska City, N.T.; view looking east
From an original pencil drawing made by Granville Stuart, April 26, 1866

FORT BENTON, LOOKING WEST (UP THE RIVER)
from Lookout hill, Choteau county, Montana; made June 9, 1866

to protect their property. The Eastern Montana Protective Association consolidated with the Montana Stock Growers' Association. Robert Ford, President of the Stock Growers' Association called a meeting to be held in Helena August 15th and 16th, 1882, and practically every stockman in the territory was present. The first meeting closed with a membership of one hundred sixty-eight stockmen. The Montana Stock Growers' Association was now one of the most important organizations in the territory.

The winter of 1881-82 was a mild one with scarcely any snow on the range. By the first of September we had twelve thousand head of cattle in our herd. I was in the saddle all winter keeping the cattle from straying off the range and the Indians from coming on.

Predatory animals were quite troublesome especially the large gray timber wolf that surpasses any other animal in sagacity, fleetness of foot, and powers of endurance. Added to these qualities is an insatiable appetite. It is said of him that he can run longer and easier, eat oftener and more, and display more cunning and ferocity in a given length of time than any other known animal. These wolves have a regular organization and travel in bands numbering from ten to twenty or thirty in a pack under the leadership of a dog wolf. To this captain the entire band yield implicit obedience.

When the buffalo were numerous these wolves followed the herds keeping near the cows and calves, watching for a small bunch to become detached from the main herd; then the wolves would separate into three divisions one slipping in between the main herd and the small bunch, the second division under the leadership of the captain would then move straight for the head of their chosen victim while the third division acted as rear guard thus completely surrounding their prey. Those in the lead would attack the muzzle of the animal while the rear guard slipped up and hamstrung him and after that their victim was helpless and easily dragged down and quickly devoured.

The cattle herds were an easy prey for these grizzly marauders as the cattle were afraid of them and ran at sight of one. The wolves being much fleeter and possessing more endurance found it easy to surround a range animal and drag it down. The range cows would fight desperately to protect their young calves but were never a match for even one large wolf, and these wolves are very large weighing one hundred twenty-five to one hundred fifty pounds. They are prolific breeders having as many as ten whelps in a litter. It is next to impossible to get within gunshot on one and almost equally as difficult to trap or poison them. With plenty of cattle on the range they would not touch a dead carcass preferring to kill their own meat. We carried strychnine with us all the time and by putting it in lard and then spreading it on bacon rinds it was a "piece de resistance" for them and we poisoned not a few in that way.

In the summer the cowboys frequently found a den and then there would be great sport roping them and shooting the awkward sprawling whelps with their six shooters. Charlie Russell the cowboy artist has immortalized this sport in one of his paintings.

The wolfer was the successor of the trapper. About the time that the beaver began to be scarce in the streams, men who had followed the avocation of trapping turned their attention to wolfing. Not until about 1866-67 were the skins of the wolf valuable but from that time on there was a good market for the pelts and wolfing became quite an important industry in Montana.

It was a hard and perilous life led by these brave intrepid men but all the more attractive to them because of the dangers encountered. Every tribe of Indians whether hostile or not to other white men was the avowed enemy of the wolfer as they lost many of their dogs from eating of the poison bait. The friendly tribes would on every occasion cut up and destroy his skins or steal his horses "setting him afoot" when the poor wolfer would be obliged to make his way to the nearest trading post without food or blankets. The hostile Indians lurked about waiting for a chance to get his scalp but were very careful not to attack unless the wolfer could be taken unawares or at a very great disadvantage. The Indian learned early in the game to keep well out of range of his deadly rifle. They usually traveled two together for company and for greater safety.

A wolfer's outfit was a pack horse, a saddle horse each, flour, beans, sugar, coffee, and salt; a pair of blankets, a buffalo robe, the best rifle he could procure, a good revolver, plenty of ammunition, a hunting knife and a supply of strychnine. These supplies were purchased in the fall at one of the trading posts and at the first freeze the wolfers took to the plains and did not return until spring.

The most valuable pelts were those of the gray or timber wolf. These wolves spend the summer in pairs on the timbered mountain sides, having their whelps in caves under the large rocks. They subsist on the fawns of the elk and deer with an occasional grouse or rabbit for a change of diet. As soon as it turns cold they collect in large packs, as many as fifty or sixty together, go to the plains and follow the buffalo.

Just after the first freeze the wolfer begins to set his baits: a buffalo would be killed and the meat poisoned. He would then follow on a short distance and repeat the operation. The baits were usually set in a circle but extended over a wide section of open valley and blizzard swept plains and the poor wolfer suffered severely from the cold while attending the baits. As soon as the wolves ate the poisoned meat they would die and the bodies freeze solid. One poisoned carcass would often kill a hundred or more wolves. When a chinook came or a thaw it was necessary to visit the baits often and skin the wolves to prevent the hides from spoiling. These visits to the baits were always attended by much danger from hostile Indians and at times the danger would be so great that the most fearless wolfer dare not venture out and many valuable skins would be lost. Occasionally a chinook or a prolonged warm spell would come at an inopportune time and hundreds of the skins would spoil, causing the loss of almost an entire season's work to the unfortunate wolfer. A good season was very remunerative, often netting from two to three thousand dollars.

The money rarely did him much good as the wolfer usually came to a trading post, disposed of his skins, and then joined in a wild carousal, drinking and gambling until the money was all gone. Then he would chop wood for the steamboats, hire out to freighters or engage in some work about the fort until winter, when he would again return to the old life of peril and privation.

The wolfer's lines of bait extended from far up into Canada to Colorado and Nebraska. Their principal trading posts were Fort Peck, Fort Benton, Fort Hawley, Fort Brown, the Crow Agency, Fort Pease, and Bozeman.

The Cattle Business

The winter of 1882-83 was a mild one and spring came early with plenty of moisture. The grass was fine. The bounty placed on wolves and coyotes made wolfing profitable once more and the wolfers were rapidly clearing the ranges of those pests. The Canadian Indians were keeping north of the line and our own Indians were slightly less troublesome. All this promised an era of prosperity to the cattle industry but there were still some dark clouds hovering on the horizon.

The sheepmen had discovered that if Montana was not exactly "a land of milk and honey" it was a mighty good grass land and several large bands of sheep were brought on the range. Herds of from two thousand to five thousand head of cattle were being gathered in Texas and New Mexico ready to start for "the land of promise" in the early spring.

The railroads had invaded Montana destroying the Missouri river transportation and the abandoned wood yards furnished splendid rendezvous for horse thieves and cattle rustlers, who were becoming so numerous and so well organized that they threatened to destroy the cattle business.

A meeting of the Montana Stock Growers' Association was called to convene at Miles City on April 17, 1883. This meeting was a memorable one. There were two hundred seventy-nine members present. The town was gaily decorated with bunting and banners and the citizens turned out in mass to welcome the cattlemen. There was a big parade headed by the mayor of the city, and a brass band and the town was thrown wide open to the visitors. The streets were thronged with cowboys dressed in their best with picturesque paraphernalia, and riding the best horses that the country afforded.

This meeting was not all parade and social enjoyment. There were conditions facing the stock growers that called for serious consideration anyone of which if not controlled, threatened the very life of the industry. First and foremost were the "rustlers." It had come to be almost impossible to keep a team or saddle horse on a ranch unless one slept in the manger with a rifle. Our detectives pursued and brought back stolen property and caused the arrest of the thieves and we hired counsel to assist the county attorneys to prosecute them but all to no purpose. The thieves managed to evade the law and became bolder each season.

The experienced cattle men worked unceasingly at this meeting. They gathered the stock laws of our western states and territories and the rules and regulations of other associations and from these were culled and arranged, by a committee of experts, assisted by able counsel, such parts as suited our locality and circumstances, and gave the best satisfaction when in force. Everything was done to bring about better conditions for the stock interests.

With hundreds of thousands of cattle valued at $25,000,000.00 scattered over an area of fifty-eight thousand square miles of territory, it was apparent to the most casual observer that there must be the closest coöperation between the companies if we were to succeed, as what benefited one, must benefit all. From this time on the entire range business was under the direction and control of the Montana Stock Growers' Association and the business run as one large outfit.

At this meeting it was agreed to employ one man in each county as a detective whose duty it would be to track up rustlers and horse thieves and do all in his power to have them arrested and brought to trial. These detectives were to be paid by the Stock Growers' Association.

Minutes of roundup meeting held at "D-S" ranch, Fort Maginnis range May 29, 1883.

Present, Granville Stuart of Davis, Hauser and Co., A. J. Clark of Kohrs and Bielenburg, Horace Brewster for Robert Coburn, Henry Sieben, Robert Clark for N. J. Dovenspeck, Amos Snyder for Snyder and McCauley, John Milliren for Adolph Baro.

It was moved and carried that every stock owner have one vote for each rider furnished and employed by him on this range and that all persons having one thousand or less cattle on the range be required to furnish one rider, or in lieu thereof pay the roundup fund $2.00 per head for branding and marking their calves, that being the price fixed for branding and marking calves for those not attending. All owners having more than one thousand cattle on the range must furnish one rider for each one thousand head or fraction of five hundred or over.

W. C. Burnett was nominated for captain of the roundup for 1883 and was unanimously elected with pay at the rate of $2.50 per day from beginning to close of the roundup.

It was decided to send three men to the lower Musselshell to the Ryan Brothers roundup to work with them and to bring back any cattle from their range found there, with instructions to brand and mark any calves. It was also decided to send two men to Fergus's range when their roundup begins to brand and bring back any cattle from this range found there.

It was decided that one man tally all calves branded and whose duty it shall be to see that there is turned out by their respective owners seven bull calves to each one hundred heifer calves. Henry Sieben was elected to attend to same.

It was also decided to elect a committee of three to inspect the bulls at each corral and to decide upon such as are too old to be of service and order them to be castrated. The owner of each bull so disposed of is required to turn out a bull calf in its place, and said committee shall count all bulls on the range and keep a tally of each brand. Horace Brewster, Henry Sieben, and A. J. Clark were elected committee on bulls.

The spring roundup is to begin on the north side of the range May 30, 1883. It was decided to begin the fall calf roundup Sept. 1, 1883, and the beef roundup to begin Oct. 1, 1883, on the north side of the range. It was decided to pay the day and night herders and the wood haulers out of the roundup funds, and the representatives sent to other ranges were also to be paid out of that fund.

GRANVILLE STUART
SEC.

We had now increased our herd to twelve thousand head of range cattle and were buying thoroughbred bulls of short horn breed to grade them up. None of our cattle were Texas long horns all being a good grade of range stock from Idaho and Oregon.

There was now, on the Fort Maginnis range, twelve outfits, – The Davis-Hauser-Stuart, the Kohrs and Bielenburg, Robert Coburn, Henry Sieben, N. J. Dovenspeck, N. W. McCaulley, C. D. Duncan, Stuart-Anderson, W. C. and G. P. Burnett, F. E. Lawrence, Adolph Baro, and Amos Snyder.

There were also twelve outfits on the Cone butte and Moccasin range: James Fergus and Son, Robert S. Hamilton, The Judith Cattle Co., Tingley Brothers, John H. Ming, Pat Dunlevy, James Dempsey, Chas. Ranges, A. Hash, C. H. Christ, J. L. Stuart, Edward Regan. From this time on the two ranges worked together in one roundup and usually held their meeting and made the start from the "D-S" ranch.

It was a novel sight to witness the big spring roundup pull out. Early in the morning the big horse herd would be driven in and each man would catch and saddle his mount. There was a number of horses that would buck and a lot of half broken colts to ride that would cause a certain amount of excitement. The horse herder in charge of the horse wranglers would lead off in the direction of the objective corral followed by the white covered four-horse chuck wagons, and then the troop of cowboys with their gay handkerchiefs, fine saddles, and silver mounted bridles and spurs.

At the "D-S" ranch there was usually an impromptu dance the night before and there would be quite a gathering of ladies to watch the start. Often they would ride to the first corral to watch the branding and have lunch at the chuck wagon.

A roundup on the range is in charge of the captain absolutely. Every man, whether owner of the largest herd or a humble roustabout, takes his orders from the captain. There were very few orders given, every man knew what he was expected to do and did it.

Work began very early in the morning. The cook was up, breakfast ready and the horse herd in as soon as it was daylight. The riders caught up their horses and saddled them and were ready to start. The men were divided into groups. The circle riders started out two together in every direction and drove to the corral all the cattle that they could find. At the corral the cattle to be branded would be cut out of the bunches and the ropers would catch and throw them. There were wrestlers and the men with the branding irons in the corral to brand and mark. Occasionally an animal would get on "the fight" and make things interesting but the rope horses were as clever as the men about keeping out of danger and rarely ever did we have a serious accident. The work at the corrals was hard and fast. The dust and heat and smell of singeing hair was stifling while the bellowing of the cattle was a perfect bedlam. At the close of the day everyone was tired and ready to roll in his blankets for a night's rest.

The spring or calf roundup usually lasted from four to six weeks. As soon as it was over the hay would have to be put up at the home ranch, range cabins built or put in repair, corrals put in shape, and stray horses gathered. If the herd was being increased we tried to get the new cattle on the range not later than September first. The fall calf roundup started about October 1, and usually required four weeks. After that was the beef roundup, the most important one of all.

The fall of 1883 we shipped from Custer on the Northern Pacific and had a drive of one hundred twenty miles. Cattle must be driven slowly and allowed to graze as they go and yet they must have water regularly. They were as wild as antelope and it required eternal vigilance to keep them from stampeding and running all the fat off. The slightest unusual sight or sound would start them off pell mell.

I well remember one night on the drive. It had been storming all day, rain mixed with snow, and a cold raw wind blowing from the northeast. Our tent blew over and the cook prepared supper over a soggy smoky fire. We were camped on a branch of McDonald creek. There was a steep cut bank on one side of the herd and cut bank coulees in every direction besides prairie dog towns which are full of holes and little mounds of loose earth. The cattle were cold and restless but they were finally bedded down. We ate our supper in the cold and wet. The night herd went on duty and the rest of us unrolled our tarpaulins and turned in. I could hear the cattle moving and occasionally their horns striking together. The boys on guard kept up their monotonous singing.

About eleven o'clock something startled the herd. Instantly every animal was on its feet and the tramping of flying hoofs and rattling horns sounded like artillery. The herders were with the stampede and in an instant every man was in the saddle after them. The night was pitch dark and there was nothing to guide us but the thunder of hoofs. They must be stopped and the only way to do it was to get ahead of them and turn the leaders so that the herd would move in a circle; "milling" it is called. Through the rain and mud and pitch dark, up and down banks and over broken ground, they all went in a mad rush, but the boys succeeded in holding the herd.

Every man had risked his life and some were in the saddle twenty-four hours before they were relieved, but there was not one word of complaint and not one of them thought of his own safety or of leaving the herd so long as his services were needed.

Our beef herd this year was in charge of William C. Burnett, a young Texan, the best range foreman that I ever met. He knew the business from A to Z, and understood the psychology of range cattle and cowboys. The herd reached the Yellowstone, crossed the river, and were loaded and shipped to Chicago where they arrived in first class condition.

Here I wish to give my impression of cowboys or "cowpunchers" as they called themselves, gathered from my ten years association with them on the range. They were a class by themselves and the genuine "dyed in the wool" ones came from the southwest, most of them from Texas. Born and raised on those great

open ranges, isolated from everything but cattle they
came to know and understand the habits and customs
of range cattle as no one else could know them.   Always on the frontier beyond organized society or law,
they formulated laws of their own that met their re-
quirements, and they enforced them, if necessary, at the
point of the six shooter.   They were reluctant to obey
any law but their own and chafed under restraint.
They were loyal to their outfit and to one another.   A
man that was not square could not long remain with an
outfit.

A herd was perfectly safe in the hands of a "boss"
and his outfit.   Every man would sacrifice his life to
protect the herd.   If personal quarrels or disputes
arose while on a roundup or on a drive, the settlement
of the same was left until the roundup was over and
the men released from duty, and then they settled their
differences man to man and without interference from
their comrades.   They often paid the penalty with
their lives.

Cowpunchers were strictly honest as they reckoned
honesty but they did not consider it stealing to take
anything they could lay hands on from the government
or from Indians.   There was always a bitter enmity
between them and soldiers.

A shooting scrape that resulted in the death of one or
both of the combatants was not considered a murder
but an affair between themselves.   If a sheriff from
Texas or Arizona arrived on one of our northern ranges
to arrest a man for murder, the other cowpunchers
would invariably help him make his escape.

They were chivalrous and held women in high es-
teem and were always gentlemen in their presence.
They wore the best clothes that they could buy and

took a great pride in their personal appearance and in their trapping. The men of our outfit used to pay $25.00 a pair for made-to-order riding boots when the best store boots in Helena were $10.00 a pair.

Their trappings consisted of a fine saddle, silver mounted bridle, pearl-handled six shooter, latest model cartridge belt with silver buckle, silver spurs, a fancy quirt with silver mountings, a fine riata sometimes made of rawhide, a pair of leather chaps, and a fancy hatband often made from the dressed skin of a diamond-backed rattlesnake. They wore expensive stiff-brimmed light felt hats, with brilliantly colored silk handkerchiefs knotted about their necks, light colored shirts and exquisitely fitted very high heeled riding boots.

Each cowpuncher owned one or more fine saddle horses, often a thoroughbred, on which he lavished his affections, and the highest compliments he could pay you was to allow you to ride his favorite horse. Horse racing was one of his favorite sports.

There were men among them who were lightning to draw a gun, and the best shots that I ever saw; others that could do all the fancy turns with a rope and others that could ride any horse that could be saddled or bridled; but the best and most reliable men were those who did all these things reasonably well.

On the range or the trail their work was steady, hard, and hazardous and with a good deal of responsibility. They were out from three to six months at a time, so when they did get to town it is not to be wondered at if they did do a little celebrating in their own way. Few of them drank to excess, some of them gambled, they all liked a good show and a dance and they always patronized the best restaurant or eating place in town and ice cream and fresh oysters were never omitted from their menu.

When on night herd it was necessary to sing to the cattle to keep them quiet. The sound of the boys' voices made the cattle know that their protectors were there guarding them and this gave them a sense of security. There were two songs that seemed to be favorites. The tunes were similar and all their tunes were monotonous and pitched to a certain key. I suppose they learned just the tune that was most soothing to the cattle. I know that their songs always made me drowsy and feel at peace with the world.

The first place they struck for in a town was the livery stable where they saw to it that their horses were properly cared for, and the barber shop was their next objective. The noisy fellow in exaggerated costume that rode up and down the streets whooping and shooting in the air was never a cowpuncher from any outfit. He was usually some "would be" bad man from the East decked out in paraphernalia from Montgomery, Ward's of Chicago.

As the country settled up and the range business became a thing of the past most of the old reliable cowboys engaged in other business. Their natural love of animals and an out of doors life led many of them to settle on ranches, and they are today among our most successful ranchers and cattle growers.

During the summer of 1882 Carpenter and Robertson moved three thousand stock cattle from Nebraska and located on the Rosebud. The Niobrara Cattle Company drove in ten thousand head of Oregon cattle and located them on Powder river. Scot and Hanks drove in a herd from Nevada and located on the Little Powder river.

In 1879 Robert E. Strahorn published a pamphlet called *Resources of Montana and Attractions of Yellowstone Park,* in which he gave interviews with prominent men and bankers, calling attention to the wonderful opportunities offered in Montana for range cattle business.

Following this came General Brisbin's book, *The Beef Bonanza* in which he pictured in glowing colors the wonderful possibilities of the range cattle business in Montana. The fame of Montana ranges had gone abroad. Eastern papers and magazines published all sorts of romantic tales about the ease and rapidity with which vast fortunes were being accumulated by the "cattle kings."

Profits were figured at one hundred per cent and no mention made of severe winters, storms, dry parched summer ranges, predatory animals, hostile Indians, and energetic "rustlers," or the danger of overstocking the ranges.

The business was a fascinating one and profitable so long as the ranges were not overstocked. The cattlemen found ways to control the other difficulties but the ranges were free to all and no man could say, with authority, when a range was overstocked.

In the summer of 1883 Conrad Kohrs drove in three thousand cattle and placed them on the Sun river range, and D. A. G. Floweree drove three thousand Texas cattle in and threw them on the Sun river range. The Green Mountain Cattle Company drove in twenty-two hundred and located on Emmel's creek. The Dehart Land and Cattle Company came in with two herds of three thousand each and located on the Rosebud. Griffin Brothers and Ward drove in three thousand head and located on the Yellowstone. J. M. Holt came in with three thousand head and located on Cabin creek. Tusler and Kempton brought in three herds of twenty-five hundred each and located on Tongue river. Ryan Brothers brought in three herds of three thousand each and located on the Musselshell. John T. Murphy and David Fratt drove in six thousand head and located on the Musselshell. Poindexter and Orr increased their herds in Madison county. Lepley brought in two thousand head, Green three thousand head and Conley twenty-five hundred and placed them on the range near Fort Benton. These cattle were nearly all Texas cattle and came up over the Texas trail. By the first of October there were six hundred thousand head of range cattle in the territory and these together with the horses and sheep was as much stock as the ranges could safely carry.

There was never, in Montana, any attempt on the part of the large cattle companies to keep out small owners, homesteaders, or permanent settlers. On the contrary every possible assistance was given to the settlers by the larger companies.

It was customary to allow settlers to milk range cows, provided they let the calves have a share of the milk and we frequently purchased the butter from the homesteader, paying him fifty cents a pound for it. The company would lend horses and farm machinery, employ the men and recover stolen horses and cattle at times when it would have been utterly impossible for a lone rancher to do so. One instance to illustrate. A settler on our range had the misfortune to break his leg and while he lay helpless in his cabin thieves drove off his span of fine mares. Cowboys immediately started in pursuit, recovered the mares and kept them at the ranch until the owner was able to look after them himself. Had they not done so the thieves would have crossed the British line and been safely in Canada before the authorities could have been notified and the team would have been irretrievably lost.

The large companies encouraged schools and their taxes largely supported them. On our range whenever as many as six children could be assembled I provided a good log school house and a six months' term of school each year. The cowboys on the range saw to it that the teacher, if a young woman, was provided with a good saddle horse and not allowed to become lonely.

At the ranch I had a library of three thousand volumes and we subscribed for the leading newspapers and magazines. At the James Fergus' ranch on Armell's creek, there was another splendid library and the leading periodicals. These books were at the disposal of everybody.

Few of the cattle outfits had any money invested in land nor did they attempt to fence or control large bodies of land. The land on the ranges was unsurveyed and titles could not be had. The cattleman did not want to see fences on the range as during severe storms the cattle drifted for miles and if they should strike a fence they were likely to drift against it and perish with the cold.

In the days of the big ranges there was never any serious trouble between the cattlemen and the sheepmen and there was never a "range war" between them in Montana. Many of the cattlemen also had bands of sheep.

It would be impossible to make persons not present on the Montana cattle ranges realize the rapid change that took place on those ranges in two years. In 1880 the country was practically uninhabited. One could

travel for miles without seeing so much as a trapper's
bivouac. Thousands of buffalo darkened the rolling
plains. There were deer, antelope, elk, wolves, and
coyotes on every hill and in every ravine and thicket.
In the whole territory of Montana there were but two
hundred and fifty thousand head of cattle, including
dairy cattle and work oxen.

In the fall of 1883 there was not one buffalo remaining on the range and the antelope, elk, and deer were
indeed scarce. In 1880 no one had heard tell of a cowboy in "this niche of the woods" and Charlie Russell
had made no pictures of them; but in the fall of 1883
there were six hundred thousand head of cattle on the
range. The cowboy, with leather chaps, wide hats,
gay handkerchiefs, clanking silver spurs, and skin
fitting high heeled boots was no longer a novelty but
had become an institution. Small ranches were being
taken by squatters along all the streams and there were
neat and comfortable log school houses in all the settlements.

The story of the Montana cattle ranges would not be
complete without a brief description of the Texas trail,
as more than one half of the Montana range cattle were
driven over that trail and almost every cowboy that
worked on the ranges made one or more drives up the
trail.

The trail started at the Rio Grande, crossing the
Colorado river at San Angelo, then across the Llanos
Estacado, or Staked Plains to the Red river about
where Amarillo now is. From there it ran due north
to the Canadian river and on to Dodge City where it
crossed the Arkansas river and then on to Ogalalla,
crossing the North Platte at Camp Clark. From Ogalalla it followed the Sidney and Black hills stage road

north to Cottonwood creek, then to Hat creek and across to Belle Fourche, then over to Little Powder river and down that stream to its mouth where it crossed Tongue river to the Yellowstone, crossing that stream just above Fort Keogh. From here it ran up Sunday creek across the Little Dry, following up the Big Dry to the divide, then down Lodge Pole creek to the Musselshell river which was the end of the trail. Texas cattle were sometimes driven clear up into Canada but never in any considerable numbers. Ogalalla was a great trading center in the range days. Many herds were driven up from Texas, sold, and turned over to northern buyers, at that place.

There were usually from two to three thousand cattle in a trail herd, and the outfit consisted of a trail boss, eight cowpunchers, a cook, a horse wrangler, about sixty-five cow horses, and a four-horse chuck wagon that carried provisions and the men's blankets. The food provided was corn meal, sorghum molasses, beans, salt, sugar, and coffee.

The cattle were as wild as buffalo and difficult to handle for the first week or ten days, until they had gained confidence in the cowpunchers and accustomed themselves to the daily routine. By that time some old range steer had established himself leader of the herd and everything settled down to a regular system.

The daily program was breakfast at daylight and allow the herd to graze awhile. The horse herd and mess wagon pulled out and then the herd started, with two cowpunchers in the lead or "point." The man on the left point was next, in command, to the "trail boss," two on the swing, two on the flank, and two drag drivers whose business it was to look after the calves that played out, the footsore and the laggards. In this order they grazed along until noon. The mess wagon would camp; one-half the crew would go in, eat dinner, change horses and go back to the herd as quickly as possible and the other half would eat, change horses and the herd would be started forward again. It would be kept moving until the sun was low and sufficient water for the cattle would be found. Camp would then be made, one half the men would go in to supper, catch up night horses and return to the herd when the remaining half would do the same. The herd would be grazing on bed ground and by dark would all be down.

The nights were divided into four periods. The first watch stood until 10 o'clock, the second until 12 o'clock, the third until 2 A. M. and the fourth until morning. In case of storms or a stampede, the entire crew was on duty and remained with the herd until it was back on the trail again, no matter how long that might be. It was no unusual thing for cowpunchers to remain in the saddle thirty-six hours at a stretch but they never complained and not one of them ever left a herd until relieved. Of all the thousands of herds driven over the Texas trail, there was never one lost or abandoned by the cowpunchers.

When the first herds started north, Indians and Mexican outlaws tried the experiment of slipping up to the herd on a dark night, popping a blanket to stampede it, with the hope of cutting off some of the lead cattle and driving them east to a market. The practice did not last long. The dead bodies of a few Indians and Mexicans found on the plains, told the story and was sufficient warning to others similarly minded. The cowpunchers were loyal to their outfit and would fight for it quicker than they would for themselves.

One of the worst things that they had to contend with on the trail was the terrific electrical storms so prevalent on the plains, and along the Arkansas and Platte rivers during the summer months. They came on suddenly with a high wind that blew the tent over and the chuck wagon too, if it was not staked to the ground. Zigzag streaks of lightning tore through the inky blackness of the sky, followed by deafening claps of thunder that fairly made the ground tremble. Over and around the herd the lightning was always worst. Every man in the outfit is out in the darkness and pouring rain, riding around the cattle, singing their weird cowboy songs in an effort to keep the herd quiet. Two of their favorites were "We go North in the Spring but will return in the Fall," and "We are bound to follow the Lone Star Trail." All at once comes a flash and a crash and a bolt strikes in the midst of them. It is too much. The cattle spring to their feet as one animal. There is a rattling of horns and thunder of hoofs as the maddened herd dashes off across the slippery broken ground and the men riding at breakneck speed to keep ahead of and turn them; for the only way to stop them is to throw them in a circle and "mill" them. If a horse should fall it was certain death to horse and rider and not a few lost their lives in that way.

In the morning the herd might be fifteen or twenty miles from camp and it would take all day or longer to get them on the trail again and all the cowpunchers would be kept in the saddle without rest or food until all were moving along again. If a cowboy was killed in a stampede his comrades dug a shallow grave, wrapped the trampled form in his blankets and laid him to rest.

The greatest responsibility rested on the trail boss.

He had to know where water was a day ahead and the
drive made according.   There was one dry drive forty
miles long.   When there was a long dry drive the
cattle would be watered and then pushed on away into
the night.   Cattle can smell water for a very long distance and if the wind was from the north next morning,
the herd would travel along all right, but if there was
no wind they would travel slow.   If the wind blew up
from behind late in the afternoon when they were suffering for water there was trouble. They would "bull,"
that is try to turn and go back to water and it required
all the skill and best efforts of every cowpuncher in the
outfit to keep the herd moving forward and then it
could not always be done.

I have seen a herd traveling along only a few miles
from where they were going in to water, when the wind
would suddenly blow from a river behind them.   The
cattle would turn as one cow, start for that water, possibly ten miles distant, and nothing could stop them.

A herd cannot be made to swim a large river if the
sunshine on the water reflects in their eyes; nor will
they go into a river if the wind is blowing and the
water ripples.   In 1885 John Lea, one of the experienced trail bosses, struck the Yellowstone river with a
herd.   The wind blew hard for three days and kept the
water rippled, and nothing would induce those cattle
to cross the river until the water was smooth.

A day's drive on the trail is from ten to fifteen miles,
but it is always governed by water.   A herd of steers
make much better time than a mixed herd.   There was
never any such thing as "resting up" or "laying over;"
the herd was kept moving forward all the time.

A company or an individual stocking range, would
go south, buy the cattle and notify his foreman to send

an outfit to some point south to receive a herd of cattle and to trail them to somewhere in Montana, and give him the brands and money for expenses.   There was a fortune in that herd of cattle but he was not worried. He knew the cattle would arrive on time and in the best possible condition.   While in St. Louis in 1884, a friend of mine told me that he had just bought three thousand two-year old steers in Texas for his range on the Musselshell.   I asked him if he was going south to come up with the drive.

"H—l, no!" was the reply.   "I am going to Miles City and play poker and be comfortable until those steers arrive."   And that is just what he did and the herd was on the Musselshell in August and the steers were fat enough for beef.

Trailing cattle came to be a profession and the trail men a distinct class.   They came north with a herd in the spring and returned south in the fall, worked in the chaparral, gathering another herd during the winter and then drove north again in the spring.   They took a great pride in their work and were never so happy as when turning a fine herd on the range at the end of the trail.

It was a pleasing sight to see a herd strung out on the trail.   The horses and the white-covered mess wagon in the lead, followed by a mass of sleek cattle a half mile long; the sun flashing on their bright horns and on the silver conchos, bridles, spurs, and pearl-handled six shooters of the cowpunchers.   The brilliant handkerchiefs knotted about their necks furnished the needed touch of color to the picture.

Cattle Rustlers and Vigilantes

At the close of the fall roundup (1883) our tallies showed that we had suffered at least a three per cent loss from "rustling." These thieves were splendidly organized and had established headquarters and had enough friends among the ranchers to enable them to carry on their work with perfect safety.

Near our home ranch we discovered one rancher whose cows invariably had twin calves and frequently triplets, while the range cows in that vicinity were nearly all barren and would persist in hanging around this man's corral, envying his cows their numerous children and bawling and lamenting their own childless fate. This state of affairs continued until we were obliged to call around that way and threaten to hang the man if his cows had any more twins.

The "rustlers" were particularly active along the Missouri and Yellowstone rivers and our neighbors in the Dakota bad lands were great sufferers. A meeting of stockmen was called at Helena on October 16 to consider what best to do. The first thing necessary was to discover the leaders and to locate their rendezvous. It was then decided to bring the matter before the Stock Growers' Association at the regular spring meeting.

The second annual meeting of The Montana Stock Growers' Association convened at Miles City on April 20, 1884. There were four hundred and twenty-nine stockmen present. The citizens' welcome was as cordial as it had been the previous year and the same

splendid entertainment offered, but the meeting itself
was not the harmonious gathering that the previous
meeting had been. Everybody seemed to have a
grievance. The members of the association that had
been members of the legislature the previous year came
in for their full share of censure. We were blamed
for everything that had happened but the good weather.

The matters for consideration were overstocking the
ranges, the dread pleuro-pneumonia, or Texas fever,
that was claiming such heavy toll in Kansas and Nebraska and how to put a stop to "rustling."

The civil laws and courts had been tried and found
wanting. The Montana cattlemen were as peaceable
and law-abiding a body of men as could be found anywhere but they had $35,000,000 worth of property
scattered over seventy-five thousand square miles of
practically uninhabited country and it must be protected from thieves. The only way to do it was to
make the penalty for stealing so severe that it would
lose its attractions. When the subject was brought up
some of the members were for raising a small army of
cowboys and raiding the country: but the older and
more conservative men knew that that would never do.

I openly opposed any such move and pointed out to
them that the "rustlers" were strongly fortified, each
of their cabins being a miniature fortress. They were
all armed with the most modern weapons and had an
abundance of ammunition, and every man of them was
a desperado and a dead shot. If we had a scrap with
them the law was on the side of the "rustlers." A fight
with them would result in the loss of many lives and
those that were not killed would have to stand trial for
murder in case they killed any of the "rustlers." My
talk did not have the conciliatory effect that I expected

and seemed only to add fuel to the fire. The younger men felt that they had suffered enough at the hand of thieves and were for "cleaning them out" no matter what the cost.

The Marquis DeMores, who was a warm personal friend of mine and with whom I had had some previous talks on the subject, was strongly in favor of a "rustlers' war" and openly accused me of "backing water." The Marquis was strongly supported by Theodore Roosevelt, who was also a member of the Montana Stock Growers' Association from Dakota. In the end the conservative members of the association carried the day and it was voted that the association would take no action against the "rustlers." In some way the "rustlers" got information about what was done at the meeting and were jubilant. They returned to their favorite haunts and settled down to what promised to be an era of undisturbed and successful operations.

While we were absent on the roundup, a party came to the ranch, stole a valuable stallion and a number of other good horses. Another party collected twenty-four head of beef steers from the Moccasin range and attempted to drive them north of the line into Canada; but when they found they could not evade the range riders, drove the cattle into a coulee and killed them, leaving the carcasses to spoil.

At the close of the roundup there was a meeting of a few stockmen at the "D-S" ranch. They and some men employed by the Stock Growers' Association had been watching the operations of the rustlers. The captain of this band of outlaws was John Stringer who answered to the sobriquet of "Stringer Jack." He was a tall handsome young fellow, well educated, and of a pleasing personality. His distinguishing features were his piercing gray eyes, white even teeth, and pleasant smile. He came to Montana in 1876 and hunted buffalo along the Missouri and Yellowstone rivers and was a conspicuous figure around the wood yards, trading posts, and military cantonments. He did not drink to excess but was an inveterate gambler. When the buffalo were gone he turned his attention to rustling cattle and stealing horses and established his headquarters on the Missouri river at the mouth of the Pouchette.

There were rustlers' rendezvous at the mouth of the Musselshell, at Rocky Point and at Wolf Point. J. A. Wells had a herd of cattle on the Judith river in charge of a herder who had eight saddle horses. On the twenty-fifth of June, Narciss Lavardure and Joe Vardner came up the river and camped opposite the Well's camp. Next day the herder crossed the river to look for some stray stock and as soon as he was out of sight Vardner and Lavardure crossed the river and drove off the seven saddle horses. They were going up Eagle creek on the run when they accidentally met William Thompson, who knew the horses and ordered them to stop. Lavardure answered by turning and firing at Thompson but his horse plunged and he missed his mark. Thompson, who was well armed and riding a good horse, gave chase. He shot and fatally wounded Vardner and after a race of six miles, captured Lavardure and brought him and the horses back to the Well's camp. Thompson and his prisoner were taken across the river in a skiff and the latter placed in a stable under guard. At 2 A. M. on the morning of the twenty-seventh the guard was overpowered by an armed posse and Lavardure was taken out and hanged.

Sam McKenzie, a Scotch half-breed, had spent two

MAIDEN, MONTANA, IN THE JUDITH MOUNTAINS, JULY 1, 1885
From an old photograph in the Granville Stuart papers

years around old Fort Hawley on the Missouri river under pretense of being a wolfer but in reality was one of the most active horse thieves. He stole horses in Montana, drove them across the line into Canada, sold them, then stole horses up there and brought them back and sold them around Benton. He had been very successful in dodging the authorities on both sides of the line because of his many friends among the Cree halfbreeds in Canada and in the Judith basin. On July 3, McKenzie was caught in a cañon a few miles above Fort Maginnis with two stolen horses in his possession and that night he was hanged from the limb of a cottonwood tree, two miles below the fort.

Early in June two suspicious characters came into the Judith basin with a small band of horses with a variety of brands on them and among them two fairly good "scrub" race horses. Word of their suspicious appearance and actions came to us and we telegraphed to several places to try to find out who the men were and whence they came.

I first met them on July 3, while out range riding, when I accidentally came on their camp at a spring just above Nelson's ranch (The old overland post office). The men were as tough looking characters as I have ever met, especially Owen who had long unkept black hair, small, shifty, greenish gray eyes and a cruel mouth. "Rattle Snake Jake," despite his bad sounding sobriquet, was not quite so evil looking as his pal, although he was far from having a prepossessing appearance. Both men were armed, each wearing two forty-four Colt revolvers and a hunting knife. When I rode into their camp, Fallon was sitting on a roll of blankets cleaning a Winchester rifle. Owen was reclining against a stump smoking and another Winchester lay on a coat within easy reach. Owen was self-possessed, almost insolent, "Rattle Snake Jake" was civil but nervously tinkered with the gun and kept his eyes on me all the time I was in their camp. I knew that they were a bad lot but had nothing to cause their arrest at that time, but decided to keep an eye on them while they were on the range.

On the morning of July 4 Ben Cline came along the road with a race horse on his way to Lewistown. "Rattle Snake Jake" saw the horse and challenged Cline for a race. Cline did not want to race, giving as his reason that he had his horse matched against a gray mare to run at the races at Lewistown and wanted to get his horse over there in good condition. After a little bantering on the part of Fallon a race was arranged between one of his horses and Cline's for fifty dollars a side, and a level stretch of road almost in front of Nelson's house selected for the race course. Owen bet ten dollars on the Fallon horse with one of Cline's companions. The Cline horse won the race and Cline and his companions resumed their interrupted journey to Lewistown.

Shortly after Cline and his friends left, Owen and Fallon packed up their belongings and set out for Lewistown. At this time Lewistown was just a small village, but they were having a Fourth of July celebration and people from a hundred miles in every direction had flocked to the town, to take part in the festivities.

Owen and "Rattle Snake Jake" arrived in town about one P. M., rode up to Crowley's saloon, dismounted, went in and had several drinks and then rode on to the race track. Here they joined the throng around the track but took no part in the betting until almost the last race when they bet quite heavily and lost their money. This, together with a few drinks of bad whiskey, put them in an ugly mood.

A young man by the name of Bob Jackson, dressed in costume, representing Uncle Sam, rode in the parade and afterwards was at the race track, still wearing the grotesque costume. For some unaccountable reason his presence near Owen gave that gentleman offense and he struck Jackson over the head with the butt of his revolver, felling him to the ground; then placing a cocked revolver to Jackson's head, compelled him to crawl in the dust like a snake. Owen then turned to "Rattle Snake Jake" and said, "Well I guess we will clean out this town" and at that shot at random into the crowd, but fortunately did not hit anybody.

The desperadoes mounted their horses and rode back to the saloon where they each had more drinks: then flourishing their revolvers in a threatening way and cursing and swearing declared that they intended to clean up the town, swaggered out into the street.

Quite a number of men who had been at the race track, sensing trouble hurried back to town, went to Power's store and armed themselves with Winchesters and took up positions in the buildings on either side of the street. Out in the street "Rattle Snake Jake" mounted his horse and Owen started to mount his, when he spied Joe Doney standing in front of Power's store. Revolver in hand he started to cross the street. When within a few feet of the walk Doney pulled a twenty-two caliber revolver and shot him in the stomach. A second shot struck Owen's hand, causing him to drop his revolver.

Doney ran into the store. Owen quickly recovered his revolver and fired at Doney just as he disappeared inside the door. The men in the store answered the shot with their Winchesters and Owen retreated up the street toward a tent occupied by a photographer. "Rattle Snake Jake," revolver in hand started to ride up the street in the opposite direction, when a shot fired by someone in the saloon, struck him in the side. He kept on for a short distance when his cartridge belt fell to the ground and he drew up to recover it. Looking back he saw that Owen was not following him but was wounded and could not get away, and turning his horse he rode back to his comrade through a perfect shower of lead coming from both sides of the street and together the two men made their last stand in front of the tent.

The citizens in the store and saloons and from behind buildings kept up their firing, while the two desperadoes standing exposed to their merciless fire, coolly and deliberately answered shot for shot, emptied and re-loaded their guns and emptied them again until they could no longer pull a trigger.

Two young men, Benjamin Smith and Joseph Jackson, were crossing an open space a short distance from the tent when "Rattle Snake Jake" caught sight of them. and dropping down on one knee took careful aim and fired on them. The first shot grazed Jackson's cheek and the second one pierced his hat and took a lock of his hair. The third one lodged in Smith's brain, killing him instantly.

A few minutes later Owen reached for his rifle, pitched forward and fell to the ground and almost at the same moment a bullet struck "Rattle Snake Jake" in the breast and he dropped. As soon as both men were down the citizens ceased firing but the bandits continued with their revolvers so long as consciousness remained. When the smoke of battle cleared away examination of the bodies showed that "Rattle Snake Jake" had received nine wounds and Owen eleven, anyone of which would have proved fatal.

In the evening Judge Toombs held an inquest over the bodies, the photographer, in front of whose tent they were killed, took their pictures and then they were given burial on a little knoll on the Pichette ranch.

On the afternoon of July 4, a telegram came to me from Buffalo, Wyoming, stating that Charles Fallon, alias "Rattle Snake Jake," and Edward Owen, were desperate characters and were wanted at several places. The two men had spent the winter on Powder river at the mouth of Crazy Woman, gambling, horse racing, and carousing. On their way north they had stolen some good horses from John R. Smith's ranch near Trabing, Wyoming, and traded them to the Crow Indians. Later on we learned that Owen was from Shreveport, Louisiana, and was wanted there for killing a negro. Charles Fallon hailed from Laredo on the Texas border and was wanted in New Mexico for shooting up a ranch and burning buildings and hay stacks.

Billy Downs was located at one of the wood yards on the Missouri at the mouth of the Musselshell, ostensibly to trap wolves, but in reality to sell whiskey to the Indians. His place soon came to be headquarters for tough characters, and it was but a short time until Downs himself was stealing horses and killing cattle. Downs was a married man and his wife was at the wood yard with him. Because of sympathy for the woman, he was warned that he was being watched and that if he did not change his tactics he was sure to get into trouble. He paid not the least attention to the warning, but continued to surround himself with the worst characters on the river and kept on stealing horses and killing cattle.

On the night of July 4, a committee of vigilantes arrived at the Downs' place and called on him to come out. This at first he refused to do but after a short parley he did come out, accompanied by a notorious character known as California Ed. Both men plead guilty to stealing ponies from the Indians but denied that they had stolen from white men, but they failed to account for the twenty-six horses in the corral, all bearing well-known brands. They claimed that the quantity of dried meat found in the house was dried buffalo meat, notwithstanding the fact that there had not been a buffalo on the range for more than two years. In the stable was a stack of fresh hides folded and salted ready to be shipped down the river, all bearing the brand of the Fergus Stock Co. The two men were taken out to a little grove of trees and hanged.

At the time the vigilante committee started for the mouth of Musselshell, another party left for the vicinity of Rocky Point where two notorious horse thieves, known as Red Mike and Brocky Gallagher, were making their headquarters. They had stolen about thirty head of horses from Smith river, changed the brands and were holding them in the bad lands. They had also been operating over on the Moccasin range and stolen horses from J. H. Ming's ranch and from J. L. Stuart.

When the vigilantes arrived at Rocky Point the men were not there but had crossed over on the north side of the river. The party followed after, and captured them and recovered some of the horses. Both men plead guilty to horse stealing and told their captors that there were six head of the stolen horses at Dutch Louie's ranch on Crooked creek.

Fifteen miles below the mouth of the Musselshell, at an old abandoned wood yard, lived old man James, his two sons, and a nephew.   Here also was the favorite haunt of Jack Stringer.   There was a log cabin and a stable with a large corral built of logs, connecting the two buildings.   One hundred yards from the cabin in a wooded bottom was a tent constructed of poles and covered with three wagon sheets.   At the cabin were old man James, his two sons, Frank Hanson and Bill Williams.   Occupying the tent were Jack Stringer, Paddy Rose, Swift Bill, Dixie Burr,[116] Orvil Edwards, and Silas Nickerson.

On the morning of July 8, the vigilantes arrived at Bates Point.   The men were divided into three parties.   Three guarded the tent, five surrounded the cabin and one was left behind with the saddle horses.   They then waited for daylight.   Old man James was the first to appear.   He was ordered to open the corral and drive out the horses.   This he did but refused to surrender, backed into the cabin and fired a shot from his rifle through a small port hole at the side of the door.   This was followed by a volley from port holes all around the cabin and in an instant the whole party was in action.

Two of the vigilantes crawled up and set fire to the hay stack and the cabin.   The men inside stationed themselves at port holes and kept up the fight until they were all killed or burned up.   The cabin burned to the ground.   The tent was near the river bank and almost

---

[116] According to Sam Stuart, a son of Granville Stuart, Dixie Burr was a son of the well-known F. H. Burr an engineer of Lieutenant Mullan, and long prominent in Montana. He was also a nephew of Granville Stuart. – Ed.

surrounded by thick brush and it was easier to escape
from it than to get out of the cabin.   Stringer Jack
crawled under the tent and reached a dense clump of
willows from which he made his last stand.   Dixie
Burr had his arm shattered with a rifle ball but jumped
into an old dry well and remained until dark.   Paddy
Rose ran out of the tent, passed back of the men engaged at the cabin and concealed himself in a small
washout and after dark made his escape.   Nickerson,
Edwards, and Swift Bill reached the river bank and
crawling along through the brush and under the bank,
succeeded in passing above the men at the cabin and hid
in some brush and drift wood.   Orvil Edwards and
Silas Nickerson were the only ones that escaped without wounds.   After the fight at the cabin the men went
down the river and spent the day looking for the men
who had escaped but failed to find them.

On the afternoon of the ninth, the fugitives rolled
some dry logs into the river, constructed a raft and
started down stream.   At Popular creek agency they
were discovered by some soldiers stationed there, ordered to come on shore and were arrested.

Notice of their arrest was sent to Fort Maginnis and
Samuel Fischel, deputy U. S. marshall, started at once
to get the prisoners and take them to White Sulphur
Springs.   At the mouth of the Musselshell a posse met
Fischel and took the prisoners from him.   Nearby
stood two log cabins close together.   A log was placed
between the cabins, the ends resting on the roofs, and
the four men were hanged from the log.   The cabins
caught fire and were burned down and the bodies were
cremated.

Paddy Rose lay all day concealed in a little washout in the bad lands and at night struck for Fort Ben-

ton, where he had wealthy and influential relatives. With their influence and assistance he succeeded in reaching the Canadian border.

There were one hundred and sixty-five stolen horses recovered at Bates Point and one hundred and nineteen at other places. After the fight at Bates Point the vigilantes disbanded and returned to their respective homes. This clean-up of horse thieves put a stop to horse and cattle stealing in Montana for many years.

Several of the men that met their fate on the Missouri in July, 1884, belonged to wealthy and influential families and there arose a great hue and cry in certain localities over what was termed "the arrogance of the cattle kings." The cattlemen were accused of hiring "gunmen" to raid the country and drive the small ranchers and sheepmen off the range. There was not a grain of truth in this talk.

There were but fourteen members of the vigilance committee and they were all men who had stock on the range and who had suffered at the hands of the thieves. There was not one man taken on suspicion and not one was hanged for a first offense. The men that were taken were members of an organized band of thieves that for more than two years had evaded the law and robbed the range at will. The fact that the stock men loaned milch cows, horses, and farm machinery to settlers on small ranches, branded their calves for them at roundup prices, established schools for them, bought their butter and vegetables at high prices and in every way helped them to get a start is proof that any law-abiding person was welcome in this country.

In 1879, when I located the "D-S" ranch, there were no sheep in that part of the country. In 1884 there were fifty thousand sheep on Salt, Dog, Armell's, Deer,

Box Elder, Black Butte, McDonald, Plumb, and Warm Spring creeks and there never was any trouble between the cattle and sheep men of Montana.

Russel B. Harrison and myself were selected to draft laws and to present them at the next session of the territorial legislature that would protect the cattle interests and make any further action of a vigilantes' committee unnecessary, and after an all session struggle we did succeed in having laws passed which did enable us to protect ourselves in this way.

A board of stock commissioners was created, and a tax levy of one mill on the dollar on the value of all cattle, horses and mules, was made each year, to be expended under the direction of the board of stock commissioners, who were authorized to employ a sufficient number of stock inspectors to inspect all cattle, horses and mules that were being driven or shipped out of the territory of Montana. The same law made it imperative that all stock of that description should be inspected by the employees of the stock commissioners before it could be driven or shipped out. All persons driving or shipping any stock out of the territory were compelled to give to the inspectors a receipt for all stock not carrying their brand. This stock could then be taken to eastern markets and sold by these shippers under the same conditions and prices as their own stock, and the money received had to be turned over to the board of stock commissioners and was by them distributed to the real owners. As an additional safeguard, the shipper was compelled to give a receipt to an inspector where the cattle were sold (usually at Chicago). You will note that the live stock interests paid all the expense, connected with putting a stop to stealing stock off the open range: but it did stop it.

I was elected president of the board of stock commissioners and served in that capacity for seven years until I went to South America.   Almost the entire direction of this immense volume of business fell upon my shoulders.   I received no compensation whatever for these years of work, except the knowledge that my initiative and labors placed the live stock industry of Montana upon a safe and businesslike basis, where it has remained up to the present time.

I say live stock industry of Montana because the vast sheep industry of the state, seeing what results followed proper legislation in the cattlemen's case, soon followed our example and procured authority for a board of sheep commissioners and inspectors and a tax levy on the sheep industry, under which they have greatly prospered unto this day.

The first national convention of cattlemen held in the United States was called together at St. Louis, Missouri, on November 14, 1884.   There were forty-six delegates from Montana and upon our arrival in the city we at once secured a room at the Southern hotel for consultation purposes and organized into a committee to work together.   R. B. Harrison was chosen secretary and I chairman of this committee.

On Monday, November 17, at 10 A. M., the convention assembled in the grand hall of the exposition building and organized.   Three thousand delegates answered roll call.   Every state and territory in the union was represented.

This convention was the greatest meeting of men representing one industry ever held in the United States up to that time.   The three thousand delegates represented the third largest industry in the United States.   It resulted in much benefit to stockmen all over the country as it brought together men from every section of the United States and each section became acquainted with the aims and aspirations of other sections and we were enabled to do better work together to our mutual benefit.

Throughout this convention the Montana delegation worked as one man and although we were small in numbers as compared with Texas, Kansas, and the Indian Nation, we were able to make our influence felt in the great convention and to greatly benefit our cattle industry.

The winter of 1884 and 1885 was another ideal one for range stock. There was but little snow and what fell did not lay on the ground but went off with chinook winds: in fact there was not enough snow to supply the cattle with water. We were obliged to keep range riders along some of the streams to cut holes in the ice so that cattle could get water.

Spring came early, March was unseasonably warm, the frost came out of the ground, the new grass started and trees and bushes budded and put forth leaves. Vegetation was as advanced as it usually is in May. There was no rain or snow in March and the drouth continued through April and May. In May we had frequent hot dry winds that shriveled the grass and licked up what little moisture there was. Water holes and small creeks were as dry as they usually are in August. Conditions on the range were serious.

About the twentieth of May, Reverend Van Orsdale,[117] S. S. Hobson and myself were passengers on the coach from Helena to White Sulphur Springs.

---

[117] Reverend William W. Van Orsdel came to Montana in 1872 as a minister of the Methodist Church. He was one of the most influential and best beloved ministers in the territory. – Ed.

Conversation naturally turned to the unusually warm weather and the continued drouth. "Brother Van" (as we all affectionately called the beloved missionary) was a jovial soul, and after listening to our complaints and misgivings about the drouth for some time, suggested that we had better quit complaining and pray for rain. Hobson and I had both been on the frontier for a long time and had to confess that we were stronger on "cussing" than we were on "praying" and we didn't believe that our prayers would be effective, because it is written in the Good Book that "The prayers of the wicked availeth nothing."

We had all been joking but "Brother Van" became quite serious and after a short silence gravely remarked: "Gentlemen, I will pray for rain."

At White Sulphur Springs we separated, Hobson and I to go to our respective ranches to start the round-up and "Brother Van" to his missionary work. On June 2, it began to rain and continued almost without cessation for three weeks. The water holes filled, every little dry creek became a raging torrent and the large streams were all out of their banks. There were not many bridges on the range but the few that were there washed out. We worked in rain and mud and swam creeks and coulees the entire roundup.

There never was such fine grass on the range before. The bunch grass grew tall and waved in the wind like fields of grain. I cannot say that I had much faith in prayers but I have always credited "Brother Van" with having a hand in bringing on that rain and saving the range.

In the spring of 1885 our outfit incorporated for one million dollars and issued one thousand shares of stock, par value one hundred dollars per share. The name was changed from Stuart, Kohrs, and Co. to the Pioneer Cattle Company. On the spring roundup we branded twenty-six hundred and twenty-two calves and two thousand and eleven on the fall roundup. The outlook for a peaceful and prosperous year seemed exceptionally good but we were not left long in this happy delusion.

During the time of and at the close of the Riel Rebellion [118] in Canada, the Indians that were more or less mixed up in that fuss, took refuge south of the line and camped in the heart of the cattle ranges. Between six and seven hundred Cree Indians, lately in open revolt against the Dominion of Canada, were allowed to move boldly, with their families, to our side of the line and locate, without any means of support and of necessity preying on citizens of Montana.

The presence of this seven hundred families of starving Indians on the range was not the worst feature by any means. These Indians were connected by blood and tribal relations with our Blackfeet, Bloods, and Gros Ventres as well as with the reservation Indians north of the line. The Indian agents at our agencies granted their wards permission to leave the reservations on pretense of visiting their relatives, at their pleasure. Those north of the line came without permission, consequently as soon as the weather was fine the entire eastern portion of Montana swarmed with roving bands of Indians whose only means of subsistence was stealing cattle on the range, and whose only source of amusement was stealing horses.

The few stock detectives that we could employ were powerless in the face of this invading hoard. Before

---

[118] For account of this rebellion see Alexander Begg, *History of the Northwest* (Toronto, 1894, 3 vols.) vol. i, pp. 373-435. – ED.

the spring roundup was fairly under way we began to find hides and parts of carcasses of slaughtered animals strewn over the praries. The stage driver reported that on one drive over his route, between Maiden and Big Sandy, a distance of one hundred and twenty miles he had counted six carcasses of cattle that had been killed by Indians and only the choicest meat taken. The rest, together with the hide, was left to spoil.

The president of the Montana Stock Growers' Association sent a letter explaining the situation to the various Indian agents and requested that they do not grant their wards permission to leave their reservations. Very few paid any attention to our request, and when we overhauled some of the reservation Indians they waved their permits in our faces and continued on their way rejoicing.

We next petitioned our commissioner of Indian affairs in Washington to prohibit the issuing of these permits for the Indians to leave the reservation but without results.

Next we asked that some of the troops that were stationed at the various military posts in Montana be distributed at the principal places where these Indians pass, one company of cavalry at each of the following points to wit. The Sweet Grass hills near Milk river, at the Piegan agency at the mouth of Arrow creek, and near the pass at the east end of the Little Snow mountains, thirty miles south of Fort Maginnis. The troops cooped up in military quarters in Montana, shooting forty shots a day at tin Indians on the parade ground were just as anxious to take the field and try their marksmanship on real Indians, as we were to have them; but they were not permitted to move without orders from the commander of the Department of the

Missouri, who was stationed at Fort Snelling, near St. Paul.

After sending petition after petition to the President of the United States, the Department of the Interior, the War Department and then clear down the labyrinth of the military authorities; we were finally granted the privilege of reporting any Indians found on the range, stealing horses or killing cattle, to the nearest military post. Blessed privilege! I will give one incident which will show conclusively what a wonderful assistance and protection this was to the pioneer settler, as well as to the stockmen. Early in July, Indians swooped down on Buchanan Brothers' ranch on the Moccasin range, plundered the cabins, taking three Winchester rifles, two hundred rounds of ammunition, three saddles, some clothing and all the provisions in the cabin and drove off eleven head of horses. Before going they cut up two sets of harness that they found hanging in the cabin, and strewed the pieces all about the corral. They also left two horses that they had stolen from a ranch in Judith basin and ridden so hard and abused so unmercifully that one died and the other was rendered worthless.

The Buchanans discovered their loss when they·returned home after an absence of two days. Buchanan rode thirty miles to Fort Maginnis and reported his losses to the commander, which required one day. The commander telegraphed to his superior officer, stationed at Fort Benton. He telegraphed to the commander of the division of Montana at Fort Shaw and he to the commander of the Department of the Missouri at Fort Snelling, Minnesota. By the same roundabout way the order came to send a detachment of cavalry from Fort Maginnis after the Indians. The order was received just eight days after the cabin had been plundered and the horses driven away.

Where were the Indians? The troops had no way of telling even the direction they had taken. A small detachment in command of a lieutenant started out in a northeasterly direction. I suppose they chose that course because it was straight out from the road leading from the parade ground. By some happy, or rather unhappy chance, this little body of soldiers ran into a Crow raiding party camped near Haystack buttes, about thirty miles from the fort. There were fourteen Indians in the party with sixty head of stolen horses. The Indians were taken completely by surprise, as they had not expected to encounter soldiers in that out of the way place. The Indians were placed under military escort and the party, together with the stolen horses, headed for Fort Maginnis. Eleven of the Indians riding eleven of the best horses made their escape, the three remaining Indians and the horses arrived at the fort.

These Indians were not the ones that had plundered the Buchanan ranch but they had come up from the Crow agency south of the Yellowstone, crossed the Musselshell west of the big bend, passed around the Little Snowies through the Judith basin and were heading for the mouth of the Musselshell, stealing horses along the route.

I, in company with one of our stock detectives, went to the fort, inspected the horses and found we could identify every brand and that the horses belonged mostly to small ranchers. I proposed to Colonel Smith, commander at Fort Maginnis, that he turn the horses over to me, I would put them in pasture and notify the owners that the horses were at our ranch.

Colonel Smith agreed to this plan and I sent notices to the owners of the horses, when a telegram arrived from General Terry, commanding the Department of the Missouri, stationed at Fort Snelling, Minnesota, ordering the horses and the three Indians sent to the Crow agency to be turned over to the Indian agent at that place. The owners of the horses, all poor men, began to arrive at the ranch, some having come a distance of one hundred and twenty-five miles only to learn that their horses were on the way to the Crow reservation under military escort. These people never did recover their property.

Shortly after this occurrence, a war party of twenty-two Crow Indians left their reservation with the avowed intention of stealing horses: and they left with the knowledge and consent of their agent. This same agent knew that his wards would have to cross two hundred miles of country, partially settled and occupied by white people, and that while on this raid they would necessarily have to live off of the white men's cattle, and that when stealing and plundering, Indians do not discriminate between white or Indian enemies. They take anything at hand. As soon as these Indians were off their reservation they separated into groups of five or six Indians each and scattered, some going north and east as far as the mouth of the Yellowstone and others into the Judith basin and north to the Missouri.

One of these parties, with thirty stolen horses, was captured fourteen miles north of the fort and brought in. About the time the Indians and horses arrived at Fort Maginnis; Charles L. Bristol of Dupuyn and William Cantrell, one of our stock detectives, came to the ranch. They were in pursuit of the Indians who had stolen eighteen head of horses from Bristol. When they learned that five Indians and thirty horses had just been brought into the fort, they, in company with Reece Anderson, from our ranch, went to the fort, stated their loss to Colonel Forsythe and asked to see the stolen horses.

Colonel Forsythe not only refused to allow them to see the horses, but was rude and insulting in his remarks, insinuating by both his word and action that they wished to look at the horses for the purpose of taking their description so as to give it to confederates who could then come and claim the horses with intent to dishonestly obtain possession of them.

Charles L. Bristol was a rancher, well-known and had his brands recorded. William Cantrell was a territorial officer and Reece Anderson was a rancher living three miles from Fort Maginnis with cattle and horses on the range and his brands duly recorded, so there could not be the slightest chance of either of the three gentlemen laying claim to any property that did not belong to them or would they have confederates who would do so. The three men returned to the ranch and the only explanation for Colonel Forsythe's conduct seemed to be, that he was considerably under the influence of liquor at the time of the interview.

In the morning I drove up to the fort and asked permission to examine the brands on the horses in order that I could state to the commanding officer who the owners were, so that he could turn the horses over to them. At this interview, Colonel Forsythe was sober but treated me with scant courtesy and refused to allow me to see the horses. Later, Colonel Forsythe, in reporting the occurrence to his superior officer, Colonel

Brooks, said that he refused to allow us to see the stolen animals as he wished to turn them over to the sheriff of the county.

Next morning we stood at our gate with Mr. Bristol and watched the five Indians mounted on five of the best of the stolen horses; escorted by a company of cavalry; drive the remaining twenty-three poor, tired, footsore, skinned-backed beasts, past us on their way to Fort Custer, one hundred and fifty miles further from the place where they had been stolen.

Eighteen of the thirty stolen horses were shot and left by the roadside because they became exhausted and could not stand the pace kept by the grain-fed, well-cared-for cavalry horses. There was no occasion for killing the poor beasts, because they were only suffering from over-driving and the abuse they received at the hands of the Indians. Had they just left them beside the road there was plenty of water and grass and they would soon have recovered.

These Indians were safely conducted to their reservation, turned loose without the slightest punishment and what became of the rest of the stolen horses we never learned.

The stockmen, through their association, asked for an explanation by what authority Colonel Forsythe or any other officer, authorized and allowed his soldiers to shoot exhausted horses that had been stolen and were being driven wilfully and knowingly directly away from their owners. A satisfactory explanation was never given.

These experiences of the citizens of Montana proved that it was harder to recover their property from the military than it was from the original Indian thieves.

This action was direct encouragement to the raiders. They had all the fun of stealing the horses and were then safely escorted through the danger zone to their reservation and turned loose, there to be a "big gun" in the tribe.

There was nothing left for the stockmen and ranchers to do but to deal with the Indian thieves as we had dealt with the white ones. If Indians came on the range they did so at their peril and there would be no more military parades across the country, in which our horses would figure prominently if we could help it.

Two weeks later a party of Crow Indians, presumably some of the same outfit that left their reservation with permission to prey upon the Piegans, appeared on the head of Armell's creek and drove off a band of young stock horses. The horses were not missed for several days but we had reason to believe that the Indians were still lurking about: so a small party from the ranch went after them. We found the trail and followed hard after them.

In the bad lands of the Missouri the Indians dropped the horses and scattered and so made their escape, and I presume eventually reached the shelter of their reservation in safety but they did not get any horses and they did not ride in state across the range with a military escort. In August a party of Piegans crossed the Missouri river at the mouth of the Musselshell and went on a raid of retaliation down into the Crow country. On their way home they crossed the Yellowstone at the mouth of Clark's fork and started north, keeping west of the Crazy mountains and east of the Belt range. On Smith's river they began to steal horses from the ranchers on the Highwoods and Shonkin ranges.

Everybody was haying and they made a point of gathering in the horses from the hay ranches which was particularly hard on the ranchers.

A party from the Shonkin range started in pursuit and we were notified that the Indians were headed in our direction and would likely come onto our range. We knew that in all probability they would try to cross the Missouri river at their favorite crossing, the mouth of Arrow creek. Our stock detective took two men and started out hoping to intercept them at the crossing or to overtake them before they could reach their reservation.

A company of cavalry was camped on Arrow creek near the mouth. There had been no Indians about and the soldiers were lounging in camp, taking things easy, when the Indians came over a low range of hills and were fairly in the soldiers' camp before they were aware of the presence of troops or before the soldiers suspected the presence of Indians. The surprise was mutual and complete, and before the soldiers recovered the Indians made their escape, but they were obliged to leave the horses, sixty head in all.

The soldiers rounded up the horses and started with them for Fort Maginnis. Ten miles from the fort, William Cantrell, our stock detective, and two men from the ranch met the soldiers bringing the horses in and turned and helped drive them. This enabled them to examine the brands and the horses.

Early next morning the party from the Shonkin range and Smith river arrived and went with the stock detectives to the fort to claim their horses, but were not allowed to see them. They then demanded that the horses be turned over to the two stock detectives, but were informed that the horses would be sent to the Crow agency and that they could put in their claims at that place. We told the commander that the thieves were not Crow Indians but Piegans and gave him proof to substantiate our statement but to this he paid not the slightest attention.

Several days later a detachment of soldiers, under command of a lieutenant, came down the road on their way to the Crow agency with the horses. As soon as the little cavalcade passed the ranch, William Cantrell, our stock detective, with two cow boys, intercepted them and demanded of the lieutenant that the horses be turned over to him. At first there was some hesitancy, but one look along the barrel of Cantrell's rifle and at the set determined face of the man behind the gun, decided the question and the lieutenant and his little command returned to the fort leaving the horses with Cantrell, all of which, but ten, belonged to white men. Six were Crow Indians' ponies and four belonged to the Piegans. The six belonging to the Crows were turned over to their agent. The four belonging to the Piegan thieves were sold and the money used to help defray expenses of recapturing the horses and the remaining fifty were returned to their owners. This was the last attempt of the military to hold horses, stolen from white men by the Indians.

From this time on, bands of roving Indians found on the range with or without permits from their agents, were promptly escorted to their reservations and warned never to come on the range again. Those caught in the act of stealing horses or killing cattle, or with the stolen property in their possession were punished just as the white thieves had been.

These methods together with the assistance of some very efficient sheriffs of the "range counties" and of our stock detectives enabled us to control the situation fairly well: but the cause of the evil which was the large reservations and our Indian policy, still remained an injustice and an injury to both the Indian and the white settlers.

In the territory of Montana, fifty-eight hundred square miles of land were set apart as Indian reservations, allowing more than three thousand acres of land to every man, woman, and child in the tribes for whom they were set aside: and of which they made no use other than as breeding grounds for a race of permanent and prolific paupers. The only mark of civilization on these immense reservations was the agency where resided the Indian agent and his few assistants. It permitted the Indians to choose isolated places where they collected in large numbers under their chief and so fostered and perpetuated their race prejudices, shift-less idleness, and vicious propensities. It kept them from the only civilizing influences possible to them; contact and intercommunication with the white settlers.

The greater portion of their lands extended along the international boundary between the United States and Canada and as the Indians were all one blood and spoke the same language, it was impossible to keep them from visiting back and forth. On these trips they stole horses and killed cattle and could not be punished because they could not be caught.

These border reservations further afforded a safe asylum for whiskey degenerate specimens of the white race, who gained residence on the reservation through marriage with the women of the tribes and by such association transmitted to the Indians their diseases and vices.

The Indian agent did not take trips of hundreds of miles over these reservations to see what was going on, and it would have done him no good if he had, for the Indians would not have informed on one another or on the white man who through marriage had become one of the tribe. The Indians usually distrusted their agent and kept as far away from the agency as possible, only going there to draw rations or annuities.

Although these Indians never had any responsible form of government they were recognized as free and independent nations, and the United States paid tribute to them in the way of appropriations to support them in vicious idleness. They were allowed to go fully armed with the latest improved repeating rifles, mounted on good horses, and given *carte blanche* to steal. When they were in danger of falling into the hands of the territorial officials and of losing their loot, they were taken under the wing of the military and triumphantly conducted to the safe shelter of their reservation.

In this environment they learned the white man's vices and forgot the red man's virtues and from almost physically perfect, self-respecting savages, they degenerated into a hoard of renegade pauper vagabonds. This was through no fault of their own. White men placed upon a reservation, armed, mounted, and isolated, and supported in idleness by the government would speedily degenerate into pauper robbers, for like the Indian they would lack the motive for honorable exertion.

In an endeavor to remedy this deplorable condition

I brought the matter before the National Stock Growers' Association at its meeting in Chicago in November, 1885, by introducing resolutions outlining a plan of procedure that would put a stop to Indian depredations and at the same time would be just to the Indians.

The following plan was recommended and endorsed by the delegates from thirty-two states and territories.

Disarm and dismount the Indians. Give them land in severalty with title inalienable for fifty years. Sell all of their surplus land to actual settlers, thus intermixing them with the whites, where they would learn to be self-supporting in a single generation by force of example, contact, and stern necessity.

From the sale of lands create a fund to start them in life and to aid them for a few years. Reduce them from being foreign nations to the level of all other citizens.

Protect them fully in all their rights of person and property and punish them for their crimes precisely as all other citizens are protected and punished.

Had this been done it would have solved the much vexed Indian question and from ignorant pauper thieves they would in time become self-supporting American citizens, for they lack neither brains nor muscle if compelled to use them.

End of the Cattle Range

During the summer of 1885 more than one hundred thousand head of cattle were brought into Montana, most of them trailed up from the South. There were also many bands of sheep driven in and these together with the natural rapid increase (under the most favorable conditions) trebled the number of sheep in the territory and by the fall of 1885 the Montana ranges were crowded. A hard winter or a dry summer would certainly bring disaster. There was no way of preventing the over-stocking of the ranges as they were free to all and men felt disposed to take big chances for the hope of large returns. The range business was no longer a reasonably safe business; it was from this time on a "gamble" with the trump cards in the hands of the elements.

During the summer we kept our beef cattle in the grassy cañons and along the rolling foothills at the base of the mountains. In these favored places the grass was good and water plentiful and the cattle did not lose flesh traveling long distances to water as they did when left down in the plains.

These cañons were very beautiful and there were many lovely wild flowers growing here that I had not found anywhere else in Montana. There were tiger lillies, Maraposa lillies, white purple clematis, laurel, several varieties of the orchid family, wild primroses, the Scotch bluebells, several varieties of larkspurs and lobelia, and the most fragrant and beautiful wild roses that I had ever seen. There were also choke-cherries, huckleberries, wild raspberries, and gooseberries.

The autumn foliage was beautiful; groves of golden quaking aspen, orange cottonwood, scarlet thornbushes, crimson rose briers, and the trailing clematis with its white cotton balls intermingling with the evergreen of the pines, fir, and spruce.

In the fall we had two thousand head of beef cattle ready for shipment when a great rush of half fat range stuff from Texas, Indian Territory, and New Mexico flooded the markets and the price of beef cattle fell to a low water-mark. We cut out all of our three year old steers and turned them back on the range and only shipped nine hundred and eighty-two head. This left us eighteen thousand eight hundred and eighty head of stock on the range after the fall shipment.

This year the National Cattle Growers' Association met in Chicago on November 17-18. The Montana delegation devoted their time and energies to two subjects, namely:

To have the government perfect and take charge of a system of quarantine against diseases of animals in all the states and territories; and to have the Indians allotted their lands in severalty and the rest of their immense reservations thrown open to actual settlers. We succeeded in having our resolutions adopted and a delegation appointed to take them to Washington and have them presented before Congress.

There was a big fight led by the delegations from Texas and Indian territory, to set aside a wide strip of country from Texas to the British line for a cattle trail and to allow the leasing from the government of the public domain. These measures did not pass.

I returned from Chicago to the range late in December accompanied by the Marquis De Mores and we stopped off at Glendive and hunted for a week. The country was dry and dusty with only an occasional snow drift in the coulees and in deep ravines. The Marquis was anxious to visit Butte, our then flourishing mining town, and as I was going there on business he continued on with me to Helena and then to Butte.

In 1885, Butte was a hustling, bustling, mining town and everything ran wide open. We arrived at seven o'clock in the evening on a little local stub from Garrison. Volumes of yellowish sulphuric smoke rolled up from the heaps of copper ore that was roasting on the flat east of Meaderville and spread over the town like a pall enveloping everything in midnight darkness and almost suffocating one. The depot was little better than a box car and the light from the windows did not penetrate the darkness. We could not see and we could scarcely breathe.

The Marquis grabbed my arm and between sneezes gasped – "What is this to which you have brought me?"

As the cab slowly crawled along the street, music from the saloons and dance halls floated out to us but we could not even see the lights in the windows. Next day it was no better and I began to feel that our visit to Butte was destined to be a disappointment in so far as seeing the town was concerned. About ten o'clock a stiff breeze blew up from the south and scattered the smoke and we were able to visit our friends, transact business, and then view the novel sights of a big mining camp.

At the meeting of the Stock Growers' Association at

Miles City, Dr. Azel Ames, F. C. Robertson, Marquis De Mores and myself were appointed a committee to confer with the people of St. Paul for the purpose of inducing them to establish stockyards and a cattle market at that city so as to relieve us from the monopoly held over us by Chicago.   We succeeded in our mission and the following autumn the St. Paul yards were ready to receive shipments of cattle.

This spring we lost quite a number of cattle from their eating poisonous plants.   It was the first trouble of the kind that we had encountered.   These poisonous plants made their appearance after the drouths and when the grass was eaten out.   Being drouth resisting they come up early, grow luxuriantly and are the first green things to appear in the spring and the cattle will eat them.

The spring roundup did not start until May 25, because with the continued drouth the green grass would not start.   The cattle were in fine condition and the "calf crop" unusually large.   Our outfit branded thirty-eight hundred and eighty-one calves on this roundup.

At this time a group of eastern capitalists offered to purchase our entire herd.   Negotiations reached the point where we were to turn the outfit over to them, when Mr. Elkins, the man who represented the eastern company, died suddenly and the sale was not consummated.

The drouth continued and in July the short grass was dry and parched, streams and water holes drying up; but in spite of the drouth and short grass, cattle were being brought in from Washington and Oregon and the herds from the south were coming in undiminishing numbers and they were all thrown on the already over-stocked ranges of Montana.

Added to the drouth was unprecedented heat. The thermometer stood at one hundred to one hundred and ten degrees in the shade for days at a time and then would come hot winds that licked up every drop of moisture and shriveled the grass. There was nothing to be done but move at least a part of the herd.

In July I started out to look for better range and after going through the lower Judith basin, Shonkin, Highwoods, Belt creek, Sun river, and Teton ranges, finally decided to drive some of the cattle north of the Missouri river, along the foot of the Little Rockies. There was more water over there and some good grass.

In spite of every precaution range fires would start and as it was so hot and dry it was very hard to put them out when they did start. Big fires along the foot of the Judith range and on the Musselshell filled the air with smoke and cinders. Crews of fire fighters were kept busy all summer.

On arriving home, I found a telegram from Conrad Kohrs stating that he had leased range in Canada and to prepare to move. He failed to state where the leased range was located. I was not in favor of taking the herd north of the British line because of the severe blizzards that swept the open treeless plains that afforded no shelter for stock and was too far north to get the warm chinook winds. It was too late in the season to move the cattle a great distance. It always injures range cattle more or less to move them and it would never do to throw them on a strange range too late in the season.

A meeting of the stockholders of the Pioneer Cattle Company decided that we would reduce the herd as much as possible by shipping to market all the cattle fit for beef, gather the bulls and feed them at the home ranches and move five thousand head across the Missouri river to the foot of the Little Rockies. To G. P. Burnett was given the difficult task of gathering and moving the herd.

The beef could not be shipped until fall so the fat steers must not be disturbed and it was very hard to drive out the others and not disturb them, for all were as wild as antelope. Extreme care had to be used so that the herd would reach the new range in as good condition as possible.

August 10 we began gathering the cattle that were to be moved. Ordinarily one could see for miles across the range in our clear atmosphere, but not so at this time. Dense smoke obscured everything and this together with the cinders and the clouds of hot dry alkali dust almost choked and blinded us, causing much suffering to men and horses.

Moving a mixed herd is always hard. The young cattle travel fast and the old cows and young calves go slowly, so the whole herd has to be driven to suit the pace of the slowest animal in it. The drive to the new range was not a long one but under the existing circumstances it was a hard one and taxed to the fullest the ingenuity of the plucky young Texan in charge of the herd.

The weather continued extremely hot, and creeks, water-holes, and small lakes, never before dry, were completely so now. The water in all the flowing streams was very low and strongly alkaline, so much so, that in places the tired and thirsty horses refused to drink. It was so bitter that one could not drink the coffee made with it. Nearly every man with the drive was ill from drinking it. For days the herd moved forward through the smoke and stifling dust across the dry parched country.

At last we were nearing the Missouri river, intending to cross at Rocky Point. The wind was from the north and the cattle smelled the water and broke for it. No power on earth could stop the poor thirsty beasts; bellowing and lowing they ran pell-mell for the water, with the cowboys in hot pursuit. There was a point of quicksand in the river just above the ford and before the men could prevent it the cattle had plunged into it and were miring down. A small steamboat tied at the landing used their donkey engine to help drag out some of them, but we lost seventy head in spite of our best efforts.

After this mishap we crossed the herd without further trouble and from here on there was more water and better grass. The herd reached its destination in splendid condition. This fall we branded two thousand and seventy-four calves.

Seven thousand head of cattle belonging to the Powder River Cattle Company crossed the Missouri river at Great Falls and were driven through the Judith basin destined for our range, but when they saw the condition of the range and found that we were moving cattle out, they continued on north across the British line and threw their herds on the range near Fort McLeod.

John H. Conrad also had two thousand seven hundred head that he intended to bring in, but later drove them north of the line to the Cypress hills.

These changes, together with the very heavy shipments of beef to the markets relieved the over-stocked condition of the range and could we have had copious rains early in the fall to start the grass and a reasonably easy winter, all would have gone well.

We did not get the fall rains. There was quite a severe storm in November. On the sixteenth the thermometer fell to two degrees below zero, with a cutting northeast wind and on the seventeenth and eighteenth six inches of snow fell, but blew into drifts. The cattle north of the Missouri being unaccustomed to the range drifted badly and kept working back to the river.

This year we noticed that the wild animals moved south. The wild geese and ducks and song birds started south early and many that were accustomed to stay with us all winter disappeared: even the range cattle seemed to take on a heavier, shaggier coat of hair. For the first time since I had come to the range, the white Arctic owls came on the range and into the Judith basin. The old Indians pointed to them and drawing their blankets more closely about them, gave a shrug and "Ugh! Heap Cold!" expressive of some terrible experience in the long past that still lingered in their memory. One old Gros Ventre warrior assured me that not since he was a small boy had he seen the owls on their reservation. Everything pointed to a severe winter and we made what preparations we could to meet it with as little suffering to the stock and loss to ourselves as possible.

December 5, there was another storm, with the thermometer twelve degrees below and four inches of snow. I returned home from Chicago December 14 and rode from Custer station to the ranch, distant one hundred and twenty miles, in a blizzard, the thermometer down to zero and high east wind that pierced to the marrow of my bones.

Between the Musselshell and Flat Willow the snow blew in our faces so that the driver could not keep the road. There were two other passengers on the stage besides myself and we took turns walking ahead of the horses with a lantern to guide them. This storm lasted three days and then cleared up warm and bright and remained so until January 9, 1887. On that day a cold wind blew from the north. It began to snow and snowed steadily for sixteen hours, in which sixteen inches of snow fell on a level. The thermometer dropped to twenty-two degrees below zero, then twenty-seven degrees, then thirty degrees, and on the night of January 15 stood at forty-six degrees below zero, and there were sixteen inches of snow on the level. It was as though the Arctic regions had pushed down and enveloped us. Everything was white. Not a point of bare ground was visible in any direction. This storm lasted ten days without abating. The cattle drifted before the storm and fat young steers froze to death along their trails.

Conditions were so changed from what they were in 1880-81. The thick brush and tall rye-grass along the streams that afforded them excellent shelter at that time was now all fenced in and the poor animals drifted against those fences and perished.

Our herd was one of the first large herds brought into northeastern Montana, consequently had been on the range longer than others. They were all northern grown range stock and occupied the best range in the northwest. We kept plenty of men on the range to look after them as best they could, keeping them back from the rivers, and out of air holes and open channels in the ice, helping them out of drifts and keeping them in what shelter the cut banks and ravines offered. The herd could be said to be a favored one, yet we lost fifty per cent of them in this storm.

There was a series of storms in February and while not so severe yet they came at a time when the cattle were least able to withstand them and there were heavy losses then. The cows were all thin and the losses in spring calves was about thirty per cent.

The herds that were driven up from the south and placed on the range late in the summer, perished outright. Others lost from seventy-five to eighty per cent of their cattle.

It was impossible to tell just what the losses were for a long time as the cattle drifted so badly in the big January storm. We did not get some of ours back for a year. Our entire losses for the year were sixty-six per cent of the herd. In the fall of 1886 there were more than one million head of cattle on the Montana ranges and the losses in the "big storm" amounted to twenty million dollars. This was the death knell to the range cattle business on anything like the scale it had been run on before.

Charles Russell, "The Cow Boy Artist" told the story of the "snuffing out of the big ranges" most graphically in his charcoal sketch, "The Last of 5000." Charlie was in charge of a herd in the Judith basin, when the owner, who lived in Helena, wrote and asked how his cattle was getting along? For answer Charlie sent him the sketch.

The large outfits were the heaviest losers as they could not feed or shelter their immense herds. Most of the big outfits had borrowed large sums of money at a high rate of interest and the cattle that they had left would hardly pay their indebtedness. They had to stay in the business and begin all over again. Eastern men who had large sums of money invested, closed out the remnant of their herds and quit.

The rancher with a good body of hay land and from one hundred to two hundred head of cattle was the man that profited He had hay enough to feed through storms and could gather his cattle around the ranch and partially shelter them, and in the spring he was enabled to buy cattle cheap. Here again I wish to say a word in defense of the "cattle barons" whom our leading newspapers abused so unmercifully at the time, accusing them of driving settlers from their homes and of "hogging" all the land. There were a good many settlers who had milch cows and a few "dogies" and did not have hay enough to feed them. The big ranches all had more or less hay and could have saved a few cattle by feeding, but instead they let the man with a family and a few cows have the hay to save their domestic animals; and they did not sell it to them at ruinous prices either but let them have it at cost of production.

In the spring of 1887 the ranges presented a tragic aspect. Along the streams and in the coulees everywhere were strewn the carcasses of dead cattle. Those that were left alive were poor and ragged in appearance, weak and easily mired in the mud holes.

A business that had been fascinating to me before, suddenly became distasteful. I wanted no more of it. I never wanted to own again an animal that I could not feed and shelter.

The spring was very wet, one heavy rain followed another in succession and the grass came on luxuriantly. We moved the remainder of the herd over on the Milk river range. I did not like the country and did not

move over there.   Conrad Kohrs took the management
of the herd.

Much has been said and written about the extravagant mismanagement of the big cow outfits, of the selfish arrogance of the cattlemen, of the wild and reckless irresponsible cow boy.

I began at the beginning and was with it to the end and I want to say that there was never a great business that was systematized and worked more economically than the range cattle business.   Some of the big outfits were owned by eastern capitalists who invested for their sons, boys who were fascinated with the free untrammeled life of the west, others were owned by men who, like myself, had been more or less in cattle in Montana for years and these small herds became the nucleus for the big outfits.   Then there were men like Conrad Kohrs who had never done anything but raise cattle, and there were cattle breeders (range men) from the southwest.

It was apparent from the first that to be successful the entire range business must be run as one outfit, hence the two strong organizations, The Montana Stock Growers' Association and the Board of Stock Commissioners.   These two organizations acted as Boards of Directors and they ran the cattle business absolutely. Their administration was just, honest, and economical, so much so that they have been in operation for thirty-five years and are still in operation.

The young men, scions of wealthy and influential families, loved the business and were anxious to learn, and under the leadership of older and more experienced heads, developed into splendid business men, many of them still in the state and numbered among our best citizens.

The handling of the herds on the range was entrusted to the cow boys from the southwest. These men were bred and born on the range and knew how to handle range cattle. It is impossible for me to describe one of them and do him justice. Their understanding of cattle was almost supernatural, their patience, ingenuity, faithfulness, and loyalty to their outfit cannot be described. They were to their outfit what a good mother is to her family and their way of handling herds has never been improved upon.

The idea of lavish expenditure was an erroneous one. I have described the headquarters ranch of a big outfit; few rude log cabins, comprising a bunk house, a cook house, a blacksmith shop, stable and corral, with hay land enough fenced to cut a hundred tons of hay. The food provided was beans, bacon, coffee, syrup, bread and beef. A can of tomatoes or oysters was a luxury.

The big outfits never imposed on the smaller ones or on the ranchers or squatters, but helped them in every way. In fact it was the big outfits that protected the little ones and made it possible for them to settle in the uninhabited country.

The big outfits brought millions of capital into a sparsely settled country and their herds converted the millions of tons of grass that had for thousands of years gone to waste into millions of dollars worth of beef. Their heavy taxes built roads and schools and did much for the advancement of civilization.

Index

Index

Breinigsville, PA USA
12 November 2010
249206BV00003B/2/P